ALSO BY BOB WOODWARD

THE COMMANDERS

VEIL:
THE SECRET WARS OF THE CIA 1981–1987

WIRED:
THE SHORT LIFE AND FAST TIMES OF JOHN BELUSHI

THE BRETHREN
(*with Scott Armstrong*)

THE FINAL DAYS
(*with Carl Bernstein*)

ALL THE PRESIDENT'S MEN
(*with Carl Bernstein*)

THE AGENDA

Inside the
Clinton White House

Bob Woodward

SIMON & SCHUSTER
New York London Toronto Sydney Tokyo Singapore

SIMON & SCHUSTER
Rockefeller Center
1230 Avenue of the Americas
New York, New York 10020

Designed by Eve Metz
Manufactured in the United States of America

5   7   9   10   8   6   4

Library of Congress Cataloging-in-Publication Data is available.
ISBN: 0-671-86486-6

PHOTO CREDITS

Ray Lustig/*The Washington Post*: 2, 8, 9, 12, 16, 20, 22, 23, 25
© 1993 Carl Cox: 3
Rich Lipski/*The Washington Post*: 4, 5, 15, 17, 19, 27
James M. Thresher/*The Washington Post*: 6
Bill O'Leary/*The Washington Post*: 7
Gerald Martineau/*The Washington Post*: 10
Carol Guzy/*The Washington Post*: 11
Bill Snead/*The Washington Post*: 13
Frank Johnston/*The Washington Post*: 14, 18, 29
Dayna Smith/*The Washington Post*: 21
James A. Parcell/*The Washington Post*: 24
Larry Morris/*The Washington Post*: 26
White House Photo: 28

AUTHOR'S NOTE

DAVID GREENBERG, a 1990 graduate of Yale University, was my assistant and a full participant at every stage of this book. David performed extensive research, reporting, writing, editing, and organizing. A tough-minded, independent, and creative thinker, he repeatedly worked to bring greater balance, fairness, and clarity to our reporting and writing. Without his resourcefulness and drive, the book would not have been possible. No writer ever worked with a more cherished or more trusted collaborator.

TO ELSA AND TALI

INTRODUCTION

AT THE HEART OF BILL CLINTON'S 1992 presidential campaign was
his pledge to fix the economy and to use the presidency to do it. The
fundamental difference between George Bush and himself, Clinton said,
was his belief in an activist role for the government. "I know how
President Lincoln felt when General McClellan wouldn't attack in the
Civil War," Clinton said when he accepted the Democratic Party's nomination on July 16, 1992. "He asked him, 'If you're not going to use
your army, may I borrow it?' And so I say: George Bush, if you won't
use your power to help people, step aside, I will." This book is about
President Clinton's effort to make good on his promise, "I will."

MY INITIAL WORK on economic policy making began in early 1992 and
focused on the Bush administration. When it became clear the economy
was the major issue in the presidential campaign, I wrote a series of
four articles in *The Washington Post* called "Making Choices: Bush's
Economic Record." The series, published in October 1992, followed the
disarray and turmoil from Bush's 1988 presidential campaign pledge of
"no new taxes," to his decision to support them in his 1990 budget deal
with Congress, and finally to his repudiation of his own deal during the
1992 campaign.

After Bush's defeat, I turned to the matter that would become this book: Clinton, his economic ideas, and his administration's handling of economic policy in the first year. Overall, more than 250 people were interviewed. Dozens of these people were interviewed many times, frequently in evening-long dinner sessions or at some length in their offices. A great many of them permitted me to tape-record the interviews; otherwise I took detailed notes. Many also provided me with memoranda, meeting notes, diaries, transcripts, schedules, or other documentation.

Nearly all the interviews were conducted on "deep background," which means that I agreed not to identify these sources. Without such a stipulation, people often will not discuss their conversations or interactions with the president or other high-level officials frankly—or at all. I took care to compare and verify various sources' accounts of the same events. The extensive documentation, and the willingness of key sources to allow me to review with them important meetings, discussions, and decisions many times, has resulted in an unusually detailed record of the first year of Clinton's presidency on economic issues.

Dialogue and quotations come from at least one participant, from memos, or from contemporaneous notes or diaries of a participant in the discussion. When someone is said to have "thought" or "felt" something, that description comes from the person himself or from someone to whom he said it directly. I have tried to preserve the participants' own language as much as possible, even when they are not directly quoted, in order to reflect the flavor of their speech and their attitudes as best I could. Quotation marks were not used when the memories of sources or the documentation was not precise about wording.

A copy of all documents, notes, transcripts, and tape recordings of interviews will be deposited with the Yale University Library. The files will be opened to the public and researchers in 40 years to provide the exact source or sources for each portion of the book.

The record will show how I was able to gain information from records or interviews, often immediately or soon after the events. I could then talk with other sources and return to most of them again and again as necessary. When this reinterviewing raised new questions, I was able to return a third or fourth time to key sources to answer those new questions. At times I conducted 20 interviews with as many as 10 sources on a single meeting or decision.

The accounts I have compiled may, at times, be more comprehensive than what a future historian, who has to rely on a single memo, letter, or recollection of what happened, might be able to piece together. At the same time, this book does not have the perspective of history, and it should not be considered definitive. Events, new information, and documentation will deepen and improve understanding of Clinton and his presidency.

Much of this book was reported while events were developing, before the outcomes and consequences were known or imagined. As a result, I believe, it contains some events that otherwise might have been lost to the record. David Greenberg, my assistant, and I have attempted to ensure that we have provided the fullest, fairest account based on the information available to us.

No journalist or historian can capture 100 percent of what happened. Neither journalism nor history provides an engineer's drawing of events. And participants often disagree. Memory, perspective, and self-interest play their parts. There are statements and events in this book that some of those involved or the sources themselves possibly will not remember —or may not want to remember. Besides, this book is about politics, and politics is about contested ground. I have, however, attempted to give every key participant in these events an opportunity to offer his or her recollections and views.

This book falls between newspaper journalism and history. In the information cycle, the newspapers, television, and magazines provide the first and second waves of explanation of events in the days or weeks after they occur. Then, generally after a long interlude, insider memoirs or histories appear. I believe there is a place for reporting that aspires to combine the thoroughness of history with the contemporaneity of journalism. This book aims to find that ground.

CAST OF CHARACTERS

THE WHITE HOUSE
President Bill Clinton
First Lady Hillary Rodham Clinton
Vice President Albert Gore, Jr.
Thomas F. "Mack" McLarty, chief of staff
George Stephanopoulos, senior policy adviser, formerly
    communications director
David Gergen, counselor to the president

THE ECONOMIC TEAM
Lloyd Bentsen, secretary of the Treasury
Roger Altman, deputy Treasury Secretary
Robert E. Rubin, director, National Economic Council
Gene Sperling, deputy director, National Economic Council
Leon Panetta, director, Office of Management and Budget
Alice Rivlin, deputy director, Office of Management and Budget
Laura D'Andrea Tyson, chair, Council of Economic Advisers
Alan Blinder, member, Council of Economic Advisers
Robert Reich, secretary of Labor

THE CONSULTANTS
James Carville
Paul Begala
Stanley B. Greenberg, pollster
Mandy Grunwald, media adviser

OTHER WHITE HOUSE STAFF
Howard Paster, congressional liaison
Ira Magaziner, health care policy adviser
Mark Gearan, communications director, formerly deputy chief of staff

THE SENATE
George Mitchell, Democrat of Maine, majority leader
Robert J. Dole, Republican of Kansas, minority leader
Daniel Patrick Moynihan, Democrat of New York, chairman, Finance
    Committee
Robert Byrd, Democrat of West Virginia, chairman, Appropriations
    Committee
David L. Boren, Democrat of Oklahoma
John Breaux, Democrat of Louisiana
Bob Kerrey, Democrat of Nebraska

THE HOUSE OF REPRESENTATIVES
Thomas Foley, Democrat of Washington, Speaker
Richard Gephardt, Democrat of Missouri, majority leader
Dave McCurdy, Democrat of Oklahoma

THE FEDERAL RESERVE
Alan Greenspan, chairman

1

ONE MORNING IN LATE AUGUST 1991 in Little Rock, Arkansas, the state's first couple awoke in the mansion's guest house. Renovation in the mansion had banished them for months to tight quarters in the small two-room house. Their daughter, Chelsea, was sleeping on the fold-out couch in the living room.

"I think you have to do it," said the state's First Lady, Hillary Clinton.

"Do you really?" Governor Bill Clinton asked his wife from their double bed.

"Yeah," Hillary said.

"Why do you believe that?" he asked.

"I think you are absolutely the right person to make these arguments," she explained. She believed that it was a rare meeting of a man and history. Her husband had just turned 45, and she was 43. They had been married 15 years.

"You really think so?" Clinton asked.

"Yeah," she said. "I really think so."

"What do you think'll happen?"

"I think you'll win."

"You really think so?"

"Yeah, I really think so!" she said.

"Well, you know," Clinton said, "a lot of people think this will be a dry run."

"I don't," she said. "I think if you run, you win. And so you better be really careful about wanting to do this and making these changes in your life." Others had been saying that if he ran well, more seasoned and powerful men in his party would come in and take it away from him, but that he would get the necessary experience, and that would be good. She did not agree.

The effort would be hard and bruising, she added. It was a question of what she called "the pain threshold," and who would take it on. The Republicans were well organized and well financed. They thought they were anointed, as if they had a right to win every time. And they played very tough.

She didn't remember exactly what he said in response that morning.

For months she had known he was going to do it, even though he hadn't yet come to realize it fully. He entertained the idea, and they'd been talking about it all summer with a new intensity. But he wasn't convinced that he was the one. "I just don't know if I want to do it," he told her once. "I don't know if it's worth it." But she knew. She had known it for months, since the spring. Since then, she had never doubted it.

2

IT WAS THAT SPRING, on May 13, 1991, that Clinton visited Harvard. He strolled into a large meeting hall at the John F. Kennedy School of Government. He moved quietly, looking relaxed, a large man, 6 feet 3, with a mop of thick, graying hair that took some of the edge off his boyish self-assurance.

Clinton came to Harvard with some ideas. He had been formulating what he felt was a powerful critique of the economics and the values of Presidents Reagan and Bush. Just two months earlier, President Bush had won the Persian Gulf War, but Clinton felt the real problems of national security were at home in the struggles of average people. Too many feared for their jobs, their health care, the educational opportunities of their children, their homes and neighborhoods, their retirement.

Though not well known on the national stage, Clinton was a leader in a movement of self-styled "New Democrats" who rejected the party's liberal orthodoxy. Mostly Southerners, they were trying to convince the middle class that the Democratic Party could be strong on foreign and defense policy, moderate in social policy, and disciplined in spending tax money and taming runaway government. While retaining the ideals of the New Deal and the Great Society, New Democrats sought more efficient activism. Clinton had been traveling the country saying that these ideas were neither liberal nor conservative, but both, and different. He cast his ideas in the loftiest terms.

At Harvard, a small, bearded, biblical-looking man of 4 feet 11 inches took the stage. "Hello, my name is Bob Reich," he said. Reich, a professor at the Kennedy School, had recently published his third book, *The Work of Nations,* which prompted one magazine to anoint him the country's "leading liberal political economist," the next John Kenneth Galbraith. Reich was leading a symposium on "Preparing Our Workforce for the Next Century," a subject central to his book.

"Bill Clinton was first introduced to me 23 years ago, when we were on a boat, on a ship heading to England," Reich said, turning to his first guest. They had been two of 32 Rhodes Scholars headed for Oxford in 1968 for two years of study. Reich explained how Clinton had nursed him through his seasickness with crackers and ginger ale.

Clinton, the nation's senior governor, in his fifth term in Arkansas, rose to the crowd's applause. "I was just thinking how much simpler life would have been for the rest of us," he began matter-of-factly, "if I'd let him die on that boat." There was laughter from the audience, which included many of Reich's colleagues.

Clinton was not widely known outside Arkansas. In 1988 he had become a national footnote when he introduced the presidential nominee, Massachusetts Governor Michael S. Dukakis, at the Democratic Convention in an interminable 32-minute televised speech. Clinton had won applause only when he said, "In closing. . . ." Though his presidential ambitions were obvious to his friends, in the spring of 1991 Clinton was not considered a leading, or even likely, candidate for 1992.

"America spent too much time and money in the 1980s on the present and the past," Clinton said to the Harvard audience, "and too little attention and money on the future. . . . I define future as investments in education, infrastructure, research and development, and the environment. . . . We have to break out of the old categories and think about whether we are going to invest in the future." Clinton spoke in a quiet tone—intellectual, reassuring, youthful but confident.

Clinton drew extensively from Reich's book, which he was toting around, with bits of paper stuck in several pages. Sentences were underlined and little stars dotted the margins for emphasis. Reich's core point in *The Work of Nations* was that a nation had only two resources within its borders—its workers and its "infrastructure" of roads, communications systems, and other common public assets—that stayed put. Other resources—such as money, factories, technological know-how—all were crossing international borders easily and almost instantly. Reich argued that a nation needed to spend money on the nonmobile resources: education and job training for its workers; roads, bridges, high-speed rail, and other forms of infrastructure. A large body of economic research showed that such investments could yield vast returns in the future, for workers and the country. Clinton was looking to bring about a government investment revolution.

Clinton was a master of sustained eye contact, hunting reactions in the eyes of an audience of one or a thousand. "If you let 10 to 20 more years go on where the middle class keeps losing ground," he continued, "this won't be the America any of us grew up in. And, I will say again, it is a question of organization, will, and leadership. It has nothing to do with the American people. . . . They have not been properly led. And I hope that this will be the beginning of turning that around. If it is, we'll owe a lot of it to Bob Reich."

Reich, sitting nearby, could imagine Clinton's talk as the prototype of a campaign speech that, while not yet fully formed, contained strands of a powerful message.

AFTER DINNER, Clinton, Reich, and Richard G. Stearns, another Rhodes classmate and a Massachusetts judge, went over to Reich's Victorian house on Mercer Circle and sat on the veranda for nearly four hours. On that crisp spring evening, Clinton turned to the topic on his mind. As his two friends knew, Clinton said, he had been thinking of running. Was this the time? he asked them. Should he do it?

Stearns had known of Clinton's ambitions since virtually the moment he met him on the ship to England in 1968. In those days, many of them had been enchanted by the Kennedys and spoke openly of their political aspirations. In 1991, however, for an unknown governor to announce such ambitions seemed to be overreaching. Stearns had been steeped in Democratic presidential politics for 20 years, having worked for candidates George McGovern, Ted Kennedy, Gary Hart, and Michael Dukakis. He had seen older, better-known, seemingly wiser Democrats chewed up and spit out in their losing White House bids. There were reasons Clinton shouldn't run, Stearns said.

True, Reich chimed in. But there were also reasons Clinton should. The three agreed to examine both sides in an orderly fashion. Stearns would list the reasons against a Clinton run, and Reich would rebut with reasons in favor. At each point, Clinton would respond—Oxford-style.

Stearns led off with the Democratic Party's fatal weakness on national security questions. With no experience in the military, in Washington, or in foreign policy, Clinton's record next to Bush's would pose a stark contrast, especially after the recent Gulf War victory. Straight off, Stearns pointed out, Bill would be forfeiting one of the most important campaign issues.

The argument seemed compelling, Clinton responded, warming to the challenge. But only on the surface. The Soviet threat was evaporating, and foreign policy would not play a big role in the campaign, he predicted. Instead, the economy would be the decisive issue. America's economic system was out of whack—great for the wealthiest 20 percent, who were getting richer, but lousy for the other 80 percent, who were sinking or treading water. The working- and middle-class alienation could help him win in 1992. These groups constituted the vast majority of voters, and they felt insecure.

Reich almost bounced with delight, as he recognized the references from his book. He relished the prospect of being chum and idea man to a presidential candidate.

Stearns moved to his second reason. Arkansas, one of the country's smallest and poorest states, had a tiny financial base. Millions of dollars were required to sustain a presidential campaign. Raising money could be not only time-consuming but also humiliating, as the candidate made the rounds hat-in-hand to the big givers and special interests. He had seen campaign debt almost wreck candidates who spent the rest of their lives trying to pay it off or hide from it.

Clinton acknowledged the problem but said there was more money in Arkansas than Stearns realized. Wal-Mart, the country's largest discount retail chain, was based there. His boyhood friend Thomas F. "Mack" McLarty III ran the *Fortune* 500 natural gas company Arkla. He had other national contacts too, Clinton said. He even accepted Stearns's challenge to build a $1 million war chest by the day he announced.

Okay, Stearns said, moving on. Clinton had promised the voters of Arkansas repeatedly in his 1990 gubernatorial campaign that he would not seek the presidency, that he would remain governor for another full term until 1994. Could he survive breaking the pledge?

That was also a difficult problem, Clinton again conceded. But if he went to the people of Arkansas and effectively asked their permission to run for president, he thought they would give it and rally behind his candidacy.

Stearns cited his next reason: Bush's immense popularity coming off the Gulf War victory. The president's approval ratings were running 78 percent in the latest polls, down from his postwar peak of 91 percent but still forbiddingly high.

Clinton again saw a twist. Oddly, he said, Bush's popularity would carry some hidden advantages for Clinton. Other high-profile Democrats—such as New York Governor Mario Cuomo, or New Jersey Senator Bill Bradley, who had just squeaked by in his reelection campaign—would be intimidated and sit out the race.

Bush would expend all his political capital in 1992, his last campaign, Stearns replied. He would convert his international activism to domestic activism and offer a dramatic set of proposals for America's problems at home.

Stearns next said that moderate Southern governors were not exactly in vogue after Jimmy Carter's failed one-term presidency. Clinton would be typecast and would have to live down the Carter legacy.

"I'm not Jimmy Carter," Clinton said firmly.

Stearns asked what the public knew about Clinton. Stearns had seen his friend revive and enliven a tipsy, late-night banquet audience with his humor and extemporaneous style. But Clinton's boring speech at the 1988 Democratic Convention, he said, had left an indelible national impression.

It had not been a great moment, Clinton acknowledged. The Dukakis campaign had written the speech, handed it to him, and insisted he deliver it precisely as written. He claimed he was just being a good soldier. "The biggest mistake of my life," Clinton said.

While on the subject of mistakes, Stearns broached a delicate subject. What about the latest rumors about Clinton and women?

Clinton had spoken to friends about the issue before. He had confided to another friend over dinner one night four years earlier the nature of his dilemma. It was the late summer of 1987 and Clinton had just decided not to run for president in the 1988 campaign.

You know why I'm not running for president? Clinton asked.

The friend guessed that infidelity was the reason. Gary Hart's affair with model Donna Rice had been publicly exposed several months earlier amid a great hullabaloo, forcing Hart to withdraw from the race. Now reporters were asking all the candidates if they'd ever had affairs. Clinton acknowledged he had strayed.

In 1991, Clinton indicated to Stearns and Reich that he thought the adultery question would prove to be 1988's passing fad. In 1992, the economy would matter.

What about the annual federal budget deficits and the $4 trillion national debt they had created? Stearns asked. Wouldn't the next president be left with the wreckage from Reagan and Bush? Wouldn't the presidency be just a cleanup job? Was he sure he would want the job, even if he could win?

Clinton said that the explosion in the federal debt was largely attributable to skyrocketing health care costs. The health system was wasteful and irrational, and reforming it would be a priority for him as president.

Reich hardly had to make the case for Clinton.

"Bill," Stearns said, "remember that presidents get in trouble not for what they do that is wrong, but what is wrong that they try to cover up."

3

S TANLEY B. GREENBERG, another important professor in Clinton's life, was also encouraging the governor to run. Greenberg, 46, was a Clinton contemporary with a rare mix of academic and practical political credentials. Intellectual and articulate, with a Groucho Marx mustache and bushy hair, Greenberg held a Ph.D. in government from Harvard, had taught political science at Yale for nine years in the 1970s, and had headed a Washington polling firm since 1980. His wife, Rosa L. DeLauro, was the congressional representative from New Haven, Connecticut.

Greenberg had been advising Clinton since his 1990 gubernatorial campaign. In 1991, he gave the governor a draft of a long article he was writing for *The American Prospect,* a liberal political journal. In part a review of three books that examined what Greenberg called "the Democrats' perceived indifference to the value of work and the interests of working people," the article was the culmination of a lot of analysis and polling. It was also a personal manifesto of sorts. Greenberg was devoted to studying the crisis in the Democratic Party and the defection of middle-class and working-class whites—the so-called Reagan Democrats—to Republican presidential candidates in the 1980s. These voters held the balance in national elections, and Greenberg argued that they wanted to return to their party, to come home. Party leaders had to reach out to this disaffected and forgotten middle class, which saw itself squeezed—paying for programs for the poor and tax breaks for the wealthy, while getting little in return from government. The middle-class crisis presented an opportunity for the Democrats. Buried in the article, Greenberg also invoked the magic phrase "tax relief."

Later, when he asked Clinton for his reaction, the governor replied, "I've read it three times."

Greenberg felt that Clinton might be the Democrat who could suc-ceed. Clinton's immersion in the small, poor state of Arkansas had provided him with a natural, immediate identification with the guy on the assembly line, on the farm, or in the coffeeshop, the average person who felt insecure about the economy. Clinton, a graduate of George-town and Yale Law School, had an unusually broad national network of political, media, and academic friends, and displayed an obvious fascination with ideas.

Clinton was also hungry. He walked and talked like a candidate, Greenberg felt. His ambition and itch for the contest was apparent in his every gesture. Yet Clinton would not fully commit to run. He continued traveling around Arkansas trying to get assurance from voters that he could break his promise not to run for president. He set August as a personal deadline for a final decision, but the deadline slipped. Clinton had no campaign manager and not much organization. He appeared locked in a perpetual debate and argument with himself and with dozens of friends and advisers. His thinking never seemed to go in a straight line. He was unable to bring his deliberations to any resolution. Greenberg was horrified at the process. It bordered on chaos.

HILLARY RODHAM CLINTON watched the forces and ideas at work on her husband. He had made several trips to Washington to talk to con-gressional Democrats, only to return each time to Little Rock to spill out his frustration. No one knew how to seize the moment, he said. Yet Hillary felt her husband's own criticism was not just economic or politi-cal but a moral critique. He was indignant about what the Republican policies had done to the average person—little or no wage increases, job insecurity, the fraying of the safety net. As governor, he had paid the price. He had told his wife once with some bitterness, "It would be great to be the president like Reagan, who cuts taxes so that every governor, including Republicans, had to raise them."

During a trip to Japan several years earlier, Hillary Clinton had over-heard a conversation between her husband and a Japanese executive. "You could do a lot to stimulate your economy," the executive told

Clinton, "if your executives in American industry weren't so greedy." Her husband replied that American executives were being given permission to grab the most at the top by the Reagan economic policies, which were designed so wealth would allegedly trickle down to those at the bottom. But those at the bottom weren't seeing the benefits. Hillary agreed. She was angry at what she called "the unacceptable acquiescence in greed that had occurred during the 1980s."

After Labor Day 1991, she saw her husband coming around, although he was still being careful. "I just don't think this country can survive without some sort of debate about this," he said at first. He often framed decisions in terms of the need for a debate. Finally, he said, "We're going to get ready to go." What she had known for a while now became conscious for him at last, and he said, "We're just going to go do this!"

ON A FRIDAY MORNING in September 1991, George Stephanopoulos, age 30, walked into a gray, painted-brick rowhouse just north of the Capitol in Washington, D.C., and climbed the steps to the second floor, the office of Stan Greenberg. A handsome bachelor of 5 feet 7, Stephanopoulos had a small, almost fragile frame, set off by a big shock of dark hair. He could roll out a grand, infectious smile as needed. Well dressed, even a little self-consciously hip, he was smooth and guarded. He was looking for a job with a Democratic presidential candidate and was here to meet with Bill Clinton. Greenberg closed the door so Clinton and Stephanopoulos could talk alone.

Clinton asked Stephanopoulos to talk about himself.

In the 1988 Dukakis presidential campaign, Stephanopoulos said, he had been in charge of rapid-response communications and joke writing, two of Dukakis's distinct failures. He said he wasn't very funny by nature, but the campaign had apparently wanted a short Greek in the room.

Clinton laughed.

After that, Stephanopoulos continued, he had worked for House Majority Leader Richard Gephardt as his floor manager the last several years. He had urged Gephardt, a presidential candidate in 1988, to run again in 1992, but Gephardt had declined.

Clinton said he was thinking of running and asked Stephanopoulos his opinion of recent political events. Stephanopoulos said George Bush was in a box after breaking his "Read my lips, no new taxes" pledge. Bush's flip-flop would help the Democrats in 1992, regardless of their candidate. The strategic question was whether the Democrats could propose raising taxes while making Bush look as bad as possible. After 45 minutes of discussing fundraising and other nuts-and-bolts political matters, Clinton told Stephanopoulos he would get back to him.

Within a few days, Clinton offered Stephanopoulos a job even though no campaign technically existed. Stephanopoulos would be deputy campaign manager—whether the sole deputy or one of several seemed to matter to neither. His salary would be $60,000 plus a housing allowance, a substantial cut from his current $95,000.

The son of a Greek Orthodox priest, Stephanopoulos was practiced at pleasing older adults and making himself essential. He was a salutatorian from Columbia and a Rhodes Scholar, and both appreciated and sought status. Stephanopoulos was the new organization man, skilled in persuasion and endurance. Charming yet vaguely aloof, he knew when to remain silent and when to step in with a burst of analysis or polemic. Stephanopoulos had come of age during the Reagan years with liberal-leftish values, and he was eager to undo the Reagan-Bush legacy. Joining the campaign would certainly be more fun than hanging around the floor of the House of Representatives with Gephardt. Although Clinton would make a very credible effort, Stephanopoulos felt, no Democrat had much chance of beating George Bush in 1992.

ONE SUNDAY LATER THAT FALL, Clinton sat down in a Washington hotel for his first extended talk with campaign consultants James Carville and Paul Begala. Football was on television in the bar area. Clinton had made up his mind to run, and in a few weeks he would announce his candidacy for president.

Carville, a 47-year-old Louisiana lawyer with a bald, pointy head and riveting, almost sinister eyes, and Begala, a rough-faced, bearded Texan 17 years his junior, made an oddball team. Emotional, often shockingly profane, and distinctly old-boy Southern, Carville had been waiting years for his moment in the political sun. He deeply resented what he saw as the Democratic Party's snotty, Northeastern elitism, and liked to inject McDonald's fast-food plain thinking into the campaigns he ran. Begala, also a lawyer by training, was a wordsmith, capable of smooth and polished speech, but he could be high-strung and caustic, even a hothead.

Clinton had asked to meet with the two consultants. He admired a speech they had helped write three months earlier for Georgia Governor Zell Miller, one of their clients and a friend of Clinton's. The speech was both a blueprint of the future of the Democratic Party and a summons to its leaders. "For too many presidential elections, we have had things backwards," Miller had said. "We have chosen to fight on social issues rather than to run on the economic issues that shape the daily lives of American families." Miller had pleaded with the party to move away from elitist social issues—civil and gay rights, school prayer, abortion rights, the arts—and return to the themes of "economic populism."

In his speech, Miller had offered a remedy. He had called for a tax cut for the middle class, a single unifying proposal that would address their economic insecurity. Clinton had studied Miller's speech and spent a marathon late-night session at the Georgia Governor's Mansion discussing it and the future of their party. Clinton told Carville and Begala that he loved the speech. He confided, however, that he was personally shy of a populist label. Populism seemed to him too anti-government and anti-business. He wanted to chart a course without reference to old labels.

Carville said that whatever the label, a presidential campaign had to emphasize these middle-class values.

Begala nearly rose out of his chair as he spouted Miller's imperatives with almost evangelical fervor. These "middle-class" or "kitchen-table economic" issues, as he called them, shaped, dominated, and even destroyed families. A good job, a college education for their kids, owning a home, affordable health care, and retirement with economic security —these were the issues voters cared about. It was almost word for word what Clinton had been preaching.

Begala had studied the strategies of Republican operative Lee Atwater and agreed with Atwater's analysis that politics was divided into populist and elitist issues. On social issues, Begala believed, the Democrats tended to take elitist positions and the Republicans populist ones; on economic issues, it was the reverse. Both parties had nominated their elites in 1988—Dukakis and Bush. Neither man nor his ideas had been embraced by the public. The 1992 campaign had to be fought on economic ground where the Democrats could brandish the populist sword, Begala said, whatever it might be called.

The session ended without any decisions being made, but there was a meeting of the minds. When Clinton announced his presidential candidacy on October 3, 1991, at the Old State House in Little Rock, Arkansas, he said that his central goal was "restoring the hopes of the forgotten middle class." He made ten references to the middle class in his seven-page announcement and promised a middle-class tax cut. "Middle-class people are spending more hours on the job, less time with their children, and bringing home a smaller paycheck to pay more for health care and housing and education," he said.

4

CLINTON SCHEDULED a series of three speeches at Georgetown University, where he had graduated in 1968, to outline his domestic, foreign, and economic policies. In preparation for the economic speech, Clinton sought advice from Robert J. Shapiro, a Ph.D. economist and vice president of the Progressive Policy Institute, a Washington think tank devoted to developing "New Democrat" policies. The think tank was in essence an attempt to put a brain behind the Democratic Leadership Council, the organization of national Democrats that Clinton had helped found in 1985 and chaired in 1991 until he announced his candidacy.

Although Shapiro agreed that Clinton should call for a middle-class tax cut, he knew it would not do much to help the stagnating economy. "The middle-class tax cut is not an economic policy," Shapiro told Clinton and his advisers. "It is a social policy." He considered it a political message to demonstrate that Clinton understood the difficult economic conditions for a broad range of people. It also underscored the theme of economic alarm in the land: Times were so bad that the government had to reduce people's taxes for them to survive.

Clinton rejected many drafts of the speech and wrote out an improved version himself, reviewing it line by line with Hillary in the Washington office of his media consultants. Hillary felt he was touching precisely what he wanted to say.

In the Georgetown speech on November 20, Clinton tried to present both a broad vision and a specific plan. He called it "A New Covenant for Economic Change." He spoke at length about his investment ideas and proposed a middle-class tax cut to be paid for with higher taxes on the rich. "In a Clinton Administration, we'll cut income tax rates on the middle class: an average family's tax bill will go down 10 per cent, a savings of $350 a year. And the deficit won't go up—instead those earning over $200,000 a year will pay more." Clinton upped his focus on the middle class to 15 direct references. The tax hike on the rich was a rather bold proposal, since in recent elections even mentioning new taxes had become taboo. But Clinton, by tying the tax to middle-income tax relief, gave a New Democrat slant to the old-line liberal prescription.

Clinton did not merely cast the middle-class themes as wise social policy or smart political choice. He raised them to the spiritual level. "These are not just economic proposals," he said, adding the immodest assertion, "they are the way to save the very soul of our nation." The speech drew modest attention.

As he approached the February 1992 New Hampshire vote, the first of the primaries, Clinton thought he needed to craft an economic plan with specifics that he could present to voters. New Hampshire was still suffering vast economic hardship, and Clinton wanted to offer a way out. He held conference calls with his advisers, including Rob Shapiro, Bob Reich, and George Stephanopoulos. James Carville and Paul Begala, who had signed up for the campaign, joined some of the calls. Ira Magaziner, a business consultant and Rhodes Scholar the year after Clinton, and Roger C. Altman, a fellow Georgetown alumnus who was now an investment banker, also offered advice.

In one phone call, the question arose whether the middle-class tax cut would get the economy moving again, act as an economic stimulus, and promote a recovery. That, after all, was what New Hampshire voters were looking to hear.

No, said Shapiro, the only economist in the group. Normally, cutting taxes did give people more money to spend, and that stimulated the economy. But in Clinton's proposal, the middle-class tax cut was to be offset by a tax increase on the rich. It would be a wash. No additional money would go into the national economy as a stimulus.

Reich disagreed. The middle class would spend all of what they received as a tax cut, he argued, while the rich tended to save more and put less of their money immediately back into the economy. The extra spending from the middle class would spur some economic growth.

Shapiro replied that the offsetting tax hike for the rich would remove their savings from the economy, reducing the amount of money available for business investment. That would hurt the economy, wiping out whatever stimulus might come from more middle-class spending, he said. So it was neutral—good social policy, he repeated, but not an economic stimulus policy.

Pressure mounted on Shapiro. He decided to be a team player and agreed to a line in a written plan that was being drawn up for release. The line read: "Putting cash in people's pockets will help build consumer confidence to start an economic recovery"—a tenuous link by economic standards.

In early January 1992, Clinton released his six-page *Plan for America's Future*. It included four steps for the short run and a pledge of college loans and health insurance for every American. The first short-term step was a 10 percent middle-class tax cut. The second step was a tax credit for families of up to $800 for each child they had. Clinton also promised to "jump-start" the economy by accelerating "fast-track" spending on highways and by expanding home and small-business loans.

Clinton taped 15- and 60-second television spots to air in New Hampshire. The ads told people to call a local phone number or visit their local libraries for a copy of the plan. The first week the commercials ran, Clinton jumped 13 percentage points in Stan Greenberg's poll.

Former Senator Paul E. Tsongas of Massachusetts, who was also running for the Democratic nomination, had been the front runner in New Hampshire as a virtual native son. But now Clinton was surging, and Tsongas attacked his middle-class tax cut proposal as a creation of political strategists. It would give the average person less than a dollar a day, Tsongas pointed out, hardly enough to make a difference. Reducing the federal budget deficit was the crucial issue. "I'm not Santa Claus," Tsongas said mockingly, to the approval of many editorial writers and columnists who preferred his anti-deficit message.

While Clinton continued to defend the middle-class tax cut publicly, he privately expressed the view to his advisers that it was intellectually dishonest. He agreed with Tsongas that a dollar a day couldn't possibly do that much for people. Tsongas seemed to be benefiting more from opposing it than Clinton was from advocating it. The former Massachusetts senator seemed to have staked out the high ground and appeared the least political of the candidates, the most willing to tell grim truth.

When Clinton began complaining privately about the middle-class tax cut not going down well with the thinking set, Begala, who was traveling with Clinton more and more, reminded him of his reason for running. "Governor," he said, "these people are hurting. The middle-class tax cut is hope and cash for them." In New Hampshire, talk of long-range global strategies and investment meant little. They were mere abstractions.

Carville agreed. "All the wrong people are against it, so it must be right," Carville said. The critics of the middle-class tax cut included Clinton's Yale friends and editorial writers and columnists from elite newspapers. Carville bristled that Tsongas was getting credit for political courage. "Political courage gets defined by the willingness to slap working-class people around," he said, adding that it was time to help working people, not bury them in political courage.

Stephanopoulos was aware of the war going on within Clinton. His heart was with the middle class, the guys in the bowling alleys of America who deserved a break. But his head was with the Tsongas voters and the harder-nosed policy analysts. Clinton was only vaguely focused on the federal deficit that Tsongas was always harping about. As a Washington outsider, he just hadn't had to worry about it.

On January 23, *The Star*, a supermarket tabloid, published a charge by Gennifer Flowers, an Arkansas woman, that she had had a 12-year affair with Clinton. Clinton danced around the allegation, appearing on CBS's "60 Minutes" with Hillary, who in effect said that if she didn't mind, why should others. When *The Star* published a second story with excerpts from tapes Flowers had made of her conversations with Clinton, Stephanopoulos felt he was almost going to have a nervous breakdown as he tried to handle the mounting allegations. A normal person would drop out of the race, Stephanopoulos felt. In the Manchester airport, Clinton spoke to Hillary from a pay phone. When he hung up, he was serene and unclouded. He began campaigning with a new resolve.

JUST AS THE GENNIFER FLOWERS STORY was dying down, the *Wall Street Journal* ran a story on February 6 about Clinton's efforts to manipulate the draft laws in 1969 to avoid military service during the Vietnam War, triggering a new round of doubts. On Sunday, February 9, with the primary just ten days off, Clinton was back in Arkansas. He had the flu, with a cough and a raging fever. Hillary was amazed he was still going. He was in terrible physical shape, totally worn out. She thought he had seen practically every doctor in New Hampshire and seemed to be taking every antibiotic known to modern medicine. Clinton gathered his top advisers in the East Conference Room of the Governor's Mansion. Stan Greenberg reported a "meltdown" in the polls in the aftermath of the draft story. Clinton's support had plummeted almost instantly from 33 to 16 percent. Other polls showed a 15- to 20-point drop. No one knew where the bottom was. Stephanopoulos, for one, thought the drop was almost fatal.

"The goddamn fucking middle-class tax cut is killing me," Clinton declared, to the astonishment of most in the room. He slammed his fist down repeatedly onto his right upper thigh for emphasis. Clinton was pounding so hard that Begala thought he might be bruising his leg. Others also couldn't help thinking that Clinton had slipped heavily into denial.

Clinton continued ranting for some ten minutes or more, holding the audience captive, spewing out his rage. The campaign should not be about his past personal life, he said, and he was not going to quit.

After Clinton was finished pounding and cursing, Hillary Clinton took the floor. "We're going to fight like hell," she said. "We're going to fight like we do in Arkansas. If this was Arkansas, Bill, you would be on every radio station, you would be out in every county fighting. In New Hampshire, they don't know you. But they're no different than people in Arkansas. We have to fight. That is the problem."

The 15-minute pep talk worked. Spirits lifted in the East Conference Room. Soon Stephanopoulos and Begala began tending to the problem. They started writing radio ads for New Hampshire, which was one sixth the physical size and one third the population of Arkansas—not all that different. They stayed up most of the night.

The next day Clinton and his team flew back to New Hampshire. In a press conference, Clinton promised to "fight like hell" to win. "For too much of the past couple of weeks," he added, "this election has been about me—or rather some false and twisted tabloid version of me —when it should have been about the people of this state." He criticized what he called the "Republican attack machine," though there was no evidence to suggest it had anything to do with the infidelity or draft stories. Clinton then threw himself at the people of New Hampshire with a punishing schedule.

The weekend before the vote, Greenberg reported that Clinton was at only 17 percent, too low to portray him credibly as a national candidate, and was preparing to brief everyone on the grim details. "I'm not coming to the meeting because Stan is wrong," Hillary declared. "I've been out there. Either everybody in New Hampshire is a consummate liar, or we're back up and we're going to do really well."

In the New Hampshire primary on February 18, Clinton received 25 percent of the vote, finishing second, 8 points behind Tsongas. "If the election went on another week," Hillary said, "we would have beat

Tsongas." Clinton quickly labeled himself the comeback kid and the national front-runner. The Clintons had pulled themselves back from the brink of oblivion.

Later the next month, during the Illinois primary, the campaign staff tested public perceptions of the Clintons. A group of voters watched videos while they adjusted dial meters to indicate whether they liked or disliked what they saw or heard. When Hillary came on, the meters dropped way, way down to the negative reading.

"They don't like her hairdo," Clinton said in a serious tone. Carville felt like sliding under the table from embarrassment after Clinton's remark, but he said nothing. He realized that much of Clinton's psychology was wrapped up in Hillary and her support and strategic guidance. In these moments no one was more firmly behind him. Perhaps it was Clinton's way of defending his wife.

The campaign was grueling, and Hillary seemed to sense when her husband needed a rest. "I'm saying it and I'm tired of saying it," she told Carville once. "Bill is tired. He needs his rest, and I have called you on that, and I am not going to call you anymore, James. I want this done. Now."

5

As THE MARRIAGE and military draft problems blossomed into a national soap opera, Clinton told his advisers that he was baffled that Bush did not use his power as president to capitalize. In the year since the Gulf War, Bush had not come forward with a dramatic, large-scale economic proposal of his own. "It's an act of economic insanity and an act of political insanity," Clinton said of Bush's passivity.

James Carville and others in the campaign searched for their own "big idea" that would capture headlines and imaginations. They needed something that embodied change and didn't smell of repackaging. "You don't get elected president by running for dogcatcher," Carville said frequently—a line Stephanopoulos and others picked up on and repeated. The point was that as a candidate, Clinton had to address squarely the problems he might face as president, and nothing less. When someone urged Clinton to make an issue out of cracking down on fathers who failed to pay child support, Clinton replied that he wasn't going to win the presidency on child-support enforcement.

Lacking a "big idea," Clinton nonetheless continued to win primaries, and in private to scapegoat the middle-class tax cut for his ongoing problems. "Goddamnit, that fucking middle-class tax cut. That's why I lost New Hampshire to Tsongas," he said in one moment of exasperation. "Earth to Clinton," Rob Shapiro thought to himself, "Earth to Clinton."

Carville rejected the idea of aggressively attacking the budget deficit, which he thought was already getting too much attention. He offered his analysis to Clinton: "I always ask the question: Why does a dog lick his dick? Because he can. Why don't we balance the budget? Because we can't."

Others also weighed in with suggestions. Reich suggested a massive, guaranteed federal retraining program for anyone poor, unemployed, or on welfare. The program would provide an income subsidy for two years. This was the kind of investment that would pay giant dividends in the future and demonstrate that Clinton was serious about human capital and willing to propose revolutionary, FDR-style programs.

Shapiro, wary of Reich's big-spending schemes, hit the ceiling. He wrote a seven-page memo attacking the idea. It was precisely the type of old-Democrat, government-is-my-brother approach that had led to the current economic problems. Shapiro estimated the cost of Reich's plan at close to $100 billion; it would create a perverse incentive to be unemployed. Besides, he added sarcastically, a two-year vacation for the poor was not exactly consistent with a New Democrat campaign aimed at the working middle class. Reich's proposal was shelved.

The disagreements among Clinton's advisers and the lack of central authority resulted in no decision. Shapiro, who worked in Washington, told Stephanopoulos that the campaign needed to hire a full-time staffer in Little Rock campaign headquarters to coordinate economic issues and reach some decisions. Stephanopoulos agreed. He gave Shapiro one specification: Find a black.

Shapiro and others scouted around but didn't find a black who they felt really fit the bill. Shapiro instead landed on Gene Sperling, a young workaholic who had assisted him in the 1988 Dukakis campaign. Boyish, earnest, and clean-cut, Sperling, 33, had a strident, urgent manner and boasted an impressive résumé: near-perfect grades as an undergraduate at the University of Minnesota, and degrees from Yale Law School and Wharton Business School.

Sperling, who was working for New York Governor Mario Cuomo, wanted to join a presidential campaign and had been crushed when Cuomo had decided not to run. Sperling also had once worked as a researcher for Reich, who had been independently encouraging him to join the Clinton team. So when Shapiro phoned about the economic policy job, Sperling expressed interest.

Shapiro pursued the possibility with Stephanopoulos.

"Great," responded Stephanopoulos, who also knew Sperling from the Dukakis campaign. "He's a genius. That's the man we want." Sperling would make the job his life's commitment. He would be a virtual clone of Stephanopoulos: young and politically obsessed, thirsty to work on a campaign. Stephanopoulos formally offered the slot to Sperling.

ON JUNE 2, 1992, the day of the California primary, Paul Begala was certain that Clinton was going to win the state and clinch the Democratic nomination with a record number of delegates. Yet Begala felt it was one of the worst days of the campaign.

Throughout the spring, even as Clinton chugged on to the nomination, the press and the polls kept showing the many doubts voters held about him. On top of that, H. Ross Perot, the Texas billionaire, had parachuted into the middle of the campaign, seized the public's attention, and effectively knocked Clinton into third place. Worse, Perot had appropriated Clinton's theme of "change." Clinton had been trying to fashion an image as the people's candidate, the outsider poised to invade Washington to set government in order, but there was no way to out-Perot Perot. As a businessman who had never held elective office, Perot seemed to represent a pure form of anti-politics.

The California exit polls showed that Perot would have beaten Clinton had he been on the ballot. Afterwards, when Clinton appeared on television to promote his campaign and his own ideas, the interviewers wanted to ask only about the new political sensation from Texas.

At the end of the day, Begala and Carville went out for a drink. Begala ordered a double martini. It was his first hard drink of the campaign.

THE NEWEST MEMBER of the campaign inner circle was Mandy Grunwald, 34, a tall, brassy, Marlboro-smoking media consultant. Grunwald came from a wealthy New York family and had a Harvard education, and shared the other consultants' populist views. She believed politics was about inspiration. The previous year, when she had heard one of Clinton's early speeches in California, she had confided to Clinton's longtime Arkansas friend Bruce Lindsey that it contained too much political science, history, and analysis. "It was an observer's speech," she had said then. "It was 'Professor' Clinton. It was not a leader's speech. You want people in the audience to listen to him and say, 'He's the one.' The speech didn't do it." This critique triggered an all-night conversation between Clinton and Lindsey on a red-eye flight back to Arkansas.

Grunwald had been recruited in the midst of the Gennifer Flowers flap to defend Clinton on Ted Koppel's ABC television show "Night-line." Both Clintons had wanted a woman upfront on defense. Grunwald aggressively and deftly turned the tables on the normally unflappable Koppel. She asked why Koppel, who prided himself on serious issue-oriented programs, hadn't done any shows on Clinton's economic proposals or on Clinton. Barreling in on Koppel, she said she was surprised that he would let "a trashy supermarket tabloid" set his agenda. "You've done a very effective job of putting me on the defensive," Koppel replied weakly.

Both Clintons had watched, and within 24 hours Mandy Grunwald had been hired and was soon in charge of media and advertising. Grunwald at first found the campaign a floating crap game. Key people were spread out; some were on the campaign plane, others in Little Rock, and many still in Washington. Politics was also about organization, and Clinton didn't have it. Everyone was throwing ideas at the candidate, who had no system to evaluate or decide among them.

Grunwald urged Clinton to hit the airwaves as much as possible, from MTV to Phil Donahue's show. Carville, Begala, and Greenberg, meanwhile, had outlined an economic message for use in the remainder of the campaign. Hillary wanted her husband to come home to Little Rock to recharge, think, and listen. "Look," Hillary told the consultants, "he may agree with you, but he has to come to it in his own way." Hillary insisted he had to "internalize" the message and the ideas. He needed in-depth exposure to the alternatives and lively debates, pushed even to the point of confusion. "He has to come to this in his own way," she repeated.

A lot of pressure grew on Clinton to move his headquarters to Washington. Some aides argued it would be easier to coordinate his campaign from there, that running it from Little Rock was inefficient. Hillary was dead set against the idea. He had to stay rooted. He was still governor, and he needed to pay attention to his responsibilities in the state. She worried that a Washington campaign would become reactive, responding to Bush and Congress, instead of active, proposing original ideas of their own. Clinton needed to stop and take a deep breath, get recentered. The campaign stayed in Little Rock.

"Specificity is the character issue this year," Stephanopoulos had told a reporter earlier in the campaign, and he continued to think he was right. Voters were measuring the candidates by their willingness to lay out in detail the specific policies they would pursue as president. Perhaps, as some had suggested, a detailed expansion of Clinton's six-page January *Plan for America's Future,* an economic plan with specifics galore, was the big idea they needed. It would grab attention and prove

Clinton's seriousness. A lot of old political hands, especially from Congress, warned against it, arguing that the cardinal rule of campaigns was to avoid setting out particulars that would be subject to attack. Details could be Clinton's undoing, they said, but Stephanopoulos felt the opposite. Clinton gave Stephanopoulos the go-ahead to draft a plan for him to consider.

In early June 1992, Stephanopoulos called Gene Sperling, the new economic coordinator, with his first major assignment. The next two weeks are going to be the most important of your life, Stephanopoulos said. Devise an economic plan, he instructed, that could serve as the centerpiece of the campaign. Most important, the plan had to have numbers, specifics. He wanted a scaled-down version of a federal budget, listing both sources of revenue and expenditures. Sperling marveled at Stephanopoulos's almost mystical sense of confidence and mission as he outlined the assignment.

Clinton, who liked being seen as the candidate of ideas, at one point orally provided an outline. He even seemed very much inclined to design the plan himself. Stephanopoulos, however, assured him they would come up with something, and Clinton agreed to leave the project to Sperling.

BOB BOORSTIN, a former *Harvard Crimson* editor and former *New York Times* reporter who had joined the campaign, was assigned to work with Sperling. Boorstin—highly intellectual, blunt, and a touch cynical—became the campaign's utility writer. As Sperling worked the budget numbers, Boorstin drafted and polished the language.

Boorstin worried endlessly about Perot, who was threatening to issue his own economic plan. Stories were circulating that Perot had teams of Berkeley graduate students pulling all-nighters to develop a plan. Boorstin feared he would again steal Clinton's thunder. If Perot used any of their ideas, Boorstin was convinced, they'd be dead. It was a race against the clock and against Perot.

Sperling too was afraid of Perot. Perot's birthday was June 27, and in the past he had shown a childlike pleasure in the importance of that day. Other rumors, frequently repeated with convincing authority, said Perot would officially announce his candidacy then. Sperling worried that Clinton would go into the Democratic Convention, scheduled for July 13, with no momentum. He wanted to have the plan ready by June 21, the day before Clinton was to deliver an important address to a Conference of Mayors.

Clinton's various political and economic advisers were spending long sessions in the basement of the Governor's Mansion in Little Rock. The mansion basement, a sort of unofficial headquarters, was distinguished mainly by its bad coffee and old Fritos, the junk food of choice, and often had the feel and appearance of a children's rumpus room. At first, when the economic and political advisers were both working in the basement, the room took on the air of an old-time college freshman mixer, with economic advisers on one side of the room, political advisers on the other, eyeing each other warily.

On Friday, June 12, Stephanopoulos urged Clinton to have a serious meeting the coming weekend in Washington with Boorstin and Sperling to review their work on the economic plan.

Okay, Clinton agreed. Let's get it done. Fly them in, let's sit down.

Stephanopoulos immediately arranged for them to come to the Washington Court Hotel. Clinton was going to speak the next day to the Reverend Jesse Jackson's Rainbow Coalition, and afterward he would meet with Sperling, Boorstin, and some of the others to review the plan. On such short notice, Boorstin and Sperling couldn't book seats together, so as they flew into Washington, they passed papers back and forth to each other, several rows apart.

On Saturday, Clinton first had to deal with Jesse Jackson, who had unsuccessfully sought the Democratic presidential nomination in 1984 and 1988. He had been considered for vice president, only to be passed over both times. Although Jackson commanded a strong following, Clinton had fared well among black voters in the primaries, and none of his senior advisers felt an urgent need to court the controversial reverend. On the contrary, Stephanopoulos and Begala saw an opportunity for Clinton to distance himself from Jackson.

At the end of a routine address to Jackson's group, Clinton criticized Jackson and his Rainbow Coalition for providing a forum the night before for a black rap singer named Sister Souljah. Clinton quoted the rapper's remarks about the Los Angeles riots: "If black people kill black people every day, why not have a week and kill white people?" Clinton said, "Her comments before and after Los Angeles were filled with a kind of hatred that you do not honor today and tonight." Jackson had just mentioned approvingly that she had been on the previous day's panel. As Jackson stared straight ahead, Clinton said, "If you took the words 'white' and 'black' and reversed them, you might think David Duke was giving that speech."

Jackson was enraged, telling others he felt personally violated. Clinton became uneasy. He worried that he had screwed up Jackson's conference. As governor, he'd held conferences and always hated it when people pulled stunts. Besides, he never liked to make an enemy, even though he wanted to signal his distance from Jackson.

After the speech, Jackson tried to hand Clinton a long memo outlining the assets he would bring to the Democratic ticket should Clinton choose him as his vice-presidential running mate.

Clinton declined. "I'm not going to put you through what Fritz Mondale or Mike Dukakis did," Clinton said.

Afterwards, Clinton told Begala and Stephanopoulos tersely, "Well, you got your story."

CLINTON RETURNED to his suite at the hotel and took a nap. Sperling, Boorstin, and Stephanopoulos were thankful. The nap gave them an extra hour and a half to polish their draft of the plan.

The meeting began around 5 P.M. in Clinton's suite. Sperling, Boorstin, Stephanopoulos, Begala, and Ira Magaziner gathered at a large glass table in the dining area of Clinton's suite. At the outset of the meeting, Jackson phoned.

Clinton took the call back in his private room. Jackson was still fuming about the rejection of his vice-presidential bid and the put-down of Sister Souljah. Jackson felt he had showed admirable restraint at the conference, avoiding a further public showdown and another round of what he called "little-boy politics." It was 20 minutes before Clinton returned to the table.

Sperling and Boorstin had prepared a two-part presentation: first some general themes for the plan, then various options for a concrete four-year budget. Sperling felt anxious. He had met Clinton for the first time just two weeks before, and now he had to present the plan that could decide this man's future. To make matters worse, Sperling learned from Magaziner that their budget numbers were off by about $90 billion. Shapiro, who had prepared the figures, had miscalculated the savings achieved by cutting defense spending. He had based his figures on those initially proposed by the Bush administration, but when Bush proposed additional reductions, Shapiro counted the original cuts again —double-counting, an elementary mistake. Sperling explained the error to Clinton in a memo dated that day, June 13.

Perot had elevated deficit reduction to topic A. Balancing the federal budget was a matter of common sense and would be simple, Perot claimed. Balanced-budget mania was now sweeping the country. The deficit problem had never been central to Clinton's vision, but the Clinton team now realized they were obliged to include specific deficit reduction goals in their overall plan. Unfortunately, Clinton's campaign pledges—new investments, a middle-class tax cut, a stimulus of fast-track spending to jump-start the economy, and health care reform—were expensive and could increase the deficit.

Promising to balance the federal budget at the end of a four-year presidential term was standard campaign fare. Clinton saw the dilemma and asked if there were any way they could credibly put out a plan that would include his promises but also balance the budget at the end of a four-year term.

No, said Sperling, supported by the others. The numbers just didn't add up, especially if they wanted significant new spending on investments. If they issued a plan, they would have to say they couldn't balance the budget in four years.

Clinton said okay.

Someone suggested that Clinton promise instead to cut the deficit in half at the end of four years, a more realistic goal.

Clinton again approved.

Turning to the investments, Clinton expressed concern that the plan didn't say enough about technology and infrastructure and didn't devote enough money to these areas. How could they justify skimping on those key investments? he kept asking.

The investments, especially infrastructure, had been a sore spot. Reich and Magaziner had been urging $50 billion a year in new infrastructure spending, while Sperling and Shapiro felt that figure was too high. At the meeting, the group settled on $35 billion a year, agreeing that it would still amount to a massive program.

They also had to decide what to do about the middle-class tax cut. Reich had been suggesting that it be dropped altogether, but Stephanopoulos and others were leery of jettisoning what had been more than an important campaign promise. The screwing of the middle class had been the foundation of Clinton's campaign. He had to offer some relief.

Sperling proposed a solution: Clinton had also been advocating a tax credit for families with children. It had been in the January plan. Instead of abandoning either tax break, why not offer families a choice between the two?

Satisfaction washed over Clinton's face. "That's a really great idea," he said. It had the appeal of helping kids, while beginning a march away from the middle-class tax cut. Under the latest calculations the either/or proposal would cost $17 billion a year, compared to $40 billion for both tax cuts together.

Perfect, thought Stephanopoulos. It was the ideal Clintonian solution —down the middle and offering a choice.

Near the end of the meeting, Boorstin turned to Clinton. "You know, Governor," he said, "Gene Sperling thought he was going to be fired today."

"Why?" Clinton asked.

"Because of the $90-billion-a-year difference on defense," Boorstin said.

Clinton went over to Sperling and put his arm around the new, much younger man.

"In my campaign, that doesn't even qualify as bad news," Clinton joked reassuringly. Everyone laughed, most of all Sperling. Clinton left to see the latest Harrison Ford movie, *Patriot Games,* based on a Tom Clancy novel.

Stephanopoulos was pumped. The meeting could not have gone better as far as he was concerned, and most importantly, Clinton had departed in a good mood. "Now stay here," Stephanopoulos said to Sperling. "Don't go home. Stay here in the hotel and work on this."

Sperling took the instruction literally. He and Boorstin stayed up, toiling away late into the night. Under close examination, they discovered other things that didn't add up.

ON SUNDAY, Sperling took a hard look at the health care numbers in the plan. They had been compiled by Ira Magaziner, another intense, driven workaholic, who prided himself on his analytic mind. Valedictorian of his 1969 class at Brown University, Magaziner had led a successful student drive for a more flexible curriculum. A tall, unkempt man, he had moved from utopian agitator to business management consultant, running his own firm called Telesis for ten years. Magaziner generally was a man for grand designs. Some of his ideas had been used in a health care plan adopted by the state of Rhode Island, and he wanted Clinton to endorse something similar for the nation. Magaziner said national health reform could eventually guarantee coverage to all Americans, including those 37 million currently uninsured, and still manage to save money by 1997. Some pegged the savings at $4 billion. The savings, he said, would be squeezed from the wasteful administrative costs that accounted for 28 percent of health care costs.

Sperling found Magaziner maniacal. Magaziner wanted to put his numbers in the economic plan, but his claims sounded absurd and implausible to Sperling. Most experts said health care reform would be an expensive undertaking. Sperling suspected that no one outside the campaign, no independent specialist, would support Magaziner. He knew that journalists would immediately check the numbers, and it would make news if no one else supported them. Expert validation was essential. He told Magaziner he wouldn't include the health care numbers in the plan unless a respected outside authority backed them up. Sperling suggested Henry Aaron, an economist at the well-established Brookings Institution and a recognized health policy expert.

Sperling and Magaziner phoned Aaron for a three-way conference call. As Sperling expected, Aaron said he didn't think health care was as waste-based as Magaziner claimed. Aaron declined to support anything close to Magaziner's estimates. He believed that only 1 or 2 percent of costs could be saved each year. Aaron added that a tax increase would be needed to pay for universal coverage.

Magaziner disagreed.

Aaron thought Magaziner was approaching the problem not as an economist but as a management consultant. Consultants believed that every business had 15 or 20 percent of fat that could be trimmed. Aaron hung up the phone convinced the Clinton team was flying by the seat of its pants. The call only reenforced his belief that campaigns were the worst environments for serious policy planning.

Sperling offered to let Magaziner find his own experts.

"They're all wrong," Magaziner insisted.

"Ira," Sperling replied, "you might be the smartest person in the world, but in presidential politics, if the experts don't verify you, you get hit on national television, and then it's a disaster."

Magaziner retreated a bit, saying that for the purpose of the campaign he would acknowledge that reform might cost $10 to $15 billion a year. Still, no one was buying.

Later in the week, back in Little Rock, Bob Boorstin took a stab at reasoning with Magaziner as they were traveling in a van to the Governor's Mansion. "No one believes you will save $4 billion," Boorstin told Magaziner. "It doesn't pass the smell test." He touched his nose and sniffed once, then twice. Smell was vital in politics. "Look, I used to be a *New York Times* reporter, and this is just not credible."

Magaziner insisted money could be saved.

6

In Little Rock, at about 4 p.m. on Thursday, June 18, Clinton met at the mansion with a number of advisers, including Stephanopoulos, Sperling, Magaziner, and Shapiro. Sperling presented his latest round of work. By using the framework of a budget, showing both the spending and revenue sides of the ledger, he made it clear that they would have to account for the cost of each new program they proposed. Immediately, problems began to appear.

Sperling suggested significantly lowering the percentage of the cost of meals and entertainment that businesses could deduct from their taxes, from 80 percent to 50 percent. Someone criticized the idea, saying it would anger restaurant owners, who depended on expensive meals for their profits. Another person said it would set off a national debate, that Clinton might be accused of taxing food. It might hint at a national sales tax and confuse people. Clinton rejected the proposal.

The atmosphere turned negative. Every minor spending cut had a downside. Clinton could be eaten up for two weeks over each one. Suggesting these cuts was like chopping the candidate's head off for nothing, because no vocal constituency would support the cut. As these problems arose, Stephanopoulos carefully monitored Clinton's mood. At one point it seemed Clinton was going to kill the whole plan, but by the end of the meeting he was still on board.

． ． ．

FRIDAY MORNING, the team gathered in the Governor's Mansion again. Sperling, looking for more revenue to pay for the new spending, had suggested additional new taxes on inheritance, securities transfers, alcohol, and tobacco.

John Kroger, a politically moderate former Capitol Hill aide who had been recruited by Stephanopoulos, erupted. Kroger worked under Bruce Reed, who had come from the Democratic Leadership Council, and the two of them had originally been assigned the plan. They had assumed it would remain their own domain and had felt ambushed when Stephanopoulos reassigned it to the more liberal Sperling and Boorstin. Kroger and Reed never would have drafted a plan like this. It was tax-and-spend, Kroger said, the old formula that plagued the Democrats, and they would get killed on it. Clinton would lose the election.

Clinton seemed to agree. The group began to review the plan, looking to minimize the taxes. Infrastructure—which Sperling had already lowered to $35 billion annually from Magaziner's proposed $50 billion—came down to $20 billion, with Magaziner fighting tooth and nail. Other taxes were scrapped, and the remaining ones were forced to account for more money. A tax on foreign corporations, which realistically might have brought in $5 billion over four years, was now saddled with the burden of bringing in $45 billion. Boorstin and Sperling knew it was a lie, a vast overestimation, but they had to balance the books and the $45 billion had come from a congressional report, providing at least some outside verification.

Kroger had prepared a separate list of spending cuts. Let's review those this afternoon, Clinton said.

In the afternoon they met at Clinton's office at the Little Rock Capitol. Kroger read through the list of spending cuts one by one. The group shot back reactions. Nothing went over well. All it took to kill a cut was for someone to say that it would hurt them in a certain critical state or with a powerful interest group.

On almost every cut, Clinton asked whether others outside the campaign had been consulted. He wanted to run the agriculture cuts by Arkansas Senator David Pryor, a close friend. He didn't want to impose water and grazing fees because he thought he had a shot at winning in the normally Republican West. Other reductions he liked but didn't want to commit to paper. How could he call this governor or that senator and simply announce these cuts? As a governor himself, he said, he would be furious if the party's presidential candidate did that to him. He needed more time to study the proposed plan, more time to consult.

Clinton was asking the right questions, Stephanopoulos felt. The plan wasn't perfect. But, he thought, they could check it and consult it to death. There was a time to leave well enough alone, and with the deadline hanging over them, he grew frustrated. He was beginning to feel that the mere existence of a plan and the act of putting it out would be more important than the actual details.

One by one, Clinton ruled out other cuts. By the end, only one specific survived: curtailing government subsidies for honeybee producers. It would save just $40 million over four years. They wound up placing other savings in a nebulous middle ground between the broad rhetoric of "cutting waste" and actual programs to be trimmed. They listed areas like "Intelligence cuts," relating to the Central Intelligence Agency and other spy agencies, and "Reducing overhead on federally sponsored university research." Words like "streamline," "reform," and "consolidate" were invoked without explanation. Even after backing off the specifics, Clinton seemed ambivalent about issuing the document without more political input.

AT 8 P.M. Friday night, the team met at campaign headquarters, the Gazette Building in downtown Little Rock, to put together a final plan. Issues that had been left unresolved earlier now had to be pinned down, and arguments broke out, with many insisting that the consensus had been closer to their own positions. Kroger and Sperling fought over how toughly to word the section on crime. Boorstin sat at the computer, trying to act as mediator.

Health care remained a question mark. Magaziner still hoped to claim some savings from reform; the others maintained it was impossible. In the end, they threw in arbitrary numbers they had essentially made up. The late-night session broke up close to 5 A.M.

DURING THE CRITICAL WEEKEND, Bob Reich was in the hospital, having both of his hips replaced. Eager to keep an eye on the investment program, Reich talked to Sperling periodically by phone, and was eventually faxed a draft of the plan. When Reich read a copy, he called Boorstin urgently. Two things were missing, he said. One was Reich's idea to create an "Economic Security Council," a vague concept for White House coordination of various economic issues. That was not a big deal, and Boorstin promised to restore it.

The other omission was crucial. The draft contained no mention of

Reich's theory of human capital, the notion that a country's most important resource was its people. This theory underpinned the whole argument for investing in education and job training; it was the link between helping people and bringing an economic revival. It meant as much to Clinton as it did to Reich. "You could do me a big favor if you put that back in," he told Boorstin calmly. Boorstin included the idea on the second page of the plan: "The only resource that's really rooted in a nation—and the ultimate source of all its wealth—is its people."

The plan still needed a catchy title. Stan Greenberg wanted to contrast the plan with Reaganomics and helping the rich. He and Boorstin also wanted to tie the plan's title to Reich's "human capital theory." But Reich's phrase, while an economist's delight, was a sloganmaker's nightmare and had zero voter appeal. They had to translate the notion into plain English. Finally they came up with a name: *Putting People First.*

ON SATURDAY MORNING, in the mansion basement, Clinton met with Stephanopoulos, Sperling, and Kroger for the final vetting. He wanted overall assessments of the plan. Sperling said it was great. Dukakis had never put a price tag on anything in 1988, and here Clinton was laying out all this detail.

John Kroger said he also believed the plan was strong, but added warily that he would prefer more deficit reduction.

Stephanopoulos felt like killing Kroger. He knew the remark would only revive Clinton's doubts. Clinton let loose. In an outburst of renewed anxiety, he said their breakneck pace was not producing a serious document. They were moving too hastily. Cuts hadn't been checked. They needed more time to consult. To Sperling, Clinton seemed to be riding a roller coaster, high on the plan one moment, down about it the next. It was all happening before their eyes—deep, near-terminal ambivalence.

Stephanopoulos was practically jumping out of his skin. He had seen Clinton act like this before, disliking, discarding, or wanting to change what he read. His initial reaction was always to resist, to say no, to force more discussion and debate.

Clinton then asked about the health care numbers, whether everyone was on board supporting them. His aides confessed that the numbers had basically been made up. They had no strong outside validation. Clinton was astounded. They replied that the widespread disagreement on the cost of health care reform meant that any numbers, though arbitrary, could not be effectively challenged.

Clinton wasn't buying. He wanted to drop health care from the plan altogether. He wasn't comfortable with the numbers and there wasn't time to check them out. His discomfort was spreading again, threatening to infect and destroy the entire plan.

"What's the backup? I'm not sure about this," he said as Hillary walked in.

"Look," she said, "if you're not sure about it, then nobody should be sure about it, because you're the one who has to stand behind whatever it is that is written. So it shouldn't be done until you are satisfied. And if that means not doing it right now, we don't do it right now."

Calmly, Stephanopoulos tried to make the case for retaining health care. It was critical they put out a plan.

Hillary suggested that they should show the plan around before releasing it, circulate it to 150 or 200 members of Congress and other elected officials to get feedback.

Stephanopoulos grew confrontational. Circulating the plan would almost certainly mean it would leak to the press. Then, if Clinton changed anything, no matter how small, he would be portrayed as caving to special interests. The news story would become not the plan but the alterations.

He turned directly to Clinton. Hey, you wanted it. "This is what you talked about," Stephanopoulos said plaintively. It was no time to back off now. The plan's unveiling was essential for ushering in the next stage of the campaign. As a practical matter, he added, they were under desperate time pressure. Clinton was to speak before the Conference of Mayors on Monday, June 22. After that, they had lined up a string of national TV appearances for him. Clinton had to have something new to present. If Clinton didn't approve the plan by that evening, he said, they couldn't get it to the printer. If it wasn't printed in time, they wouldn't be able to hand out copies to the mayors. Stephanopoulos knew how much Clinton liked being able to hand things out to an audience.

Clinton seemed convinced. Still, he said, he wanted a conference call to settle the health care issue. He had to drive to a meeting elsewhere in Arkansas, and wanted to have the call when he returned at 1 P.M.

Kroger stayed behind to try to track down various health care experts who had been advising the campaign. It was a Saturday morning, and he had to round them up for a major conference call in an hour. People were all over the place. Stephanopoulos thought it was crazy.

.   .   .

CLINTON RETURNED to the mansion midday for the health care call and took a seat in the kitchen, with Kroger sitting beside him. Hillary came in and out of the room. Fresh coffee was brewing. The third round of the U.S. Open golf tournament at Pebble Beach, California, was on the television.

Magaziner, who had gone home for the weekend, launched into his familiar spiel, and soon the various experts were delving into the complicated, technical minutiae of the costs. He maintained he didn't recognize some of the new numbers, but insisted that money could be saved if universal coverage were delayed until 1998. "I can't say that," Clinton replied.

Stephanopoulos and Sperling, together in Stephanopoulos's office, tried to gauge Clinton's response from his voice over the phone. Sperling was in pain as the conversation dragged on. Stephanopoulos detected a positive sign. Clinton was losing interest, and seemed to be melting away.

In the kitchen of the mansion, Clinton's eyes veered over to the golf match. As the experts debated, Clinton turned to Kroger. "So, you golf?" he asked. Kroger said he hadn't played in a while.

Finally Bruce Reed, on the line from Washington, asked why they needed to include health care numbers at all. He suggested they take out the numbers, but leave the basic principles and language.

"Yeah," Clinton said hesitantly. He paused. "Maybe we could do that."

Few seemed to pay attention. The debate continued.

Clinton turned again to Kroger. Did Kroger think specific health care numbers would bring any political benefit? Clinton asked. Kroger said no. Any numbers, as they all knew too well, would be somewhat arbitrary.

Clinton returned his attention to the conference call. They should describe the health care component of the plan as revenue-neutral, he said, with no estimated costs and no estimated savings. If anyone asked questions, they could say they would issue more details later in the campaign. Someone else added that they could even release a separate health care initiative later and get another bang out of it. The solution seemed clear.

Stephanopoulos was elated. "Okay, okay, we're done," he exclaimed. "Okay, okay, let's go!" Just close it up, he urged. The call had already lasted about an hour.

But others kept talking. Stephanopoulos had another emergency conference call to take. He thrust a finger into Sperling's chest. "You end this call!" he whispered vehemently. *"End this call!"* Stephanopoulos left.

Sperling finally jumped in during a rare opening in the conversation. "Well, I think the governor is busy, and we've taken enough of his time," he said.

Clinton laughed.

The experts kept at each other. Sperling tried again. "Let's let the governor get back to his golf," Sperling said. He punched the button ending the call.

The no-numbers compromise seemed to have saved the day. It had been close, Sperling knew. Magaziner, he felt, had nearly killed the entire plan.

By about 5 P.M., the plan was off to the printer, so it could be ready for release on Sunday. Boorstin, Kroger, Stephanopoulos, and Sperling went out for a Mexican dinner to celebrate.

Carville liked the plan for strategic reasons; he didn't involve himself much in the nitty-gritty of policy. If the Bush or Perot people started arguing about the plan or attacking it, he told Clinton, Clinton would win. Even if he were to lose that particular debate, he would still win in the scheme of things, because he would demonstrate how serious he was about fixing the economy. He would have shifted the campaign spotlight to the economy, precisely where he wanted it. Any debate on the economy could only highlight Bush's record and his indifference to real people, and that debate Bush could only lose.

Clinton announced the plan on Sunday, June 21, at noon. The release of the 22-page document kicked off a week of favorable coverage. The timing of its release was fortuitous. That same day, *The Washington Post* ran a long story documenting investigations Perot had launched of Bush, in particular that he had paid a law firm $10,000 to see if Bush had helped his former business partner obtain a $48 million tax deduction. Anxieties were crystallizing about Perot's penchant for investigating his opponents or enemies, and a sound-bite feud between Bush and Perot followed. Clinton turned the feud to his advantage. While Bush and Perot were investigating each other, he said in campaign appearances, he was investigating the American economy, as the unemployment rate reached an eight-year high.

7

O**N THE EVENING** of Tuesday, June 30, Clinton was holed up at the Capital Hilton in downtown Washington to interview possible running mates. Though the choice of a vice president would probably not decide the election, it certainly could generate months, or even years, of favorable or unwanted press. That night, Clinton's visitor was Senator Albert Gore, Jr.

A sturdy, dark-haired Tennessean, Gore, 44, was a son of Washington. Gore's father had been a senator, and Gore had grown up in the city and learned its culture; he still referred to the hotel he was visiting as the "Statler Hilton," as it was called in his youth. Gore had served eight years in the House and eight more in the Senate, acquiring a reputation for uncommon earnestness and studiousness. No one was going to trump him when it came to seriousness. Stiff and plodding in his speech, he exuded a sense of diligence. A Harvard graduate, he boasted a whiz-kid mastery of the technical details of opaque policy issues such as arms control and, his current obsession, the environment. His book, *Earth in the Balance,* a diagnosis and prescription for the world's long-term ecological problems, had just been released and was on its way to becoming a best-seller.

Gore and Clinton had talked at length only once before, in 1987, when it was Gore who was running for president. He had visited Clinton in Little Rock ostensibly to solicit the governor's endorsement, though his real purpose had been simply to keep Clinton from endorsing his fellow governor and friend Michael Dukakis. Gore had presented to Clinton what he considered a theory of the mutuality of their interests. When the histories of late 20th-century American politics were written, Gore believed, they would show that the only politicians capable of uniting the Democratic coalition were Southern moderates such as Lyndon Johnson, Jimmy Carter, and, Gore argued, himself and Clinton. If Gore succeeded in his bid, Democrats would build on this pattern of success and turn to those like Clinton. Gore said that the two of them should regard themselves not as rivals or antagonists but as allies, working toward the same goals, able to succeed together. Gore sensed that Clinton shared his outlook. In the 1988 primaries, Clinton remained neutral.

Now, in a suite at the hotel, the tables were turned, though the irony remained unmentioned. The conversation picked up right where they had left off five years earlier. For about three hours they talked, discussing the nature of a good partnership and working relationship. A year before, when Gore was contemplating a 1992 presidential run, he had heard from mutual friends that Clinton would sit out the race if he ran, but Gore himself had voluntarily pulled back. His six-year-old son, who had been hit by a car in 1989 and nearly died, was still recovering, and Gore didn't want the campaign to tear him from his family. By 1992, however, his son was healthy and Gore felt renewed about life. He told Clinton that although he would happily consider running for vice president, he wasn't lusting for the nomination. If Clinton wanted to pick someone else, that was fine.

Afterwards Clinton told his advisers that he had been surprised at the rapport with Gore, and that he thought he would select him. The senator had staked out arms control and the environment as areas of expertise, persisting with both issues—an admirable trait, Clinton said, likening it to his own concentration on schools and jobs in Arkansas.

Begala probed for a deeper reason. Why Gore? he asked.

"I could die, that's why," Clinton said.

As Clinton deliberated over the next ten days, he also received a piece of advice from one of Gore's closest friends. The friend praised Gore's intelligence and stamina, and then added: "And most importantly he won't stab you in the back—even if you deserve it." Clinton laughed heartily and the next day announced Gore's selection.

IT BECAME a bad three weeks for Perot, and the morning of July 16, in the midst of the Democratic Convention, he announced that he was not going to run. His decision turned the presidential race upside down and provided a substantial boost to Clinton. That evening Clinton accepted the Democratic Party's nomination for president "in the name of the hardworking Americans who make up our forgotten middle class."

The next day, Clinton gathered his top campaign staff and advisers in New York. He was setting up a new system, he said, with Carville in charge. A strategy center in Little Rock would clear and coordinate all work. "Strategy will determine everything," Clinton said. "Strategy will determine the schedule. Strategy will determine the message. Strategy will determine the budget." It would determine what he and everyone else said and did, when, why, and in what order. Carville would be in charge of strategy.

Carville, who had been trying to put off the day of obsessiveness when he would become fully immersed in the campaign, moved to Little Rock. He and Stephanopoulos set up a coordination center. Hillary dubbed it the "War Room."

Their job was focus. Carville posted a sign in the War Room to remind everyone of their three-pronged message, which Stephanopoulos called a haiku:

> Change vs. more of the same.
> The economy, stupid.*
> Don't forget health care.

AT A CAMPAIGN STOP in Macon, Georgia, on September 1, 1992, Clinton spoke to a group of elderly citizens in the town square while thousands of locals were roped off from the event. "Your people told us they didn't want any Macon people here," a state representative told Clinton right afterwards. "This is a national event." Clinton was furious and went over to the ropes, spending hours shaking hands in the summer heat. He demanded to know who on his staff had made the decision to exclude the Macon people, which he said violated all his principles, but none of his aides knew. He then directed one senior staffer to return to Little Rock and discover who had made the mistake. "I want him dead, dead," Clinton said in blind fury. "I want him killed. I want him horsewhipped." Clinton was in a steady rage for three days, complaining to his staff about the utter stupidity and incompetence. Many remembered it as the angriest they had ever seen Clinton.

The senior staffer returned from Little Rock at midnight of the third

---

* This was later modified in the popular vocabulary to become the widely quoted catch phrase, *"It's the economy, stupid."*

day. "I want to know who did this. I want him fired," Clinton said, downgrading the punishment. The campaign headquarters had been turned upside down to locate the culprit—a functionary who was plodding in his work and had made an innocent mistake. Clinton knew him personally. "Damn it," Clinton said, "I hope he gets a real talking to."

THE MORNING OF OCTOBER 4, 1992, Clinton called Stephanopoulos into his suite at the Grand Hotel in Washington. Clinton was grumpy. He was scheduled to travel to North Carolina to deliver a speech on the North American Free Trade Agreement (NAFTA).

Free trade, a cause normally championed by Republicans, was a tough issue for any Democrat, but especially for Clinton. He had been wrestling most of the year with the particular agreement that Bush had negotiated with Canada and Mexico. Clinton knew that backing it would alienate organized labor, a key part of the Democrats' constituency, and hurt his chances in big union states such as Michigan and Ohio. Michigan could be lost on the single issue if he endorsed it, Stan Greenberg had concluded. But Clinton believed in free trade, and as governor he had run personal campaigns to attract foreign investors to Arkansas. In addition, the New Democrats generally favored the agreement. He had considered finessing the issue by saying simply that he could not support any agreement that was Bush's work.

Finally, however, he had decided to endorse it, based on raw political calculation. Stephanopoulos, Carville, and Greenberg had argued that an endorsement would put Clinton and Bush on the same side, remove the issue from the table, and neutralize it. The campaign could then remain focused on domestic economic issues. Clinton would make his support contingent on acceptable side agreements with Mexico and Canada on environmental protection and worker safety. That way, Stephanopoulos had concluded, Clinton, if elected, could use the side agreements as a pretext for bailing out on the treaty.

That morning, the exact speech text had not been finished, and Clinton began yelling at Stephanopoulos about the draft. Stephanopoulos had grown accustomed to tirades like this. He sometimes thought his primary function was to get yelled at first thing in the morning, to bear the brunt of Clinton's anger, to take the punches. Clinton seemed to have to vent and expel all of his ire and frustration, and then he could proceed with his decisions and his day. After a while that morning, Stephanopoulos felt that Clinton's heart wasn't really in his yelling.

Clinton finally stopped screaming. Sitting across the bed from

Stephanopoulos, the candidate looked at his aide. "Do you think we're going to win?" Clinton asked.

Stephanopoulos was eternally the pessimist. But the pollsters had just conducted their final survey testing every argument—their best argument, Bush's best argument—and had essentially found that Clinton couldn't lose. Although a loss was always possible, especially with the crucial national television debates still ahead, the polling showed that Clinton had won the main argument of 1992: change and the economy. For the first time, Stephanopoulos believed it might be real.

"Yeah," Stephanopoulos said. He did think they would win. He couldn't quite believe he'd said it out loud.

"I do too," Clinton said.

Stephanopoulos felt a great shot in the arm. It was the first time Clinton had openly acknowledged that he expected to win.

That day in his long speech at North Carolina State University in Raleigh, Clinton endorsed the free trade pact; but as *The Washington Post* said, he did so "in a speech full of dire warnings about the damage the treaty could cause if the nation did not change its overall economic policies."

"Clinton's speech amounted to a tightrope walk," the *Post* article continued. "As is his wont, he sought to define his as a third position on a polarized issue." On the campaign trail, Clinton started to moderate his promise of economic restoration. He started talking about how the country didn't get into this economic mess overnight, and if elected president he wouldn't be able to get the country out of the mess overnight.

CLINTON RETURNED to Arkansas that week and talked with Carville at the Governor's Mansion. *The Washington Post* had published a four-part series of articles that week about Bush and the making of his economic policies. Many of Bush's economic advisers had criticized their own president and one another in the articles, often using harsh language. Richard G. Darman, Bush's budget director, was reported to have said privately that Treasury Secretary Nicholas F. Brady was a "dolt" who could not pass an introductory economics exam in any American university and was "probably the weakest Treasury secretary in the history of the country." At one point, the articles reported, Michael Boskin, the chairman of Bush's Council of Economic Advisers (CEA), had threatened to resign so he could meet with the president to convey some bad economic news. Clinton had the articles in front of him and pointed at them.

"They are snakes," he said to Carville, referring to Bush's economic advisers. He poked his finger hard into Carville's shoulder. "They're jumping ship." He poked Carville's shoulder again.

"You can't say that about your friend Mary Matalin," Clinton said. Matalin, a top campaign spokesperson for Bush, was romantically involved with Carville—certainly the oddest pairing of the 1992 campaign. Matalin had on her wall a picture of Hillary portrayed as the Wicked Witch from *The Wizard of Oz*. The caption read: "I will get you, my pretty, and your little dog too." Matalin often attacked Clinton personally and had once called him "a philandering, pot-smoking draft dodger." In the context of Bush's apparently disloyal economic team, however, Clinton seemed to admire her loyalty. "She's sticking," Clinton said, as if delivering some important message as he continued to poke Carville.

"But they're rats," Clinton said. "Jumping the ship. George Bush made them. They were nothing before."

SOMETIME AROUND 1:30 P.M. on election day, November 3, 1992, Stephanopoulos and most of the campaign staff realized the election was over. The exit polls conducted by the television networks showed a solid Clinton victory. But it was not over for Hillary Clinton. She paced nervously around the Governor's Mansion throughout the day and night. Others were celebrating; she paced. She didn't believe exit polls. Back in 1980 when Clinton was running for his second term as governor, a TV station general manager had called her. "Oh, I'm so pleased," the manager said. "Our exit polls are showing Bill at 58 percent." Hillary and Clinton both expected a close contest and felt that the election could go either way. She didn't think 58 percent was credible. "Your exit polls are wrong," she told the manager. "They're lying to you." Her husband lost by 32,000 votes.

Now, 12 years later, she waited for the final tally of electoral votes. Finally, Ohio put him over the top. Clinton was elected President of the United States with 43 percent of the popular vote and 370 of the 538 electoral votes. Bush received 38 percent and Perot 19 percent.

Clinton went over to his wife. She told him that she loved him very much, she was very proud, and she couldn't imagine anyone going through what he had gone through and keeping his spirit and optimism. And, she said, he would be a great president.

"You really think so?" Clinton asked.

"Yeah," she said reassuringly, "I really think so!"

8

For the most important year of the most important part of his life to this point, Clinton had lived on the campaign trail—an insular and often surreal world of planes and buses, hotel rooms, podiums, microphones, hands and faces, brutal punches and brutal counterpunches. The first thing he had to defeat was the exhaustion; simple survival had seemed like a triumph. Now he didn't stop to savor his victory or collect himself. He took no real vacation.

After his victory, Clinton remained in Little Rock, the small capital city—population 132,000—of his small state, population less than 2 million. Clinton had dominated the state politically for the last decade, running it largely with a Rolodex of 100 important telephone numbers. Now he had 78 days before he would be running the biggest operation in the world, headquartered in the alien culture of Washington. He plunged into the transition, the uncomfortable interlude of neither campaigning nor governing, knowing he had to create an administration and a government from nothing.

Clinton did not set up a central transition authority. Some of his political advisers, such as Stan Greenberg, concluded that Clinton had not liked ceding so much authority to the War Room during the campaign and was now reclaiming what he had surrendered, placing his own hands on the levers of power. Stephanopoulos could see dangerous mistakes in the making. They should have taken two weeks, picked a White House staff, and then systematically selected the cabinet, he felt.

Stephanopoulos and Gore had had a tense relationship during the campaign, in part because they were jockeying for proximity to Clinton. After the election, Gore virtually moved to Little Rock. Stephanopoulos noticed that while Gore lacked a certain political deftness and creativity, he was disciplined. When Hillary's close friend Susan Thomases, a New York lawyer, tried to push Gore out of the inner circle, Gore methodically moved to shore up his support. He met with everybody who might be relevant and never left the room when Clinton was having an important meeting or discussion. He was relentless.

Clinton appointed two lawyers, Vernon E. Jordan and Warren M. Christopher, as formal heads of the transition team. Jordan, a former civil rights activist and head of the National Urban League, was a successful and canny lawyer, and a fixture in Washington's political and social worlds. Christopher had been the number-two man in President Jimmy Carter's State Department, but had been out of Washington for 12 years, practicing law in California. A small man, with a wizened face and a hesitant voice, Christopher was known for his caution and ability to lawyer any problem to death.

With Hillary, Christopher, Gore, and Bruce Lindsey, Clinton would pick his cabinet. No action would better define Clinton and his administration than these selections. He realized that picking a person was easier than picking a policy, but he basically knew what policies he wanted. The selections would be the rawest, and, at least on the surface, the least complicated exercise of power.

Clinton assigned Bob Reich to head the transition's economic policy team. He was to study and write exhaustive reports, translating their 24-year-long tutorial and debating society into policy options for the new administration. Reich was also a sure bet for a top administration job. At one point Reich thought he might want to be the chairman of Clinton's Council of Economic Advisers, the trio of economists formally charged with analyzing economic data and policy for the president. But Reich was not a trained economist, and when his name was floated, professional economists rose up in protest. The CEA chairman's main constituencies were the economic professionals and economic technicians from academia to Wall Street. Clinton did not need someone with his own credibility problems.

Reich was also a leading candidate to head the new super-committee of cabinet members and other key White House officials that Clinton had pledged to create, now being called the National Economic Council. The position, overseeing all economic policy, was potentially a powerful one. But in a conversation with Stephanopoulos in an airport over a hot dog and a beer, Reich made it clear that he had come to see that he was exactly the wrong man for the job. First, he would have to be an honest broker, filter and weigh others' opinions, and not advocate opinions of his own. He would have to present options to Clinton in a neutral manner. He would also need to maintain low visibility, not give many interviews or appear on the TV news shows. Reich, however, loved developing and pushing his own ideas, and he loved the media spotlight just as much.

Reich repeated these points to Clinton. He would prefer another position, he said. They finally settled on Labor Secretary. It was a cabinet post in a department that had long been neglected during Republican administrations, and labor was a key Clinton political constituency. And it was where Reich could try to put some of his theories into practice.

TREASURY SECRETARY, traditionally the chief spokesman for economic policy, would be Clinton's key appointment. During the campaign in the summer, Texas Senator Lloyd Bentsen, the Democratic chairman of the Senate Finance Committee, had joined Clinton on a campaign bus swing. Clinton had known Bentsen for 20 years. During the trip, the thought had struck him, "God, I'd really like it if he were secretary of the Treasury."

Bentsen, 71, could have come from international finance ministers' Central Casting. Tall, with a leathery face and a mat of silver hair, he had a restrained, aristocratic air that alternated between friendly and sour, collegial and stiff. Bentsen believed important business should be done not in public, but in private, among gentlemen.

Bentsen also had 30 years of Washington experience. A millionaire insurance man, Bentsen had been a Texas congressman and in 1970 had defeated George Bush for the Senate. In 1988, as vice-presidential nominee, his gentlemanly charm, along with his stinging and memorable "You're no Jack Kennedy" slap at Dan Quayle in their debate, lifted him to the top tier in politics. He was the only one of the four national candidates in 1988 to emerge with his reputation indisputably enhanced.

Clinton liked the way Bentsen played politics. During 1992, Bentsen devoted much time to the Clinton campaign, once spending hours in a TV studio flacking for the nominee in a series of monotonous satellite hookup interviews. It was the kind of small, almost piddling favor that someone of Bentsen's stature undertook only when he wanted something himself.

Clinton had also been told a story about Bentsen's dramatic efforts to court Ross Perot to Clinton's side before Perot decided to reenter the race. Bentsen had visited Perot in Dallas on September 27 as part of a team of Clinton advisers. After what Bentsen realized was too much idle chatter, he interrupted his fellow Texan. "Ross, this is real nice," Bentsen said. "But we've got something serious to talk about today. We know you want to change this country. But I am worried that you are going to reenter the race, and there are three things that could happen. First, you reenter the race and do poorly. People who don't like you will use that against you forever. It will destroy everything you've worked for, destroy everything you've accomplished. Two, if you reenter and do well, you still won't win. You can't win. What you will do is bring votes from the only candidate who stands for change, Bill Clinton. Third, you today could endorse Bill Clinton. In doing that, you could effectively end the election today. I doubt if there are many moments in history where one person has such a chance to make such an impact or to have that power. Ross, you have that power today." Knowing that Perot was sick about a newsmagazine cover that had pictured him with the headline "Quitter," Bentsen added, "You'd be the one person that elects the president. I've never seen that before in this country. One person. I can see that cover of *Time* magazine and it says, 'Kingmaker.' " Although Perot did reenter the race, Clinton said he appreciated Bentsen's sense of political gamesmanship and advocacy.

Privately and delicately, Bentsen let it be known that he was interested in the Treasury post. Clinton now had the choice of making Bentsen an elder statesman in his cabinet, or being stuck with a spurned chairman of the Senate committee that would be central to the passage of his economic plan.

When Bentsen visited Clinton in Little Rock on November 24 for a long talk, he had the impression he was being offered the job, but Clinton didn't ask directly. Clinton still had an out, and there was some equivocation.

Bentsen made two main points to the president-elect. First, the Treasury Secretary had to have direct, unimpeded, and total access to the president. There could be no obstructionists on the White House staff to interfere with that relationship. Second, it was critical that Clinton develop a relationship of trust with the chairman of the Federal Reserve, Alan Greenspan. The Federal Reserve set key short-term interest rates, and the chairman would be either a help or a serious problem for the new administration, Bentsen said. He sensed that no one had quite underscored the importance of Greenspan to Clinton before.

For Clinton, the only downside to Bentsen was how a 71-year-old man would fit into an administration that was supposed to represent youth and vigor. Clinton delayed in making a final offer, wanting to make sure he was comfortable.

FOR THE TREASURY POST, Clinton was also considering Robert E. Rubin, the multimillionaire co-chairman of Goldman, Sachs & Co., the premier New York City investment banking firm. Rubin, 54, was a graduate of Harvard College (*summa cum laude,* Phi Beta Kappa) and of Yale Law School, and for years had been a major fundraiser for Democratic candidates. He raised large sums of money for Clinton, giving the candidate a needed lift in the early going, and he had peripherally advised the campaign later on. A slight man with soft eyes, Rubin was no showboat and gave off no airs. He too visited Little Rock on November 24 for an interview with Clinton.

Two people were on his short list for Treasury Secretary, Clinton said, Bentsen and Rubin himself.

Bentsen would be better, Rubin said. He knew Congress and the media. Rubin explained that he did not seek or want a high profile.

Would Rubin be interested in deputy Treasury Secretary? Clinton inquired.

Rubin made it clear he would not.

Afterward, Rubin told a friend about the meeting. "I don't know what that was about," he said, describing the conversation as "very confusing." The two-hour discussion had been undirected and strange. He assumed it was Clinton's way of getting to know him.

Clinton wanted someone who knew Wall Street and the bond market close to him in the White House. One of the criticisms of Jimmy Carter had been his woeful lack of understanding and appreciation of the bond market. Carter had allowed interest rates to skyrocket, probably one of the mistakes that had doomed his presidency. Rubin had also proven he knew how to run a team. He was sweet and gentle. Though fabulously wealthy, Rubin cared about the poor.

Soon, Warren Christopher called Rubin. What about heading the National Economic Council? Christopher asked. Rubin didn't know much about what Clinton envisioned for this new White House coordinating position. The candidate had said only two and a half paragraphs about it during the campaign and had never laid out details. Rubin was used to Wall Street deals that involved hundreds of pages of explicit agreement.

On December 3, Christopher produced a one-and-a-half-page memo on the new position of assistant to the president for economic policy.

The person would rank on a par with the national security adviser, make recommendations on all key economic issues, be "an honest broker," "prepare the presidential decision memoranda," and finally serve as "an implementer of the president's economic policy" and "an organizer of the president's activities in this area." (Later, the job description was downgraded on paper to say he would not be "an implementer." Instead, he would "monitor implementation of the president's economic agenda.")

Rubin accepted the job. He believed that if the country did not soon get its arms around the economic problem, it would enter a steady, long-term, maybe permanent decline. Rubin also nurtured a strain of idealism. Being a Democrat on Wall Street in the 1980s had not been easy. "Why isn't the underclass as much a crisis as Vietnam?" he asked around Washington during the transition period, displaying a newcomer's naivete.

Clinton, meanwhile, personally offered the Treasury job to Bentsen. Bentsen accepted.

ROGER ALTMAN had been a year ahead of Clinton at Georgetown, where they had been the most politically active students in their respective classes. A thin man, with graying hair and a polished manner, Altman had been an assistant Treasury Secretary in the Carter administration, and then went to Wall Street, where he made millions as an investment banker. Having assisted the Clinton campaign, he had hoped for a top economic post. During the transition, however, Christopher called with a message, "I have bad news." Bentsen and Rubin had been selected for the top jobs. At Clinton's suggestion, Bentsen soon picked Altman as deputy Treasury Secretary.

9

ACROSS WASHINGTON, in a comparatively modest classical office at the nation's central bank, Federal Reserve Chairman Greenspan sat at his desk beside a large plaque proclaiming: "The Buck Starts Here." He pecked on various program keys on his computer, his window to the world economy, looking out for signs of inflation—a rapid increase in prices. Here Greenspan regularly summoned up the very latest charts and data on stocks, bonds, currencies, interest rates. Click: he had the stock market prices at five-minute intervals. Click: the most forbiddingly technical charts on currency relationships. From these countless flea-sized particles of economic data, he hoped to glean some hint of whether inflation was on the rise, which would mean interest rates might have to be increased to choke it off. Of course, Greenspan was not glued to his terminal all the time. On a calm day of trading and economic activity, he checked it only once every half hour.

A shy Republican economist who wore thick-lensed glasses and unspectacular dark suits, Greenspan, 66, looked and dressed like a 1950s New York intellectual. He walked slowly, with a slight stoop, giving off a sober, sometimes gloomy air. Greenspan spoke in a weary drone with an overly abstract precision, elevating "Fedspeak," as the jargon-filled language of the Federal Reserve was often called, to a higher form all its own: "Greenspanspeak."

Now, after the election, Greenspan puzzled over what Clinton's victory might mean for him. Other than the president, Greenspan was perhaps the most powerful economic actor in the government and likely the most powerful Republican left standing in Washington. While the White House and Congress set government tax and spending policy, Greenspan and the Federal Reserve made important decisions on interest rates, the government's other main economic policy lever. Chairman of the Federal Reserve was supposed to be an independent position, like the FBI director, appointed by the president and confirmed by the Senate for a fixed term. President Bush had appointed Greenspan to his second four-year term as Fed chairman, meaning he could serve through March 1996. Greenspan would be overseeing interest-rate decisions for most of Clinton's term.

Throughout its history, the Federal Reserve, known as the Fed, was often at war with the White House. The Fed tended to want interest rates high enough to keep inflation low. Higher interest rates reduced credit opportunities and economic activity. The White House, in contrast, typically urged lower interest rates to give people and businesses easier access to credit, promoting economic growth.

During the Bush presidency, dominated by a recession and a sluggish economy, Greenspan had dropped short-term interest rates from nearly 10 percent down to a mere 3 percent, the lowest in decades. But the rates still had not been low enough to boost the economy substantially or to help Bush. Many in Bush's circle blamed Greenspan for Bush's political demise—particularly Treasury Secretary Nicholas Brady, who wanted interest rates dropped faster and further. Brady, who had worked three decades on Wall Street and been chairman of the investment banking firm Dillon, Read & Co., pressured Greenspan to lower rates. Brady even, bizarrely, tried to intensify pressure on Greenspan by dropping all his social contacts with the chairman. He ceased all breakfasts, lunches, and dinners—"Whoosh! Boom! Stop!" as Brady once characterized it privately. The strategy didn't work. Greenspan, a longtime Republican insider, concluded that Brady had some profoundly naive and outdated beliefs that interest rates could be lowered dramatically without triggering dangerous inflation. Still, the episode left Greenspan sour. If he couldn't coordinate a strategy with Republicans, how was he going to work with Clinton, a Democrat, in the White House?

Greenspan wore the Fed chairmanship comfortably, like one of his suits. It fit perfectly and it looked like he had been in it all his life. The Federal Reserve was a conservative institution, seeking a stable currency with little or no inflation and moderate but sustained economic growth. Greenspan felt that his time as Fed chairman could be judged a success if nothing happened. His vigilance against inflation ran deep. As a graduate student at Columbia in the 1950s, he had studied under the conservative economist Arthur F. Burns (later himself a Fed chairman). One day, Burns had asked his seminar, "What causes inflation?" After soliciting the students' answers, the professor announced: "Excess government spending causes inflation." The lesson was seared into Greenspan's mind. In Greenspan's view, in 1992, with the federal deficit still out of control, any further lowering of interest rates would risk higher inflation.

Greenspan's patrons also ran to the core of the Republican Party. His political involvement began as a domestic and economic policy adviser in Richard Nixon's 1968 presidential campaign. Greenspan had had little contact with Nixon until a meeting of campaign insiders in Montauk Point, Long Island. Nixon opened the meeting, and in three or four sentences uttered more four-letter words than Greenspan knew existed. Greenspan was floored. It was not the words themselves that shocked him, but what he saw as Nixon's dual personality. The discrepancy between Nixon's earnest public persona and this profane private side, Greenspan thought, was very weird. Uncomfortable, he was the only senior person in the group not to take a position in the Nixon administration.

In the mid-1970s, however, he joined the Ford administration as chairman of the Council of Economic Advisers. Over the years, he forged friendships with all the Republican Party heavyweights. His confidants included former Secretaries of State Henry Kissinger and James A. Baker III and Defense Secretary Richard Cheney. In 1987, he was first appointed Fed chairman by President Reagan, and then reappointed by Bush.

No one understood the Fed's power, and the radical limits on its power, better than Greenspan. The Fed's basic tool, the setting of short-term interest rates, seemed small. But those short-term rates gave the central bank substantial, at times brutal leverage in the credit markets over the long-term rates paid by businesses, consumers, and homeowners on mortgages.

Greenspan knew the economic numbers like few others. Few things pleased him more than an evening poring over newly released industry statistics or a Sunday paging through the *Survey of Current Business*. Even as a young man, when Greenspan played tenor saxophone in a 1940s big band, he was good at reading music, "reading the sheets," but incapable of improvising—a fatal handicap for a jazzman. While fellow musicians drank or smoked dope, Greenspan became the band's bookkeeper and spent his time reading economics and the spreadsheets.

In the 1950s, he entered into the small circle attending the popular philosopher Ayn Rand, champion of laissez-faire capitalism and author of *The Fountainhead* and *Atlas Shrugged*. Greenspan spent his Saturday nights debating with Rand and her acolytes, one of whom, Nathaniel Branden, dubbed Greenspan "the undertaker." A follower of the philosophy of "logical positivism," which held that nothing could be known rationally with absolute certainty, Greenspan argued to the group that his own existence could not be conclusively proven and therefore had to be doubted. Branden wrote in his memoir that he and Rand privately ridiculed Greenspan's radical skepticism. One day, after Greenspan finally conceded that he must exist, Branden said he asked Rand, "Guess who exists?" She replied, "You've done it? The undertaker has decided he exists?"

Branden also wrote that he and Rand admired Greenspan's intellect but viewed him as a social climber preoccupied with worldly success. Apart from a nine-month marriage in 1952 that ended in divorce, Greenspan was a lifelong bachelor. He dated NBC-TV White House correspondent Andrea Mitchell and became a fixture on the Washington and New York social circuit, where he seemed to love mixing with the glitterati—a social craving that mystified many. He projected the uneasiness of a professor at a cocktail party at times and seemed, given his high position, the world's most underconfident man.

In a private lunch after Clinton's election, Greenspan had cautioned a longtime friend from New York who was in line for a top administration post about the perils of Washington. "This is a town that is full of evil people," Greenspan said starkly. "If you can't deal with every day having people trying to destroy you, you shouldn't even think of coming down here." Washington was insular and self-absorbed, Greenspan indicated, in need of a periodic witch trial. A permanent political aristocracy peered out the windows every day to see who was being taken to the stake or the guillotine. (Though the person failed to get the post, he was deeply impressed by Greenspan's words.) Greenspan felt that lots of people in politics behaved in all respects as normal human beings but could nonetheless look someone straight in the face and lie. This was no hypothesis. It had happened to him, and it was done without blinking. The lies were a technique to gain a certain advantage, Greenspan felt. "And to me that is morally evil," he once said.

Memory, even of recent events, Greenspan knew could be shockingly selective and self-serving. When the Federal Open Market Committee, the group that set the key short-term interest rate, met behind closed doors, the proceedings were secretly tape-recorded. The committee's secretary kept a confidential verbatim transcript. The existence of the tapes and transcripts was kept secret from the public, from Congress, and even from some of the committee members themselves.* Greenspan had had occasion to consult the transcript when there was doubt about what had been said.

Some colleagues said that Greenspan had perhaps only made one mistake as chairman. At a time when he was up for reappointment in 1991, during a telephone conference call of the Open Market Committee, he had proposed a drop in interest rates, largely on the basis of some overnight numbers showing no inflation. The confidential 25-page transcript of the April 12, 1991, discussion showed that a strong majority disagreed with his recommendation. Rather than be outvoted—a potentially debilitating vote of no confidence that could cripple his authority—Greenspan simply adjourned the conference call. The law requires that a record of "action" and the "reasons underlying the action" be kept and reported to Congress annually. Not changing interest rates, especially when the markets expect a change, was technically an action, as Greenspan knew. Neither the existence of the meeting nor any details were reported. Upon reviewing the transcript, Greenspan was surprised to discover that his own memory was faulty and imbued with recollections that were self-interested but not true.

About four weeks after the election, Greenspan received the most important invitation of the season: a call for a private meeting with President-elect Clinton in Little Rock. This visit presented a significant opportunity for Greenspan. He believed his role as Fed chairman was to work closely with the president while retaining the Fed's independence—always a tricky balancing act, even during the Republican administrations. Greenspan understood that the Fed's power reached far beyond economics and had a psychological and a political dimension. His visit with Clinton was scheduled for December 3.

Because there was no direct flight to Little Rock, the trip took Greenspan five hours. He was irritated that he couldn't take a government or a private jet. It did not benefit the taxpayers one bit, he felt, to have him cooling his heels in the airport for an hour waiting to change planes.

At the Governor's Mansion, Clinton told Gore beforehand that he wanted to meet alone with Greenspan to ensure there would be "one-on-one chemistry." When Greenspan and Clinton sat down alone, Clinton had questions and observations on subjects ranging from Bosnia, Somalia, and Russian history to economic issues such as job training and

---

* Greenspan publicly disclosed the existence of the tapes in congressional testimony in October 1993.

education. As they talked, Greenspan immediately saw that Clinton's reputation as a policy junkie was richly deserved. He was remarkably knowledgeable. Greenspan had seen four Republican presidents up close —Nixon, Ford, Reagan, and Bush. Clinton was going to be a different kind of president. He wouldn't need a chief of staff. He would be his own. The president-elect was not just engaged, he was totally engrossed.

For about 15 minutes, discussion turned to the Federal Reserve. Greenspan outlined his message, one of the most important he might ever send as chairman. There was no magic to coordinating the economic efforts of a president and Congress with the Federal Reserve. But there was a crucial new reality. The short-term rates the Fed controlled were at about the right level. The critical interest rates were the long-term rates, the rates that mattered to businesses with large debts and to people paying mortgages. Lower long-term rates would leave businesses and people more money to spend, causing the economy to grow. Perhaps no single overall economic event than a drop in long-term rates would do more to help the economy, businesses, and society as a whole. The long-term rates were also most sensitive to the federal budget deficit. Credible evidence that the federal deficit was going to be controlled could cause long-term interest rates to drop.

Clinton felt that the long-term rates had been too high for too long. The middle class, he felt, could not improve its condition unless the rates came down.

Clinton's concern was properly placed, Greenspan said. The president-elect's eyes and his manner made it clear he was listening. So Greenspan gave his economics lesson. Though the lesson was not long and its logic not particularly tortured, few took the time to understand it. The long-term interest rates for 10-year, 20-year, and 30-year securities, Greenspan said, were an unusual 3 to 4 percent higher than the short-term rates. Historically, the rates had been closer. The large current gap was basically an inflation premium. Bondholders and traders were sophisticated and anticipated that the federal budget deficit would continue to explode for many years. The anticipated cumulative growth of the deficit over those years was so large that it was perceived to be unstable. History showed, Greenspan said, that with such vast federal expenditures, inflation would inevitably soar at some point. The double-digit inflation of the late 1970s had been induced by the budget deficits from the Vietnam War. Investors were now wary and demanding a higher long-term return because of the expectations on the federal deficit.

With focused sincerity, Greenspan added that if the new administration removed or altered that expectation by exerting some control on the deficit, the market expectations would change. Bond traders would have more faith that inflation would stay under control. Long-term rates would drop, galvanizing demand for new mortgages. And since homeowners increasingly used refinancing as a source of consumer credit, they would be able to buy more automobiles, appliances, home furnishings, and a whole variety of consumer goods. This spending would expand the economy—a significant payoff.

In addition, Greenspan said, as inflation expectations dropped, investors would get smaller returns on bonds. As a result, they would shift their money to the stock market. The stock market would climb—another payoff.

Finally, Greenspan said, because the federal budget deficit was so high and unstable, the traditional argument that deficit spending increased jobs did not hold. On the contrary, the economic growth resulting from deficit reduction would actually *increase* employment—a third payoff.

If Clinton's economic plan were not credible with the bond markets, an effort by the Federal Reserve to lower short-term rates would likely backfire, he said, and drive up long-term rates. The market these days was too sophisticated to be fooled. Businesses and individuals had gone on a debt binge in the 1980s, borrowing vast sums of money, perhaps unrivaled in 50 years. The debts were being paid off. The lower the long-term interest rates, the better and easier this effort. The economy was rebounding, but there was no predicting the endgame of the current business cycle, no telling whether the recovery was solid. The current momentary upswing could fall on its face. Addressing the long-term deficit was essential, Greenspan repeated. In addition, he said, as a practical matter, it was impossible to jump-start the economy with a short-term stimulus package, as Clinton had suggested in the campaign. It would be fiddling at the margins. But—and here was the key—keeping the long rates down would trigger economic growth, even more growth than the conservative estimates that had been circulating.

Clinton had many questions and ideas. But also he had enough information to make the critical decisions and choices, Greenspan believed. The conversation continued for two and a half hours. Greenspan had not intended to stay for lunch but eventually lunch was offered and appeared. Greenspan easily recognized the atmosphere of academia. Clinton was very close to being an intellectual. He was at home with ideas and knowledgeable about history. The chairman was quite surprised at the level of abstraction of their conversation. Yet he also knew that intellectuals, himself included, tended to know too much on both sides of an issue and sometimes found it hard to make decisions. He wondered if Clinton would be like Hamlet, afflicted with the problems of the thoughtful. Was he too thoughtful for his own good? Too thoughtful for politics?

In his five-hour trek back to Washington, Greenspan had time to ponder. He had not found it necessary to share his observation that Washington was full of evil people. After all, Clinton was a practicing politician. Yet Greenspan tried to evaluate the president-elect's sincerity. Was it possible that Clinton was pulling his leg? That it was all a show? That, Greenspan felt, would be really impressive. He would be disturbed if someone was that skilled at deceiving, but it would be remarkable. Clinton's performance was too straight. The president-elect, Greenspan concluded, was an intellectual pragmatist. He didn't like to use the phrase because he considered it slightly pejorative, but it captured Clinton's style. Besides, it could also apply to Greenspan himself.

Greenspan reflected on a shift in the public economic debate he had seen over the years. Two or three decades ago, a great ideological chasm in economics had divided Republicans from Democrats, but now on many issues a consensus was emerging. No longer could Alan Greenspan be so easily distinguished from Bill Clinton. Greenspan thought that Clinton's plans for his administration even resembled President Ford's in the 1976 Republican platform.

On Clinton's all-but-imminent tax hike on the rich, Greenspan was open-minded. In the 1970s, Greenspan had publicly taken strong stances against such taxes, viewing them as a dubious use of the state's power and a punishment of those who created economic growth. He still described himself as a libertarian, distrustful of the power of the state, and opposed, in theory, to taxes and regulation. But times had changed, and so had Greenspan's job. He appreciated the irony of a libertarian heading one of the government's chief regulatory agencies. He now considered the deficits such a threat to America's future that higher taxes in the name of deficit reduction just might be worth it.

For his part, Clinton felt that Greenspan was not a typical Republican banker who would try to have it both ways. He did not plead to bring down the deficit but protest against raising taxes on the wealthy. In fact, the tax hike hadn't even come up in their discussion. Clinton told Gore after the meeting, "We can do business."

The prospect of more real economic growth lodged in Clinton's mind. Four days later, on December 7, he publicly addressed the overall economic conditions. "We may or may not be coming out of our recession," Clinton said. For the moment, the president-elect sounded as though he had taken an introductory class in Greenspanspeak.

10

On December 6, Stephanopoulos and Greenberg took a trip to Fort Lee, New Jersey. There they spent four hours listening to voters who had supported either Clinton or Perot. First, ten women discussed the political campaign for two hours. Then ten men did the same. Greenberg and Stephanopoulos watched the focus groups through a one-way window.

The significant finding was the dog that didn't bark. When the moderator in the discussions asked the participants to name Clinton's campaign promises, no one mentioned the middle-class tax cut. When asked about it directly, the voters, who were middle class, said they did not expect it. Some of them accurately recalled that in one of the debates Clinton had refused to make a flat pledge to cut middle-class taxes. Many also indicated they did not think such a tax cut would be good policy. It was clear too that these people wanted to make some sacrifice if they believed the problems of the country were being faced. A tax cut seemed too much of a quick fix and sounded like a Reagan and Republican idea.

Greenberg and Stephanopoulos realized that Clinton's economic plan would have a stronger appeal if everyone was asked to contribute something to the recovery effort. Greenberg felt he had discovered a critical point about the post-election psychology of voters. They seemed to feel if they didn't pay for something, it had little value.

HOUSE MAJORITY LEADER RICHARD GEPHARDT, the real organizer of the House Democrats, had pressed Clinton to choose his close friend Leon E. Panetta, 54, the chairman of the House Budget Committee, as his budget director. Gephardt had gone almost overboard praising Panetta, a 16-year California House veteran, as a technical, personal, and political wizard. Panetta was a loyal lieutenant to the House leadership and someone the House members considered one of their own, Gephardt argued, a straight shooter and the polar opposite of Richard Darman. Clinton hardly knew Panetta and didn't think he would select him. He wanted a woman among his top tier of economic advisers, quite possibly as budget director. In deference to Gephardt and numerous other Panetta boosters, and out of his own curiosity, Clinton decided to have Panetta down for a private talk.

During the campaign, Panetta had publicly challenged some of the numbers in candidate Clinton's economic plan, and Panetta felt that had doomed any chance of landing an administration job. During the transition, Panetta was at his home in Carmel Valley, California, when Warren Christopher called. "The president-elect would like to talk to you," Christopher said. For the first time Panetta thought, Oh, shit, this was for real.

Panetta flew to Little Rock and at a table in the library of the Governor's Mansion, over a couple of Cokes, the two met alone. With his happy-go-lucky smile, Panetta exuded congeniality; he seemed laid back and at times even downright giddy. In response to Clinton's questions, Panetta said his chairmanship in Congress required that he try to cut spending and bring down the deficit. "I'm a deficit hawk," he declared, but added that he also considered himself a traditional Democrat. Investments like those Clinton advocated absolutely had to be made. The money didn't exist now because of the refusal of past presidents and the Congress to exercise discipline over the budget, he said.

Clinton liked Panetta immediately. Panetta's energy did it for him. About 15 minutes into the talk, Clinton thought this was an extraordinary talent—a good human being, smart, and knowledgeable about Congress, someone to help him with the alien culture.

The president-elect asked some practical and political questions. How would he piece together an economic plan? What needed to be done? Who was important? What were the timetables?

The approach had to be bold, Panetta said. This would involve risks, political risks. The message out of the November election was for the president to take on this issue, he said.

What about the Republicans? Clinton asked.

"As always," Panetta said, "if you can build a bipartisan base for it, it's a hell of a lot better, but my experience, particularly on the House side, is that Republicans are not going to support anything that involves any tax increases." Bush's 1988 "Read my lips" pledge, though abandoned briefly in 1990, was now hard Republican dogma.

On the topic of investments, Panetta said that for progressive Democrats such as themselves to govern, they had to first show they were tough on the deficit and controlling spending. If Clinton and the Democrats demonstrated they had the guts to make tough decisions, they would have room later to target investments for the future. That was the only way Democrats could make the process work.

After about an hour and a half, Clinton talked about the importance of the budget director's post. He inquired if Panetta would be interested in the job.

Panetta remarked that he had not sought the position. "I want you to succeed," he said, "and if you say to me that you need me as part of the team in order to succeed, I would not refuse that. I feel strongly enough about the opportunity to make a Democratic administration successful." Clinton did not offer the job, but afterwards he made it clear to others that it was Panetta's.

Several nights later, Panetta was attending a black-tie Kennedy Center celebration. In the middle of a performance, an usher handed him a note to call Warren Christopher in Little Rock. Panetta made his way to a phone booth and called Christopher, who asked him to come down for the announcement on Thursday.

"Am I being asked, you know, for that position?" Panetta inquired cryptically from the phone booth.

"The president-elect wants to ask you to accept that position," Christopher said.

CLINTON HAD NOT YET SELECTED a chairman for his Council of Economic Advisers. Larry Summers, 38, a wunderkind Ph.D. economist who had won full tenure from Harvard at the extraordinarily young age of 28, seemed like the certain choice. But a memo that Summers had written as chief economist at the World Bank, suggesting that toxic waste might be dumped in "underpolluted" African countries, had leaked. Gore scuttled Summers's nomination, and Clinton was left without a Council chairman.

Clinton was still looking for a woman among his top economic advisers. During the summer, he had met with Laura D'Andrea Tyson, 45, an economics professor at the University of California at Berkeley, and she had impressed him. A longtime friend of Bob Reich, she had worked on the campaign periphery doing opposition research on Bush's economic record and statements. As a student in MIT's prestigious economics program, she had written her doctoral dissertation on inflation in Yugoslavia, and now she specialized in trade and technology policy.

After the election, she had worked, at Reich's request, on transition booklets on trade, technology, manufacturing, and small business. Then unexpectedly Warren Christopher called and invited her to Little Rock for an interview with Clinton. Christopher mentioned the Council of Economic Advisers, and Tyson assumed she was up for a deputy position.

About an hour before her interview on Wednesday, December 9, Tyson had lunch with Gene Sperling. "Do you know why you're here?" Sperling asked.

Tyson said she assumed it was something about the Council of Economic Advisers.

"Well," Sperling said, "you're actually here to be interviewed for the chair."

Tyson was stunned. She felt as though she were scheduled for an oral exam and only learned the topic an hour beforehand.

She met alone with Clinton. The president-elect quizzed her in detail about what policies she thought made sense. He asked her if she believed in the monetary aggregates for measuring the money supply, previously a key index used by the Federal Reserve in setting interest rates.

Tyson knew that the monetary aggregates, because of technical problems, were no longer reliable, and said she basically dismissed their importance.

What did she think was the mission of the Council of Economic Advisers? Clinton asked.

Since she hadn't prepared, she said she had no reason to think it would change. The Council served a useful function analyzing the economy for the president.

How did she think it might change?

In some ways it wouldn't, Tyson replied. Because of her special interest in technology and trade policy, the Council would probably give more attention to those matters.

Clinton said it had been nice and thanked her. He did not offer her the job.

Very late that night, Tyson was awakened by a call from Christopher. She had done herself a big favor that day, he said, and she should stay in town.

How long? she asked.

They would probably know something tomorrow, Christopher said. On Thursday afternoon, Christopher called again. An announcement was scheduled for the next day, he said. That was it. This was bizarre, she thought. Neither Clinton nor Christopher had ever formally offered her the job. Only from Reich did Tyson learn the offer was being made.

Before the press conference to announce Tyson and Reich's appointments, Clinton, Stephanopoulos, and the new appointees met to practice answers to some possible questions. Stephanopoulos posed some mock questions. How can you two both be in the same administration, Stephanopoulos asked, since you have different views on things?

"What do you mean, they have different views?" Clinton asked. "They have similar views, don't they?"

Tyson said that she and Reich once had an academic debate in *The American Prospect* on whether the nationality of a firm was important.

"Yeah, Laura was wrong," Reich said.

Clinton looked as if a light had switched on in his head. "I didn't know that you wrote that," he said to Tyson. "I forgot that. You know what? You were right, and Bob was wrong."

How many people in the country, Tyson wondered, read *The American Prospect?*

GENE SPERLING had been working closely with Bob Rubin during the transition, but it wasn't at all clear that he would be chosen as Rubin's deputy. Sperling thought that his selection should be almost automatic. He, after all, had given his life to the campaign and Clinton's economic program. He was Clinton's historical memory and he had support from key people such as Stephanopoulos and Reich. But as the days passed, Rubin said nothing about it. Then Sperling realized that Rubin was checking up on him, phoning some 20 people, asking whether Sperling was a substantive person, verifying his academic record. Sperling was pissed, then offended, and now ripshit. At one point, Rubin raised the subject. "Look, neither you nor I have been in the federal government," Rubin said. "We don't have any experience." Eventually, however, Rubin settled on two deputies: Sperling and W. Bowman "Bo" Cutter, a former Carter administration official.

STEPHANOPOULOS SAW THAT CLINTON, himself, and the rest of the team were beginning to come to grips with the big new reality of unexpectedly large budget deficits. As early as August an explicit warning had arrived, but Clinton had been consumed with winning the election and little else had registered with him. At a transition meeting on December 7 at Blair House, the White House guest residence, Reich and Summers had presented new budget estimates showing a greater deficit. "What?" Clinton yelled, blowing his top, "I thought we'd been through all that!" Then on December 14, at Clinton's Economic Summit in Little Rock, a grand teach-in on the economy, John White, who had drawn up Perot's deficit reduction plan during the campaign (but had later endorsed Clinton), reiterated the point. Most recently, Stephanopoulos learned that Darman's budget office was going to come out with new official figures, projecting the deficit to be roughly $50 billion more than previously expected.

Reich's teams had put together two three-inch-thick briefing books labeled "Economic Transition #1" and "Economic Transition #2," which had been delivered to Clinton. The 600 pages were full of undigestible tables, charts, forecasts, theories—with no overall theme to the pudding, no line of reasoning at all.

Sperling tried to summarize it all in an introduction titled "Economic Overview," dated December 23, 1992. "You have inherited a two-part challenge of historic proportions"—the federal budget and the public investment deficits. "Either challenge by itself would be daunting but manageable. Both challenges together, with their contradictory elements (cutting the deficit, while increasing the deficit) amount to a formidable task."

Bob Boorstin was among those who read the memo. *You have inherited a two-part challenge of historic proportions,* he read. In other words, he thought, you've been fucked.

Ira Magaziner had written a four-page memo on deficit reduction for the briefing books, laying out Clinton's problems and the contrast with the campaign. "There are political risks to deficit reduction," Magaziner warned. "It would potentially anger most major interest groups. . . . It would require a change from campaign rhetoric and positions which did not stress the deficit as a problem."

In his memo, Sperling addressed the campaign promise on the deficit. "If you are displaying significant courage and making serious progress on reducing the deficit," he wrote, "it is unlikely that failure to bring the deficit in half will be that consequential."

FOR THE LAST FLING of the year, the Clintons joined in an annual New Year's gathering, somewhat pretentiously called Renaissance Weekend, at the seaside resort of Hilton Head, South Carolina. It was a blend of seminars, networking, exchanging phone numbers, recreation, and serious discussion—Clinton's idea of a good time. Clinton invited Ken Adelman, who had headed the Arms Control and Disarmament Agency under Reagan and now wrote a conservative syndicated newspaper column, over to his beach house.

"There are four things I can tell you, Governor, that will really surprise you in the White House," Adelman said.

"First, the difficulty you will have getting good, solid information. People are not very honest. Numbers will be disputed. People will shade things all the time. So you'll confront an epistemological question: How do you know?" Adelman added, "I've been in the room many times, when a cabinet officer would not correct something the president had said, when it was clear it was wrong."

"I've noticed that since becoming president-elect," Clinton said.

"You haven't seen anything yet," Adelman said. "People, strong people, will come into the Oval Office and bow and scrape, be disgusting in ways you cannot imagine.

"Second, you will not have accountability from your cabinet members until you fire someone," Adelman said.

Clinton blanched. "That was never my strong suit," he said. "Why can't you just fix things?"

Because it is hard to discipline the bureaucracy, Adelman responded. "Third, when you make a mistake, you'll be surprised how difficult it is to find out what really happened, who to blame and how to fix it." He proposed that Clinton assemble a "Whoops Squad" of friends from Arkansas and elsewhere who had no stake in the government, to come in for a few days to make a clear-eyed, dispassionate analysis when blunders occurred.

Clinton indicated that he was hoping to avoid big mistakes.

"Governor," Adelman said, "you'll screw up in some way, probably by May, certainly by June."

Adelman's fourth point was more like a suggestion. "Find a defining moment in your first few months, something that you do or say that gives a clear definition to your presidency."

The next day Clinton told Adelman that he had mentioned the four surprises to Hillary. Upon reflection, Clinton said, he particularly agreed about the difficulty of getting good information. The budget numbers seemed more and more confusing. But how could he solve the problem?

"Reward those who stand up and correct you," Adelman said, or those who dig out and give you the information even if it's bad news.

"Hillary said that we are getting 3,000 résumés a day from those who want to work in the administration," Clinton said. "And she said maybe we should just intentionally hire a turkey so we'll have someone to fire."

"No problem, Governor," Adelman said. "You'll have a turkey no matter how hard you try not to. You won't have to strain yourself on that."

ON JANUARY 6, 1993, Sperling and Stephanopoulos went to Clinton to give him another heads-up. Darman was set to release his new budget numbers, they told him, showing that the deficit for 1997 would be up another $60 billion.

Clinton was disbelieving. He turned to Gore, who was with him, and laughed. "Why?" he asked. "What has changed so much?"

No one had good information.

11

Bob Rubin, Gene Sperling, and a few others were working furiously to prepare to meet Clinton's campaign promise to pass an economic recovery plan in his first 100 days. Rubin had suggested holding meetings between Christmas and New Year's, but the transition was so unwieldy he couldn't get anything going. It wasn't clear whose hands were on the steering wheel. Clinton was busy with his remaining cabinet selections, and beyond the president-elect, there was no central authority, just a lot of people doing a lot of separate work, much of it seemingly unconnected to any concrete plan.

Rubin concluded he had to insist on an initial meeting of the National Economic Council and get it on Clinton's agenda. The date of that initial meeting would drive their work. He went to enlist the help of Thomas "Mack" McLarty, Clinton's friend since kindergarten and the designated White House chief of staff. McLarty, 46, the CEO of the Arkansas-based natural gas company Arkla, Inc., was friendly and unassuming, the opposite of the stereotypical hard-driving executive. A short man, with soft features and a Southern graciousness, McLarty had taken over his father's Ford dealership after graduating from the University of Arkansas. Active in Arkansas Democratic Party politics for years, he had worked closely with Clinton on some of his gubernatorial campaigns. He was attentive to others, at times even a bit unctuous, and had succeeded more through diligence and personal relationships than vision or smarts. He had questioned Clinton hard on whether he was the one to run the White House staff, but Clinton had insisted he needed him.

Rubin had known McLarty for ten years. "Mack," Rubin said, "we need to talk about this meeting. How do you think he wants it structured?" Rubin asked about Clinton. "I'm very concerned if we don't have an agenda." The meeting could easily degenerate into one of the endless, rambling policy seminars that Clinton loved. Rubin didn't want to presume to chair a meeting that Clinton might want to lead, but he felt the proceedings would need a focus and a crispness.

Having known Bill Clinton for four decades, McLarty understood all too well. He told Clinton directly, almost sternly, that the meeting could not be taken lightly. It had to be constructive and productive. All the participants would have to arrive in Little Rock the night before to make sure that the weather or other excuses did not delay the prompt start of the meeting. Rubin had to have the authority to keep the discussion moving so they didn't get off track. Clinton agreed. The date was set for later than Rubin wanted: Thursday, January 7, 1993, just 13 days before Clinton's inauguration.

"We have to present in five hours to President-elect Clinton what is normally presented over five months," Rubin told Sperling. "So we better get our act together." Rubin gave specific assignments to Sperling, Bentsen, Panetta, and Tyson, as well as to Deputy Treasury Secretary–designate Roger Altman and Larry Summers, who was now in line for a top Treasury job. They and other members of the economic team conducted full telephone conference rehearsals to make sure the meeting would run smoothly. Deliberately, Rubin chose to make no presentation himself. He would protect everyone else's position—and, he hoped, establish his own position by making it clear that he planned to be a coordinator, not an advocate.

Rubin designed the meeting as a framework for making decisions on overall domestic policy. This was not going to be a narrow budget exercise. A plan had to be assembled from scratch. All of the campaign promises—the investment program, the middle-class tax cut, health care reform, a stimulus package of fast-track spending, and deficit reduction—were bumping up against each other. They all had to be reevaluated in the context of the new economic situation they faced. The group had to step back and ask: What were their goals? What was possible?

WELL AFTER THE APPOINTED 9 A.M. starting time on January 7, the economic team started gathering in the Governor's Mansion in Little Rock. Clinton, known for his tardiness, had not yet arrived. The team members milled around, reluctant to take seats, since it was unclear where Clinton would sit. Gore arrived and sat down near the door, marking it as the head of the table. The others took seats at the opposite end of the table, under a large mirror. Soon, however, a photographer showed up and said Clinton was planning to sit near the mirror, so Gore came rushing down, forcing a reshuffling.

Finally, Clinton appeared at the door, instantly the center of attention. He walked around the table, shook hands with everyone, and then took a seat—right by the door. Gore again rose and strode down to take the seat to the president-elect's left. Bentsen, who would occupy the senior domestic cabinet post and was the senior person by 15 years, sat at Clinton's right. The others slid back toward the gap under the mirror.

Rubin, the master of ceremonies, welcomed everyone with a brief hello. He quickly turned to Leon Panetta.

Sounding as sharp an alarm as he could in his amiable way, the budget director designate said that the annual federal deficit was shooting out of control, worse than expected. By 1997—the year they would use to frame their budget plan—the deficit would be somewhere around $360 billion, a record. By the turn of the century, it would soar to $500 billion, a truly unmanageable level. The explanation for the increase? The collection of tax revenue had fallen, largely because of the recession and sluggish economy, while federal spending on entitlement programs, particularly government health insurance—Medicare for the elderly, Medicaid for the poor—had risen astronomically.

As the nominee to chair the Council of Economic Advisers, Laura Tyson was responsible for presenting a neutral analysis of the economic conditions. She began with a presentation on the current state of the economy and what was expected for the near future. Most likely, she said, the American economy would grow at a modest, unspectacular rate of 2.5 to 3 percent in the next 12 months. That meant that although a recession was unlikely, so was a robust recovery. An economy that could kick up or down, it was clear, would leave Clinton in political limbo.

Next to take the floor was Alan Blinder, a mainstream liberal economics professor from Princeton who was Tyson's deputy on the council. Blinder's forte was the large issues of taxes, spending, and budgets, so-called macroeconomics, that were traditionally the focus of the CEA chairman. "I've been asked to do the pedantic stuff," Blinder said, getting a laugh. Why were they hearing that the federal deficits needed to be reduced? Blinder asked. Why was that goal important?

Lowering the deficit would help the national economy, he said. It was not just to clear the decks or because the founding fathers were Puritans. Blinder, equipped with slides, flashed on the wall a chart entitled "THE LONG-RANGE BENEFITS." A lower deficit, Blinder said, meant the federal government was borrowing less from the pool of national savings—the money of all its citizens that was invested rather than consumed. Most of that freed-up savings could then go to private investments such as new plants and equipment or better worker training. These investments would eventually yield more efficiency and greater productivity per worker. And increased productivity—and here was the key—would eventually mean an increase in the standard of living for most Americans. Standard of living was the name of the game, as the president-elect had emphasized during the campaign, improving the lot of the average person. The 1980s, for most Americans, had brought stagnant or declining incomes.

How much would their standard of living improve? With a credible deficit reduction program, Blinder said, nothing over the first two years. But over four years, perhaps, just perhaps, there would be an increase of .4 to .8 percent, his chart showed. "At the high end, you will get the 1 percent better standard of living after four years," Blinder said, realizing that while it might be economically significant, it would be negligible in people's lives. Clinton was looking grim.

So what would be the downside of deficit reduction? Blinder proceeded to ask. He moved to a chart headed, "THE SHORT-RUN COSTS." Reducing the deficit meant cutting government spending. Just as increased government spending caused the economy to expand, diminished government spending caused the economy to contract. Taking $60 billion of federal spending out of the economy in a year—about 1 percent of the country's total economic output, called the Gross Domestic Product or GDP—could lead to a 1.5 percent decrease in economic growth. From Tyson's projection of 2.8 percent annual growth, Blinder subtracted the 1.5 percent caused by 1 percent of deficit reduction. The result of such deficit reduction, he said, would be an economy expanding by 1.3 percent a year—the edge of recession.

"The worst-case scenario," Blinder continued, "is a recession no worse than George Bush enjoyed." His chart of short-run costs said explicitly that cutting the deficit would decrease overall economic growth and "costs jobs"—although, Blinder added, those effects would shrink over time and effectively disappear after five years. Clinton had promised to "grow the economy" and create more and better jobs. The irony was palpable. Blinder realized he was presenting Clinton with a political loser.

It was time for some good news. Deficit reduction of this magnitude *could* be "costless," Blinder ventured, saying the magic word. Little appealed to Clinton more than a "costless" decision, a chance to have it both ways, to eat ice cream and still lose weight.

Three events could offset the contraction from cutting the deficit, Blinder said. First, traders could buy and sell bonds at lower long-term interest rates, which would mean consumers and businesses would pay less to borrow money and would have more money to spend. Second, the Federal Reserve could lower short-term interest rates, an action which generally (but not always) caused long-term rates to fall. Third, increased foreign buying from more trade could provide a boost to the American economy. With a fully cooperative Federal Reserve and bond market, Blinder explained, deficit reduction could be relatively costless. The increased economic activity that would result from lower interest rates could offset the contraction caused by the $60 billion of diminished government spending. Lower interest rates were the key.

"Two possible but *unlikely,* ways out," the chart on the wall said, the word *unlikely* underscored. It was possible that the Fed would lower rates, and it was possible that the credibility of a deficit reduction plan would cause inflation fears to recede and the bond traders to cut long-term interest rates, their inflation premium.

Clinton recognized that it was the exact argument that Greenspan had made to him the previous month: Deficit reduction could mean lower long-term interest rates.

"But after ten years of fiscal shenanigans," Blinder quickly pointed out, referring to the unrealized promises of Reagan and Bush to cut the deficit, "the bond market will not likely respond."

At the president-elect's end of the table, Clinton's face turned red with anger and disbelief. "You mean to tell me that the success of the program and my reelection hinges on the Federal Reserve and a bunch of fucking bond traders?" he responded in a half-whisper.

Nods from his end of the table. Not a dissent.

Clinton, it seemed to Blinder, perceived at this moment how much of his fate was passing into the hands of the unelected Alan Greenspan and the bond market.

Stephanopoulos also saw that it was a crucial moment in Clinton's growing realization. It was no longer a political campaign. They faced new economic realities and had to start all over again. Their first audience would have to be the Fed and the bond market.

THE ADMINISTRATION WOULD have to come up with a credible plan it could sell, Clinton said.

Larry Summers interjected some optimism. A favorable response on long-term rates from a good deficit reduction plan, he said, was not so unlikely. The inflation premium was abnormally high now, he noted, and a good plan would convince the markets that inflation was not that much of a problem and long-term rates should fall.

Blinder flashed his next chart, which summarized the costs and benefits of a $60 billion annual deficit cut. The costs would be immediate: the sharp 1.5 percent drop in economic growth from the 2.8 expected annual growth that was projected. The benefits, on the other hand, lay far off: perhaps a 1 percent increase in growth after four years, perhaps 2 percent after 20 years, and a 2.7 percent increase at "infinity." The professional economist's esoteric models had come to presidential decision making. Blinder realized that it was ridiculous to talk to a politician about the distant future. To mention "infinity" was patently absurd. More vividly, Blinder saw he was presenting Clinton with costs that would be paid in his presidency and benefits that would come several presidencies into the future.

Clinton asked about job creation. Would they get the 8 million new jobs he had promised?

The contraction caused by deficit reduction could cost several million of those jobs, Blinder said. Only lower interest rates could offset the loss.

Clinton wanted to connect deficit reduction directly to job creation, but Blinder and Tyson repeated that it wasn't the correct link. Deficit reduction might lead to more jobs down the road, but in the near future, it would have exactly the opposite impact.

Summers, again optimistic, said that the contractionary impact of deficit reduction might not be as great as economic theory predicted. Drawing from his experiences as the former chief economist of the World Bank, Summers described how a number of European countries had cut their deficits substantially without impeding economic growth; it had even happened in the United States one year during the 1980s. Other countries that had cut their deficits had not wound up with the predicted job losses either.

Blinder flashed his final chart, listing five options for deficit reduction. Each set a different deficit-level target for the year 1997. The most severe option was to chop the deficit in half in four years—Clinton's campaign promise. That meant lowering the 1997 deficit by nearly $200 billion. A less severe option involved stabilizing the ratio of debt to the gross domestic product (GDP)—in other words, making sure that the deficit was not growing at a faster rate than the economy as a whole.

This required cutting the deficit by $100 billion or less. Blinder focused on a middle option of reducing the deficit by $145 billion.

Rubin pointed out that Blinder's chart assumed no new public investments. To afford the new programs Clinton wanted, they would need even more spending cuts than Blinder suggested.

Without strong deficit reduction, Tyson summarized, "There is a long-term risk of financial collapse." Deficit reduction would put the government in a position to respond to crises. The point seemed to register on the president-to-be.

LEON PANETTA was up next. Campaign aides had told him that Clinton was deadly slow to make decisions. "The worst thing about him is that he never makes a decision," Stephanopoulos had said. "He's not going to give you an answer," Sperling had echoed. Although Panetta figured it was unlikely, probably impossible, that Clinton would make any decisions at this meeting, he wanted the president-elect to see the abstraction of "deficit reduction" translated into specifics. Panetta handed out 47 pages of new charts and tables.

He ran through three main areas of spending. First, he listed five options on how much to cut defense spending, recommending an option right in the middle. Next, he reviewed a long laundry list of possible nondefense cuts. Finally, he turned to entitlements. Panetta reminded everyone that entitlements—especially Medicare and retirement programs—were the category of programs growing most rapidly, yet also, politically speaking, among the most difficult to cut.

Alice M. Rivlin, the 61-year-old budget expert and economist who was designated to be Panetta's deputy, said that Clinton's campaign promise to cover those Americans without health insurance would use up any savings that could be squeezed from Medicare or Medicaid. "The best thing to assume is that health care will be budget-neutral," Rivlin said. Her blunt analysis struck at the heart of Clinton's plan to save money from health care reform.

Ira Magaziner noted that others agreed with Rivlin, but he did not. He suggested setting up a commission to examine the health care options. Skyrocketing health costs would eat up a third of the country's economic growth over the next seven years. Reforming the system and containing costs could realize huge savings in the federal budget by 1997, he said. As much as $89 billion might be saved. "This will involve some tough political choices," Magaziner said, but it was better to concentrate on one major reform than on the scores of small items in the budget, such as grazing fees charged for using federal land. The small items would never save as much as health care reform and would entail lots of political skirmishes instead of one big battle. Reform could both achieve universal health care coverage and appeal to conservatives by saving money, he added. Clinton agreed to create a team to look at the overall health care problem.

Should we assume health savings for deficit reduction? Panetta asked. Clinton had not responded to Rivlin's suggestion that health care reform be treated as deficit-neutral. Panetta and Rivlin both knew people who had worked years to get a handle on health care costs. They knew this was a key question.

"This will take about two weeks, I think, to get a handle on that issue," Magaziner said. Two main questions would be addressed, he said: how to control costs and how to get the savings to the federal government. Clinton expressed optimism that they could pass a health care reform bill fairly early.

Panetta resumed his presentation. He said that in the 1990 budget deal they had looked at delaying the cost-of-living allowances (COLAs) for Social Security recipients for three months. Every year, all Social Security beneficiaries got an increase in their checks to account for inflation; delaying these increases was often discussed but rarely done. A three-month delay, Panetta said, would save $20 billion over three years.

For the first time, Gore jumped in, saying Social Security should be an option. Like taxes, Social Security was usually considered untouchable, but Gore wanted to be tough-minded.

HILLARY CLINTON had taken a seat on the sidelines against a wall, not at the main table. She wanted mostly to listen, but she also wanted to be sure that everyone at the table was thinking about the real lives behind their decisions. These decisions were not abstract. She had running through her mind a movie of the thousands of people she and her husband had seen on the bus trips and the rallies over the last year. These people had come and clutched his hands, her hands. They had supported Clinton, she felt, because they believed that as president he would pay attention to their concerns.

The mention of cost-of-living allowances triggered a reaction from her. The advisers were talking about the $20 billion they wanted to save, a nice, round, important number. "Does anyone have numbers regarding people with COLAs?" Hillary inquired. How many people received the cost-of-living allowances and had other income to help them out?

No one had an answer. She knew it was a basic issue for millions who lived on Social Security. There were lots of ways of taking on Social Security costs, and delaying the increases would be about the least progressive among them. The poor, who often rely on Social Security as their only source of retirement income, would be hit the hardest.

Panetta concluded by presenting three possible goals for the 1997 deficit: $240 billion, $220 billion, or $195 billion.

TREASURY SECRETARY–DESIGNATE BENTSEN, slated next for a presentation on taxes, opened with some broad remarks. "It's critical that this bill pass," Bentsen declared. "Anything we do on revenues is going to be difficult politically, and if the bill doesn't pass it will be a very, very serious blow to the administration."

Bentsen entered into a brief disquisition on power and the importance of winning. Perception of strength was everything in Washington, and strength was measured by winning. The importance of this first battle could not be underestimated. Whatever their ideal program, they had to pass some sort of economic program. If Clinton succeeded, he would be strong and able to do good things for his presidency. But if he didn't, he would be perceived as weak and not get anything.

The plan would have to move through Congress quickly, Bentsen added. Therefore, on taxes, they had to propose familiar options. There would be little time for education. They should look at the options provided by the Congressional Budget Office, the well-regarded, non-partisan analysis arm of Congress. Those options mostly represented good policy. If all the options appeared equally desirable as policy, their political acceptability should be the decisive test. Bentsen also urged presenting several different taxes rather than one single tax, so a loss on one wouldn't mean the loss of the entire tax package.

Bentsen had a single sheet listing various possible taxes. It included Clinton's campaign promise to increase income taxes on the wealthy. Other options included an increase in the corporate tax rate; taxes on cigarettes and alcohol; a decrease on the portion of business meals that would be tax-deductible; a 4-cent-a-gallon gasoline tax increase; and several other technical adjustments that could bring in new revenues. The sheet also listed the amount of new revenue that these various tax increases might bring in over a five-year period. The highest level was $250 billion.

AFTER BENTSEN FINISHED, Gore stepped in. Gore felt that Clinton and he had been elected in part because of their promises on the environment, and he saw himself as steward of that part of the mandate. He had not told Clinton that he was planning to make a statement about using tax policy to help the environment.

Gore told the group he favored a broad-based energy tax—something not on Bentsen's list—such as a tax levied on the use of the British thermal units, or BTUs, a basic measure of energy. A BTU tax would be environmentally sound, he said, because coal, the dirtiest fuel, would be hit the hardest, though oil and natural gas would also be taxed. This emphasis would create political problems in coal states, he acknowledged, such as Pennsylvania, Michigan, and Ohio, which were key to Clinton's election. It would also hit West Virginia, home of Senator Robert C. Byrd, who chaired the powerful Senate Appropriations Committee that had to approve all spending. But such a tax would put the United States on the side of the environmental angels, Gore felt, because the Europeans and Japanese had said they would enact their own broad-based energy taxes if the United States did.

What's the best year we could have? Clinton asked, momentarily diverging from the tax discussion. If a genie were to give us our best possible year politically and in policy, what would we ask for? The news so far had been sobering, but Clinton's optimism resurfaced as he answered his own question. He listed a credible deficit and investment package, greater spending cuts, and progressive tax increases. He said he liked Gore's energy tax. He also listed health care reform and some of the bills that Bush vetoed. That would be an ideal year.

NEXT ON THE AGENDA was the proposal for a short-term stimulus to the economy. Roger Altman and Larry Summers had prepared a 108-page memo for Clinton on the subject as if it were a term paper to be graded on its length. They had proposed some $20 billion of fast-track spending and tax reductions for businesses to boost the economy.

"It would be quite risky to do nothing," Summers said now. He and Altman had estimated about a 20 percent chance of a recession. A stimulus package, he urged, would provide insurance against a recession.

"That's one of the strongest arguments for doing this," Clinton replied.

In addition, Summers said, a stimulus would position the administration to take credit if the economy did pick up. Clinton agreed and said a small stimulus that included a summer jobs program should be part of the economic plan.

GENE SPERLING brought out three sets of charts on possible levels of investment to achieve by 1997. In contrast to the short-term stimulus, these were the spending proposals to help the economy in the long run —the investments in job training, education, and rebuilding America that Clinton frequently called "the things I got elected for." Sperling too felt they constituted the core of Clinton's agenda. It made moral, political, and economic sense to Sperling, who had spent so much time putting together the campaign's *Putting People First* economic plan.

First of the three options was the full Clinton wish-list from *Putting People First,* at a cost of $88.8 billion. The second option, a "core" package, would cost $63.9 billion, and it included the middle-class tax cut. The third, a so-called bare-bones package, would cost $40.1 billion. Clinton made it clear he thought the $40 billion was far too low, even pathetic.

With vigorous enthusiasm, Sperling advocated a big investment package. "If Gene could get this budget," Stephanopoulos said at one point to those around him, "he'd be satisfied with a one-term presidency."

AFTER THE FORMAL PRESENTATIONS, the conversation moved to the question of the 1997 deficit reduction target. Blinder and Panetta had both laid out a variety of options. Reich, hoping to retain money for investments, began by arguing for a target on the smaller end of the range. But Clinton proposed a figure around Panetta's middle option: cutting the 1997 deficit by $145 billion, to bring the deficit for that year to about $220 billion.

Rivlin, Panetta, and Gore each made a case for a strong dose of deficit reduction. Rivlin said they should shoot for a 1997 deficit below $200 billion, noting that it would give them a better bargaining position with Congress, which would surely balk at their proposed cuts. Panetta said that businessmen, Wall Street, congressmen, the media, and academics all would watch their plan closely, and only steep deficit reduction would persuade these groups of the administration's seriousness. Gore agreed with Rivlin on the target, adding that, realistically, the two opportunities to be "bold" were with retirement and taxes. A bold plan with a BTU tax would create a synergy that would convince the markets they were serious, he said.

Tyson then expressed concern about the contraction that deficit reduction would bring with the economy still soft. Summers, however, again dismissed the worries. "You're going to get lower interest rates," he said confidently. Others weighed in on the issue. Altman disagreed, saying that interest-rate cuts would come more slowly. "The markets will adjust only when they see results," he maintained. Sperling urged caution.

Clinton said that the work done for Ross Perot's more radical deficit reduction plan showed no decline in long-term interest rates until the end of the decade, and wondered how they would get help from long-term rates.

Blinder said that if the package were credible, the markets would respond. "But you need some pre-assurance from Greenspan," he added. Bentsen, for one, knew this suggestion was potentially explosive. Greenspan and the Fed were independent, and the Bush administration had not succeeded in trying to pressure or work out agreements with Greenspan.

When Tyson warned that people would falsely expect short-term benefits from deficit reduction, Gore countered that a positive public response would not hinge only on short-term benefits. Throughout the meeting he had been arguing that the new administration had already captured the nation's imagination by realistically assessing the economic conditions after 12 years of Reagan and Bush, and that the mood in the country was upbeat. By seizing control of the deficits and their economic future, Gore argued, they would be doing what was politically unpopular but right. Potential critics from either the left or the right would be silenced by the popular sentiment that Clinton was trying to do the right thing. So the benefits of deficit reduction did not have to be short-term. When people saw the boldness, there would be a surge of support for the plan. Gore, who had been saying that boldness was the essence of Franklin D. Roosevelt's program, again pointed to the New Deal legislation. "Look at the 1930s," he reminded.

"Roosevelt was trying to help people," Clinton shot back. "Here we help the bond market, and we hurt the people who voted us in."

Gore said they could phase the energy tax in over time. "If you're bold," he said, "people will come around."

Panetta again took the floor. You really don't have a choice, he said bluntly to Clinton. If he didn't act on the deficit, a balanced-budget amendment might well pass Congress, forcing Clinton to surrender his presidency to a few players in Congress. "They will come up with some other way to basically take the presidency away from you," Panetta said, whether through a balanced-budget amendment or legislation like Gramm-Rudman—the 1980s law that tried to enforce lower deficit levels. "So you can't afford not to confront this issue."

Panetta said they had to realize the Fed would likely raise short-term interest rates if the deficit kept going up. Rather than cooperate, the Fed would be working at cross-purposes with the administration. That would lead to a foundering presidency, an inability to get anything done. A credible plan, however, would ensure that the Fed wouldn't bail out on the president and would likely work in the same direction as he was. There simply was no alternative.

Clinton said he was still concerned about a deficit reduction package that would harm the economy. "If average people don't see something good happening, they won't be impressed," he said. But he said they should focus on a $225 billion target for 1997, the position that seemed to be the consensus—and also consider a steeper target, below $200 billion. He added that he also wanted them to look at the all-fuels BTU energy tax.

The meeting ended after nearly six hours.

12

Gore told Clinton that he wanted to confidentially sound out some moderate Republican deficit hawks he knew in Congress about quietly exploring a bipartisan agreement on a Social Security COLA freeze. Clinton gave his approval, and Gore said he would do it in his own name to preserve Clinton's deniability on such a touchy political subject. Gore spoke with four Republicans in the Senate and several in the House. He had rarely received such point-blank refusals. He reported to Clinton that not one would agree to even discuss it. The new administration and the Democrats in Congress were going to have to make cuts on their own. Gore noted that these were the Republicans who pounded hardest on the federal deficit, but since he had promised to keep his exploratory conversations with the Republicans in confidence, he was prevented from going public with their hypocrisy.

On Wednesday evening, January 13, 1993, Stephanopoulos arranged for Sperling to brief some of the consultants and political people on how the economic plan was shaping up. Stephanopoulos knew the consultants felt cut out, and he wanted some political feedback. Greenberg, Begala, and several others attended the briefing in a conference room on the fourth floor of the transition headquarters in Little Rock.

Using slides, Sperling showed that the $50 billion in additional anticipated deficit could devastate Clinton's plan. It was bad news for the campaign promises. A middle-class tax cut would be difficult, the opportunity for investments reduced. Worse, he reported, Gore was gunning for an energy tax, which would hit the middle class. Social Security benefits might be taxed more or the Social Security cost-of-living increases frozen. Even with all that, it would be hard to uphold the campaign promise of halving the deficit in four years. Clinton might have to slip on that too.

The consultants and others bombarded Sperling with skeptical and angry questions.

Afterwards, at about 10 P.M., Stephanopoulos, Sperling, Greenberg, Begala, and others adjourned to Doe's Eat Place, their campaign hangout, a downscale diner with a screen door and cheap tables that specialized in steak and tamales.

"Why did we run?" Stan Greenberg asked, pounding the table. The whole transition had been screwed up—insular, with no political screen or input. Deficit hawks and the Washington establishment had stolen Clinton's presidency. "The presidency has been hijacked," Greenberg said flatly. A near-fatal disconnection had taken place. The team of political advisers that understood Clinton and his extraordinary mix of political traditions—true Democrat, populist, Southern pulse-taker and man-of-the-people, brainy policy student—was out in the cold. As a result, the vital link between Clinton and the voters was being severed. It was more than breaking promises; it was forsaking the visceral understanding of a candidate who had lived among real people. And the idea of new taxes that would fall on the forgotten middle class was in contradiction with how they had sold his candidacy.

Sperling said without a broad new tax, the deficit would probably be something like $250 billion for 1997.

Unacceptably high, Begala acknowledged.

Furious, Greenberg questioned both their analysis and the numbers.

Look, Sperling protested, the numbers just did not add up. Some ideas and promises that had seemed simple in the campaign were turning out to be very hard. Stephanopoulos backed him up.

The conversation wandered back and forth into the night. They asked Doe's to stay open past closing time, as they had done many times during the campaign.

Sperling felt pulled in both directions. On one hand, the economic team had not really accepted him and was growing increasingly skeptical of his insistence that Clinton stay true to the campaign themes. On the other, the consultants, his friends, were angry and were blaming him, the messenger, for the bad news. Sperling still felt the consultants were the cavalry behind him and would surely prevail.

Stephanopoulos felt beaten down. He realized that Clinton's promises didn't hang together. He couldn't cut middle-class taxes, cut the deficit in half, and finance a big investment program. Although Bush's attacks on Clinton's program during the campaign had been sufficiently untrue to merit denial, Stephanopoulos had to admit that the charge that his promises didn't add up had some validity. Now the larger deficit projections only gave the charge more credence.

THE NEXT MORNING, Clinton again gathered his economic team in the Governor's Mansion for a second large meeting before the inauguration. The negative drag that deficit reduction would have on economic growth seemed startling, and Clinton wanted to be sure he understood the potential impact.

Laura Tyson began. She said they had looked hard at the numbers. Assuming no help from the Fed and no stimulus package, the maximum growth in the years 1993 and 1994 would be 2.8 percent, and 2.5 percent thereafter. The economy was weak and wouldn't get to 3 percent growth without help, she said.

Alan Blinder repeated that deficit reduction would slow down the economy in the short run and yield only long-run benefits. Should the economy slow down for any other reason, he said, "then you have a recession similar to the Bush recession."

The effect on Clinton was electric. The dangers of the emerging deficit reduction package seemed clearer. "If we do all this and bleed all over the floor, and Greenspan doesn't help," he said, "we're screwed."

Yes, Blinder said. He added that he had run the numbers on a stimulus package and it would not give the economy a strong enough boost to offset the drag of deficit reduction. To forget about the stimulus was possible, but that might risk a financial crisis.

Roger Altman had been assigned to brief on the Federal Reserve. For Altman, Greenspan was a true prisoner of statistics: The Fed chairman looked at the numbers and let the policy flow from them. Senior contacts inside the Fed had told Altman that the central bank followed only one-month plans and did not look beyond that. The Fed's view, Altman said, seemed to be that if the administration showed enough courage on deficit reduction, the response of consumers, the bond markets, and others would neutralize the negative impact on the economy.

"There is too much intuition going on here," Tyson said. Cutting federal spending would drag down economic growth. Courage did not substitute for known laws of economics.

Altman felt that economic policy making was more an art than a science, and that the economists' models were often wrong. He nonetheless did not argue and attempted to explain how the Fed worked. Even if the Fed helped in the short term, it was impossible to predict what it would do further out. And the Fed couldn't really affect long- and medium-term interest rates. Altman said that the administration could not get a quid pro quo or advance assurance from Greenspan. That wasn't the way the independent Fed worked.

Why don't we get as tight a deficit reduction package as possible in the first year, with a stimulus? Clinton asked. He floated a range of $210 to $230 billion for the 1997 deficit target. Then, if that and the health care plan passed, they could come back with an eight-year deficit reduction plan later. If we accomplish all that on our economic and domestic agenda, we will have done what we were supposed to do. If we do all that, he added, do we just go play golf?

Bentsen said that Clinton should not simply focus upon what showed up as scorable savings under the budget in the first four years. If he did something that had an impact in the later years, and locked it in, that would also affect the bond markets. The markets looked at what would happen 10, 20, even 30 years out. The 30-year bond was the benchmark for measuring the long-term interest rates.

Others continued to suggest strategies and deficit reduction targets. After Reich repeated his preference for a less severe goal of $240 billion for 1997, Clinton offered his view. It seemed designed to please nearly everyone. The target, he said, should be $240 billion—Reich's suggestion—or 10 percent lower than that—about $216 billion, enough presumably to satisfy Bentsen and Panetta, though not perhaps Rivlin and Gore.

The key was courage, Gore said, returning to his favorite motif. If the country believed that Clinton was acting courageously, he said, that would change the chemistry in Congress. The administration had to make spending cuts, especially in entitlements. And Clinton should not shy away from politically difficult taxes. Gore added that the key was the Federal Reserve. He repeated his preference for a deficit target below $200 billion.

Rivlin agreed, adding authoritatively that $240 billion would not be credible.

Sperling and Panetta raised questions about the political risks and the feasibility of cutting programs such as Medicare, but Gore would not relent. "We have a chance to create a new reality," he said. "If you don't belly up to it now, it will never happen." This course would involve uncertainties, but the alternative was to drift. Panetta finally suggested that he and Bentsen talk to the congressional leadership about Social Security cuts.

As requested by Clinton the previous week, Bentsen presented details on a broad-based energy tax such as a BTU tax, now item number seven on a new chart he had prepared of possible revenue raisers. If properly designed, the tax would discourage use of high-pollution fuels such as coal. "We should start with a BTU tax as an opening bid," he said, withholding his private concerns that the tax would meet serious political resistance.

Gore took Bentsen's statement as an enthusiastic endorsement. Delighted, he agreed the tax had to be carefully written. "We may blow it if we do it wrong," he said. He added that consultation with Congress would be critical, and Clinton said he would have a private conference call with Senate Majority Leader George J. Mitchell, Speaker of the House Thomas Foley, and Gephardt.

Clinton turned to a more sensitive subject. How far could they depart from campaign promises and remain consistent with his values? he asked.

Stephanopoulos had come to realize that the middle-class income tax cut, the centerpiece of Clinton's early campaign, just wasn't in the cards. It had really hit home the night before. Now, on Clinton's cue, Stephanopoulos came out and said it: The middle-class tax cut should be abandoned. For one thing, the money for it didn't exist. Further, the media didn't expect it, and Clinton would get more criticism than praise for honoring a promise now widely viewed as unrealistic. Lastly, Stephanopoulos had seen the reaction of voters to the tax cut in the Fort Lee focus groups, and Greenberg had done other polling—all suggesting that people never really expected the tax cut.

Bentsen and Panetta both agreed it should be dropped. Panetta noted that the politically difficult Social Security cuts would bring in some $16 billion, and to lose that money right away to a middle-income tax giveback just didn't make sense.

The discussion turned to a timetable for devising the plan. Stephanopoulos suggested that the entire economic and domestic plan be presented to Congress on February 4, three weeks away. It was critical to pass the economic package in the first 100 days, as Clinton had stated. Gore proposed February 11. Clinton instructed Rubin to come up with a timetable.

Clinton then summed up his wishes. He said he also wanted numbers on Social Security and Medicare cuts. The cuts didn't have to yield savings early—maybe even in the next century was okay—as long as the bond markets took them seriously. Clinton spoke with firmness, making it clear that he understood Bentsen's argument about credibility in the bond market, and that he had signed on to the financial markets strategy. The technical approach to fixing the economy suggested by Greenspan, reenforced by Bentsen, Panetta, and others, now seemed more likely to work than some of his campaign proposals. To Clinton, a long-term effort to reduce the deficit could not be adopted simply to appease the bond market, but to help the middle class, the working families, those who had voted for him. Would the financial markets strategy help them too? The calculation was a gamble, he realized, and like most gamblers he was not certain of his choice.

AFTER THE MEETING, Bentsen came up to Altman. "I liked that presentation very much," Bentsen said, giving his intense but distant smile. He paused. "That's because I agreed with it."

Bentsen then went to see Greenspan. He told the chairman of the groundswell of support for deficit reduction within the new economic team, especially on Clinton's part. The Fed chairman, first among deficit hawks, smiled at the news. For years, Greenspan had repeated his view in public and private that it was time to act seriously and courageously on the deficit. He was careful not to give the impression of making an overt deal with Bentsen. He wanted the public to believe that he was not offering his views on specifics—on the particular mix of various spending cuts and new taxes that would achieve the sought-after deficit reduction. *How* the new administration and Congress chose to address the deficit was up to them, and was important, but *that* it be done was crucial.

Bentsen reported to Clinton about their meeting. "He's not going to give us a deal," Bentsen said. "There can be no quid pro quo." Short of that, however, Bentsen said, it looked good. "Greenspan will be supportive within limits, but those limits are great," he said. It was the best Clinton could get.

The communication with Greenspan was better than a deal. Greenspan appreciated what Clinton intended to do, and the administration knew what Greenspan had to do. There was another element: Lower interest rates made Greenspan's job much easier. For one thing, he would be spared the usual barrage of criticism for raising rates. And the administration's plan would also help Greenspan fight inflation—his chief responsibility.

13

PAUL BEGALA had virtually lived with Clinton during the campaign. He often had been the one to wake the candidate in the morning, to hand him a towel and the latest newspaper when he stepped from the shower. He had traveled on the campaign plane and hovered alongside Clinton at rallies, speeches, and bus tours. The campaign had been grueling and exhausting, in some ways worse for Begala and the other staffers than for Clinton. Clinton got an adrenaline boost from being at the center of attention, while they were merely part of the entourage, frequently waiting, watching, talking on the phone, haphazardly snatching food and sleep, often unshowered and overfed, with awful airplane air blowing over them. In his role as part-time valet, Begala had established a personal closeness with Clinton and had gained envied confidence as a tireless friend and defender.

Since election day, however, Begala had become isolated from Clinton and the locus of decision making. After so much proximity, he felt almost estranged. His campaigning skills were not seen as governing skills. Instead, high-powered lawyers such as Vernon Jordan and Warren Christopher had run the transition. The new administration was going to be populated with Washington insiders like Gore, Bentsen, and Panetta, and Wall Streeters like Rubin and Altman. Begala worried about these new people around Clinton and the influence they might have.

Begala had a simple philosophy: You win elections by appealing to real people, and you have to have them with you when you take over the government and try to run it in their interest. He had always considered Clinton a populist. The new crowd had little in common with the struggling working- and middle-class voters who had been the motive force in the campaign. Clinton succeeded because he connected to these people. In the Democratic primaries, when Paul Tsongas and others had talked about impersonal issues like the deficit numbers, Clinton had asserted that the campaign was about people and their economic security. In a sense Clinton had run against the Democratic Party elites. Now, however, he seemed to be courting them. The elites, Begala felt, had taken Clinton's body and were after his soul.

The morning of the inauguration, January 20, 1993, Begala received a phone call telling him he would not be sitting on the podium outside the U.S. Capitol where Clinton would be sworn in. Instead, he was assigned seats down front. He and his wife picked up their tickets that morning, only to find their seats were located in the last reserved section, down front, but way, way back. They went, and his wife wept.

James Carville, who was also bumped from the podium, was so upset he didn't attend the swearing in at all, watching it on TV instead. Carville saw that he held a less exalted status in the new order. The political people like himself had been the mercenaries hired to clean up the town, he reasoned, and they had done so and been shunted aside. The "experts and schoolmarms," as Carville sarcastically called them, had been brought in to govern.

Soon after the inaugural, Hillary Clinton called Begala. A low-level inaugural functionary had taken Carville and Begala's podium tickets for his own family, she explained, and she was outraged. "We love you," Hillary said. "We're sick about what happened." She invited Begala over to the White House and then to Camp David, the presidential getaway in the nearby Maryland mountains, for an upcoming weekend retreat to be attended by the cabinet and the senior White House staff.

STEPHANOPOULOS, the designated communications director for the new administration, had felt unsettled during the transition, in part because while the economic plan was being hammered out in the confidential discussions, he had not been able to answer any questions about economic policy. Expectations were so great, Clinton's rhetoric so full of promise, that Stephanopoulos worried that Clinton might have to deliver a preliminary speech or release some outline of his plan just to satisfy the press and public. The news vacuum was already being filled with stories about gays in the military that were diverting attention from the upcoming economic plan. Stephanopoulos proposed that the economic team get together right after Clinton's inaugural speech to see if some partial step could be taken publicly before the congressional recess at the beginning of February.

Rubin, Sperling, Altman, and Panetta gathered with Bentsen in Bentsen's Senate office. Stephanopoulos, delayed with the president, did not attend. Sperling noted the pressures for a preliminary step, wondering what remained to be done since their meeting in Little Rock just six days earlier.

Panetta said getting the plan done by mid-February was going to be brutal, let alone ten days earlier.

"Whatever you do, you're going to be stuck with it for a long time," Bentsen said in his careful, clipped voice. His eyes traveled around the room, systematically staring the others down. "So whatever and however, you've got to make sure that it's right." In the long run, minor communications victories would be meaningless. "Getting it right is all that's important," he said. The others agreed.

Sperling called Stephanopoulos afterward. "Bentsen squashed me like a bug," he reported.

ON THE SATURDAY after the inaugural, January 23, Bentsen arranged to go to the White House to meet with Stephanopoulos, Rubin, and Sperling. Bentsen, who had already been confirmed as Treasury Secretary, was about to make his television debut as Treasury Secretary the next morning on NBC's "Meet the Press." As a spokesman for the administration, he wanted to make sure what he planned to say would fit with White House plans. Bentsen brought along his press secretary of two decades, Jack R. DeVore, 54, a cagey, cigar-smoking Texan who believed in giving the media the truth but not too much of it. DeVore once said that a press secretary's job was to manufacture a steady stream of doggie biscuits for the press, who would gleefully lick the hand that fed them, thumping their tails as long as there was news. But, DeVore said, if you ran out of treats or news, the press would eat your arm and try for more.

At the White House, Bentsen said he was accustomed to appearing on the Sunday talk shows and saying whatever he wanted. If they wanted him to say something or not say something, he wanted to know and get some guidance. For example, there were bound to be questions about Zoe Baird, Clinton's nominee for Attorney General, who had just withdrawn because she hadn't paid Social Security taxes for her child's nanny.

If that comes up, change the subject, Stephanopoulos suggested.

It wouldn't be that easy, Bentsen said. The only way to turn attention from Zoe Baird was to offer a new, more compelling subject. Bentsen or DeVore proposed several ideas, but they were shot down. Stephanopoulos, even more nervous, pessimistic, and cautionary than usual, would agree only that Bentsen say Clinton's economic plan would be ready in mid-February—hardly juicy enough to make news.

When the meeting broke up, Bentsen remained unsatisfied. Rubin, Sperling, and he went into the empty office of Press Secretary Dee Dee Myers and shut the door for 15 minutes. What should I say if asked about an energy tax? Bentsen asked. They all knew that the BTU tax was almost certainly going to be a central component of the president's plan.

Sperling was adamantly opposed to releasing any single part of the plan. All the elements had to be presented together as part of an interlocking whole, he said. Let any one part out, especially a new tax, and it could get creamed or become the subject of endless, negative press. Floating the energy tax would only lead to more questions about the middle-class tax cut that was almost certainly headed for demise.

They all agreed that Bentsen would say merely that an energy tax was on the table, just as everything was on the table, but he would not signal that Clinton was going ahead with it.

Don't worry, Bentsen assured them. He made these sorts of television appearances all the time. He wouldn't slip up.

The next morning, Bentsen and DeVore went to the NBC studios on Nebraska Avenue in Washington. When asked about taxes, Bentsen said without qualification, "Some consumption tax is going to take place." He said he could not pin down its size or type. "A broad-based energy tax is certainly one of those that is on the table as an option to be considered," he added, noting with praise that it would promote energy conservation. He then went on to eliminate various other kinds of consumption taxes.

How did it go? Bentsen asked DeVore afterwards.

No mistakes, DeVore said, and no major news.

Sperling, spending a typical Sunday at work, his first at the White House, came to the same conclusion, focusing on what they intended to say rather than on what had actually been conveyed. The Associated Press, however, and other news services quickly put it together. No single sentence or sound bite said it all, but an unmistakable impression had been left. Bentsen had said some consumption tax was "going to take place." The broad-based energy tax was "certainly" on the table. He praised it and eliminated the others. The story was the lead on most evening news shows and on the front page in the next day's newspapers.

Sperling was baffled when he saw the news coverage. He spent the morning drawing up two pages of likely questions and possible answers on the subject for Clinton. On the phone, he insisted to reporters that Bentsen hadn't said an energy tax was necessarily coming. Clinton, too, in his comments to reporters that day, challenged the press's reading of Bentsen's remarks. "I wasn't sure that I was reading about the same interview in the press this morning," Clinton said in a brief exchange with reporters. "He said that no decision had been made, and no decision has been made."

At Treasury, Bentsen came to work braced for the reaction. He had probably gone out on a limb. DeVore could see that the normally uptight Bentsen was even more uptight. Soon news of the reaction in the bond market poured into Treasury. By the afternoon, Bentsen was all smiles. The yield on the government's 30-year bond fell throughout the day from 7.29 to 7.19 percent, signaling confidence. "You might note that the long-term rates are down to a six-year low," Bentsen said to DeVore smugly at the day's end. It was one concrete result that could be posted by the new administration before a bill had even been proposed or a single vote taken in Congress. The financial markets strategy was beginning to work.

Mandy Grunwald, for one, did not share the jubilation. She believed that the bond market thrived on bad news for the middle class. The reaction seemed to indicate that if Clinton didn't plan to screw the middle class, he was not serious about deficit reduction.

As CLOSE AS HE WAS, Stephanopoulos felt he was watching the president and First Lady through a glass. There was no way to know their real relationship. Why did some couples stay together and others grow apart? An outsider could not know. One thing was evident: Hillary was his most important adviser and she wanted a senior post in the White House. Initially, she wanted to be the top White House domestic policy adviser. Stephanopoulos, Greenberg, and several others were alarmed. It would be politically explosive, send the wrong message, and invite attention and Lady Macbeth stories about her as the true source of Clinton's ambition and drive.

The domestic policy post went to Carol Rasco, a longtime Arkansas friend and political aide to the Clintons. Hillary said she still wanted an office in the West Wing of the White House, the business and policy hub where the president's Oval Office was located. Traditionally, the First Lady worked out of the East Wing, the opposite side of the White House, that contained the social offices. During the transition, some Clinton advisers had tried to talk her out of it, but had failed. Stephanopoulos was relieved when they decided to fall back on the model that had worked in Arkansas—give her a project to supervise.

Clinton decided to put her in charge of a health care reform task force —the most important and influential role ever explicitly assigned to a First Lady. Clinton had initially asked Gore to head the task force, but Gore had declined the job, which could have demanded all of his time. Clinton had also considered offering the assignment to Senator John D. "Jay" Rockefeller IV of West Virginia, a close friend who had studied the issue closely, but Majority Leader George Mitchell had warned against having a senator head an executive branch task force.

The same Monday the bond market responded so favorably to Bentsen's comments, Clinton called together his staff and key cabinet members in the Roosevelt Room after lunch to announce that his wife was going to head the task force. She was to be treated like anyone else, Clinton said, and be challenged and questioned like any other member of the cabinet. Bentsen thought the president was taking a hell of a risk appointing his wife, but didn't feel he knew Clinton well enough to tell him. Clinton then read a statement he planned to give to the media.

Just after 2 P.M., Clinton read the statement publicly. He said he wanted to submit legislation to Congress within 100 days. When asked if the 100-day deadline was "hard and fast," Clinton gave a modified yes. "If it were 101 days, I wouldn't have a heart attack."

THE NEXT DAY, Senate Minority Leader Bob Dole told Clinton at the White House that the Republicans probably wouldn't give him any votes on his economic plan. Clinton would be raising taxes, and if the tax hike didn't work, Dole said forthrightly, that would permit the Republicans to blame Clinton. Clinton appreciated at least the candor. Dole wasn't going to let him have a honeymoon. It was funny and sad, Clinton felt. He had viewed Dole as one Republican who had been willing to stand up to Reagan and Bush on taxes and adopt what Clinton thought was a more balanced and realistic approach. Now, Clinton concluded, Dole had become one of them, securing his position as leader with the many conservative, anti-tax Republicans in the Senate. Part of

Dole's motivation might also have been his own political ambitions. Clinton realized he wasn't the only one who was operating as if the 1996 presidential campaign began the day he became president.

AT 2 P.M. on Wednesday, January 27, Clinton invited to the Oval Office the Democratic heavyweights from Congress. From the Senate were Majority Leader George Mitchell; Robert Byrd of West Virginia, the Appropriations Committee chairman; Daniel Patrick Moynihan of New York, the Finance Committee chairman; and Jim Sasser of Tennessee, the Budget Committee chairman. Their House counterparts were there as well. These were the men whose support Clinton would need to pass his economic plan.

Moynihan, 65, looked around the room. He had first been in the office 32 years earlier, at the start of the Kennedy administration. Back then, he had been the youngest person in the room; now he was the second oldest after Byrd.

Panetta told the senators about the plan to cut back the cost-of-living adjustments for Social Security. A simple three-month delay would save an extraordinary $20 billion over five years. The COLAs that had been applied during the double-digit inflation of the 1970s had contributed significantly to the current explosion of entitlement costs. This would be politically feasible, Panetta said, because the three months would pass before anyone could gear up to oppose it. He felt Clinton ought to do it. Panetta also had a plan for bigger six-month and one-year freezes. Under his plan, those at or below the poverty line would still get their adjustments.

Both Clinton and Gore indicated they liked the idea. Several of the House members also expressed support.

Mitchell, a 59-year-old former federal judge, departed from his normal judiciousness. "This is wrong," the majority leader said. However it was fashioned, such a freeze would be regressive and hurt those least able to afford it. The typical Social Security recipient was an elderly woman with little or no other income, who just barely survived, he reminded them. Such a proposal would also be politically unwise and wouldn't pass the Senate.

None of the others said anything.

Over the next several days, news stories appeared suggesting that a cost-of-living freeze was still under consideration. Gore, for one, was still pushing, arguing that such cuts would be necessary for an equivalent effort to increase taxes on Social Security benefits on the wealthy.

Moynihan thought that Clinton had interpreted the silence of the other senators as disagreement with Mitchell's assessment, when, in fact, they had agreed. Moynihan decided to teach the new White House a lesson. In a TV interview, he said that cutting cost-of-living increases was unthinkable—never, not a chance. "That's a death wish," he said, "and let's get it out of the way and forget it right now."

Clinton was displeased with both Moynihan's reaction and his style of delivering it. Panetta, aware that the House leadership was willing to go along, was also upset that the Senate was resisting. Bentsen tried to explain that the freeze would be "political suicide" for many senators, and there was no way they would pass it.

As Panetta watched Clinton struggle, he felt it was the beginning of what the budget director began to call Clinton's "slow and torturous awakening" to the ways of Washington.

BENTSEN AND RUBIN had kept Alan Greenspan up to date on the status of the White House discussions on the economic plan, and they wanted him to visit with Clinton face to face at the White House. They arranged a meeting for the morning of Thursday, January 28, the beginning of Clinton's second week as president.

With Bentsen and Rubin sitting in, the chairman expanded upon what he had said to Clinton the previous month in Little Rock. His words this time came in a significantly different context: Clinton was now president. Greenspan realized his words took on great new meaning.

The chairman dropped a bomb, one of the most sobering messages a president could receive. His concern, he confided, was not for the next two or three years. With defense spending dropping precipitously, the deficit could be controlled for a short time and the basic economic problem would be obscured. But after 1996, the data showed, the outlook changed drastically. At that point, Greenspan said, the deficit would climb back up and the interest on the debt would explode. The system would become unstable.

"That's what financial catastrophe means," Greenspan said plainly. The phrase "financial catastrophe," with its overtones of the stock market crash, the Great Depression, and Herbert Hoover, could not but resonate with a brand-new president. Clinton was now sitting in the Oval Office as a result of a financial situation far short of catastrophe, simply the economic doldrums of the Bush years. The stakes, political as well as economic, were obvious.

Greenspan continued. To prepare for any unanticipated financial disasters, and to assert control while the president still had some leverage,

Greenspan told Clinton, "You've got to act well in advance." Bentsen and Rubin obviously agreed. Clinton made it clear that he received the message, and that a major deficit reduction plan was already in the works.

14

CLINTON ARRANGED to have his entire cabinet and senior White House staff gather at Camp David for their retreat the weekend of January 30–31. Begala, Greenberg, and Grunwald were all able to attend. Clinton took Greenberg aside before the discussions began. "We've lost track of why we ran," Clinton said. Deficit reduction was overwhelming the economic plan, he said, in part because of the effective efforts of Panetta and Rivlin. He asked Greenberg to make a presentation so those people who had not been in the campaign would understand why he ran.

Greenberg felt that a wonkish tone had pervaded the transition, set not only by Clinton, the lover of policy, theory, and discussion, but also by Gore. Gore had seemed to want to drive politics out of the decisions and do what was pure and right. Greenberg wanted politics back in.

After they convened, Mandy Grunwald led off with a discussion of what the American people thought they had voted for. She provided a snapshot of what she called middle-class economic anxiety. People were more scared of the status quo than they were of change. Those who worked hard and played by the rules didn't win any more. Clinton had promised that he would address their concerns about jobs, retirement, education, homes, and health care.

Greenberg said that people generally believed that government had failed them, but they also wanted what he called a Reichian solution from an activist government on jobs, education, training, and investment. "People are anti-government and pro-government at the same time," he said. "This is a complicated notion. Don't confuse the desire for deficit reduction with a presumption that people want small government." Clinton had to convince voters that he would use their tax money more efficiently and effectively.

In his focus groups and polling, Greenberg said, he asked voters to name Clinton's most important promises. The first answer was the promise to create 8 million jobs, the second health care reform, the third welfare reform. All of these ranked above deficit reduction. If deficit reduction was going to require new taxes on the middle class, the president had to be seen as fighting for the middle class in every other way. If deficit reduction had to be emphasized, it couldn't be portrayed as an end in itself, but as a means to accomplish the other promises of the campaign.

Hillary Clinton interjected. The event which had gripped the public most during the inauguration celebrations, she said, was the White House open house, where she and her husband stood for hours greeting the public. People had the feeling that others "like me" were in there, she said. Making it clear she was backing Greenberg's point, she said the people needed to feel that Clinton was in touch with them and their problems, such as jobs and health care.

Clinton then turned to some of the broad themes for his presidency, while others listened or took notes. He spoke of hope and opportunity, and the difference between them: Opportunity, he said, was an objective reality. Hope was the faith that things could be better. FDR created hope long before he created opportunity. Clinton talked about "making change our friend." He reminded everyone that things were worse than he had thought before taking office, that the American people had been misled, and that the economic situation had deteriorated. He wanted to keep faith with the middle class. "It's scary to be a little person," he said someone had told him in the line at the White House. America had a special place in the world, and the eyes of the world were upon them. But more important, he said, "the eyes of our children are upon us." If we do our jobs, and reform health care, he said, "We'll return to office."

Then Hillary took the floor to address some practical questions. The problems from the 12-year Republican mess would not be solved overnight, she said. The administration would have to communicate to people that the country was going on a journey—a long journey, with milestones along the way to mark progress.

Let me tell you how this guy works and how we operated in Arkansas, she said. During his first term as governor, he set about attacking all the problems all at once. He was the darling of the reform-minded, liberal press. But he didn't communicate a vision or describe the journey he intended. In 1980, she said, when Clinton lost his bid for reelection as governor, the lack of a coherent story had disconnected him from the people he was trying to help. In 1983, when he came back, they had devised a simple story, with characters, with an objective, with a beginning, middle, and end. And it all had come from a moral point of view.

They had taken on education reform, the hardest issue, whose benefits would not be seen for a generation. Talk about a long journey, she said. They realized the need for a story, complete with enemies and villains. They even villainized the teachers' union, which had been their ally, for resisting "accountability" when it opposed teacher testing.

"You show people what you're willing to fight for when you fight your friends," Hillary said. Though the battle was long and a painful political experience, there were benchmarks of progress every two years or so along the way: Class sizes shrank, teacher testing was implemented, reading scores improved slightly. "It took years to see results," she said. But by the end of Clinton's time as governor, people understood his commitment to education was genuine. Isolated initiatives worked less well, she added. "People have got to understand where he wants to take the country."

And in 1985, when they were devising a strategy for economic development in Arkansas, she said, they made sure that Clinton was telling a story to voters, not delivering a speech to politicians. As it went along, they noted the markers of their progress. They pointed out that the state government was sacrificing, too, by limiting perks, and people felt served and included. They didn't avoid fights with the legislature, but rather used them to move the story forward. The overall story, she said, has to be sold before the details are put forth.

In Clinton's acceptance speech at the 1992 convention, he had used that wonderful quote from Isaiah, " 'Where there is no vision, the people perish,' " Hillary said. The vision, she said, was in a sense the plan for the journey ahead. They could not get bogged down in bond market talk and deficit reduction numbers. Those were just tools. They were not the vision; they were not the journey.

President Clinton then stepped up and enumerated his priorities. He reeled off a dozen items from the campaign, ranging from a stimulus package for short-term economic growth to health care. Maybe health care could be sent up to Congress, he suggested, to begin the process while lowering expectations on the timing.

Secretary of State Warren Christopher suggested some lawyerly caution. The administration should narrow the priorities, he said, since everything on the list was tough.

Hillary then gave a ringing speech in favor of just the opposite—doing everything. "Why are we here if we don't go for it?" she asked at the end.

Afterward, Begala almost grabbed the First Lady, taking her aside. She had pinpointed what was wrong, he said. "That's the problem with the economic plan," he said. "There's all this discussion of minutiae." The news was full of stories about program cuts, possible taxes, Social Security, God-awful numbers upon numbers. The story was precisely what was missing.

"The economic plan is being defined by leaks," said Mandy Grunwald. The president was being killed for even considering cuts in Social Security, for instance. She knew he was never going to do it, but no one had swatted the idea dead.

Hillary started nodding. Clinton walked up. She turned to her husband and said they were talking about the need for a story they could tell beforehand to sell the economic plan. Thus far, there was no context for people to understand what the new administration was proposing to do. "People can't process information they don't have," she said.

"Why don't you do it?" the president asked Begala and Grunwald.

Yes, sir, Begala said. At times he thought that without Hillary, Clinton would have wound up as merely the most popular law professor at the University of Arkansas, where he had taught before entering politics.

Hillary turned to Begala and Grunwald. "You write the communications plan," Hillary said. "You know the journey." Get some of the Navy guys who run Camp David to drive you back to Washington in a van, she instructed. Take notes, she said, get others involved, and get back with a plan for telling the story. "Can you fax it up to me tonight?" she requested.

Grunwald was delighted to see the First Lady moving things. She was a great planner. In the first days of the administration, with attention focused on Hillary as the potential dragon lady, Hillary had posed for photos in a great dress, the attentive hostess overseeing the kitchen and dining rooms. The photos were intended to soften her image. Now Grunwald could see some of that similar planning would finally be directed where it was needed most, at the economic plan.

IN THE VAN, Begala and Grunwald made some notes. Back in Washington, they called Greenberg and took what amounted to his deposition on the issue. They reached Carville and put him on the speakerphone. Carville said things were spinning out of control. The first week of the administration had been chaos, with all the media attention focused on the controversy over allowing gays in the military and on Zoe Baird's nanny problems. The White House needed more political awareness, he said.

The four consultants had their assignment and soon were working the problem. It was exciting, just like the campaign. By the end of the day, they had drafted a three-page memo that was addressed only to Hillary at Camp David.

It read: "We need a communications strategy—a campaign to sell the president's economic recovery plan in the days leading up to the Address. . . . Time is extraordinarily limited. There are certain steps that need to be taken immediately. . . .

"First, we need survey research and focus group data to tell us what the American people know about the state of the economy and what they expect from the economic plan—most importantly, if their perceptions and expectations have changed since the campaign has ended. Stan is working on that.

"No matter what, the American people need to be told that things are every bit as bad as we thought they were in the campaign, indeed, even worse." They wanted to recreate the urgency of the campaign. "This piece of information must be communicated *now: before the Super Bowl*"—the football game was to be played the next day—"the President should tell the media the upshot of this working weekend is:

"1. We've inherited one hell of a mess. Layoffs around the country are worse than they should be and worse than we thought they'd be." At the time, the unemployment rate was standing at 7.3 percent, better than the worst months of the Bush administration but still exceptionally high.

"2. The *real* budget numbers are far worse than we dreamed. The government has misled the American people. The President's attitude should be as outraged and betrayed as the attitude of the free Russians when they saw firsthand how the Communists screwed up their country. (Don't forget: FDR dumped on Hoover for years and Reagan *still* blames Carter and 'the bureaucracy.') This can be done without mentioning Bush by name.

"3. Our government is frighteningly ill-equipped to deal with the dimensions of the problems caused by its neglect." The memo turned to some minor but symbolically important examples: "There are six chefs at the Department of Transportation, but not one phone in the White House on which the president can make a conference call." It briefly dwelled on fancy executive dining rooms and limousines, juicy targets to provoke popular outrage.

Begala had come to grips with the fact that the middle-class tax cut was dead. Under No. 4, in boldface and underscored, the memo read: *"We are not going to call on middle-class Americans to do more with less until their government finally does more with less.* This will get us through tomorrow."

"We know the broad contours of The Story," the memo said, elevating the strategy with capital letters: "government failed us, betrayed our people and our values. . . . Every day between now and the address to the Joint Session, the president should be in the media with an economic event stressing cuts in government and taxes on the rich."

In a parenthetical remark referring to the First Lady's performance, the memo added: "(The lesson you raised from teacher testing in Arkansas is instructive here: Showing you have the guts to do what's tough on interest groups buys you the maneuvering room to do other tough things.)"

The memo recommended that, over the next week, Clinton launch a media blitz to emphasize his plan to eliminate the deductibility of excessive corporate executive pay. "We should also leak the upper-income tax increase, then go to a crowd of Wall Street honchos," it said, where Clinton should demand they pay their "fair share."

The memo proposed a mobilization of the White House and government to sell the program. "It needs a campaign manager to coordinate its efforts." It recommended Paul Begala for the job and volunteered the services of the other three consultants.

"One final point," the memo said. "Although we don't believe we need the details of the plan to outline The Story, the sooner we make fundamental decisions about the package's contents the clearer our task will be."

CLINTON AND HILLARY asked Begala to come work full time at the White House. To avoid any conflict with his ongoing political consulting business, Begala decided to work without pay. He reported to work Monday, February 1.

Clinton told him to talk to deputy budget director Alice Rivlin, who was in charge of the book the administration was going to issue once the economic plan was made final. At lunchtime, Rivlin asked Begala and David Dreyer, a deputy to Stephanopoulos, to come by her office in the adjoining Old Executive Office Building.

A small, elfin woman with a quick mind, Rivlin had shuffled between government jobs, including the directorship of the Congressional Budget Office, and the Brookings Institution, one of the most elite think tanks, for 35 years. She had a Ph.D. from Radcliffe and had written several heavily analytic policy books with titles such as *Microanalysis of Socio-economic Systems*. During the transition, Clinton had interviewed her in Little Rock for the budget director post, and she had gone in planning to pitch deficit reduction to the president-elect. To her surprise, Clinton made the pitch to her, and she left feeling that this was an administration she wanted to join. Clinton, however, made it clear to aides that he found her prickly and lacked the easy warmth and humor that he liked, and opted for Panetta instead. She settled for deputy.

When Begala and Dreyer arrived, Rivlin was on the phone and eating a chicken salad sandwich, which Begala noted was dripping from her chin. "So what do you guys want?" she asked.

Begala said they first wanted to discuss the dimensions of the risk to the economy if the administration did nothing about the deficit.

He was preaching to the choir. Rivlin said that was terrific, right on track. What else? she wanted to know.

"We have to walk people through the journey the president has gone from November to February. We have to explain why the deficit got worse and how it got worse," Begala said, focusing on The Story.

"That's nonsense," Rivlin said bluntly, her voice cold with assured professionalism. "Bill Clinton knew where this deficit was going," she said, adding that they had to face the fact that the campaign fundamentally misrepresented the situation. There was no need to revisit that journey, she said.

Begala was steaming. To him, Rivlin symbolized all that was wrong with Clinton's new team of Washington hands, and represented the Volvo-driving, National Public Radio–listening, wine-drinking liberalism that he felt had crippled the Democratic Party for decades. He tried his argument again. They needed to explain how the situation had changed.

Rivlin repeated herself, this time more tactfully omitting Clinton's name, but rigidly maintaining that "the campaign" had been "dishonest" and its statements "untrue."

Begala was astonished. "I don't think Bill Clinton is a liar," he said. He got up and walked out.

Begala reported his encounter to Stephanopoulos and several other campaign workers who were now on the White House staff. They did not share his vexation. Stephanopoulos showed no interest in doing anything about Begala's altercation with Rivlin. It was not a matter of principle, and she was a member of the team. Begala also described the incident generally to Bentsen and Panetta without identifying Rivlin, but they, too, were busy with other matters. He decided not to mention it to Clinton or Gore.

Begala concluded that he would have to create a train wreck, to draw attention to the clash between Rivlin's jaded attitude and his desire to shake up the system. If Clinton didn't govern as he had campaigned, he felt, it would be a betrayal. Begala produced a seven-page memo to the president. He began by invoking Hillary. "As Mrs. Clinton stressed at Camp David, we need to define The Story of the economic plan." Begala said the story had to have "heroes and villains," and offered "a first cut at The Story."

He sounded a class-struggle theme: "We need to reject the greed and short-sightedness of the past . . . [reject] sitting idly by while an elite few profit as our economy erodes. . . . There will be a 'ladder of contribution.' . . . When it comes to sacrifice, we will turn first to the government, then to the special interests and corporations, then to the rich, all before we ever talk about asking still more from the beleaguered middle class."

For each part of the plan, the memo proposed a critique and solution. Under "CHANGING THE GOVERNMENT," it said that government "has served only itself and the economic elite . . . government's been lying to the American people about it with phony cooked numbers and hidden off-budget spending . . . the very rich can buy government bonds, which are used to finance the debt and get rich off the very deficit that was created by their own tax breaks."

The next section, entitled "CORPORATIONS AND SPECIAL INTERESTS," said that "Corporations can no longer expect something for nothing from our government." It raised the specter of the "forces of greed and defenders of the status quo" who would fight the plan. Other sections focused on "THE RICH" and "THE MIDDLE CLASS." The memo concluded by reiterating that the plan's opponents should be equated with greed and the status quo, and by urging Clinton to say, "I ask that you join me in fighting them."

Clinton agreed to try some of these ideas in a speech he was to give on February 3 to the employees of the Office of Management and Budget. But instead of attacking government, Clinton praised the workers effusively, saying no one worked harder than they did. "Everybody should come to work for the Federal Government," the president said. And instead of blasting the rich for their greed, Clinton said, "The wealthiest Americans enjoyed the fruits of their labors."

Begala was beside himself. The more discussions and meetings he attended with the economic team, the more he realized that they had all converged on deficit reduction. It was no longer just catechism repeated to appease a certain constituency; it had become the religion. There was no discipline or coherence to the message they were trying to send. He wrote a stream-of-consciousness-style memo, peppering it with strong language—"shit" and other four-letter words—for emphasis. The president read and approved it, and Mack McLarty suggested that Begala rewrite it, retaining the main points but cleaning up the language so it could be handed out to the cabinet.

"This is an Economic Growth Package," the memo began. "It is not a deficit-reduction package, a shared sacrifice package, or a pain package." Warming to the task of instructing the cabinet, he wrote, "The first thing out of your mouth when you're talking about this package should be, *'President Clinton's economic growth package will create jobs and increase incomes for millions of Americans . . .'* "

He continued with his second point. *"This package represents fundamental change.* Always, always, always steer the discussion to what a wonderful world it will be if we have the courage to make the changes we must, and how terrible things will be if we do not." At the end of this paragraph, in capital letters, he wrote: "[SEE RULE ONE]"—the line that it was an economic growth package, not a deficit reduction package.

Third, the contribution would be fair and shared. He said to use the word "contribution" instead of "sacrifice." "It sounds less painful, more voluntary and has a patriotic ring." The rich would pay, but, Begala noted this time, "none of this is punitive, all of this is necessary and fair."

Other points addressed the theme of responsibility ("We hope to create more millionaires than Ronald Reagan ever did—but they'll have to pay their fair share in taxes"); of the power of special interests ("Don't shy away from the fact that the powerful interests, preferably powerful economic elites, will not like this package"); of not letting the press turn the discussion to "pain" or the betrayal of campaign promises; and of the long-term payoff of the plan.

In conclusion, Begala wrote: *"It's NOT the deficit, stupid."* He repeated Greenberg's point from Camp David. "Reducing the deficit is not the end. It is a means to the end of increasing incomes and generating jobs." Begala read the memo to the economic team and it was handed out to the cabinet.

15

 EARLY IN CLINTON'S PRESIDENCY, House Majority Leader Richard Gephardt and the congressional leadership met with Clinton, and Gephardt offered him some advice. It wasn't enough that the congressional leaders knew the direction of the plan, Gephardt said. A freshman representative or a member from a less prominent state also needed to hear directly from Clinton that the plan was going to be the paramount issue in the administration's first year. That way they could feel personally invested. Clinton agreed.

Begala had earlier worked as a speechwriter for Gephardt and he followed up with his old boss. Gephardt said he didn't want any surprises. He asked to be kept informed. Congress would pass what Clinton proposed, he assured Begala, but to keep everyone from pouncing until the plan had been fully explained, Clinton would have to listen to each member who wanted to speak. If Gephardt was going to deliver the members for Clinton, he would have to be able to deliver Clinton to the members for these interchanges.

Gephardt said he would help arrange half a dozen meetings at the White House for Clinton to meet with the House Democrats, limiting each gathering to only 20 to 30 members. He would see to it that each group included at least two to four avowedly pro-Clinton—"shills," as Begala dubbed them—who would vocally support the president. Gephardt also promised to scatter any potentially anti-Clinton members throughout the groups to dilute their impact. Each member would get only about two minutes to speak, but they at least would be able to report to their constituents, "What I told the president was . . ."

FEBRUARY 17 WAS SET as the date for Clinton to give his main address to a Joint Session of Congress. In an eight-page memo, David Dreyer outlined a day-by-day strategy, from February 6 through February 22, for management of the media in selling "The Story" of Clinton's new economic plan.

On Sunday, February 7, "The morning papers reveal plans by the Clinton Administration on significant policy issues related to taxing the rich and powerful. As a consequence, the 'hit the rich' theme is pursued by each of the three weekend talk shows, and the comments by Tyson, Reich and other Administration spokespeople highlight that apparent policy decision. Events of the day drive the message that the plan involves hurting the special interests."

On Monday, several Washington think-tank political scientists such as "Norman Ornstein, Richard Neustadt, Tom Mann, Charles Cook, etc., are equipped with talking points and media contact lists to 'message out' praise for the President's decision. The cuts are deep and they are unprecedented." *

The message was to be controlled as much as possible. "Stephanopoulos to discuss the number of canned chefs and drivers," or McLarty offered as a guest to the various news shows, "strongest message advocates of the President program (Bentsen, Gephardt) are pitched to the weekend shows."

Similar instructions were enumerated for virtually every day over the next two weeks. On February 11, child immunizations and an attack on "the evil pharmaceutical companies" would be stressed. Clinton, Mrs. Clinton, and others would visit a child health facility, along with a "neutral authority figure" such as former Surgeon General C. Everett Koop, who would be recruited to comment.

For February 12, both Clinton and Bentsen would give the same

---

* This plan was apparently never followed up. All four said they had not been contacted by anyone in the White House. "I would have been a little more reassured if they had tried," said Norman Ornstein of the American Enterprise Institute. In his writings he both praised and criticized Clinton's plan. Neustadt, a scholar of the presidency at Harvard, laughed when told of the memo, and called it "someone's harebrained scheme." Thomas Mann of the Brookings Institution said he was amused at the idea but that he never heard from the White House. Charles E. Cook, a political columnist, had both kind and unkind words for Clinton's plan. "I am not a flack," he said. "Everyone gets spun a little but they haven't bothered with me."

speech to business groups: "Double shots of Clinton and Bentsen ensure score for evening news broadcasts." February 13 would be more criticism of special interests, defined as "drug companies, restaurants, and the rich and powerful." Beginning February 14, the Democratic National Committee would seek out support for Clinton's upcoming plan, "with the goal of having 500 telephone calls per Congressman and Senator" by the end of the day after the State of the Union address.

The political staff and the Democratic National Committee would "begin meeting with vulnerable members of the House and Senate to assure support for those members with tough 1994 races who support the program." On February 15, they should "stress the deceit of the past two administrations," and on February 17 use an administration official "to prepare members of Congress for 'reaction interviews' following the speech." Clinton and Gore were to do some public event as "affirming footage" for the evening news shows.

After the speech, the memo continued, "President departs for Chicago, Illinois for barnstorming tour. *If consistent with ethics rules, the President takes real people with him on Air Force One.*" Cabinet secretaries would fan out across the country to stump for the plan. Nobel Prize-winning economists would testify before Congress in support. On February 19, "In Chicago, the President participates in uplifting people events." On the morning of Saturday, February 20, Clinton would participate in a "Kids Town Meeting" on ABC, stressing what his plan "means to posterity." The following Monday, Clinton and Reich would announce the administration's plans to extend unemployment benefits. Amid all this choreography, one person had been overlooked. A footnote on the last page of the memo read: "Left unaddressed is the issue of Perot."

IRA MAGAZINER had landed the position of White House senior adviser for policy development, and given his health care experience had joined the First Lady on the health care task force. They met early with Carville to hear his views on the politics of health care reform. In contrast to these two students of policy, Carville came as the plain-speaking, outside voice, a role he relished. He didn't want to become a member of the administration, even a temporary or unpaid one like Begala. Besides, he was getting fat speaking fees on the lecture circuit as the Democrats' Svengali and the man who made Clinton. The master of focusing Clinton's message during the campaign, Carville now had his ideas for how the administration should structure its agenda. Carville felt that Clinton should first pass the economic plan, and then present and pass the health care plan. That way, he could direct his energies at one issue at a time and deliver a one-two punch.

During the transition, a 16-member team had sent an 84-page health care reform memo to Clinton, warning that reform would be expensive and its actual cost would hinge on "the extent to which you employ short-term price controls." It listed four options for proceeding. Each one included an analysis of "1996 election politics," and each forecast a dreary road ahead, with one interest group or another outraged.

Carville saw a way out. "Get this economic plan passed," he explained to Hillary at the meeting, "and get credit for that. And then next year do the health care plan, and you'll get credit for that." The first victory would spill over and help build momentum for the second.

"You don't understand," Hillary replied. "If we don't get this done this year, we are three years away from the benefits. And the only savings will be in the fourth year. So we've got to get it done right away, or we're going to be beaten in 1996."

This was serious, Carville realized. Both he and Begala had one doctrinaire belief about 1996: Clinton could be defeated if people believed he hadn't brought about change. If there were only the same old, stale feeling in the air, Clinton would be doomed.

After the meeting, Carville told Magaziner, "I now see this as real. When I do a campaign and fuck up, someone just loses. But if you fuck up, you fuck up the country." Magaziner just rolled his eyes.

ON FRIDAY, February 5, Bob Rubin sent a short memo to the president saying that the economic team was going to meet over the weekend to discuss Hillary and Ira Magaziner's desire to incorporate health care reform into the economic plan. If Clinton passed an economic and a health care plan in the opening months, he would enter the history books. And failing to pass a health care plan early could be politically dangerous.

Rubin also forwarded a 15-page memo from Bowman Cutter, his other deputy along with Sperling. Cutter's memo laid out the options on the deficit reduction target for 1997, and recommended the second option: cutting the 1997 budget deficit by $140 billion. Rubin noted that he and McLarty both agreed with its recommendations.

"Greenspan believes that a major deficit reduction [above $130 billion] will lead to interest changes *more than offsetting* the demand effect," the memo said, referring to the contractionary impact of deficit reduction. "He therefore believes that the probabilities of the program hurting the economy are low. He also believes that the reality and credibility of the program are more important than the numbers."

On a copy of the memo that Lloyd Bentsen had seen, he had scrawled with his lead pencil next to the reference to Greenspan: "He urges 140 or above." The notation disclosed the most confidential exchange of communications between Bentsen and Greenspan. Though both publicly said they didn't talk specifics, in the course of their conversations, Greenspan had offered his view that the goal of cutting $140 billion or more by 1997 would be credible to the financial markets and likely result in lower long-term rates. Bentsen had to be careful with this information. The administration and the Fed could coordinate, but traditionally each was supposed to do its own job and not the other's. The administration and Congress set the deficit targets, just as the Fed set the short-term interest rates. But no one knew the financial markets better than Greenspan, and his specific analysis was invaluable as Bentsen worked to ensure that the new administration established credibility on Wall Street.

Cutter's memo continued: "The various markets—in my view—now expect a major deficit reduction program including some form of energy tax. The financial markets will regard a deficit reduction much below the top end of our range as a disappointment." Here Bentsen had written in the margin of his copy, "Strongly agree." McLarty, Rubin, and Bentsen were all recommending a target of at least $140 billion.

Clinton didn't need to be hammered over the head. The $140 billion target had been emerging as a consensus view since the first economic team meeting a month earlier. It seemed to be just enough but not too much. Of all the options, it offered the best chance to have solid economic growth for 1996.

HILLARY CLINTON and Ira Magaziner continued their push on health care and invited the economic team to a meeting in the Old Executive Office Building over the weekend of February 6–7. Both said that they saw tremendous advantages in including some of the health care plan in the economic plan. Under Senate rules the economic plan only required a majority of 51 votes to pass, but a health bill outside the overall plan would require 60 votes in the Senate if the administration had to break a filibuster.

The members of the economic team all argued against this firmly but gently. The chief reason was they did not and could not have a health plan ready in time. They suggested it wasn't realistic.

"George Mitchell and Dick Gephardt don't think it's crazy," Hillary said. She had spoken with both. Mitchell had urged that health care be included from the outset, knowing how long it took to get things done in Congress.

Magaziner said they had to consider some form of price controls on health care costs. He did not like explicit government controls and knew all the arguments against them. He preferred to let competition in the marketplace set costs; but they needed health savings, and for the government to clamp on controls by fiat would be more certain to pull in savings in the near future. The administration could not continue to allow health costs to skyrocket while they wrote their detailed plan.

There was silence around the table. No one favored the controls, but no one seemed to want to speak up. Who was going to fall on the sword first?

Alice Rivlin stepped forward and ripped the notion hard. Nixon had tried price controls and they had failed, she said. An intricate health care system would require equally intricate price controls, a complicated task that would take weeks or months to figure out.

Her remark started an avalanche. Laura Tyson wondered how price controls might be put in place. How would the government gather the data? How would doctors and hospitals and others report? It probably would take a year to 18 months to implement even short-term price controls, she said. And that would presumably be the point at which full reform would begin and price controls would supposedly not be needed.

Alan Blinder said that one of the first messages from the new Democratic administration should not be to put one seventh of the American economy under the command and control of the federal government. That would only reenforce the notion that Democrats didn't like free markets.

Hillary was noncommittal at the end of the meeting.

Stan Greenberg did not attend the meeting but he had his own doubts from the political end. Putting health care in the economic plan would jeopardize both, he felt. The idea, he confided to others, was completely insane and impossible. He decided not to share his views with Hillary.

16

In PUTTING TOGETHER the economic plan he would present to Congress, Clinton wanted to be in on all the details. He instructed that the key domestic cabinet members and senior White House staff meet with him days, nights, and weekends if necessary until they had discussed, and he had approved, each part of the plan. The meetings were held in the Roosevelt Room, a large White House conference room decorated with pictures and artwork of both Theodore and Franklin D. Roosevelt. The room, just a few steps from the Oval Office, became the president's base of operations.

On Sunday, February 7, Hillary and Magaziner took their argument for a medical price freeze to the Roosevelt Room. There was lots of resistance from the economic team.

"That's Nixon," said Health and Human Services Secretary Donna Shalala, comparing Magaziner's idea to the Republican president's largely unsuccessful price freeze in the early 1970s.

Hillary argued that an immediate freeze would save an estimated $28 billion.

President Clinton backed his wife. He wanted to do something and was angry at the resistance. "They'll say this is an admission of defeat," he said. "It's screwing up before we start. We're going to keep screwing everyone."

Alice Rivlin took the president on. "That's not right," she said.

"We're being asked to put health care out in May, not now." Clinton had announced a 100-day deadline to give them time, she said, "in order to avoid a half-baked plan now."

Stephanopoulos suggested something in between. In Clinton's speech to Congress presenting the plan, now scheduled for February 17, the president could say that a health care plan would be forthcoming and it would include still more deficit reduction.

Clinton wasn't buying. "If I don't get health care done," he said, "I'll wish I didn't run for president." He added that he would have to do another huge budget agreement after this one.

Joining health care and the economic plan had the virtue of requiring only 51 votes in the Senate, Hillary reminded them.

Panetta had already pointed out the plain practical problem that health care reform was intricate and complicated, and could not be solved in the next ten days.

"You can wait on health care," Gore said, lining up with those in favor of delay. Congress would take a year or more on health care, and the administration ought to respect that inevitable rhythm. It did not have to be in the February 17 speech, he said.

Hillary backed off a little. "We could signal several themes on the 17th, which would be included in a later health care plan," she said.

Clinton suggested that on the 17th he could say they were putting forward a health care plan that would avoid a rising deficit during the second four years. It was clearly difficult for him to decide. His wife and Magaziner were pushing one way, while everyone else, especially his budget experts, pushed the other. He finally offered his solution: They would have to wait, but it wouldn't be that long.

Magaziner was incensed. Delaying would be costly. Price controls would save everyone $101 billion over four years, Magaziner said, referring to a thick sheaf of charts and tables. Hillary too was visibly angry.

Clinton was still sorting out the implications of heavy deficit reduction and he moved on to the subject of jobs. "Don't ever say our program could cost jobs in the short run," he said. For one thing, he didn't think it would. Besides, many Democrats would have to run in 1994, and such comments would be free ammunition for the Republicans.

He was also growing uneasy about skimping on some of his investments, and he wanted to underscore his commitment. "If I do too little investment," he said, "then some other candidate won the election, not me."

The meeting turned to a long discussion on freezing Social Security cost-of-living adjustments. Though Clinton said it was the right choice, still supported by Panetta and others, the adamant opposition of the

Senate leadership was now loud and clear. Clinton finally said to drop it. He added, however, that he still planned to propose an increase in the percentage of Social Security benefits subject to taxes, even though it would mean a big jump for middle-income retirees. "All the voters live in Florida," he noted only half-jokingly. The implications for the 1996 reelection were clear. Clinton had lost the state in 1992, but it would surely be lost again. "Bye-bye Florida," he said.

DESPITE THE SINGULAR INTIMACY of the presidential campaign, Carville and Begala still had one fundamental question about Clinton, particularly in their moments of frustration. Once Carville took a piece of paper, drew a little square, and tapped it with his pen. "Where is the hallowed ground?" he asked. "Where does he stand? What does he stand for?"

For Begala, too, that was the most perplexing question about the man. Begala had seen two sides to Clinton over their year together: a Southern, populist, religious side that connected with the average hardworking middle class; and a Northern, elitist, Yale Law School side that craved approval from liberal intellectuals and the journalists at *The New York Times* and *The Washington Post*. The populist side was real, Begala felt, but Clinton was too willing to stray from it, and Begala never knew how far. Now, on the deficit issue, the elitist Clinton seemed to be overpowering the populist Clinton. The deficit had never been central to Clinton's case in the campaign. In spite of all Begala had done to downplay the deficit reduction emphasis, he could see that some of Clinton's new advisers didn't get the message. There was much public talk about pain and sacrifice, little about contribution, much about deficits and taxes, little about growth, jobs, or fairness. Begala felt as if he were from a different country than some of the senior Clinton officials, or certainly as if he worked for a different boss.

The worst of them, Begala felt, was Leon Panetta, the former congressman from Carmel Valley. Begala felt that of all 435 congressional districts, Panetta's was least representative of America—the pure, elitist, unreal world of California dreaming. Panetta seemed to love talking about nothing more than deficit reduction and all the truth-in-budgeting discipline he was imposing, rejecting the rosy scenarios of the Reagan era. Rosy scenarios didn't mean anything to real people, Begala felt, and in private, he began applying a new label to the budget director: "The Poster Boy for Economic Constipation."

After about a week of working in the White House, Begala decided to confront Clinton. Clinton liked frankness, and Begala was a natural with direct communication. Begala went to Clinton and said the deficit obsession could have awful political consequences. He added that it seemed that as president, Clinton had changed allegiances from putting people first to putting the deficit first.

"That's not the way it is," Clinton protested. "The deficit is $50 billion worse each year." There was no way around those numbers. It was possible to conceal them, using accounting tricks and phony numbers, but he had taken a strong position against gimmicks. They were going to use the numbers from the nonpartisan Congressional Budget Office. Alice Rivlin, who used to head that office, supported the decision, as did its current officials, as did the rest of the economic team.

"Mr. President," Begala said, "why are you listening to these people? They did not support you. It's not what you're about."

"We need them," Clinton said, his temper rising. "We can't do anything for people unless we reduce the deficit." The Republicans certainly created the legacy, but they didn't make up the numbers. They were real and Clinton had to deal with the problem he had inherited.

"Mr. President, we're just driving at a number. That number, it's like there's some magic in it." How did that happen? Begala asked.

"They love their country," Clinton said of his economic team. "They're working hard at this. What do you want me to do? We can't lie about the deficit. Can't do that."

"I agree," Begala said.

"Then stop," Clinton ordered.

"I think we're too obsessed with the deficit. This is all about how elite economists see this."

But the conversation was over.

OFTEN STEPHANOPOULOS, Begala, and Sperling felt that the Roosevelt Room meetings were stacked against them. They were just three pipsqueaks fighting the assembled Washington and Wall Street economic establishment as the largest and smallest budget items were tested for economic and political feasibility.

They believed, however, that the campaign themes which ran in Clinton's blood were where his heart and head worked together. One of Clinton's favorite campaign themes had been to promise that anyone who worked full time and had a child would not have to raise that child in poverty. The message, which came under the campaign heading of "Rewarding Work" in the *Putting People First* campaign plan, had a broad appeal. The working poor, the conservative middle class, and many others seemed convinced that many poor people had an incentive to go on welfare instead of working. Clinton said he would expand a tax break called the "Earned Income Tax Credit" to provide enough additional tax refund for low-income working families with children to provide an incentive for them to continue working. The full plan would cost some $27 billion.

At several points Bentsen said it was unrealistic to expect they would be able to implement this program immediately. It would have to be phased in.

Sperling had been challenging the Treasury Secretary regularly, invoking various campaign promises. The millionaire, dapper Bentsen just did not seem in a position to comprehend the implications of this important Clinton promise, Sperling felt, and at one point said as much.

"What did you say?" snapped Bentsen, turning abruptly in his seat. He was not accustomed to being challenged, especially by someone less than half his age with precisely four weeks of government experience.

"The president said in the campaign we want to push everyone above the poverty line who works," Sperling replied.

The Roosevelt Room was very quiet.

Roger Altman intervened. Why don't we let Gene and Lloyd go out and settle this in the hall? Altman joked. Everyone laughed.

"If that happened," Clinton said, "after about three months, we'll be sitting around saying, 'What ever happened to old Sperling?' "

Though Clinton seemed to be backing Bentsen as the best man with his fists, he reminded the group that the tax credit had been one of his best applause lines during the campaign. "I've never seen a program for working poor people be so enthusiastically supported by the middle class and in the suburbs," Clinton said. It had appealed to both his traditional and New Democrat constituencies.

Later Clinton spoke with Sperling. He wanted the campaign promises pushed. "You stick at it!" Clinton said dramatically, waving his hand at Sperling. "You stick at it!" Clinton eventually approved the full $27 billion for the tax credit.

As the marathon sessions in the Roosevelt Room continued day and night, Clinton found no detail too small for his attention. At one point they were reviewing rural and agricultural programs, cutting away at what most of them considered indefensible special-interest subsidies.

"Mr. President," Rivlin said enthusiastically, "I've got a slogan for your reelection." Taking off on his campaign promise to "end welfare as we know it," she proposed: " 'I'm going to end welfare as we know it for farmers.' "

Clinton stiffened, looked at her, and snapped, "Spoken like a true city dweller." The former governor of Arkansas leaned across the table dramatically in her direction and added, "Farmers are good people. I know we have to do these things. We're going to make these cuts. But we don't have to feel good about it."

A chill fell over the room. Begala, who sat on the sidelines behind Gore so he could see Clinton, almost cheered.

ON THURSDAY, February 11, at 5 P.M. the group was back in the Cabinet Room to discuss taxes, especially the proposed BTU energy tax. Despite Bentsen's public pronouncement and subsequent indications it was in the works, Clinton still had qualms. Not only would he be unable to cut middle-class taxes as he had promised, but he would be raising taxes on the middle class. "These are the people who got screwed in the 80s," he said. "And it's a heck of a thing for me to propose this."

Bentsen, the resident tax expert, noted that in theory a broad-based tax on all consumption—not just energy but all consumer spending—would increase savings and help the economy significantly. Such a tax would be an administrative and political nightmare, and he opposed it. But if the president was determined to go ahead, the BTU levy—taxing just energy consumption—had an advantage.

The case could not be made on economic grounds alone, Bentsen explained. The politics of the tax had to be addressed. He said he realized the kind of negative campaign commercials the Republicans would run against Clinton in 1996. He could understand why Clinton was worried to death. But it might not be as politically dangerous as they feared. His experience had been that energy taxes drew much more criticism when they were proposed than after they passed. Everyone soon forgot. Voters wouldn't hold it against Clinton. In Bentsen's almost 30 years in the House and Senate, he had voted for many energy taxes and had never received many complaints or angry letters. The public's bark, he said, was worse than its bite.

Gore, too, kept pushing for it, arguing for the biggest possible tax. "The public is more willing than we realize," he said at one point. He stressed again that the tax would encourage energy independence and conservation. It would be environmentally sound.

Clinton at last gave the final okay to the BTU tax. They would propose taxing oil, coal, and natural gas. Turning to a new subject, the president mentioned that he had been in Michigan the day before. "Last night, at a town meeting, a woman asked about child care," Clinton told his aides, "and I realized we don't have anything there." At the public town meeting in Detroit, Clinton had told a different story, saying, "Well, I think there are two or three things we can do that we're working on now." Clinton pushed a discussion of a child-care credit.

As the group went through the budget line by line, Clinton had more questions. "Why are you taking out the incentives for small business," he asked, objecting strenuously, "and putting back in the stuff for big business?" They all had very weak answers. Clinton scrutinized all the business incentives and insisted they go to the small firms.

It was Bentsen's 72nd birthday and everyone sang to him. The most noticeable thing about the Treasury Secretary was that he looked dead tired.

FROM OUTSIDE THE WHITE HOUSE, Carville was furious. He knew the policy people and the president had to make the decisions on the economic plan. But he told others that if an energy tax were actually proposed, he would break ranks and personally lead the war against it. "The Republican Party is in shambles," Carville noted. A new tax could provide a rallying point. "This could be the issue that galvanizes them." The new taxes in 1990 had effectively caused the right wing of the Republican Party to rise up against Bush. Even Bush had finally admitted the new taxes were a political mistake. It was the one thing Republicans might agree on.

IN THE ROOSEVELT ROOM on Friday, February 12, the goal of cutting $140 billion from the deficit for 1997 was being questioned all over again. Someone defended the $140 billion as important for the bond market.

The newest addition to the group was Howard Paster, 48, who had been chosen as Clinton's chief lobbyist with Congress, a post Paster had wanted all his career. A short, personable man, with a Brooklyn accent and an appealing scrappiness, Paster had worked as a senior aide in both the House and Senate. He had then become a lobbyist on both sides of the ideological street in Washington, first for big labor and then as the resident Democrat in a major Republican firm, representing banks, oil companies, and even the National Rifle Association. Still, he remained a liberal Democrat and preserved his ties to the party leadership in Congress.

Paster viewed the economic plan through the lens of Congress. At one point in the budget planning, all the highway demonstration grants, money for building roads that typified the kind of beneficial pork programs that all congressmen loved, had been zeroed out. One of the canceled grants was in Portland, Maine, the home of Majority Leader George Mitchell. The political shortsightedness reminded Paster of President Carter's mad attempt to cut the equally beloved water projects, a move that had engendered permanent hostility from Congress. Paster decided to be blunt.

"How many votes does the fucking bond market have?" Paster asked. "We've got to win votes on the Hill, not Wall Street. If it looks like Jimmy Carter's water projects all over again, we're dead." It was crucial that the plan not be dead on arrival at the Congress, he explained. Such a plan wouldn't reduce their bargaining position, it would eliminate it.

Panetta and Rivlin wanted to stick with the $140 billion goal. They emphasized that it would be only an opening bid with Congress, which had never been inclined to budget austerity. If the administration sent up a $140 billion cut in the 1997 deficit, Congress would not swallow it all, as sure as they were sitting there.

Even though Clinton had indicated support, Laura Tyson was pretty sure he wouldn't go for the $140 billion. She figured that he would be convinced it was too risky. Several weeks earlier she had written a memo to Clinton outlining her views on deficit reduction. Since the benefits were long term, she said, it made sense only to stabilize the size of the debt relative to the country's overall economic output or GDP. That meant a cut of $120 billion or $125 billion would be sufficient. But now, at the Roosevelt Room meeting, it was clear that no one was buying that. Tyson proposed aiming for a $135 billion cut.

Panetta and Rivlin were steadfast, almost barking out their nos. They warned that if they proposed a $135 billion cut, they would end up with $125 billion from Congress, and that was clearly not enough. They needed the maximum as a bargaining position, Rivlin asserted.

"Okay," Tyson said, "I am going to say this because it's my role in this room." Tyson viewed herself as a neutral arbiter in these situations. She didn't oversee any federal programs and had no budget turf of her own. Her job was simply to give pure economic advice. She rocketed into a speech some later referred to as the "$140-billion-has-no-clothes speech."

"Mr. President," she said, "I can't prove to you that there is anything magical about the $140 billion. There is a point where the bond market will take your program seriously. I don't know where that point is. Maybe it's at $135 billion or $140 billion or wherever. I can't tell you." A life-or-death effort for $140 billion made no sense, she said forcefully.

Clinton looked taken aback.

The hawks pounced. Bentsen, Panetta, and Rivlin said the plan was going to be debated heavily in Congress; it would be a political debate of some intensity. Congress did not like pain, and the president's position would certainly be trimmed back, they reiterated. Bentsen had not disclosed the sensitive fact that the $140 billion was Greenspan's recommendation.

Tyson noted that these were political judgments, no doubt correct, but they were not economic arguments. The economic realities argued against a blind adherence to the $140 billion figure. Begala, Blinder, Reich, and Sperling all agreed with her. Stephanopoulos in particular argued for stopping a little short of $140 billion.

Clinton ignored them all. He pressed forward, looking for ways to meet the goal. They could get $2 billion here, he offered off the top of his head, or perhaps $4 billion there.

The meeting dragged on into the evening, dissolving into virtual chaos. Everyone was tired, and there was no clear direction, much less a consensus. Begala—seeing the situation was crazy and the meeting no longer productive for Clinton—went over to McLarty, who had said little during the sessions. The chief of staff was not an expert on economics or budgets, or on Washington or politics.

"Mack," Begala said, "you've got to get him out of here." Stephanopoulos pressed McLarty as well. But the discussion continued, until, finally, Clinton had to leave for another event.

On Saturday morning, they gathered again. Their work was unfinished, Clinton told reporters before the meeting, "otherwise I wouldn't be asking them to meet on Saturday." They sat down to business and picked up where they had left off. Numbers were flying around—$134 billion, $137 billion, $142 billion—and there was still no resolution. Clinton had to leave for his Saturday radio address. "I will present my plan to generate jobs and increase the incomes of the American people," he said in the speech. In the Roosevelt Room, Rubin, Altman, Sperling, Panetta, Rivlin, and others all crowded around Bentsen, who sat at the table, dressed in a light brown sweater-vest, trying to work out a final number.

After some discussion, Rubin said he thought that if they took another 15 or 30 minutes with the president, they could work it out. Later, several of the key people gathered in the Oval Office, and the scene was captured in a private White House photo. Clinton, wearing a tie and blue blazer, sat perched on the front of his desktop facing the seating area. He gazed skeptically at Bentsen, who stood before him holding a legal pad with numbers. Stephanopoulos sat in a chair listening and looking at his fingers. Panetta, in a dress shirt and a tie, stood to Bentsen's left with his arms folded. McLarty, in a light blue sweater and with his hands in the pockets of casual weekend trousers, stood to Bentsen's right, looking at the floor. Rubin, in casual attire, sat awkwardly on the arm of one of the couches. Gore, in a dark suit, was pacing.

Bentsen suggested dropping the administration's proposal for welfare reform, which was estimated to cost some $3 billion. During the campaign, welfare reform had been a critical promise. But as with health care reform, Bentsen said, there was no way to know the exact cost. How much would a plan that wasn't even written cost? he asked. And they had to get to $140 billion.

Clinton was skeptical. Stephanopoulos thought the relentless drive to the $140 billion goal was bullshit. But Bentsen, joined by Panetta, pushed hard. Gore wanted to be bold as usual. McLarty said little. Rubin joined Bentsen and Panetta favoring the $140 billion.

They would drop welfare reform, Clinton finally decided, to reach the $140 billion. It was the last big decision.

They continued all day, working out some fine points. As 6 P.M. approached, Clinton declared, "I love this stuff."

Clinton had the group come to the White House again on Sunday. Wearing jeans and a jeans jacket, he reviewed the final package with a sense of triumph and harmony: $140 billion in deficit reduction in the year 1997. There was much discussion about how to get the crucial support of Ross Perot and perhaps also that of the original Democratic deficit hawk, Paul Tsongas.

Clinton implied that something more was needed as well. "The highlight of my campaign was the Richmond debate when I talked to the woman," Clinton said, referring to the questioner from the audience who had asked Clinton, Bush, and Perot how the deficit had affected each of them personally. Bush had acted as though the questioner was from Mars and totally muffed it. Clinton had walked toward the woman and replied smoothly that he knew people in Arkansas who were unemployed or whose businesses were suffering, conveying empathy and understanding. "Americans respond to specificity and a human touch," Clinton said.

BOB REICH was very unhappy with what had happened. The Sunday newspapers almost exclusively described Clinton's forthcoming plan as a deficit reduction package. "Clinton's Deficit Plan to Be Unveiled This Week," proclaimed one headline. "Mr. Clinton believes that the Government's biggest contribution would be to stop draining the nation's investment funds," read another article.

The next day, Reich wrote a two-page memo to the president, using his annoyance with the newspapers as an opening. The subject heading: "Educating the public about the deficit, this week." He began by quoting from a sampling of the Sunday papers. "They make you sound like Calvin Coolidge," Reich said bluntly. "Your plan isn't a deficit plan; it's an investment and growth plan, whose purpose is to create better jobs."

First, he reminded Clinton of the economic logic behind deficit reduction: "The American economy won't grow unless the private sector uses the resources freed by deficit cuts to invest in the future productivity of all Americans."

"American business must NOT use the added resources to (a) speculate as they did in the 1980s, (b) pad their executives' salaries, (c) improve productivity by buying new machines merely to replace their workers, (d) hire platoons of lawyers to sue one another, (e) hire consultants to bust unions, or (f) build new factories abroad." Clinton should stress the positive ways for business to use the resources: worker training, apprenticeship programs, research and development, and so on. "Deficit cuts won't improve the lives of average Americans unless American business chooses [that] path," he wrote.

Next, Reich wrote of the need for government, business, and labor all to "invest in the nation's future rather than feather their own nests." Government would pledge to cut fancy perks and invest in education, training, transportation—the usual litany of investments. But others would have to pitch in also: labor would have to make compromises; business executives would have to "stop rewarding themselves huge salaries" and concentrate instead on the well-being of their workers to make them more productive; and Wall Street must begin "investing in the real courses of future growth, the skills of the American workforce, and the machines and equipment necessary to fully utilize those skills."

Finally, Reich wrote, "The goal is to shift our sights from the present to the future, and to do so fairly." Raising taxes on the rich was not enough. Antitrust laws should be enforced to keep companies, such as pharmaceutical industries, from profiting at others' expense. The deductibility of executive pay should be capped, to "close the widening gap separating them from their workforce." And "The rich and well-educated must not secede into suburban ghettos (gated communities, residential compounds, exurban villages) and turn their backs on the rest of their countrymen."

Reich gave the memo to Clinton's staff secretary, John Podesta, who passed it on to the president.

17

KNOWING HIS ECONOMIC PLAN would contain some controversial elements—the energy tax and the omission of the middle-class tax cut —Clinton decided to address the nation from the Oval Office that Monday night, February 15, two days before his longer, formal speech to the Joint Session of Congress. A ten-minute televised speech would allow the White House to get a jump on putting out the message it wanted, to lay out themes, anticipate criticisms, and deflect accusations about the taxes. At 9 P.M., Clinton appeared in his first address from the Oval Office. Looking youthful and a bit unaccustomed to the office, he seemed out of place in contrast to the older faces of Reagan and Bush.

Clinton broke the news, which had already been leaked to the media, that he wouldn't offer a middle-class tax cut in his plan. Following Begala's storyline, he said he was first going to cut White House staff and federal government costs. Then he would turn to "the wealthiest Americans" for more taxes.

Finally, he said, he had hoped to spare the middle class. "I've worked harder than I've ever worked in my life to meet that goal," he said. "But I can't." He lashed out zealously at the 1980s and "the big tax cuts for the wealthy." He said that 70 percent of his new tax proposals would be paid by those who earned more than $100,000 a year. "And for the first time in more than a decade we're all in this together."

The stock market dropped almost 83 points the next day.

. . .

McLARTY TOLD the president that the speech had an edge to it that was divisive. "It's not the Bill Clinton I knew in Arkansas," he said. In Arkansas, businessmen had been welcomed. That was what being a New Democrat was about. The speech, in contrast, had been judgmental and critical of businessmen such as some of their friends from back home. McLarty mentioned one. "I don't think that's what you believe," the chief of staff said. Of course, it was Clinton's choice, McLarty said, but he ought to know how it had sounded. Clinton indicated that he agreed.

Bentsen mentioned to the Clintons that he had previewed the plan for Alan Greenspan, who seemed to like it. Howard Paster, who was in charge of the administration's allotment of tickets to the Joint Session speech, suggested, "Why not put Greenspan up there?" He could be offered a seat near or next to Hillary—a certain television shot.

"Great, if he'll come," Clinton said.

Over at the Federal Reserve, Greenspan's office received a call from the White House. The chairman was invited to sit in Mrs. Clinton's box for the speech. Greenspan accepted. He figured he would be seated in the back, probably next to someone like Alice Rivlin. Then, the day of the speech, a friend who had seen the seating chart called him. Did the chairman know where he would be sitting? Was there another A. Greenspan?

Oh my God, Greenspan thought. When he looked at his ticket, he noted it was for seat A6. He knew "A" meant the front row. The seat would place him squarely between Hillary Clinton and Tipper Gore, the vice president's wife—the most prominent seat, and a magnet for the TV cameras. Greenspan consulted some of his senior staff and colleagues on the Federal Reserve. The Supreme Court came to these joint sessions and sat in the front, and was able to remain neutral, Greenspan noted. He also tried to argue that protocol dictated that he not refuse an invitation from the First Lady. He could only decline under extraordinary circumstances. The occasion, he claimed at one point, was in some ways ceremonial, not political. And though it was social, it was also, of course, the most political event of the season.

Greenspan was never one to shy away from a social event at the center of the action. In this case it was where he belonged. After all, going back to his December 1992 meeting with Clinton in Little Rock, he had been privately advising the White House and Bentsen of his views. The chairman of the Federal Reserve was in some ways the ghostwriter of the Clinton plan.

. . .

ON WEDNESDAY, February 17, Clinton rose about 6 A.M. Chelsea needed help with her math homework. The problem was perplexing, something about Harry having six more vests than Sally while someone else had one more than half of Sally's.

Altman called Stephanopoulos that morning. All the talk in the press about extreme sacrifice and pain for the middle class was exaggerated, Altman said, and should be corrected. Long-term interest rates were still heading down and the reduction would more than offset the $9-a-month direct impact of an energy tax on the average middle-income family. It was an important point, and Altman followed it up with a memo.

At the White House, about 2 P.M. Rubin and Bo Cutter reviewed the draft of the speech. Both were unhappy. At 4 P.M. Hillary, looking drawn and tired, had Rubin and Altman into her office. She was also displeased. The communications people and the substance people hadn't communicated, she said. Altman drafted a paragraph for her saying that since the election, interest rates had dropped on mortgages and consumer loans more than enough to offset the proposed energy tax.

She approved it, and took Rubin and Altman down to the Roosevelt Room where the speech drafting was continuing. In the room with Clinton was a collection of helpers ranging from Begala to Harry Thomason, a television producer and friend of the Clintons from Arkansas. The speech had to be delivered in five hours. "Okay," Clinton said, "it's time to get serious. Page one." Moans and what seemed like at least one angry growl were heard.

Clinton complained that the speechwriters had given him a campaign speech. He noted its emphasis on the new programs. "This is just spend and spend," he said sharply. He went through more and more of it. This is not me, he said. This is not what I'm going to do, this is not what it's all about. The speech seemed to be in a hundred messy pieces. Mandy Grunwald was given one section to work on. Other sections were farmed out. Pages seemed to be flying around.

Clinton took out his pen, slashing and adding. He worried about the BTU tax, the part of his plan that would be most objectionable to middle-class families. What was this about the energy-tax cost? Clinton asked.

There were more moans and growls, low but audible. Altman made his point about the $9-a-month direct cost.

What about the additional indirect cost? someone asked. Manufacturers and businesses that would have to pay the energy tax would pass the cost along to consumers. But no one was sure how much that would be. Call Treasury, Clinton instructed. Altman came back with a total of $17-a-month in both direct and indirect costs. The number was plugged into the speech.

Other problems arose. Someone noticed that the first 11 pages of the speech didn't contain a word on economics. A reference was quickly inserted.

With several hours to go, Hillary said that her husband needed time for a full rehearsal. "Unless he reads it out loud," she said insistently, "he won't know what's missing." Words might be left out. The speech might not track.

They all went over to the White House theater. Clinton practiced the speech, scrawling on the draft as he talked. One of the few specific spending cuts mentioned was a proposal to reduce interest subsidies to the Rural Electric Administration. Clinton decided to cut it.

After the practice session, Grunwald and Greenberg huddled with Clinton. The specific spending cuts were missing, they said. Write some in, Clinton said, changing his mind and deciding to restore the rural electrification cuts. He would add something about how painful this would be for his home state. He exited. There was no time left.

Stephanopoulos went back to the Roosevelt Room with Grunwald and Greenberg to find more spending cuts. They took some examples to the typists, but they knew they were weak. The staff, writers, and helpers gathered. There was a bad feel. The speech was good perhaps, but it was supposed to be great. Many felt that in this, Clinton's first major moment as president, they had let him down.

ABOUT 15 MINUTES before the speech was scheduled to begin, Clinton left to change his tie before leaving for Capitol Hill.

Over in the House Chamber, Gore took his place on the dais with Speaker Foley. As Clinton was introduced, entered, and walked down the aisle, Gore had an angle on the TelePrompTer window where the speech was to appear. He could see the text was being changed in the computer as the operators furiously scrolled up and down throughout, typing additions and deleting.

Clinton came to the podium just as the audience was finishing a second standing ovation. The TelePrompTer was a blur scrolling back to the beginning just as Clinton began: "Mr. President, Mr. Speaker . . ."

Stephanopoulos stationed himself in the House cloakroom with an open phone line to the White House. Grunwald was on the other end. "He's riffing," she said, trying to follow the supposedly final version of the text. "He's making it up!"

Greenberg had viewers in Dayton hooked up to his dial meters to report their instant reactions. With a copy of the speech in hand, he went down to the White House communications office where he had a phone to Dayton. Every two seconds, he got the readings from the dial meters—65, 67, 69—quite positive numbers. He tried to write the numbers down next to the portions of the text so he could review what had worked and what hadn't. Quickly he realized he couldn't follow at all and began thumbing through his copy wildly. He glanced at a television monitor showing House Minority Leader Bob Michel, who was supposed to deliver the Republican response to the speech right after Clinton finished. Greenberg took solace that Michel too was fingering through his text, as bewildered as anyone.

Altman was stunned that the speech had actually fallen into place. As a piece of rhetoric, the 58-minute presentation was fabulous: a sensational delivery, straight talk, clear—interrupted constantly, it seemed, by standing ovations. The full economic plan, Altman felt in contrast, was only good, not great. Clinton, who had not run against the deficit, was proposing a plan to attack it. He had played against type. Still, Altman felt that they might have been able to do more, that they did not take full advantage of their rare opportunity.

Begala had helped draft the speech, and there was one line he had put in for defensive purposes. Knowing that Republicans would accuse Clinton of not cutting the budget enough, he suggested that Clinton offer to entertain other cuts but insist that they be specific. "Next I recommend that we make 150 specific budget cuts, as you know, and that all those who say we should cut more be as specific as I have been," Clinton said. Begala hoped that those who called for cuts but were afraid of the political consequences would be seen as posturing, while Clinton would be seen as serious.

UP IN SEAT A6, the chairman of the Federal Reserve was on full display. The cameras drifted over to show Hillary with the chairman of the central bank dutifully at her side, applauding stiffly. His presence in the balcony could only seem like an endorsement. Greenspan believed he had never told the White House or Bentsen that he would approve of their plan. He had only approved of its general thrust of deficit reduction, not the specific cuts or taxes. But specifics mattered less than symbols, and this was a symbolic moment.

Greenspan, still a little astounded that the White House would put him on display this way, did not feel he had been politically naive in accepting. He might be indirectly supporting Clinton and his plan, but it was a two-way street. The White House was also conferring enormous power upon him, elevating him and the Fed to a position of even greater prominence and power. If he were to criticize Clinton's speech or plan, he could do great damage. He could almost destroy them, he believed. Clinton had taken an enormous risk.

Greenspan thought that his original political mentor, Richard Nixon, never would have taken such a chance. Nixon would have calculated that he was putting power in someone else's hands. After his resignation, Nixon had said that he had greatly assisted his political enemies. "I gave them a sword, and they stuck it in. And they twisted it with relish." Greenspan realized he had been handed a sword.

Hillary had met with Greenspan recently on health care and had found him appreciative of the tough decisions her husband was willing to make on the deficit. Greenspan didn't seem to be seeking partisan Republican advantage, and seemed to avoid thinking about the 1996 Republican primary in New Hampshire, for example, something that was occasionally on her mind. Hillary did not know that it was Greenspan who had recommended the deficit reduction target of $140 billion that had been adopted.

She was pleased with the speech and the overall plan. They reflected a coherent strategy, she believed. First, they delivered the goods to her husband's political base. Second, they explained to those in the middle who hadn't voted for him where he hoped to take the country. Third, they were aimed at Wall Street and the bond market. At least they showed that her husband was not a Communist.

Rubin had been meeting with her privately, explaining how the financial markets strategy would work. She believed that Rubin was a true Democrat, who cared about the cities and the poor. He hadn't given them a 100 percent guarantee that the financial markets strategy would work, but he had said it was their best hope. Although she couldn't accept that the bond market was that crucial, she had come to appreciate that other people took it seriously and that it was an important element to consider. Still, at times she found it hard to take the bond market seriously as it responded to absurd rumors, moving up and down for silly reasons, even something that could be a joke.

REICH LISTENED carefully to the speech from the House floor. He saw for himself the great tidal wave of deficit reduction that had been pounding at Clinton. All the freshman congressmen, mostly New Democrats, conditioned by the Ross Perot summer, were talking only about the deficit. Any time somebody leaned over to tell Clinton to be bold, they really meant to be bold about deficit cutting. Investments, Reich's issue, the centerpiece of the campaign, had faded. Although Clinton talked about investments, they seemed distant and abstract. There was no neat summary or number to wrap them in. The speech had been deficit reduction, health care, and stimulus. Maybe the public and the government, Reich rationalized, couldn't keep a fourth issue—investments—in their heads at the same time.

Clinton had a private rationale for not playing up the investments that much. "No matter what I proposed in the way of investment programs," he later claimed to others, "I was going to be operating around the margins of a very large economy. And that, in the end, having control, some control over the discipline and the direction of the economy, was going to be a precondition to making my investment programs work." He felt he had preserved a good deal of his investment programs in the plan he sent forward.

He had also reached some core conclusions about economics, Washington, and Wall Street. There was no question in his mind that interest rates had been too high for too long, that the middle class could not improve its lot until interest rates came down so people could refinance their homes, businesspeople could expand and feel free to hire again. Clinton believed he could get more overall economic growth from a drop in interest rates than suggested in conservative economic estimates by what he considered conservative economists.

"All the folks that I ran to help would be more hurt by a slow economy than they would be helped by a marginal extra investment program," he said later. He was not trying just to help the bond market, he claimed. The bond market was just the vehicle for helping the middle class.

THE IMMEDIATE PUBLIC REACTION to the speech seemed favorable. One poll, conducted by CNN and *USA Today*, showed that 79 percent of those surveyed supported the plan and only 16 percent opposed it. Most of the criticism came from congressional Republicans, who even before the speech were calling it a tax-and-spend program. Even Ross Perot, whom Clinton had called earlier in the day, managed some qualified praise for addressing the deficit.

Clinton hit the road in campaign-style appearances to sell the plan to the people. The day after the speech, Thursday, February 18, he flew to St. Louis. Addressing a crowd of 15,000, he repeated his preemptive strike at his critics. He heralded the "150 tough cuts" he had proposed. "Now, let me say I've already heard some people on the other side of the aisle say, 'Well, he should have cut more.' And my answer is: show me where, and be specific. No hot air."

Clinton's strategy was subtle. It was not only a challenge to the critics to be specific, but a ploy to direct their fire away from a balanced-budget amendment or an entitlement cap. Both of those proposals sounded good and simple on the surface and would be popular, but both would mean drastic cuts. For example, limiting the growth of entitlements to the inflation rate plus the population growth rate sounded reasonable. But Medicare had been growing at 13 percent a year, and such a formula could mean throwing some of the elderly out of hospitals. If the debate on the budget had shifted away from Clinton's plan to a balanced-budget amendment or the entitlement cap, he could have been in real trouble. But the debate stayed on his plan for the moment. In the White House, Sperling was coming to realize that no one ever received credit for averting a crisis that never happened. No one was passing out compliments for keeping the balance-budget or entitlement-cap genies in the bottle.

Grunwald was not happy with the focus on Congress. The legislative strategy was becoming the communications strategy. Clinton was at his best talking to the larger populace, which then would pressure the Congress. "It's a bank shot," she explained to others. "What you say to the American people bounces back to the Congress."

BOB RUBIN and Alice Rivlin were assigned to visit the floor of the New York Stock Exchange. After Clinton's Oval Office speech, investors had grown panicky over Clinton's soak-the-rich rhetoric, afraid that he would hit corporations hard in his economic plan. Some were quoted as saying that taxing people who earned $100,000 or more was setting the standard for the wealthy too low. The Dow Jones Industrial Average had plummeted. Rubin and Rivlin had to reassure Wall Street that there was more for them to like than dislike in Clinton's plan, that it would reduce the deficit and help the economy in the long run. They met with stock traders and corporate executives, urging them to look at the positive response of long-term bond yields, which continued to fall.

In the evening, Rubin and Rivlin attended a private, off-the-record dinner in New York City hosted by Laurence Tisch, the head of CBS.

Tisch had assembled a group of CEOs of some of the nation's largest corporations, including American Express and RJR Nabisco. The support of business leaders was essential to confidence, the delicate foundation underlying all business decisions.

The executives were in a rage, at times a quiet slow burn and at other times openly hostile. Rubin and Rivlin faltered. Rubin looked exhausted; Rivlin parroted back ideas and lines from Clinton's speech with seemingly little thought. One executive wondered aloud what the differences were between Clinton's plan and something that George McGovern might have proposed. Rubin brushed off the question.

The executives took issue especially with Clinton's attack on the wealthy, some claiming they were personally offended. Many had started with little and had worked hard to reach the top. They said they did not worry about how the tax increase would affect them personally, but they said they were concerned that taxes would sink the economy. The taxes, along with the class-warfare implications in Clinton's rhetoric, would erode business confidence. When do you think I'll make a decision to expand, make big equipment purchases, and hire new people? one executive asked sarcastically.

The next morning, Rubin went to the Oval Office to report to Clinton on the dinner. They beat the hell out of us, Rubin said. "Mr. President, you're being seen as anti-business. You're seen as punishing the rich." The executives felt that the speech and plan insinuated that it was immoral to be rich. To have worked hard and been well paid did not make them guilty of 1980s-style greed. Particular criticism, Rubin said, had been leveled at the president's line, "We're all in this together," when it seemed to them that the wealthy were being singled out.

Begala, who was present, was not surprised at the reaction of the New York elites. The "We're all in this together" line was not inconsistent with Clinton's message, Begala said. It meant that for 12 years the rich had been held up as heroes, but no longer would they get such special treatment. Now everyone was going to be treated the same and pay what they could afford.

Begala's remark triggered a strong negative reaction from Mack McLarty. He agreed that Clinton was being seen as anti-business. Mr. President, he said, you don't want that perception.

Rubin said he didn't have a personal problem with demonizing the affluent. But to do so would have a serious practical consequence. The economy would thrive only if there was confidence among the business community. If businesspeople felt the administration didn't believe in the capitalist system, business wouldn't expand and hire, thus hurting the economy. Anything that made the economy worse had to be bad for the president politically. Candidate Clinton could say what he wanted about the rich and business; but President Clinton was constrained.

Clinton appreciated Rubin's argument, and in his public statements he began scaling back, and even cutting out altogether, his rhetoric about taxing the rich.

ON FRIDAY, February 19, Alan Greenspan was to appear before the Senate Banking Committee. By this time, he had waded through the details of Clinton's plan. Greenspan meant it when he said the details really didn't matter. It was the overall that mattered, and since it was Greenspan's recommendation, it couldn't be better. Greenspan felt Clinton had been courageous, and deserved commendation. It would have been an act of injustice not to say so, and although Washington was a town often short on fairness, Greenspan believed, there had to be a little. Before addressing the Senate, he had discussed the plan and his assessment of it with members of the Federal Open Market Committee, the group that sets short-term interest rates. He wanted to make sure that no one could stick so much as a razor blade between his views and those of the other members of his committee.

Greenspan arrived at the Dirksen Senate Office Building on Capitol Hill and took his seat before the horseshoe of senators, all eager for their ritual semi-annual grilling of the chairman. After enduring 45 minutes of their opening statements, Greenspan began in his gloomy monotone. He talked at length about interest rates, business restructuring, and other technical matters before finally, in his conclusion, mentioning Clinton's plan. "The President is to be commended for placing on the table for debate," he said, an economic plan that was both "serious" and "plausible." He didn't dare state further his belief that Clinton had displayed rare political courage. For the cautious Greenspan—so often the essence of Republicanism, conservatism, Wall Street, big banking—to go as far as he had was already a highly unusual embrace. There was no more important approbation Clinton could receive.

In its lead story the next day, *The New York Times* said that Greenspan had "endorsed Mr. Clinton's proposal to cut the budget deficit." *The Washington Post* headline read: "Greenspan Vows to Help Clinton." The *Wall Street Journal* Monday headline said that "Greenspan Takes Positive View of Clinton's Strategy." Some of the coverage was a little off the mark. Greenspan, after all, had not endorsed any specific elements of the plan, just its goal of deficit reduction, and had taken pains to point out that the appropriate combination of taxes and spending cuts was a decision for the politicians, not himself. He had chosen every single word of his testimony carefully. It focused and drew attention to the issue of his noninvolvement in the taxing and spending questions. None of the senators knew of his involvement in recommending the deficit target of $140 billion. Yet he was not unhappy that the reporters had received his underlying message that he supported Clinton's financial markets strategy. It was best that no one knew the extent to which the strategy was also Greenspan's.

THOUGH THE OVERALL economic plan had been presented to Congress, many details in the full administration proposal had to be worked out or changed. The tension between Begala and Rubin lingered for several days. In a discussion between the two on February 23, they erupted at each other over Clinton's campaign pledge to limit pay for corporate executives. Clinton's idea was to prohibit companies from taking tax deductions for CEO salaries above $1 million a year. Rubin said business didn't like the idea one bit, and he himself thought it was stupid.

Begala suggested an alternative: linking salaries to the CEOs' performances, or to the increase in productivity of their companies.

Rubin scoffed. How would anyone measure a CEO's performance fairly? he asked.

Fed up, Begala said then they should simply make the cap $1 million or perhaps $2 million. Period.

Rubin called Roger Altman, Clinton's other Wall Streeter, for his opinion. "He disagrees with me," Rubin reported frankly, "and says the business community really doesn't care." Begala was struck that Rubin was willing to report Altman's different view. "But I disagree with Roger," Rubin persisted. He maintained that a cap would be stupid, both punitive and ineffective.

Rubin and Begala then took their argument directly to Clinton. The president decided on a middle position. He would support caps, but would permit them to go up if the CEOs' firms performed well. Rubin said he still disagreed but added that the proposal would not have a significant impact.

They all walked over to nearby Constitution Hall, where Clinton addressed the U.S. Chamber of Commerce at 11:15 A.M. "Just yesterday, due to increased confidence in the plan in the bond market, longterm interest rates fell to a 16-year low," Clinton noted. For the first time since the government began issuing the 30-year bond, its yield dropped below 7 percent.

That day the 30-year bond rate dropped another .11 percent. Carville was beginning to understand real power. He told *The Wall Street Journal,* "I used to think if there was reincarnation, I wanted to come back as the president or the pope or a .400 baseball hitter. But now I want to come back as the bond market. You can intimidate everybody."

In his own small retirement plan, Carville had some 30-year bonds that his financial planners had suggested he buy when the prevailing interest rates had been a high 8.75 percent. He sold them as the rates moved below 7 percent. Because the value of bonds goes up as the prevailing interest rate drops, Carville made over 50 percent on his investment.

INTEREST RATES KEPT FALLING, bringing some tangible benefits. On Thursday, February 25, the *Wall Street Journal's* main story was about Clinton and the bond market. After noting the irony of a populist president embracing the markets, the article said that Clinton was taking a huge risk. "After all, part of the rush to buy bonds comes from people who think the Clinton program will lead to a stagnant economy," the article noted, since a weak economy would bring low interest rates.

But the low interest rates made Bentsen a hero of sorts. They also emboldened him. The day after Clinton's speech, in testimony before the Senate Budget Committee, Bentsen had identified three components to Clinton's economic plan: the stimulus package, investments, and deficit reduction. He used the same order a week later before the Senate Finance Committee. But by March 10, he was elevating one component to special status. In testimony, he told the House Ways and Means Committee, "Deficit reduction is the key."

18

With the apparent success of Clinton's February 17 speech, some of the political and media spotlight shifted dramatically to the head of his health care task force. In her meetings with congressional and other groups, Hillary had so far been treated with deference, almost reverence. She seemed smart and attentive and often took notes. She was also a novelty. Now, however, both publicly and within the White House, she was suddenly under enormous pressure to follow up her husband's performance with an equivalent success on health care.

To some of her staff, she seemed at times skittish and vulnerable. Not only was health care reform a central campaign promise, but health care costs were responsible for a large part of the deficit problem. Hillary was working and talking as if what she did or didn't do could harm her husband's presidency. She and the president had said at meetings that Clinton would be a dead man politically if he didn't reform health care in the first year. She had accepted the need for the earlier delay and now set May 1 as the deadline for submitting legislation to Congress.

As governor, Clinton had learned volumes about the health care system and wanted a radical overhaul. It was the stupidest financing system in the world, bleeding billions of dollars in bureaucratic and insurance costs away from actual health care. Hillary and Ira Magaziner set out to educate themselves by consulting experts, doctors, and members of Congress. Some of her staffers talked about this period as the idealistic phase of the health care task force, but she thought it was nonsense to think of idealism. This was pragmatic problem solving.

Beyond designing policy, they also were designing strategy, which Hillary loved. As with the economic plan, she told her staff, they had to find a story to tell, with heroes and villains.

Bob Boorstin, now working as her media adviser, was undergoing successful drug therapy for manic depression with the controversial drug Prozac. He had seen the price of a Prozac tablet jump from about 60 cents to $1.10 in just three years, and knew firsthand how drug companies were profiting off the ill. Research showed the enormous profits of drug companies, and Hillary was poised to denounce them.

Hillary wanted to find more villains. She ruled out family doctors, since most people liked their physicians; but she had no problem going after specialists, such as plastic surgeons who performed face-lifts and other expensive cosmetic operations. The American Medical Association, one of the best financed and most powerful lobbying groups in the country, was an obvious, lush target, but for the very reason of its power would have to get a pass. She decided on the insurance companies: They raked in huge profits; they restricted who could get insurance, often preying on the sick; and they saddled people with needless, burdensome paperwork. Her staff would even get the forms from the 1,500 insurance companies and wallpaper a room with them to point up the absurdity of the paper bureaucracy.

On February 25, Magaziner went to Capitol Hill to see some of the key House leaders and committee chairmen. Those in the room were filled with worry that Clinton would propose another tax increase. Representative Dan Rostenkowski, the 34-year House veteran and Illinois Democrat who chaired the Ways and Means Committee, was the most alarmed. Magaziner said that if they didn't solve the health care problem, the economic plan would not work, jeopardizing the Clinton presidency and the Democrats' control of Congress. Some tax increase might turn out to be necessary to fund reform at the outset, he had come to realize.

"You guys don't get it," Rostenkowski shot back. "You can't send up another tax."

HILLARY WAS UPSET about some of the initial media coverage of her reform effort. The coverage often lacked seriousness, she felt, with stories appearing in the lifestyle sections of the newspapers, which traditionally covered First Ladies, rather than on the front pages as a critical question of national policy. She had learned to detest the media during the campaign, and knew all too well that journalists were drawn to stories about controversy or failure. It spooked her at times. To ward off potentially negative stories, she decided that the meetings with 500 experts who were going to advise in the drafting of the legislation would be conducted in private. She also refused initially to release the experts' names. The cloak of secrecy prompted much criticism and even a lawsuit, bringing health care out of the lifestyle sections onto the front pages. Hillary was upset that the dispute took so much time and attention from the designing of the policy.

UP ON THE FOURTH FLOOR of an annex building to the main congressional offices, Robert Reischauer, the director of the Congressional Budget Office, was going through some very tense days. He had been poring over Clinton's economic plan with his staff for two weeks and had to release a preliminary evaluation. A tall, relaxed old Washington hand, Reischauer was the economic equivalent of the National Bureau of Standards, the ultimate nonpartisan arbiter of budget statistics. With a playful sense of humor and a mischievous smile at the corner of his mouth, he cultivated the air of the last sane man in a town gone crazy. His numbers were the official figures used by Congress, and although they were usually dismissed by the White House, this year in his February economic address Clinton had formally enshrined them as the official administration numbers as well.

Reischauer knew that Alice Rivlin, his old boss when she headed the Congressional Budget Office (CBO), had called the Clinton budget baby beautiful. But Reischauer found some problems. The analysis he and his staff conducted showed that over five years the plan reduced the deficit by some $50 billion less than the administration had claimed—a point Reischauer was going to state publicly in his official assessment of the plan for release on March 3.

The announcement could be an embarrassment. Reischauer expected real problems, since his assessment would contradict the core of the administration's promise of no tricks or gimmicks. The office Clinton had held up as an authority would be undercutting his own team's figures. After hearing of Reischauer's assessment, the White House prepared a seven-point defense. The defense focused on the deficit reduction for the year 1997, noting that the CBO figure for that year was only $1 billion off from theirs.

Later Reischauer discussed the numbers with Leon Panetta. We hated you for a day, Panetta said. But it had turned out fine. Congress had adopted the administration's original target numbers as their own targets, and then, using the stricter CBO numbers, cut spending even more to meet those goals.

Reischauer also received a visit from Magaziner and one of his notetakers to talk about health care. "You're trying to restructure 14 percent of the economy," Reischauer said, "and doing it gradually and right is more important than fast."

Magaziner quoted back to him many of Reischauer's own statistics and testimony that the deficit could not be controlled without slowing down the growth of health care costs. Medicaid costs for the poor, for instance, had jumped 30 percent the previous year.

To reform rapidly, Reischauer countered, would involve too much pain and readjustment. For example, cutting out waste in the medical system could wind up eliminating one third of the physician specialists, who would then have to go into general practice or leave medicine. Reform would likely eliminate 20 percent of all hospital beds. These reductions might make economic and policy sense, but they would shock communities that were built around their doctors and hospitals. Tampering with the social fabric rashly would not be wise.

Magaziner said he disagreed.

SENATOR DAVID L. BOREN of Oklahoma had a mixed view of the Clinton presidency. The round-faced Boren, 51, was a Democrat who had served in the Senate for 14 years and tried to present himself as a maverick. He was both a natural ally and a natural rival of Clinton's. Also a Rhodes Scholar, Boren had served with Clinton on the regional Rhodes selection committee in New Orleans two decades ago. Back then, both in their twenties, the two would occasionally dine together and engage in the save-the-world talk of aspiring politicians. In 1974, Boren was elected governor of Oklahoma, and four years later Clinton was elected to his first term in Arkansas. Both wore the mantle of "New Democrat," despite Clinton's more liberal sentiments and Boren's conservatism.

In the 1992 campaign, Boren had held off from endorsing Clinton during the early primaries. He thought Clinton was playing populist demagogue, and he preferred the anti-deficit platform of Paul Tsongas, a close friend from the Senate. Boren supported Clinton after he won the Democratic nomination, serving in the campaign as a communications conduit with Ross Perot, another anti-deficit favorite of Boren's. After

Christmas, Boren had made the pilgrimage to Little Rock for a private, two-hour meeting with the president-elect.

During Clinton's early days as president, Boren attended an hour-long White House meeting with the congressional Democratic leadership on campaign finance reform, one of his pet issues. Some of the Democrats present had adopted a condescending tone toward Clinton and spoke of their real-world experience, leaving a thinly veiled threat that said, Don't tread on us or you'll be sorry. Boren felt that Clinton hadn't responded forcefully enough. He had acted as if he weren't in charge and seemed so eager to please that he would not defend his own ideas. So Boren had muscled in.

"Mr. President," Boren had said, playing to the gallery, "I want to invite you to step on our toes and make us mad. If you sit up here and you're going to be viewed as getting in bed with all the Washington insiders, the people that sent you here are going to feel you let them down."

Boren had admired Clinton's February 17 economic address. As he listened from his seat, Boren sensed a change halfway through the speech. He could virtually see and feel Clinton become president before his eyes—strong and emphatic, speaking with a new voice of self-conviction. But when Boren examined the details of the plan in the days and weeks afterward, he believed they didn't match the rhetoric.

In particular, Boren had reservations about the stimulus package, which Clinton had finally set at $16 billion of quick spending. Conceived when the economy was still weak, the stimulus was designed to help people in hard times; but now that the economy was growing faster, at a rate of close to 5 percent in the last three months of 1992, Boren did not feel it was necessary. The Clinton plan called for spreading money through 14 major departments and agencies.

Boren considered the spending as just a thin layer of federal sugar, something for everyone. Although the package included $4 billion in extended unemployment benefits, $1 billion for job training and employment, and funds for transportation and environmental construction grants, Boren focused on items such as the $281 million for rural water and sewer grants, the $9 million for the National Library of Medicine, and the $148 million for Treasury information systems. Boren knew these sorts of federal programs were full of studies, commissions, consultants. He wasted no time in advertising his dismay. "It would send the wrong message to the country," he had said publicly two days after the speech. "If the first thing they see us do is pass a stimulus package, it's going to destroy our credibility. A lot of us will be extremely uncomfortable with voting more money for anything before we lock in deficit reduction."

But although Boren made clear his opposition to the small stimulus package, he backed Clinton's overall economic plan. After sampling public opinion, which was responding positively to Clinton's speech and the White House's massive offensive, Boren declared his unconditional support. "I support the package unreservedly," he said in a remark quoted in a *New York Times* front-page story on February 28. "I'll try to fine-tune it, to improve it. But even if I can't get anything changed, I'm going to support it."

The White House rejoiced. "I believe that when the history of this is written," Begala responded publicly, "one of the key points will be the day David Boren stood up and announced he was going to support it. When we heard about Boren's statement, a resounding cheer went up." In the White House communications office, there was a celebration.

SENATOR JOHN BREAUX, an affable Louisiana Democrat and a close friend of Clinton's from the Democratic Leadership Council, was also displeased with parts of the economic plan. He too objected to the stimulus package and, along with several others from gas- and oil-producing states, he had problems with the BTU tax. A tall, avid tennis player, Breaux, 49, was politically ambitious. Like many Louisiana politicians, he had mastered the Washington insider game, yet frequently displayed an independent, rogue streak.

At a meeting at the White House to discuss the stimulus package, Breaux reported that the early sentiment in the Senate was pointing toward trouble. He suggested the administration retain those programs in it that would directly create jobs and cut out the pork.

"That's a good idea," Gore said.

"That sounds like a way to solve this problem," Clinton agreed.

McLarty also endorsed the idea.

Boren too spoke to the president about the stimulus. "People can't receive two messages at once," Boren said. "You've gotten them all believing they've got to get the deficit down. This is mission one, and now you're confusing them by coming in with a spending program. That mixes the message. It's causing cynicism to already set in." Boren said he supported some new spending initiatives for summer jobs but not the pork. He and Breaux were going to pursue an amendment to the stimulus bill.

"I understand," Clinton said. Confidentially, the president repeated his line that all the newspaper editorial boards and a hundred economists would praise the stimulus package, but "walkin'-around" people would wonder why the deficit had to be increased in order to be lowered. Clinton didn't say outright that he agreed with Boren, but the senator felt he had dealt with presidents long enough to know when he had assent.

Boren had more reason to think Clinton agreed with him after speaking with Bentsen. Bentsen and Boren had been close friends in the Senate; on the Finance Committee, they would work out compromises together in private, and Bentsen would tug his ear twice when Boren was supposed to offer an amendment to a bill. As they spoke about the stimulus package, Bentsen told Boren he agreed with his concerns. The Treasury Secretary said he was not enthusiastic about the small stimulus package. It was so small at $16 billion that it would not make a difference in the overall economy, even in the short run. Long-term interest rates were the key, Bentsen felt. Bentsen liked the Boren-Breaux proposal. It would bring the conservatives along by delaying the pork spending.

Bentsen had talked with Clinton and praised the Boren-Breaux approach. The senators had identified an internal contradiction in the economic plan—the austerity and cuts in the overall plan versus the stimulus package of a piddling $16 billion that was sufficiently pork-infested to seem like a wild spending spree. It looked like the administration was working at cross-purposes with itself, Bentsen said. He was glad to hear Clinton agree.

Then Boren heard from another friend, Chief of Staff Mack McLarty. More than 15 years earlier, while governor, Boren had struck up a friendship with McLarty, who had just come aboard the natural gas company Arkla. Natural gas was a giant business in Oklahoma, and over the years the two had stayed in touch. When McLarty told Boren that he too was "strongly" in favor of Boren's suggestion, it was all Boren needed to hear.

Boren took the somewhat unorthodox step of making calls to some moderate Democrats in the House. They seemed to like a stimulus compromise. But a Democrats-only strategy would kill Clinton, Boren felt. Senate Republicans were there for the asking if they could give the stimulus package a conservative cast.

Boren called Howard Paster. He suggested that the House vote on his compromise plan before the Senate did. That way, the Senate could just pass the same version of the bill that the House did.

Well, no, Paster replied. The House committee was doing just fine on the president's version of the stimulus, and the White House couldn't bail out on them. It was going to be a hard fight, Paster said, and the White House didn't want to start talking compromise and be seen as wavering right out of the box.

In that case, Boren asked, did Paster intend to negotiate with the moderate Democrats like himself when the stimulus bill came to the Senate?

It would depend on the vote count, Paster said.

Okay, Boren said, if that was the way they were going to play it, Paster could round up his votes and Boren would round up his own. Despite the earlier encouragement he had received, it was now apparent that the White House was changing course. If the White House was going to use brass knuckles instead of compromising, Boren felt, so could he. By the middle of March, Breaux claimed that he and Boren had identified 15 of the Senate's 57 Democrats who shared some of their concerns.

But the House continued on track. Late in the evening of Thursday, March 18, the House, by a vote of 243 to 183, passed the resolution approving the broad outlines of Clinton's five-year plan. Clinton's un-adulterated version of the $16 billion stimulus package then passed in the early-morning hours Friday.

These were just the first of many steps in the protracted legislative process and carried largely symbolic meaning. Unlike an actual budget bill, the resolution outlined only how the government *intended* to collect and spend its revenues over the next five years. Two major votes in each house had to follow. First the House and the Senate would have to pass their budget reconciliation bills; then those bills—which were bound to have some differences—would have to be reconciled in a conference bill; and then the conference bill would again have to pass each house for those taxes and spending choices to become law.

Yet it was still cause for celebration. On March 19, Clinton had the House members over to the White House for an 8:30 A.M. breakfast in the East Room. The president was full of laughter and praise. He spoke about "change" and looked forward to a "historic year."

That afternoon Senator Robert Byrd, 75, the powerful chairman of the Appropriations Committee and the former Senate Majority Leader, was ushered into the Oval Office to meet with Clinton and Paster. Byrd was the Senate floor manager for the stimulus package. As Appropria-tions chairman, he controlled all 13 regular appropriations bills that would follow. "Robert Byrd controls your life," Paster explained to Clinton. Formal, pompous, and parochial, Byrd was given to quoting from Cicero or Thucydides' history of the Peloponnesian wars. With his mane of gray hair, he was the oldest of the old Democrats, having won his first elected office in the West Virginia House of Delegates in 1946, the year Clinton was born.

Paster handed Byrd a copy of a letter from Clinton urging him to move the $16 billion bill without changes.

"I'm going to do this for you," Byrd said proudly, "and let me show you how I'm going to do it." Drawing on a large manila envelope, he sketched out a complicated amendment tree for the president. Byrd was a master of the Senate's arcane rules of parliamentary procedure. By offering a series of amendments, he explained, he could effectively block all other amendments, ensuring that the bill would be voted on without alteration. He looked at the president wistfully. The House Democrats had delivered for the new president without a single word change. Byrd was going to make sure the Senate did the same.

"Thank you, Mr. Chairman," Clinton said in a businesslike manner. "Let's pass the bill." He had thrown in his lot with Byrd.

ON FRIDAY, March 19, Hillary's father, Hugh Rodham, 81, suffered a stroke and was hospitalized in Little Rock. She went to him immediately. Clinton joined her in Little Rock for much of Monday and Tuesday. The stroke was very severe, and Hillary dropped most of what she was doing in Washington. She stayed out of the nitty-gritty of the economic plan, and even put health care on the back burner.

SOON AFTER the House vote approving the budget resolution, the core members of the National Economic Council gathered in Room 476 of the Old Executive Office Building, next door to the White House. Panetta passed out copies of a sheet that broke down the numbers in the House resolution. Here's what we have, he told the assembled. Heads bent downward as they thumbed through the pages and skimmed over the columns of figures.

Alice Rivlin offered the first endorsement. Look at that, she said. Their deficit reduction was not only completely intact, it was strengthened. She had expected the House to dilute the administration proposal and was delighted to find it was increased. Though the $140 billion in reductions for 1997 had been the focus of discussions within the White House while the plan was being drawn up, the five-year total reduction proposed had added up to $473 billion. That five-year total became the basic index. Rivlin noted that the House's version of the five-year package added up to more than $500 billion in deficit reduction.

You're darn right, said Bentsen, as he hit the table with his hand triumphantly. We held up, Bentsen added proudly. Panetta, too, nodded and agreed, his face breaking out into his Cheshire Cat grin. Satisfaction filled the room. The group seemed ready to break out the champagne.

Gene Sperling's eyes, however, landed on the pages summarizing the investments. The plan Clinton had sent up had included a total of $231 billion in investments for the five years. Though some was old, much of it was new. But the House resolution contained less than $1 billion in new investments for the first year, 1994. Sperling couldn't believe it. And it didn't get much better. The number for 1995 was less than $6 billion.

"I hate to be a dissenter here," Sperling said, "but I do not think this is particularly good. This is not all good news." The president's investment package was in deep trouble. Sperling pointed to the numbers. "I think we should be looking at this as a partial victory and a partial *crisis*."

Ron Brown, the Commerce Secretary, agreed. Brown said that he and Vice President Gore had been working hard to craft an initiative for investing in cutting-edge technologies, very positive stuff. The president really believed in it. How could they proceed with the initiative without the funding?

Laura Tyson saw the low investment numbers as confirming her concerns about the headlong drive for the 1997 target deficit reduction of $140 billion. She said the numbers vividly demonstrated that they had tilted too far toward meeting that goal.

Bob Reich, godfather of the investment program, was absent from the meeting. His right-hand man, policy adviser and chief economist at the Labor Department, Larry Katz, was at the table in his place. Katz, a 33-year-old Harvard economist, had recently heard Reich predict devastation for the investments. But Labor's own budget analysts had disagreed, and no warning had been sounded. Katz could predict his boss's reaction, but he didn't want to speak for him.

The fault line between the deficit hawks and the investment hawks, once just a hairline fissure, now cracked open. Right after the meeting, Sperling, Tyson, Brown, and Katz caucused.

You know, Gene, Tyson said, you used the word "crisis." That summed it up right.

Did they think the president realized some of this? Ron Brown asked. Sperling said he would talk to Rubin at once, and he asked Katz to talk to Reich.

The alarm went out. Reich was flooded with calls. Tyson phoned. Katz reached him late that night. "There needs to be a meeting with the president," Reich said. The issue was so important that Clinton could not just be casually informed. Sperling also called late that night. They all feared that the essence of the Clinton presidency was about to be demolished. Bentsen and Panetta did not know Clinton's heart, they agreed.

Clinton's investments had been decimated because of the caps on spending for the years 1994 and 1995 that had been part of the 1990 budget deal. In 1990, the caps seemed a wonderful way to get some $100 billion in future deficit reduction without any immediate pain. But the future had arrived and the caps were now an ironclad reality. Reich and Sperling, newcomers to budget rules and law, thought they had been too dependent on Panetta, who felt deficit reduction in his gut, as they felt the investments in their guts. Jeopardize the deficit reduction and Panetta would go into orbit, but the possibility of losing the investments had never seemed to alarm Panetta. He had explained that they would fight to raise the caps.

Had Reich been the budget director, Sperling felt, the discovery of the caps would have triggered a response along the lines of: "Crisis! There is a crisis here! Stop everything! We have to go into an all-day session. We need to call Gephardt here. We need to do everything. What can we do?" But Panetta had downplayed the issue of the caps whenever it was raised, as if it would be easily handled. Panetta had never given anyone reason to get worked up about it while something could still be done.

Sperling talked to Rubin. Did the president know? Sperling wondered. Rubin wasn't sure. Sperling felt Clinton had to be informed. The problem had to be underscored at once, immediately. As the presidential gatekeeper on economic issues, Rubin had reservations about allowing a special meeting with the president. The National Economic Council had to remain the vehicle for economic decisions, with everyone participating. Rubin had to maintain scrupulous neutrality, or the whole process would break down. In drawing up the economic plan, the NEC process had been largely observed—full and open discussion, no special pleadings to Clinton, no *ex parte* contacts. Rubin did not want to undermine the honest-broker reputation he had won in the first months by rushing in to the Oval Office in violation of his own rules.

Sperling pressed. This was a crisis, he insisted. Rubin realized that Clinton might be in the dark about the fate of his investments and would want to know. It was only fair that Reich and Sperling, the keepers of the investment flame, brief the president on what had happened. He gave the okay. It would take several days to get everyone together. As he waited for a meeting with Clinton, Sperling was going nuts.

19

THE WHITE HOUSE had run up against its first obstacle on the long-term investments in the overall economic plan. But the short-term $16 billion stimulus package was proceeding nicely. After the bill passed in the House, Byrd pressed for passage in the Senate. On Tuesday, March 23, he reported the full stimulus package out of his committee and brought it to the Senate floor. The bill still included a small amount of funding for such projects as swimming pools, golf courses, whitewater canoeing facilities, and studies of fish, alongside the programs designed to create jobs. "I think in the end we will pass it," Clinton said of the package the next day in an interview with Dan Rather of CBS News, "because, first of all, I think the public would just be outraged at the thought that we have a chance here to create half a millon new jobs and to do things that are good that need to be done and this would be slowed up."

On Thursday, after finally passing the budget resolution, the general outline for Clinton's overall economic plan—a big victory for Clinton —the Senate turned to the $16 billion stimulus, a comparative footnote in the overall scheme of things.

Byrd introduced his amendment tree to prevent further changes to the package. Boren and Breaux saw the move as a strong-arm tactic and in protest staged a four-and-a-half-hour filibuster to prevent the $16 billion stimulus package from passing. Byrd repeatedly challenged Boren, who said he was acting in Clinton's interest. "I offer this proposal not in the spirit of opposing the president, but in the spirit of enthusiastic support for the president," Boren said. He said he was acting on Clinton's goal of reducing the deficit.

"Does the senator doubt the statement of administration policy that is on the desk of senators dated today in which President Clinton stated that the administration opposes any efforts to delay passage of this critical legislation?" Byrd countered.

That Sunday, March 28, Breaux went to the White House to meet with Panetta and Paster. He hoped once again to convince them a compromise was in their interests.

Panetta wanted to consider a compromise, but Paster insisted the Boren-Breaux proposal wouldn't get significant Republican support, if any at all. The compromise would only drive liberal Democrats such as Senator Howard Metzenbaum of Ohio up the wall, he said.

Clinton had probably been Metzenbaum's fourth choice among the Democratic presidential candidates, Breaux said. What could they possibly owe him?

Paster said that the liberal wing of the party could not be taken for granted. He wanted a cohesive strategy. Clinton had insisted there be no modifications in the House, and it had to be the same in the Senate.

ONE MODERATE REPUBLICAN, Senator William S. Cohen of Maine, had been maintaining that as long as Republicans could get fair consideration for their amendments, he was willing to let the stimulus go forward for a vote. But Byrd's heavy-handed maneuver, he felt, was like a chemical catalyst, instantaneously fusing the left and right wings of the Senate Republicans together. It was a foolish move, Cohen felt, since Clinton was personally extending a hand to Republicans such as himself. At a lunch with Senate Republicans just a week and a half earlier, the president had been jovial and conciliatory. "We're willing to work out our differences," he had asserted.

Just before his April 1 departure for a West Coast swing that included a Vancouver summit meeting with Russian President Boris Yeltsin, Clinton again reached out. He invited Cohen to a White House dinner with six Democratic and six Republican senators. Clinton spent several hours soliciting the views of each senator as he carefully went around the table, asking about Russia and an aid package for the Russians. Cohen felt he was getting more attention from Clinton, a Democrat, than he had from his fellow Republican Bush.

Clinton left town for four days, and the Republicans, galvanized by Byrd's tactics, picked up and continued the Senate filibuster with relish. The filibuster delayed a planned recess. Forced to pursue a compromise, Paster began talking to Republicans and by Saturday, April 3, had received hints of a possible concession and a willingness to compromise. He called McLarty, who was on Air Force One headed to Vancouver. Do we want a deal? Paster asked the chief of staff.

McLarty went to check with Clinton and came back. "No," he said, "we don't want to deal at this point."

In the early hours of Monday, April 5, Clinton returned from Vancouver. Later in the morning, he boarded a train to Baltimore for the Orioles' opening-day baseball game, where he was asked about the Senate logjam. Clinton called the filibuster "just a political power play." He added derisively, "In the Senate, the majority does not rule. It's not like the country."

Byrd and the Democrats needed to break off just three Republicans to get the 60 votes needed to end debate, but they could not find a single defector. Clinton called Bill Cohen to ask for help.

"People on our side are willing to compromise," Cohen told the president.

"But Dole is not extending his hand," Clinton replied.

"I see it the other way around," Cohen said. "The administration is not extending its hand."

Clinton extended it. "I hope you're willing to support us."

"Some of us are hoping there'll be negotiations," Cohen said.

"I don't see it coming out of the Republicans," the president noted.

"I was at a meeting of all of us and I think Dole wants to reach an agreement," Cohen answered.

"That's not my impression," Clinton said.

The next day, Tuesday, April 6, Mitchell adjourned the Senate for a two-week Easter recess, the filibuster intact. Over in the budget office, Panetta attributed the problems to a dual failure: no effective message operation to counter Republican charges, and no backup plan to keep the package moving. Success in these situations required movement. Clinton's economic plan seemed stalled.

Clinton had run into two old, unsettled pieces of business in Senate politics: Byrd's old-baron style and Dole's desire to prove he was the party leader who could hold the various Republican factions under one tent.

THE TUESDAY that the Senate adjourned, Hillary Clinton flew to Austin, Texas, to deliver a speech. For the last 18 days her father had lain in a hospital bed. His stroke was so serious that the family was going to have to decide about discontinuing life support—a wrenching decision. Hillary had been back and forth to Little Rock many times. Her father had turned 82 just a few days earlier and had had a long history of heart trouble.

The speech she gave had been germinating for a long time. She called for a national awakening, saying that the country was suffering a "sleeping sickness of the soul." To counteract what she called a "crisis of meaning," she called for what would amount to a new politics of kindness. Teenage mothers and "angry boys with guns" were only part of the overwhelming sense of "alienation and despair and hopelessness" that filled the country, she said. The speech was an outpouring of religious ideas and 1960s concepts, full of better-world rhetoric that reached beyond politics to the spiritual.

Her declaration of war on weak morals attracted much media attention, some of it skeptical. *The New York Times Magazine* ran a long cover article about her the next month headlined: "The Politics of Virtue." She posed for a cover photograph in a pure white satin suit. A drawing inside next to the headline, "Saint Hillary," showed her dressed as Joan of Arc, replete with sword and halo. Another headline described her as "More Preacher Than Politician." Some noted that during the 1992 presidential campaign, when Republicans were attempting to stress "family values," she had said, "American women don't need lectures from Washington about values," and yet in Texas she had plunged deep into the question.

Some in the White House, such as Stephanopoulos, were suckers for the theme. Others believed that while the speech was sincere, it was an emotional expression of the distress she was feeling at the moment. "Hillary's a lawyer, not a philosopher," said one official who worked with her daily. "She contradicts herself because she's very good at giving arguments on both sides. She could give the lecture on why lectures on values shouldn't be given and turn around and give the lecture on values —both with equal effectiveness."

THE NEXT DAY, April 7, at about 1 P.M., Rubin, Reich, Sperling, and Stephanopoulos went to see Clinton on the investments fiasco. Along with a couple of other top advisers, Rubin was routinely allotted 15 minutes each day on Clinton's schedule. If he didn't have a pressing matter, he canceled the time, a highly unusual action for White House aides, suggesting utter confidence and eliciting much comment from others in the White House; personal time with the president was to many the yardstick for measuring influence and importance. When the four men went into the Oval Office, Rubin again did the unusual. He turned the floor over to his deputy.

Mr. President, Sperling began, we wanted to make sure you were focusing on how bad the budget resolution has turned out. This was the same resolution that Clinton was embracing daily. The administration had focused with incredible intensity on the deficit and now the stimulus flap, Sperling said, but he and others thought they should be focusing with the same intensity on winning more investments.

It was instantly apparent that the president didn't grasp what had happened. The magnitude and import of the House's action had never sunk in.

Sperling explained how the caps in the 1990 budget agreement had come home to roost. The House had slashed the investments to ribbons. The bottom line, he said, was less than $1 billion for new investments in 1994 and about $6 billion in 1995.

The president began to yell and shout questions. How? Why? When? Sperling, always slightly intimidated by Clinton, felt that the messenger bearing bad news should be rewarded, not blamed. But Clinton was angry.

What? the president asked, astounded. Panetta had said he would get the House to rewrite the caps to accommodate the proposed investments.

The House, Sperling said, had responded to the changing political climate and climbed on the deficit reduction bandwagon. They had stuck with the old caps. Reischauer's Congressional Budget Office had, as the president knew, found the administration's plan fell some $50 billion short over five years of its stated deficit reduction goal, so the House had just found that much more to cut. The money had come largely out of the new investments.

Slamming his fist down on the end of his chair, Clinton let loose a torrent of rage and frustration. He said he felt blindsided. This was totally inconsistent with what he had been told. Why hadn't they ever had a serious discussion about the caps? Day after day, in dozens of hours in the Roosevelt Room going over the smallest programs and most trivial details, there had been no meeting, no discussion of the caps? The president turned red in the face. Why didn't they tell me? he asked. This is what I was elected for, he said. This is why I'm here.

Clinton seemed to check himself. He said he was not putting down what they had accomplished. It was important, it was good. "We have just gone too far. We're losing our soul."

Reich could see that the president felt betrayed, and was struck by Clinton's use of the pronoun "they." The president, it seemed to him, was referring to Panetta and Rivlin, the budget experts, almost as if he were accusing them of sabotage or incompetence. They were the old hands, familiar with and in control of the numbers and the process. Reich knew they loved the caps; they were an excellent device for constraining the budget. Reich, however, could not believe that anyone had intentionally subverted the process, whatever their love for deficit reduction.

Reich also sensed a sheepishness in the room. All of them had let Clinton down. All of them should have seen this coming. Reich himself had testified before the committees on the Hill and should have realized this. There simply was no excuse.

Stephanopoulos thought everyone was being defensive. They all should have known. Stephanopoulos knew what to do in these occasions: Weather the Clinton storm, don't get fazed, and focus on the next step.

Sperling believed he knew how Clinton felt. It was like having your telephone suddenly disconnected over a late bill, only worse. He knew the feeling of having been done an injustice because the phone company had not issued a full alert: "Stop! Warning! Major Problem!" The whole encounter was uncomfortable as the president seemed to be expressing two contradictory emotions: fury at Sperling and Reich for not being on top of the problem, yet also some gratitude that they were watching out for his investments. Beneath it all, Clinton indicated that he felt isolated, that too many of his senior advisers didn't think and feel as he did.

After Clinton's explosion, Rubin pressed ahead. All they wanted, he said, was an okay to convene a meeting for establishing a few priorities among the investments. Given the limited money Congress allotted, they had to decide what they should fight for first and hardest. The resolution was not the final plan, and with work, some investments could be salvaged.

Yeah, Clinton said, distracted. He was still consumed. Why hadn't someone raised the flag? It was maddening. He felt he was getting the worst of all worlds. The investments he cared about—"the non-Wall Street elements," he called them sarcastically—kept getting slashed. He had to keep telling himself that getting control of the deficit and the process would put him in a position of strength. Then, later, from that position of strength, he could move to what mattered. He could fix it later.

. . .

SPERLING LEFT DEVASTATED. Back in February, when they were making the decisions on the plan in the Roosevelt Room, Clinton had control. But once the plan moved outside the Roosevelt Room over to Capitol Hill, it was out of Clinton's hands. Congress had subjected it to its own process. Multiple committees, powerful personalities, special relationships, and special interests the White House didn't understand took over. From a distance, Congress seemed a world of subtlety, a labyrinth. Sperling found he couldn't tell where a congressman stood unless he spoke to him directly. If he heard that a congressman had said no to something, Sperling wouldn't know whether that was an absolute no, a no for bargaining purposes, or a no for other strategic reasons. In this world of uncertainty, they had lost control of their program.

"IF YOU COULD FEEL THE MOOD on the Hill, Mr. President," Panetta said to Clinton later, trying to explain what had happened. They all had grossly underestimated the forces coming out of the November election and the power of Perot's deficit reduction message. In the economic plan, Panetta had proposed an increase in the spending caps so Clinton would get his investments. But then they had hit a brick wall: deficit mania. The leadership and key members of Congress were determined to take the administration package and do it one better. Panetta explained how his successor as House Budget Committee chairman, Martin Sabo, the Minnesota Democrat, had said that the only conceivable way to keep the conservative Democrats on board was to obey the old caps. On top of this, the White House pressure to move fast and get passage in record time meant these decisions had been made under immense time constraints. The Senate side was stacking up the same way, only worse. If they tried to change the caps, the issue would be subject to a point of order in the Senate, and it would take 60 votes to overcome a likely filibuster.

Clinton indicated that he had never quite connected the earlier discussions of that seeming abstraction, "caps on discretionary spending," with their impact on his investments. He had never fully grasped the relationship.

. . .

ABOUT TWO HOURS LATER, Clinton, still fuming, went to the Roosevelt Room for a meeting with his economic and health care advisers. The administration had publicly set a deadline of May for announcing its health care reform package, and it was pretty clear that Congress would at that point still be in the thick of the debate on the economic plan. Clinton had to decide whether to push back the health care package another two weeks so it wouldn't collide with the economic plan. Seated underneath a picture of Teddy Roosevelt, the president settled in for the arguments. The mood was already tense.

Begala suggested that the administration come in with health care right away and regain the political offensive. The economic plan, with the emphasis on deficit reduction, wasn't playing well, he explained. The proposed new taxes, especially the BTU energy tax, were unpopular. People couldn't see the benefits or know where their money was going. Deficit reduction was too intangible, too abstract. "Taxes for deficit reduction is something for nothing," he said. People, on the other hand, would more likely accept taxes for a concrete benefit such as health care reform. "If I wake up in the middle of the night and hear my baby cry, I identify with that," he said. The baby's health was central to his life, one of his kitchen-table issues.

Stephanopoulos felt that Begala didn't understand that the system could not handle two things at once. He knew that Hillary and the consultants were angry about anything that might delay health care reform and harbored suspicions that the senior economic people were ready to undercut health care, particularly if it turned out to require new taxes.

Gore took issue with Begala. "That's the problem," he said. "Congress may abandon our economic plan and only go for our health plan." He suggested that they postpone the presentation of the full health plan and make sure they consult with everyone on the details. Such a tactic could help protect the economic plan.

"May 15 is the earliest possible date for completion," Hillary said of the health plan. Although that meant a two-week delay was inevitable, she didn't want more than that.

"We need enough time to do good numbers," Panetta said, implying that Magaziner's numbers work was unsatisfactory.

"Agree completely," Bentsen said tartly.

"Let's be careful," Donna Shalala added.

Clinton was still simmering from the earlier Oval Office meeting on the scuttled investments, and now there was an implicit challenge to Hillary and health care. Furious once again and racing over the various other problems, Clinton took the floor. "Moynihan's very angry over welfare reform, that we dropped it out of the budget, *and he's right,*" the president said. No one missed that shot at Bentsen, who had urged dropping welfare reform to hit the early $140 billion target. "Congress thinks it can run in '94 on this budget, plus GATT and NAFTA," he added, referring to the two pending trade agreements. *"They're crazy. . . ."*

"Where are all the Democrats?" Clinton bellowed. "I hope you're all aware we're all Eisenhower Republicans," he said, his voice dripping with sarcasm. "We're Eisenhower Republicans here, and we are fighting the Reagan Republicans. We stand for lower deficits and free trade and the bond market. Isn't that great?"

The room was silent once more.

He erupted again, his voice severe and loud. "I don't have a goddamn Democratic budget until 1996. None of the investments, none of the things I campaigned on." His voice dropped. Clinton said he would bow to political reality and delay health care, but only for two weeks, and he didn't like it one bit. "We must have something for the common man. It won't hurt me in '94, and I can put enough into '95 and '96 to crawl through to reelection.

"At least we'll have health care to give them, if we can't give them anything else," he added.

The old campaign hands, Stephanopoulos, Sperling, and Begala, were used to the temper tantrums. But the senior cabinet members like Bentsen and Panetta hadn't seen that much of it. To most of them, this marked the day that Clinton lost his formality with his cabinet and opened up about his feelings and his conflicts. It also marked the day the cabinet lost its virginity with Clinton.

Rubin didn't take the tirade too seriously. He had seen Clinton make as many as ten pronouncements on a subject; most would be temperate, and several might be extreme. It would be a mistake, he felt, to view extreme pronouncements or outbursts as Clinton's real conclusions.

Tyson thought the president had accurately captured the situation. The administration was appearing too Republican, too oriented toward deficit reduction, free trade, and the bond market.

Gore was the first to speak. He tried to smooth things over, noting that they faced some very tough questions.

"We must get reconciliation on a faster track to make room for health care," Panetta said. Reconciliation was shorthand for the overall budget act that would implement the economic plan, and Panetta suggested they press Moynihan to move up the date when the Senate Finance Committee would begin considering it.

Clinton wasn't through. He turned to the free trade agreement. "I'd like to pass NAFTA this year, but the bottom has fallen out of support for it. No one in California will vote for it." He landed again on the investments and blamed Reischauer of the Congressional Budget Office, whose estimates had led Congress to cut another $50 billion from Clinton's plan. "We've gutted our investment program by turning the government over to Reischauer!"

"There are so many Senate Democrats up in '94, we could lose the Senate that year," Clinton said, returning to politics. "People are ready for a huge deal on health care. We must convince people that our plan will improve every American's security. The only way they can beat us is by making people feel even less secure over our plan."

Hillary thought her husband had a good point that they were too Republican. He had convinced her that nothing else could be accomplished until the economic plan passed. He needed that victory to build on. He kept saying that it was going to be a marathon, not a sprint. She looked on it as trench warfare.

"We've done the responsible good-government thing which will get Democrats beat," Hillary lamented. She tried to put the best face on the situation. "We cleaned up the mess we inherited. Once we pass reconciliation, however, there'll be another boost in terms of public reaction."

Panetta had never seen Clinton so angry. Clinton, he concluded, must have naively thought he could implement his full agenda, according to his own timetable. But the spirit and enthusiasm of the presidential campaign just did not automatically or easily become a legislative program. After the bitterness of his tirade, Panetta saw calm overtake Clinton. The blowup, he thought, marked another step in the president's slow and torturous awakening to the ways of Washington.

20

Later that night, Hillary learned that her father had died. The next morning, she and the president flew to Little Rock for a memorial service to be held on Friday. On Saturday they flew to Pennsylvania for the funeral, and then on to Camp David to spend Saturday and Sunday nights. The three weeks of her father's illness had stalled the health care task force, "the work-stop phase," some staffers called it. Though planning and briefings continued, nothing of substance was accomplished while she was gone.

Magaziner's strategy on health care reform had been to run two tracks of briefings. First, he held a series of briefings and meetings attended by the Clintons and the administration's key health and economic advisers. For the second track, Magaziner met with just the president and Hillary alone for private briefings, updates, and discussions, as the Clintons had requested.

One day at one of the larger group meetings on the fourth floor of the Old Executive Office Building, Bob Boorstin was summoned away on an unrelated matter. Not wanting to miss what he thought was an important meeting, he complained to Magaziner.

Magaziner said not to worry. The meeting was not that significant. He was having regular private, confidential meetings with the Clintons.

Boorstin knew that the economic team was already deeply suspicious of Magaziner and suspected there were some informal, back-channel contacts. Eight departments in the federal government were involved in health care reform, and they all needed to be included. A regular series of secret sessions was explosive, Boorstin felt.

"If they find out," Boorstin told Magaziner, "you're a dead man. You're digging your own grave. Not only will the policy be dead, but it will be dead for less than a good reason. It will be because these people feel cut out."

Magaziner ignored Boorstin's warning. The private briefings for the Clintons continued.

ON WEDNESDAY, April 14, while the Senate was still in recess, Clinton spoke with Dole, who was visiting New Hampshire, the first presidential primary state. Clinton was ready to work out a stimulus compromise. Dole, relishing his newfound power, wasn't budging. He had stopped the new president for three weeks at a point when momentum was crucial. Though the stimulus constituted a mere fragment of the overall plan and only 1 percent of the annual federal budget, the struggle over it was assuming huge symbolic importance.

Later in the day, Clinton attended one of Magaziner's large health care briefings in the Roosevelt Room. Hillary, Gore, Rubin, Tyson, Panetta, and about ten others were there. The president announced grimly that he had just talked with Dole.

"Mr. President," Magaziner began, taking note of Clinton's mood, "if you're not in a good mood, I'm going to make it worse." He had a dozen charts on health care costs and timelines. They told an ugly story, depicting explosive costs and few new options to raise extra money. Any way they looked at it, the reforms were going to cost about $50 billion to $100 billion in the short run, before the savings could be realized. Most of the tax options couldn't come close to raising this kind of money. A $1-a-pack increase in cigarette taxes would raise $10 billion to $15 billion. A tax on guns wouldn't raise even $1 billion.

Only some kind of consumption or Value-Added Tax (a form of national sales tax) could bring in $60 billion to $80 billion. Although a VAT would encourage investment, it would fall hardest on low- and middle-income people. It would make policy sense in many ways but would be politically explosive. Clinton had already rejected a national sales tax in his economic plan, and various White House officials had asserted publicly that it would not be proposed. But it was mentioned in various internal documents, and in recent days both Alice Rivlin and Donna Shalala had suggested publicly that it was under consideration.

Throughout the discussion, the president seemed uncomfortable, and Gore seemed positively ill.

That same day, Stephanopoulos had to put the best public face on the contradictions. "I'm acknowledging that the task force has studied this proposal," Stephanopoulos told reporters. "I am also stating that the president has not made a decision on it."

HILLARY WAS IMMERSING HERSELF in health care and spending a good deal of time briefing members of Congress on Capitol Hill. Prior to one gathering with 50 senators from both parties later in the month, two of her staff members noted that the senators were likely to ask about costs. "I don't care how they do things here," Hillary said defiantly. "If they can't take the truth, at least they're going to get it from me."

In the meeting when the question of cost arose, Hillary casually tossed out the $100 billion figure. Senator Jay Rockefeller, a close administration ally on health care reform, dropped his jaw. If they were planning to spend $100 billion, a large new unpopular tax would be unavoidable. After the meeting, Rockefeller had to be sent out to clean up the damage.

One of Hillary's staffers took her aside and expressed concern about using the $100 billion number. "That's the truth, and they'd better get used to it," Hillary replied.

A number of staffers noticed an increasing self-righteousness in Hillary. She acted as if she had seen the light. There was a new, deeply anti-Washington flavor in her tone. Hillary expressed her views in the White House. "I believe in evil and I think that there are evil people in the world," she said. But Washington especially, she believed, brought out in people a need to act out of self-interest. The culture of the city led people to lose sight of what was important, the larger values in life, and focus on petty personal and political concerns. The social clawing was particularly ugly. One prominent woman told the First Lady, "What you don't understand about this town is that they can fight about issues all they want, but they don't really care about them. What they really care about is who they sit next to at dinner." Hillary claimed that she had been shocked.

CLINTON MEANWHILE CONTINUED to act as if his investment programs had suffered nothing less than a sneak attack. Panetta wanted to deal constructively with Clinton's frustration and presented the president with three options.

One was to try to get the House to change the caps. But, he explained, the politics of the House and Senate had just shown that it couldn't be done. Even Sperling and Reich realized this. It would kill the administration and undermine all their credibility. They might as well put a "Big-Spending Liberal" sign on Clinton's forehead.

Second, they could try to find more money from other parts of the budget, such as defense. But the defense number was locked in, and any other maneuver would be a gimmick, which they had pledged to avoid. To try something that might look underhanded would also unnecessarily risk their credibility.

Third, they could face the hard truth that if they wanted more investments they would have to find offsetting spending cuts in other programs. Once again Clinton had no attractive choice.

A few days later, the National Economic Council met to pursue the third option of finding more spending cuts. Panetta, Sperling, and a representative from Treasury had drawn up a list of ideas. There was some discussion that the initial investment plan was unrealistic. Starting up their new programs would take a while, and they would not suddenly be able to spend large sums of money in 1994 and 1995. Panetta said they could nonetheless do better than $1 billion for the first year. They should identify the most important investment programs, he said, and begin discussions with the Senate and House Appropriations committees to get money from other programs.

Panetta and Sperling formed an informal subcommittee to identify their top priorities. But Clinton had too many favorite projects, and they couldn't whittle the list down to fewer than 33 items for the first year. Panetta said they wouldn't get all of them. So that night, Sperling returned to the office, knowing they had to go further. He chopped the list down to 20 items; he and Panetta then estimated the total cost would be about $3.5 billion. They sent the list to Clinton.

Clinton returned it, saying they should make sure not to cut any corners on three programs: the 1990 Ryan White Act for funding AIDS treatment, Head Start pre-school education, and his proposal to put 100,000 more policemen on the streets. Clinton and his administration had once again settled into a state of lessened expectations.

THE PLIGHT of the stimulus package was almost a national embarrassment. Dole was getting more and more coverage as a giant-killer. In an effort to rescue it, Howard Paster made a new run at the moderate Senate Republicans. He visited Mark Hatfield of Oregon in his office, then Ted Stevens of Alaska; he called Minnesota's Dave Durenberger and Missouri's John Danforth. Several others were tracked down by phone. Senator James M. Jeffords of Vermont intimated to Paster that he might break ranks if Paster could find at least one other Senate Republican to join in the defection, but Paster failed. The recess, supposedly the only respite from the mind-numbing series of personal sales calls, turned out to be no recess at all.

Gore, McLarty, Bentsen, Panetta, and Stephanopoulos had all urged compromise at various points, but Byrd was dug in. "This is important to the president," Byrd claimed to Breaux. "This is what he's asked for. And we can't compromise."

Paster agreed. "You can't screw the House," Paster insisted to Clinton, noting that the House Democrats had dutifully marched in lockstep and passed the stimulus, in some cases based on commitments from the White House that Clinton wouldn't abandon any part of the package. "Those guys are out on a larger limb, and you'll pay forever with these people if they think you screwed them. You can't sell out people whose trust you'll need."

"I don't know this place," Clinton told his staff. Byrd presumably did. "He's been around here almost as long as I've been alive," Clinton added. "How do I not go with him?"

On Monday, April 19, when the Senate reconvened, Dole still held all the 43 Republicans, who showed no signs of splintering. The filibuster continued unabated.

CLINTON'S MOUNTING POLITICAL EMBARRASSMENTS demonstrated that the quick-response team from the campaign was needed and gave the outside consultants a new lease on life. Stan Greenberg wrote a draft of a long memo to Clinton and reviewed it with Carville, Begala, and Grunwald. Dated April 20, the memo said for the first time that the four consultants believed that Clinton's presidency was off the tracks in a fundamental way. The president had failed to communicate both the central values of his presidency and an organizing idea for his economic program. Side issues such as gays in the military were still getting in the way, resulting in caricatures of Clinton and the new administration. If the stimulus package failed, the memo warned, the president would be blamed for gridlock. It recommended that Clinton return to *Putting People First* and recreate the vision of jobs, work, and responsibility.

At 10 A.M. on April 20, the four consultants came to the Oval Office to meet with Clinton, McLarty, and Stephanopoulos. The president was agitated, not just about his situation but about the memo. McLarty said that he had talked with all the former chiefs of staff to Democratic and Republican presidents. Don't worry, they had all said. There was no way for a new administration to be prepared. The first months were always bumpy.

One by one, the consultants gave their analyses, which mirrored much of the television and newspaper pundit talk. It got down to one word: focus, the celebrated campaign success. The goals and priorities of his administration and economic plan simply were not clear.

"I know what's *wrong!*" Clinton finally screamed. "Give me a strategy!" The rhetoric and analysis were of no use to him, he said. He needed a plan of action. What immediate steps should he take? One, two, three.

Begala thought that Clinton was like a boxer in the ring throwing wild punches. Exhausted and enraged, he couldn't land a solid blow. They might have to pull him out of the ring.

The consultants continued talking about abstract themes, communications, values and ideas.

"I know that," the president snapped several times at their comments. "That's all I get is analysis. I never get a strategy. I never get a plan," Clinton complained. He wanted something right away, something concrete.

The consultants went to work and drafted a second memo with the same date. As an immediate matter, they recommended that Stephanopoulos be transferred from communications director to head a political policy group, and be given the title of deputy chief of staff. Currently, Stephanopoulos had three jobs, they noted: principal policy adviser to Clinton; principal spokesman; and manager of 60 people in the communications shop. They suggested that Mark Gearan, the deputy chief of staff, take over as communications director.

Clinton also had to bail out on the stimulus package at once, they said. The package at one point might have seemed like a sensible cushion and insurance policy, but now it was evident that its size was trifling and it had little to do with the president's larger values or ideas. The stimulus package was now dangerous for the president. He had almost come to the point of hollering, my kingdom for a stimulus package. At a minimum, he had to get the episode behind him. The longer it dragged on, the worse he looked.

Clinton decided to wait on the recommendation on Stephanopoulos, but to move on the stimulus package. That meant first resolving a serious disagreement between Mitchell and Byrd. Mitchell, who had to try to run the Senate for the long year ahead, wanted a quick resolution on the stimulus. If the stimulus had to be sacrificed to get on with Clinton's agenda, so be it.

Byrd preferred going all the way. Keep the Senate in session around the clock, he advised. Let's have an old-fashioned filibuster. He was going to fight. Bring in the cots to the Senate floor and put the Republicans' feet to the fire. At one point in a burst of enthusiasm, the 75-year-old senator was so confident of success he gave Paster a high-five.

Paster felt like he was running a shuttle diplomacy between Byrd's office on the first floor of the Capitol and Mitchell's on the second.

Byrd wouldn't compromise, saying it would be wrong. No one would tell him what to do with his committee, the chairman protested. He would not take the word of either Mitchell or Paster about Clinton's decision. He insisted that Clinton phone with his personal assurance that he wanted to abandon the fight. Clinton did so.

The next day, April 21, Clinton threw in the towel publicly. "I'm very disappointed about this," Clinton said to reporters. "And frankly, a little surprised about it. It doesn't make a lot of sense. A lot of the Republican senators told me they wanted to work something out, and I went out of my way to meet them halfway, and then some." Clinton vowed to regroup and come forward with a new bill. The Senate quickly passed the $4 billion in extended unemployment compensation that had been part of the stimulus package, and the House followed, but any real stimulus was dead. At 70 years old, Dole was hailed in Washington as the heavy among Republican presidential contenders for 1996.

IF THE DEFEAT was not enough, Greenberg reported to Clinton some distressing poll data. First, the defeat of the stimulus package had set off a sharp decline in Clinton's approval ratings, Greenberg said. Second, the prevailing wisdom that Clinton had been tainted by fighting for a pork bill wasn't quite accurate. It was worse. Greenberg's research showed that many people were under the impression that Clinton's entire economic plan had been defeated or was headed for defeat. The death of the stimulus meant to people that gridlock still reigned supreme in Washington, that Clinton was not strong enough to overcome the forces blocking change. Overall, Greenberg reported, he found a sharp rise among people feeling the country was on the wrong track. The mood of the country had turned bleak, its sense of hopefulness abated. People had lost a sense of possibility, he explained.

Hillary thought the stimulus was important to get some action going so people could see immediate results, a visible milestone in the journey.

But the White House had failed to prepare adequately or explain its importance. She was still astonished at the different environment in Washington, the slower pace of Congress, the president's lack of control over it. In Little Rock, she had been used to 60-day or 90-day regular legislative sessions in which Clinton was able to bring up a whole agenda. As governor, Clinton had had an office in the Capitol Building and had served as his own floor manager, staying up late and directing every step.

Clinton realized that the stakes had been enormous on something that was in fact very small. It was too small to make an all-out plea on national television, to argue to the country that the economy would crash if he didn't have this $16 billion bill. He had been hamstrung because the scale had been so small.

Later, Clinton unleashed his fury. "I'm never going to be so vulnerable again," he asserted. "That bill had too much pork in it," he said. "It was designed to ring the bell of every committee chairman." Rostenkowski wanted this, another chairman wanted that, and he had granted it instead of offering a real investment package.

"Damnit," he said, "I'll have to do it myself now." He said he would never let the stray forces of Washington dictate his course of action. "It's not enough to be advised," Clinton said. At one point, Clinton even blamed Panetta, saying the budget director seemed too worried about standing by his former House colleagues who had approved the full stimulus package.

IN AN ON-THE-RECORD MEETING with a small group of reporters the next Monday, April 26, Panetta let fly with his frustrations and his pessimism. The administration's economic proposals were in deep trouble, Panetta said. He was urging a delay in the health care proposals and said that the proposed North American Free Trade Agreement was "dead." "The optimism that came out of the November election and the Christmas shopping," Panetta said, amounted to only a "shadow recovery. . . . I sense that confidence has diminished somewhat. I think there's a weakness out there." His remarks were the kind of gloomy, introspective, but honest assessments that ran totally counter to all the happy talk that politicians normally expressed.

The Washington Post ran Panetta's remarks as the main story on page one under the headline: "Panetta: President in Trouble on Hill; Agenda at Risk, Trade Pact 'Dead.' " The story created a momentary furor.

Panetta apologized abjectly to Clinton. He said he was down. "I said those things. I thought they were off the record. I'm sorry," he told the president.

"You're Italian, you're Catholic, I understand," Clinton replied after Panetta's confession. "But you know, you got to stay up." The president was not all that upset with his budget director's public remarks. They were not all that different from some of his own private remarks. What Clinton hated much more were anonymous leaks from inside criticizing the White House or him. Clinton naturally identified with screw-ups, having endured his own share. He was drawn to suffering, and clearly Panetta was hurting. A joke among Clinton's aides was that it was better to fuck up really big rather than have a series of daily minor mistakes, since Clinton identified with the celebrated, all-points fuck-up.

The next afternoon in a Rose Garden ceremony honoring the national collegiate basketball champions, Clinton was asked about Panetta. "I just think he's been working 60 to 70 hours a week, and he got discouraged," Clinton said. "He's done a wonderful job for this administration. He's got a lot of credibility. . . . He had a bad day yesterday because he got his spirits down. I want to buck him up."

Begala saw Panetta later. "Leon, I was in Europe and saw your picture all over the front pages," Begala said. "The stories were in German or French and I couldn't understand them. I thought you were dead. But then I read it was worse: You were attacking the president." Panetta laughed.

For Begala, the Poster Boy for Economic Constipation was acting in defiance of all sound tenets of political warfare: Define and create the reality you want. Panetta instead was creating a bleak reality of despair, which was precisely what they didn't want.

THAT EVENING, April 27, the Clintons invited Pat Moynihan and his wife Elizabeth to the White House for a private dinner. Moynihan was not happy with the overall economic plan, and felt he had not been consulted enough about it. In effect, the White House had just handed it to the House and Senate, saying, here, pass this.

Moynihan wanted to introduce Clinton to sensitive real-world politics. For example, there was one item in the economic plan that would have to be dropped, a proposal to eliminate the tax subsidy for U.S. corporations doing business in Puerto Rico. Known by its title, section 936, the subsidy was, Moynihan granted, of course, indefensible. One company received a tax break of about $500,000 per worker. Some pharmaceutical firms got $150,000 per worker.

But that wasn't the point. Moynihan painted a doomsday scenario of what would happen if the tax credit were dropped. First, American firms would pull out of Puerto Rico, causing the unemployment rate to double to about 30 percent and creating an economic crisis. A political crisis would follow. Puerto Rico faced an upcoming plebiscite on statehood, and if the tax break were eliminated, the politicians could argue that it never would have happened if the territory had two U.S. senators. Statehood would then pass the plebiscite, Puerto Rico would apply for statehood, and Congress would of course reject the application. In all, it would be a political nightmare. How would the United States look in the world? So the tax, which would save some $5 billion over four years, just couldn't be done, Moynihan said. He could never let such a proposal out of the Finance Committee—for reasons, he noted, that couldn't be explained publicly.

Clinton promised to consider the point.

The president broached other topics. Who might we have problems with on the Finance Committee? he asked.

David Boren, Moynihan said.

"Oh, no," Clinton said. "He has said to me that he would *never* be the cause of the defeat of my plan. And he said that he's for it, in fact." Clinton was sure that Boren's problems ended with the stimulus package.

"I don't think you can depend on that," Moynihan said.

21

THURSDAY, APRIL 29, was Clinton's 100th day in office, a symbolic day for presidents since FDR. Clinton had repeatedly held out the day as a benchmark for accomplishing many of his goals. At a senior staff meeting, McLarty brought a *Wall Street Journal* poll and its accompanying analysis. Clinton's approval rating was at 55 percent, the lowest in recent times of any elected president on his 100th day. Kennedy had had 83 percent approval, Carter 63 percent, Reagan 68 percent. Only Bush had a similar rating of 55 percent after his first 100 days.

McLarty read from the analysis, headlined: "Clinton Zigzags Between Politics and Policy." Reagan, McLarty read, "focused on delivering a basic message to voters and left the policy details to others." Reagan just articulated principles. McLarty said that every little compromise or setback in the congressional process was being interpreted as a personal loss for Clinton because he was seen directing the details. They needed to move him to a broader message.

McLarty continued conferring with Boren. As a matter of legislative position, Boren maintained that the president needed to be a centrist and seek bipartisan support. "Otherwise, he's the prisoner of the left," Boren said. Boren reviewed the mathematics of the situation. In the House of Representatives, Clinton could afford to lose the 30 or so conservative Democrats. He would still prevail without a single House Republican if he yielded to the wishes of the 65 or so left-leaning Democrats and the Black Caucus. That meant as long as he pursued a Democrats-only strategy, Clinton was beholden to the left. By reaching out to moderate Republicans, he could move to the bipartisanship center, where he belonged and where he would be stronger, in Boren's view.

Boren told McLarty that he and several other Democrats had been meeting with five moderate Republican senators. They were hoping to devise an alternative or modification of Clinton's economic plan that could attract centrist support. Involving moderate Republicans in the Senate would help win over moderate Republicans in the House, Boren reasoned.

"That's good to explore," McLarty said. "Except, of course, we can't sign on board. We can't say we're blessing it, but I hear you. I understand it." The chief of staff cautiously gave a green light. "Just see how it works out. Maybe something will happen."

On Wednesday, May 5, Clinton called a strategy session in the Roosevelt Room. They had to regroup to ensure passage of the final economic plan by the House the next month. In attendance were Hillary, Gore, his wife Tipper Gore, McLarty, Stephanopoulos, Begala, several other communications staffers, and Carville, who was coming by only about once a month now. None of the senior members of the economic team were present—no Bentsen, no Rubin, no Panetta, no Tyson.

Clinton complained that the spending-cut war with Congress was out of hand. He was again pounding his right thigh for emphasis. "These people, these bastards," the president said, "are trying to take all our investments."

Carville took the floor, tuned up to issue a dose of supercharged populism. The administration had lost the edge on the economic issue. "Mr. President," he said, "you've got to get outside of Washington thinking." Carville believed that nothing was harder in political strategy than to think as you didn't think naturally.

Clinton began to take notes furiously.

The war was not about spending cuts or deficit reduction, Carville explained, his voice rushing with his confident, back-home Southern rhythm. "You've got to get to the big things and the big ideas. Washington is about getting small things. The whole culture is built around this idea of the old. In Washington, the Democrats say, we'll give you a fish. The Republicans say, we'll take your fish and give it to the rich."

There was appreciative laughter.

"What we are going to do is teach fishing to people," Carville continued. "We're going to empower people." He reviewed the campaign litany—health care reform, even the Bentsen-rejected welfare reform, the middle class, the much-reduced investments, the things for working people.

"The $16 billion stimulus package," Carville reminisced tartly, his Southern accent rippling half in condolence, half in humor. "The $12 billion for people who work and $4 billion for those who do not. What does Washington do with it?" He paused, resting for a dramatic conclusion. "They pass the $4 billion for people who don't work."

The president continued to write it all down. His notetaking gave the words extra weight.

Carville preached against the inside-Washington game of minutiae and process, negotiating with Boren and Dole. "Change versus more of the same," he reminded them.

The president, however, could not suddenly drop the inside game. They were already committed.

HOWARD PASTER URGED that the president meet with Democrats on the Senate Finance Committee in person to begin the committee's home-stretch on the economic plan. At 6:15 P.M. on Thursday, May 6, all 11 Democrats on the Senate Finance Committee gathered with Clinton in the Cabinet Room of the White House. With 11 Democrats and 9 Republicans on the committee, a single Democratic defection would mean a 10-to-10 deadlock. Clinton's plan was hostage to any Democrat on the committee. Each of them, for all practical purposes, held a veto.

Moynihan saw the meeting as an opportunity for Clinton to understand that he lacked 11 solid votes, to see up close the potential fickleness of Democratic Party solidarity in the U.S. Senate. The important issue was to pass a budget of some form that could be called Clinton's plan. Although some of it was miserable and awful, Moynihan felt, details were almost irrelevant. Failure would mean the report would go out: The United States again doesn't have a government, another failed presidency.

At the beginning of the meeting, Moynihan reminded the group that Senator Bob Packwood, the senior Republican on the Finance Committee, had candidly and convincingly told Moynihan that Clinton would get none of the nine Republicans on the committee to vote for the plan. So Moynihan pointed out the obvious and vital importance of holding all 11 Democrats. "Eleven votes in the Senate Finance Committee and the presidency will be a success," he said directly. "His presidency will begin once we finish this bill." They were all Democrats, and the purpose of this meeting was to show their cards, not to shield any problems they had, he indicated.

Senator Kent Conrad of North Dakota, the junior member of the committee and his state's former tax commissioner, spoke long and vociferously, making it clear he was almost off the reservation. Nearly 25 percent of North Dakota's population lived on farms or ranches—the highest percentage in the nation—and the proposed BTU tax would be onerous to farmers in his state, he said. If these agricultural interests could not be satisfied, he said he might have to vote against the plan. Winding up in a rhetorical flourish more suitable for Fargo, North Dakota, than the White House, Conrad said, "I won't cut the throats of my people!"

Many eyes turned to Clinton. This was the president's meeting in the president's house. It was a close-quarters presidential moment. The junior member of the Senate committee was challenging his bill. Moynihan and others were looking for Clinton to manage the situation with force, clarity, and warmth. Surely Clinton would find a way to say, in effect, Please don't talk that way but we can work this out.

The suspense lasted a few more seconds.

"Uh-huh," Clinton responded neutrally, and turned to the next senator to speak. "Jay, what do you think?"

Senator Jay Rockefeller gave a long, impassioned speech saying that the Democrats had to stick together. Now Democrats had the chance to show they could govern. They could not split apart. One or two senators who had problems shouldn't lock up the entire process, he said.

"Now, Jay, let's remember," said George Mitchell, the majority leader and a committee member, recalling Rockefeller's efforts to hold up another piece of legislation because of coal interests in West Virginia. Mitchell was trying to stop short any choosing up of sides between Clinton loyalists and defectors, gently pointing out that no one held the high moral ground. While they all had their own interests, those interests didn't have to present obstacles to cooperation.

From his seat at the table, John Breaux felt that too few of them were being frank with Clinton. They were falling into a trap, the natural tendency to say what they thought the president wanted to hear. Breaux spoke up and voiced reservations, especially about the BTU tax. It was a bad idea whose time has not come, he said, calling it downright "goofy" and unworkably complicated. He said he would prefer some other tax.

"The last thing I want to do is to be somebody that causes you not to pass the bill," Boren said. But the doubts of a few—Conrad, Breaux, himself—were real. The plan didn't contain enough spending cuts, not enough on entitlements. And the BTU tax was terrible, he said.

Wait, Moynihan said, hadn't Boren said he was unconditionally for the package?

Well, Boren replied, shifting ground, he had been unconditionally for the president's speech, but the package was not quite what they were promised in the speech.

Moynihan grew angry. His power and influence were being tested. He knew his doubters in Washington considered him a great debater and seminar leader, but said he wouldn't be able to play hardball well enough to control his committee. They were going to have Senator Boren's vote, Moynihan asserted. He knew they would—no matter what—before it was all over.

Discussion turned to 1982, when the Republicans were the majority in the Senate. The Republicans on the Finance Committee employed a so-called unit rule, meaning they would caucus in private and even if an issue was decided by a single vote among them, they would all come back and vote a straight party line in the full committee, overwhelming the Democrats, then in a minority.

Mitchell said that the Republicans operated that way because they were cohesive and disciplined, but he didn't think it possible that Democrats ever could. "Although," he added in judicious understatement, "it would be nice if once in a while we could agree." Even if Democrats were too independent for rigid, formal unit rule, he said, surely they could work together informally. Mitchell carefully was not asking that they deliberately exclude all Republicans, though he didn't imagine any would join them.

Gore went a step further. With his earnest, determined body language, he tightened up, and asked that they promise not to work with the Republicans on amendments or talk to Republicans about the bill. They should work and talk only with Democrats. The moment was confusing. To some it even seemed that Gore was asking for a show of hands for those willing to take the pledge. Others thought he was not that emphatic.

Some hands almost went up. Boren did not raise his. Clinton and McLarty knew Boren was already working with Republicans.

Wait a minute, Boren said, growing panicky. His seat was on the same side of the table as Clinton's and he pushed his chair back so the two could see each other. "I want to raise my hand on the contrary proposition. I will work with Republicans on this as hard as I possibly can to get a bipartisan consensus and to get some Republican votes on the Finance Committee to pass this package because I think bipartisanship's imperative."

Gore laid down a challenge. If Boren couldn't promise to be for the bill, then surely he could at least promise not to embrace the Republicans openly. "Can we all agree that we're going to work it out together?" Gore asked.

Boren wouldn't.

"Eleven votes, Mr. President," Moynihan repeated, poking his finger on the table for emphasis. "Eleven votes right here, Mr. President. People here know that 11 votes and your presidency is secured. And of course we will get those 11 votes, because, Mr. President, this is your presidency on the line. If you get this, you are a strong president. If this fails, you are a weak president."

Clinton said little. Moynihan could see that the president was beginning to realize that his private little understanding with Boren was not necessarily in place. Moynihan turned to Clinton, and repeated his mantra, Eleven votes. He hoped the indirect communication had been received: You, Mr. President, have to tackle this, you have to realize you don't have those 11 votes.

Clinton just nodded.

Boren took Paster aside after the meeting and said the rumors he was trying to get Paster fired were not true. Every journalist who had called him to inquire, he had set straight.

Paster felt that Boren was protesting too much.

After the meeting, Moynihan felt pretty good. Conrad could be appeased with some $1 billion in agricultural exceptions on the BTU tax that would hold his vote. Breaux's statements, though strong, seemed framed in a positive enough way, and Breaux, who had leadership ambitions, was not likely to break with Clinton, a longtime friend. Boren was another matter. He might bolt. But his opposition seemed soft. Boren had not spoken the language that every committee chairman understood; Boren had not said, "I can't have this," or, "I have to have that."

Lawrence O'Donnell, the staff director of Moynihan's Finance Committee, wanted to make sure that the Democratic senators understood the implications of their votes. At a meeting of the key staffers to each of the committee senators, he said if the plan passed, "you will find out what it is to have a chairman who is your best friend for eight years." If the plan failed, he said, "you'll find out what it's like to have his undying bitterness."

SENATOR BILL BRADLEY had sat through the meeting and not said much other than to voice support. He had heard that Boren had been trying to secure a personal meeting with Clinton just before the Finance Committee session so he could walk in with the president. At least Clinton had been astute enough to avoid that. Bradley was going to vote for

Clinton's plan even though he was disappointed with it. The plan was a nest of contradictions: deficit reduction but more spending for investments; cutting some spending but increasing spending elsewhere for political reasons; raising tax rates but not closing tax loopholes. The biggest disappointment, though, was that it brought deficit reduction but not change. Clinton was not changing the way business was done. It should have been bolder, a plan designed to transform the debate from business as usual to a higher plane, some larger purpose. Clinton should have tried to force a change in the way people thought about public spending, reduce the transfers from one person to another in the entitlement programs, shed some of the baggage. Clinton should have forced a choice, made it the vote of a legislator's lifetime. But this didn't come close.

Mitchell told Clinton that no matter what he did, he would be criticized. If the president took an inflexible position and refused to negotiate, as President Carter had on several occasions, he would be attacked for not knowing the ways of Capitol Hill or having the experience to win. If on the other hand, Mitchell said, Clinton participated and made the necessary compromises to get the plan approved, he would be attacked for being too willing to give. "You cannot escape criticism in this process," the majority leader said. Mitchell remembered that in response, Clinton didn't say anything.

TWO DAYS LATER, in his regular Saturday-morning radio address, May 8, Clinton unleashed 17 paragraphs of what Carville and Begala saw as the old Clinton. He began on the theme of "struggle" and his efforts to create "more jobs and better incomes and opportunity for hard-pressed working families." He spoke of "special interests" blocking his effort for new investments in education and training. He said he wanted health care reform, and student loans that would "make it possible for every young person to go to college."

He returned to the populist rhetoric, saying that "banks and their allies are out in force since they make enormous profits from the current student loan system" and were opposing his plan. He lashed out at "big money and the special access it buys."

AFTER A WHITE HOUSE CEREMONY on May 7 to introduce the administration's campaign finance reform bill, Boren had told both Clinton and Gore in brief, separate conversations that in the final analysis they shouldn't worry too much about his playing footsie with the Republicans. Gore considered it a commitment that Boren would be with them in the end.

But Boren wanted to explain to the president directly the reasons for his distress, and pressed McLarty to arrange a longer meeting with the president. Early the next week, McLarty called Boren at about 5 o'clock. A meeting had been set for 5:30, he said.

Boren raced down to the White House. He entered the Oval Office, where Clinton was sitting in his high-backed armchair by the fireplace. Boren took the adjacent armchair. McLarty sat on the first seat of the sofa.

There had been a misunderstanding on the stimulus package, Boren began, and he didn't want to have another disaster. He said he wanted to walk the president through his thinking. "I'm saying this as a friend," Boren said, claiming that he felt his own reaction mirrored that of the public.

Boren said he had been euphoric about the president's February 17 speech, unconditionally supportive of it, perhaps even, some would say in retrospect, foolishly optimistic about it. But so had been the American people. Someone disappointed was angrier than someone who never believed in you, Boren said, and people were now disappointed by Clinton and turning cynical. Clinton deserved tremendous credit for preparing them for the right proposals—he just hadn't delivered those proposals. The stimulus package, Boren said, made them feel like they'd been had because of the pork spending.

Clinton didn't disagree. He said he understood Boren's reading.

Boren continued his lecture. Clinton couldn't afford to lock himself into something in the House that couldn't pass the Senate, where he would need bipartisan support. Clinton could only be reelected, he said, as a centrist Democrat. That, he added, was for the good of the Democratic Party and for the good of the country. Right now, however, Clinton was failing with the people and was fighting with those who had been his philosophical soulmates.

Clinton listened cordially, sitting passively, agreeably, seeming to reflect on the analysis.

Boren said he didn't want to make Clinton feel bad, but that's what people were saying.

No, the president replied, he wanted to hear.

Boren said he was working with Senator Danforth, some other Republicans, and some Democrats. Their goal was to come up with an alternative bipartisan plan and present it publicly.

"If you could help get bipartisan support for my plan," Clinton said, "if you could help make my plan into a bipartisan proposal, it'd be the best thing you could do for my presidency."

McLarty almost sprung off the sofa. "Now, David—" he interjected. He wanted to clarify Clinton's remarks. "I don't think, Mr. President, you meant to be saying to him you're going to endorse his plan. I don't want him to misunderstand."

"No, no, no," Boren said. "I understand the president's not endorsing my plan."

"No, no," Clinton added. He could not offer an endorsement sight unseen.

Boren said he was going to hit entitlements harder, since they were the real budget problem. He didn't want to wait for a health care proposal. Clinton would never have more leverage, Boren said, than right then, when he was asking for all these taxes. Boren also said they had to do away with the BTU tax.

Boren proposed that his alternate plan be a trial balloon. All he was asking, he said, was that the White House not shoot it down, that they let it rise or fall on its own. He said he hoped they would welcome it, because it represented the first bipartisan initiative. Even if it contained details they couldn't accept, at least it would be a starting point. Boren said he would send them the specifics once he had them in writing.

Boren left feeling optimistic. He expected the next step would be for Clinton to invite Democrats and Republicans to join in bipartisan talks. When Boren arrived home, his wife Molly noted that he was in a wonderful mood. "I'm the happiest I've ever been," Boren replied. "The president and I are on the same track. We're thinking just alike on this. He really understood everything I said. He understands why we've got to have bipartisanship. He sees the mistakes of the stimulus package."

STEPHANOPOULOS KNEW that it was a mistake to assume that any one moment with Clinton, any one conversation, day, or even week reflected Clinton's true feelings or unchanging fundamental attitude about something. With any single audience or person, Clinton was generally consistent and had mastered his rap. But he could articulate a totally different, even contradictory rap to the next audience with genuine sincerity.

Clinton was more than capable of seeing and feeling different things at different times. This was the intellectual, ruminative side of his personality. Stephanopoulos realized that in making decisions, a range of arguments should be presented forcefully so the boss could reflect and change his mind. But given Clinton's predisposition for deliberation, his inclination to listen sympathetically—at times too sympathetically—Stephanopoulos questioned whether they did this too much. Clinton would push debate to the point of chaos. The process seemed confused. Stephanopoulos concluded that the staff had to stifle this tendency, so cleaner, clearer, faster decisions would be made.

"You've got to always keep in mind," Stephanopoulos said to one of his closest associates, that watching Clinton "is like a kaleidoscope. What you see is where you stand and where you're looking at him. He will put one facet toward you, but that is only one facet." Every time, the kaleidoscope would reflect the fragment of stone at the bottom in a unique way, showing a different facet; every person would see a different pattern. It was real, but it could change in an instant, as soon as Clinton turned.

ONE CONCRETE RESULT of the discussions with the consultants was Clinton's decision to get out of Washington. He would go to the real world. On May 10, he traveled to Cleveland. Begala went along. It was like a campaign, with people cheering, overjoyed to see their president. "I'm trying to govern in a bipartisan way," Clinton claimed, even though he was seeming increasingly committed to a Democrats-only strategy.

That night Begala faced off against Republican media consultant Roger Ailes on Ted Koppel's "Nightline" television show. "Basically, Bill Clinton got elected saying he wanted to go to Washington and fix things," Ailes said. "He's been there two months and now he doesn't want to be in Washington."

"Bill Clinton's strength is his outside game," Begala replied. "He's always going to be someone who's better with the American people than he is with the Beltway politicians and pundits."

"The translation of that is," Ailes responded, "you heard one of his top advisers say he's lousy at governing, but very good at campaigning."

Back at the White House, Hillary greeted Begala enthusiastically. "My hero!" she declared, delighted they were again fighting.

On May 12, to counter the charges that the new taxes would be spent and not go to deficit reduction, Clinton announced his support for a "deficit reduction trust fund." All the money raised in his plan from tax increases and spending cuts would go into a special pool, devoted to deficit reduction. Although no more than a bookkeeping and labeling issue, the move was intended to reassure taxpayers that the saved money would not simply be spent on something else. But Alice Rivlin said to the *Wall Street Journal* that the trust fund would have no real effect and was essentially just public relations. "It's a display device," she said.

Begala, who was closely monitoring the media coverage, called McLarty when he read Rivlin's remark. "You've got to fire her," Begala demanded. "If this isn't disloyalty, what is?"

McLarty said that he too was upset. Panetta had just been in his office to discuss Rivlin's remarks. "I told him to go get a life raft, you're in deep water," McLarty said. But he added that it would be counterproductive to fire Rivlin, the fiercest of deficit hawks. It would only make her a martyr and call into question the president's commitment to deficit reduction.

22

LATE ONE AFTERNOON in the middle of May, about 5 P.M., ten consultants and White House staffers convened for a meeting on political scheduling. They gathered in the Ward Room, a private, windowless room with a standard-issue rectangular table, located just off the White House mess. They were mostly the young people who knew each other well from the close-quarters trench warfare of the campaign. The discussion quickly turned to the question of the day: Had Clinton betrayed the principles of his presidential campaign?

Mandy Grunwald, sounding the consultants' theme, argued that Clinton was coming dangerously close to the point of betrayal. The emphasis on deficit reduction was way out of hand, she said. The public no longer identified Clinton's plan with his campaign themes.

Sperling had for months believed the same thing, but lately he was changing his view. He explained the need for the shift. The representatives and senators, he said, had liked the deficit reduction message and felt they could take it home to their constituents. Many, particularly in the House, felt abandoned on the stimulus package, and now relations with Congress were obviously tenuous. The members had to be satisfied.

The president, Grunwald replied, had to be able to pivot away from the legislative fight and address his broader message to real people. He couldn't just focus on getting the economic plan passed. There was much more than that to the Clinton administration, she added dryly.

"Excuse me?" Sperling interrupted. "That was the most unbelievable thing I've ever heard."

The Clinton presidency was not about deficit reduction, Grunwald said angrily.

"Mandy, it's me," Sperling replied, feeling she had forgotten his dedication to the investments and other campaign centerpieces. "I am the one who fought, who almost risked my credibility fighting so hard for investments in there," he said, almost sputtering as he gestured toward the Roosevelt Room. "If I thought there was any other way—nobody cares more about investments than I do."

"I'm not so sure anymore," Grunwald snapped.

Sperling felt he had been kicked hard. For a moment he wanted to cry. He was awash in self-pity. Working 16 to 20 hours a day, he had taken on Bentsen in front of the president and had for days left the Roosevelt Room meetings wondering, Am I ruined forever? Now Grunwald was hitting him from the other side, questioning his loyalty to Clinton's philosophy. His voice about to crack, Sperling replied, "There's nothing I care more about. But I want him to succeed. We have got to pass this package for us to have any strength to do anything good. We just cannot do anything good if we don't pass this package. And we've got to focus on that." Sperling said he didn't want to be making this argument. But it was imperative they gain and hold congressional support.

Grunwald argued that the biggest impact on Congress would come from constituents fired up by the president's rhetoric. What Clinton said to the public, she reasserted, would bounce back to Congress. Sperling was being captured by the insularity of the legislative process. "At the end, your friends are no longer at the table," she said. "You're dealing with the last intransigent conservatives in talking about what they want." Clinton's populism was being drowned out and they had to start reviving it right away. They couldn't waste another day, she said.

Sperling said he feared they could wind up with nothing. The selling of the plan needed clarity and focus. A beautiful speech that stressed everything was like birdshot. Only one message came through on the evening news, and if the message was new investment spending one time and deficit reduction the next, it was a wash—and the Republicans had a free swing to pound Clinton on taxes.

They had only several weeks to save the plan, Sperling reminded Grunwald and the others. If they could convince people the deficit reduction was tough, they could buy credibility. Credibility could push the package through. They were fighting for their lives, he said.

Grunwald was furious. Clinton was off-message, she insisted. Soon she was shouting and Sperling was shouting back.

Immediately after the meeting, Stephanopoulos heard about the fight. "You have got to be nice to Gene," Stephanopoulos told the consultants. They were treating him unfairly, cruelly. Their arguments might be sound, but campaign purity was irrelevant. This was now about winning and passing the economic plan.

Grunwald later said that Sperling's body had been snatched by the Washington insiders and the deficit hawks. "Gene has become a pod person," she said, referring to the movie *Invasion of the Body Snatchers,* in which people abducted by aliens inhabit large pods. Grunwald felt that outside, hostile forces were stalking the halls of Clinton's White House.

Begala then had a session with Sperling. "Look," Begala said, "all this shit about reducing the deficit through your taxes. It's just not our plan. It shouldn't be. What's happened?"

"I realize it is not the best of worlds," Sperling answered. "It is not even the second-best world. We are operating in the third-best world." Frankly, he added, they had to hope the lower interest rates would keep the economy from stalling out.

Begala repeated his old argument that deficit reduction could not be sold as an end in itself.

"This is what we're left with," Sperling said. "We've got to get something through the Congress." The difference between ends and means had dissipated.

Begala felt fatalistic. There was no way to pretend, not in detail, not in spirit, that the plan before Congress was the *Putting People First* plan. It was a lie, Begala was saying. Carville agreed with him.

Sperling regarded Carville and Begala as mentors. But in this case he felt they had lost sight of the fundamentals. Their most valuable contribution to the campaign had not been the populist themes, he felt, but the realization that messages had to be simple, clear notions that voters could grasp. With only several weeks until the House voted on the plan, Sperling thought they had to go with what he called "the most achievable, feasible, nontax message."

Stephanopoulos could see that Clinton was fighting for his political life. Victory was all that mattered. During World War II, General Dwight D. Eisenhower had argued vehemently for hours with British Prime Minister Winston Churchill over the strategy for the D-Day invasion of Europe. Eisenhower, as Supreme Commander, had finally prevailed. Later Churchill wrote to Eisenhower, "Historians will consider and describe it as a great military movement, but I must tell you, my dear general, it was the fourth-best possibility." That was precisely what Clinton had to accept.

. . .

EIGHT BLOCKS AWAY at the Federal Reserve, Alan Greenspan was facing a new perplexing problem of his own. In the month of April, the consumer price index had shot up .4 percent, much higher than expected. It was one of a series of indicators suggesting that inflation, which had been relatively low, might be creeping back up. Based on historical models, however, there should have been little to no inflation. What was happening? Greenspan wondered. Could it be just a seasonal problem? He pored over charts and data, spent hours at his computer looking at raw information and trends. All the technical indicators—a weak economy, little demand for loans, underlying weakness in the international economy, stable growth in the money supply—should have added up to no inflation problem. This dumped a gigantic two-headed problem in Greenspan's lap, political and economic.

On the political side, the early inflation signs meant the Fed might have to raise interest rates. A rate hike could upset the applecart. Few things could be worse for Clinton. With no Republican support, a move by Greenspan could radically undermine confidence in Clinton and his plan and send long-term rates soaring. No matter how logical or sound, no matter how Greenspan might dress it up, a rate hike would be a reversal of Greenspan's earlier endorsement, a broadside that could shock the financial markets he had been trying to reassure.

On the purely economic side, Greenspan's problem could be graver. New forces could be emerging that he and the Fed experts did not understand. He likened their situation to Galileo's problem: The old models didn't describe what was happening. For nearly four years, since the middle of 1989, Greenspan had always felt he understood fundamentally how the economy was working. His numbers might not have been right all the time, or the trends might have been off a little bit, but in those four years he had never had to contemplate something entirely new or different. Now he was starting to get scared.

In many respects, he had prepared most of his life for a situation like this, one that called on all his knowledge of politics and economics. The unexpected inflation needed to be studied from every possible angle. Greenspan summoned his senior staff to his office. It would be unacceptable if they failed to understand what was happening, he said. They needed to shake themselves up, look at the data again. As he saw it, two possible explanations existed. Most likely, they were seeing a short-term aberration. Possibly, however, some fundamental change had occurred, creating a new set of forces that they could disregard only at their peril.

If inflation started to rise suddenly, how would they explain it to the world? What if it turned out that all the elements that they believed drove the system in a weak economy didn't drive the system?

No one had an immediate answer.

Greenspan said he wanted them squarely to address this scenario: Suppose, he said, two months from then they were in his office and inflation had continued to surge. "What could have caused us to be wrong?" Greenspan asked. "What is wrong with our structure of analysis, our body of concepts, which can explain it? In other words, I'm not asking you to construct a concept which forecasts. I'm asking the reverse."

If inflation had taken hold, Greenspan noted, it would be extraordinary, the first time without a high demand for loans and credit. It would be the economic equivalent of the "immaculate conception," he said. More alarming, if inflation took hold, it would also likely mean that the basic economy was in far worse long-term shape than they imagined and potentially in fundamental dislocation.

In a speech to the Economic Club of New York on April 19, he had warned that runaway inflation was not necessarily under control. "It is an open question whether we have learned enough to skirt the dangers of budgetary and monetary excess that have triggered past episodes of debilitating inflation," he said. Now Greenspan began to take serious precautions.

At 9 A.M., on Tuesday, May 18, Greenspan convened the regular meeting of the Federal Open Market Committee, which would determine whether to increase short-term interest rates. He began by suggesting a strategy for dealing with the inflation threat. The recent inflation numbers were too high. It might be a bubble or a blip, he said, a reversible or an irreversible trend. He proposed that they signal the markets that they were ready to raise interest rates—but stop short of actually raising them. This move would be sufficient to reassure the markets. The problem, after all, was not inflation itself but the expectation of inflation. The signal would be a preemptive strike against inflationary expectations in order to prevent real inflation.

Greenspan saw Clinton's plan as the greatest potential short-term stabilizing force in the economy, but as the new president seemed to falter, it fell into jeopardy. "There is deepseated pessimism in the country," Greenspan said to the committee, somewhat elliptically, but making his message clear. The suggestion of the Fed's added responsibility was obvious.

Greenspan said his initial inclination was to have the committee "lean" toward higher rates. This was done through a formal directive giving him the authority to raise rates at any time during the six weeks

2

Robert Reich, Clinton's Rhodes Scholar classmate and an intellectual godfather of his plan for more public investment, became Labor Secretary in the Clinton Administration.

3

Stanley Greenberg, a former Yale political science professor who became Clinton's pollster, helped develop the key 1992 campaign theme of appealing to the economic needs and insecurity of middle-class voters.

Senator Albert Gore, Jr., and Governor Bill Clinton on election night '92.

James Carville *(left)* was the chief strategist for Clinton's campaign but remained an outside consultant once Clinton was elected. His partner, Paul Begala *(center)*, traveled alongside Clinton during the campaign and argued for an economic plan that stressed helping the middle class rather than reducing the deficit. George Stephanopoulos *(right)*, one of Clinton's earliest campaign aides, was initially White House communications director and then became general policy and strategy adviser to the president. Stephanopoulos spent more time with Clinton than any other White House aide.

5

Mandy Grunwald, Clinton's media consultant, felt that the way to win congressional support for Clinton's economic plan was by appealing directly to the American people.

6

8

9

Laura D'Andrea Tyson, an economics professor at the University of California at Berkeley, was chosen to chair the Council of Economic Advisers. She cautioned against a headlong rush to meet an arbitrary deficit reduction target and catering too much to the bond market.

Alan Blinder, a Princeton economist who became Tyson's deputy, was an expert on the large budget issues of taxes, government spending, and economic growth.

Robert Rubin (left), a former Wall Street investment banker, ran the White House council for economic policy, with his deputy Gene Sperling (right), who helped craft Clinton's economic plan in the 1992 election.

Leon Panetta, a former California congressman, became Clinton's budget director and witnessed the president's slow and torturous awakening to the ways of Washington.

Alice Rivlin, the deputy budget director, was a leading deficit hawk in the new administration. She is pictured here with Senator Daniel Patrick Moynihan, the new chairman of the Senate Finance Committee, which had to approve Clinton's plan.

13

Howard Paster, a former lobbyist for both labor unions and big business, became the president's chief negotiator with Congress and resigned before the end of Clinton's first year.

Mack McLarty, the White House chief of staff and Clinton's friend since they attended kindergarten together in Arkansas, dealt with some of the moderate and conservative Democrats on the economic plan.

Lloyd Bentsen, the veteran Texas senator, relinquished his
independence to become the senior economic statesman
in Clinton's cabinet as Treasury Secretary.

Roger Altman, the
deputy Treasury
Secretary, ran
the White House
War Room to win
passage of the
president's eco-
nomic plan.

17

House Speaker Thomas Foley, President Clinton, Senate Majority Leader George Mitchell, and Senate Minority Leader Bob Dole in the White House Cabinet Room, January 26, 1993.

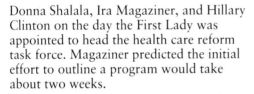

Donna Shalala, Ira Magaziner, and Hillary Clinton on the day the First Lady was appointed to head the health care reform task force. Magaziner predicted the initial effort to outline a program would take about two weeks.

18

President Clinton at his desk in the Oval Office.

19

Federal Reserve Chairman Alan Greenspan between Hillary Clinton and
Tipper Gore at Clinton's speech to Congress unveiling his economic
plan, February 17, 1993. Greenspan maintained he was surprised to
learn that he would be seated right next to the First Lady.

David Gergen, a veteran of
three Republican admin-
istrations, joined the White
House to help turn around
its relations with the press.

Senator Robert Byrd
(above), the powerful West
Virginia Democrat, insisted
on fighting for the $16
billion stimulus package,
leading Clinton eventually
to feel let down by the old
hands of Washington.

Senator David Boren *(left)*
of Oklahoma, a longtime
Clinton friend, abandoned
the president and voted
against the economic plan.

Clinton, McLarty, Bentsen, and Gore on May 27, 1993, the
day of the first narrow victory for the economic plan in the
House of Representatives.

Senator Bob Kerrey, Democrat from Nebraska, was the last vote
Clinton needed to pass his economic plan and wavered right
until the end when he finally voted yes.

Hillary Rodham Clinton, the congressional leadership, and President Clinton.

Gore and Clinton having lunch at the White House, February, 1993.

An official White House photo of the Clintons, February 3, 1994.

until their next regular meeting. If granted that authority, he said, he would hold a full telephone conference consultation with the members before taking any action. Two of the committee members wanted to raise the rates .25 percent at once, but Greenspan prevailed in a 10 to 2 vote. The decision to raise rates, for the next six weeks, would be left at Greenspan's discretion, exactly as he wanted it.

Since the Fed's debate and decisions were made in secrecy, and Greenspan had not decided to exercise his discretion, the Fed would be buying or selling bonds in the market to signal the change. No formal news of its meetings was supposed to be disclosed until a very much shortened version of its meeting minutes were released six to eight weeks later. This time the news leaked, and fast. Only six days after the meeting, the *Wall Street Journal* reported accurately that "Federal Reserve officials voted to lean toward higher short-term interest rates." After the *Journal's* story, the bond market once again pronounced favorable judgment at least temporarily and the interest rate on the Treasury's 30-year bond fell. Although the reaction played into Clinton's financial markets strategy, *The New York Times* predicted that the White House "would view such action as a declaration of war. And it would probably direct its heavy artillery at Mr. Greenspan."

REALIZING SUPPORT for the economic plan on the Finance Committee was shaky, Clinton and Gore met with the key Congressional Democrats in a closed-door session at the Capitol in mid-May. Before the meeting, Gore approached John Breaux, who had been openly critical of the BTU energy tax. "Well," Gore asked, in a voice intentionally loud enough for others to hear, "are you going to screw us or not?"

Breaux just chuckled.

Gore tried again. "I want to know if you're going to screw us."

Breaux again gave no answer.

During the meeting, Gore made a strong pitch for the Democrats to unite on all aspects of the plan. "Let's just cut to it here," the vice president said, looking straight at Breaux. "The question is whether one or two Democrats are going to betray us." Breaux, who felt no awe of Gore, simply glowered back. Throughout the meeting, Breaux was the only one not to speak up.

Afterwards, Clinton walked out with Breaux. "What was the problem?" Clinton inquired.

"I didn't say anything because I was afraid of what I was going to say," Breaux replied.

"I knew something was wrong," the president answered.

. . .

As far as Howard Paster was concerned, Clinton was taking too many road trips and needed to direct his mind and energy on Congress. Passing the plan meant winning congressional votes, Paster felt, not hopscotching around the country. The campaign that mattered was in Washington. He prepared a two-page memo to McLarty on Tuesday, May 18.

"The House of Representatives is scheduled to vote on the reconciliation package in ten days, on Thursday, May 27," Paster began. Though straightforward, the suggestion that the White House chief of staff might not be aware of this carried a trace of sarcasm, as Paster intended. "It is possible to be hopeful about the outcome; it is dangerous to take success for granted," Paster warned.

Paster said that the president's schedule had to be cleared for him to work on getting the plan passed in the House. He recommended specific steps. First, Paster said, the president should speak to the House Democrats and make a "very specific request for support, not a vague nor a casual speech." Clinton, he felt, had a tendency to be too patient, to talk too much and not close the deal or win explicit promises. Paster liked to say that the aluminum-siding salesman who didn't get his order blanks signed didn't sell much siding. He also urged hosting a meeting with the House committee chairmen and, knowing the White House tendency to shuffle its schedule at the last minute, stressed that an upcoming scheduled meeting with the House and Senate Democratic leaders could not be rescheduled.

Paster also called for more sales calls: "The President should send a strongly worded memorandum to the Cabinet admonishing all Cabinet members to contact a minimum of 20 Democrats and 5 Republicans by May 26 to solicit their votes." He listed nine key House members for Clinton to phone. Last, he said, "The President needs to meet separately with Senators Boren, Breaux and Conrad for the express purpose of asking them in the most explicit and most emphatic terms to cease and desist from any additional public comment on the reconciliation package until after House action. Every time the senators on the Finance Committee talk of basic changes in the package, it weakens our positions in the House. These senators owe it to the President to keep their comments private at this time."

Paster was unaware that McLarty had been keeping up with Boren's plan to devise an alternative bipartisan plan. He did not get a response on his memo the next day from McLarty. But later in the day all hell broke loose. Mitchell told Paster that Boren had a group perhaps of eight senators—four Democrats, including Breaux, and four Republicans—talking about a compromise plan that would drop the BTU tax and cut entitlements another $114 billion. Paster saw all his hard work being sabotaged.

Clinton had arranged a meeting that night with Breaux, so Paster sent McLarty a personal note. "Mack, If nothing else is accomplished in the president's meeting tonight with Senator Breaux it is essential the president secure a commitment from Senator Breaux that he NOT join in such a group and that he NOT sign on to the Boren initiative. I cannot stress how strongly I believe the president needs to use his personal relationship to ask Senator Breaux for his help."

McLarty passed Paster's memo about Breaux to the president. That night Breaux agreed that he would not join Boren's group.

IN THE MIDST of the fight to pass the economic plan, two media flaps exposed the lack of organization and discipline within the White House. First, the White House had fired some of its travel office personnel, citing "gross mismanagement," and then hired a cousin of Clinton's, prompting accusations of nepotism. Then Clinton delayed his departure on Air Force One from the Los Angeles Airport so he could receive a ridiculously expensive haircut—some reports said $200—from a Beverly Hills stylist. For a while, reports incorrectly said the haircut delayed other flights. Though neither story had long-term implications, they reflected basic management problems that Clinton did not insist be addressed.

Perot was also back, zinging the travel office and haircut episodes and joining the Republican's attack on Clinton's plan as tax-and-spend. Perot spoke to the freshman House Republicans on May 19, urging them to defeat the plan, and lined up TV and speaking appearances for the days before the House vote. A number of Democratic senators and congressmen also seemed to conclude that opposing the president was politically advantageous. In the current mood of the country, political fortune was to be made not as a Republican or a Democrat but as a fiercely independent, seemingly nonpartisan outsider.

Consternation gripped the White House. Rubin, for one, just didn't understand the desertion of the Democrats. It was inconceivable that Democrats would vote against their president. Sperling had a knot in his stomach for days. He viewed Perot, with his influence over freshman members and his power to mobilize waves of voters to call or write

Congress, as perhaps the most dangerous enemy, and gathered data to hit the Texas billionaire hard.

Taking the economic plan in Perot's book *Not for Sale at Any Price*, Sperling contrasted Perot's plan with Clinton's, and with Perot's own rhetoric. Perot's plan, Sperling pointed out in an internal memo on May 24, actually proposed more taxes than Clinton did. Perot's plan hit the poor and middle class harder than Clinton's while going easier on the rich. In addition, Sperling discovered, Perot used out-of-date numbers from the Congressional Budget Office to reach his balanced-budget goal. "PEROT RELIES ON AN INDISPUTABLE $133 BILLION MISTAKE TO SAY HE BALANCES THE BUDGET," Sperling wrote in a bold headline. "INDEED, WITH ACCURATE BUDGET NUMBERS, THE PEROT FINAL DEFICIT IS HIGHER THAN CLINTON'S."

Sperling sent copies of the memo to Stephanopoulos, Rubin, and McLarty. "His level of hypocrisy is stunning," he noted. "How much should we hold our fire? I would love to share this with some people." Later news stories appeared making some of the same arguments.

BOREN HAD FAXED the details of his alternative economic plan to McLarty. His plan would drop the BTU tax, which was expected to bring in $72 billion, and drop other taxes, mainly on the wealthy and businesses, totaling $50 billion. To make up the revenue, he would cap the growth of Medicare and Medicaid, reduce some cost-of-living adjustments, and slash Clinton's expanded tax credit for the poor.

With Breaux and some others deciding to stick with Clinton's plan, Boren had lined up only three other senators for his alternative. His main Republican ally was John Danforth of Missouri. The only ordained minister in the Senate, Danforth had served for 16 years and, apart from his unflinching support for Clarence Thomas, a friend and former employee, for the Supreme Court in 1991, was generally considered the essence of moderation. Also on board were Democrat J. Bennett Johnston of Louisiana and Bill Cohen, the moderate Republican from Maine.

The four senators gathered on Thursday, May 20, to announce their plan. Waiting for their press conference to commence, they congratulated each other on their effort to resurrect bipartisanship. Suddenly, Boren was summoned to the phone. Clinton was calling.

How are you, Mr. President? Boren asked.

"I've had better mornings," Clinton said. "I really wish you wouldn't do this."

Boren said it would be impossible to cancel the press conference now. But he explained that he was just presenting what he had faxed to McLarty days earlier. Boren promised he would praise, not criticize, Clinton's effort. "I'm not asking for your support," Boren said. "All I ask is you just don't shoot it down."

"Well, I don't know what I'll do," Clinton replied. "I just wish you weren't doing it. But I guess you have to do what you have to do."

"Well, I do," Boren replied.

The unveiling of the plan made instant news on the wire services: Key Finance Committee Democrat Bites Democratic President.

"Yes!" Mandy Grunwald said when she got word of the details, raising her arms in the air like a referee signaling a victory touchdown. This provided the point of contrast with the right wing of the Democratic Party they had been seeking. Compared to Clinton's plan, Boren's would take tens of billions of dollars from the poor and middle class and give it to the rich and the oil industry. She was aglow with the prospect of Clinton attacking Boren for caring more about oil than people. Boren could not have designed a plan more open to a blast of populism.

Up at the Capitol, Mitchell reviewed Boren's proposal. Boren had kept him informed about it and told him about his contacts with McLarty. But Mitchell didn't consider the proposal serious. It certainly couldn't be enacted, and Boren wouldn't try to bring it to a vote because he and the others wouldn't even vote for it themselves. It was simply Boren's attempt to force a compromise and scuttle the BTU tax. Mitchell sent word to the White House: Call off the dogs, don't attack. They would need Boren for a deal. Grunwald, hearing the instructions, went into a tailspin of near depression as the attack was canceled.

Clinton's public criticism of Boren's plan was mild. He called it a "mistake" that contained "bad things," including a shift of $40 billion of the tax burden to the elderly and working people. "Otherwise," he said, "I'm glad to have people talking and coming up with new ideas."

News accounts described the plan as both challenge and obstacle. *The Los Angeles Times* began its front-page story: "In a potentially devastating blow to President Clinton's economic program . . ."

RUBIN WAS WORRIED that he and the other economic advisers—Bentsen, Panetta, Tyson—were not sufficiently involved in health care reform. By now the president had made it clear that he saw them as his fuddy-dud conservative economic advisers. To some Clinton had even called them "incrementalists" who didn't understand his vision. Rubin feared a massive plan springing out of Ira Magaziner's process that they would never be able to get back in the bottle. Rubin proposed that two teams be set up to debate in front of the Clintons the key question of the size of the health care benefit package that should be proposed.

The debate was set for Thursday, May 20, at about 6 P.M. Full rehearsals had been conducted. More than 30 people crowded into the Roosevelt Room as the Clintons arrived and took their seats.

Len Nichols, a professor on leave from Wellesley College working at the budget office, presented the first option, a plan designed to provide care for serious or catastrophic illness—smaller in scope and less costly. Although some privately called it the "bare-bones" package or the "Rubin Plan," officially it was dubbed simply "Plan A," so that no value judgment would be implied.

Nichols said that Plan A was not only less costly but more feasible. Plan A would also allow flexibility; individuals could choose less coverage and more risk if they wanted. This option would, naturally, increase business support for the plan, he noted. The option would also allow benefits to be increased later if desired. It was less wasteful than the alternative because it would not provide benefits that most people simply did not need.

Both Clintons interrupted Nichols with lots of detailed questions. The president was conversant, citing his experience as governor and the endless memos and studies he seemed to have mastered. The more questions he asked, the more apparent it became that he was not thinking small. Some of those in the room detected beneath the friendly surface of the questions a skepticism about whether such a plan could meet Clinton's goals.

"Plan B" was presented by Atul Gawande, a 26-year-old Harvard medical student, also on leave, who had worked on health care in the presidential campaign and was now an adviser on developing the health care plan at the Department of Health and Human Services. Gawande made the pitch for a broader package of so-called comprehensive benefits. A comprehensive plan would guarantee real health security to all Americans, move closer to the coverage available in other developed countries such as Germany and Japan, and establish health care as a right for all citizens, he said. It would provide measurable benefits that the public could see, such as lower deductibles, an essential ingredient of reform, something that addressing just those with serious illness wouldn't do, he said. Gawande realized that his pitch sounded attractive in part because the health care team still hadn't calculated how much savings could be reached. In the absence of an absolute cost, a comprehensive package naturally sounded much more attractive.

Gene Sperling followed with a political argument for the comprehensive plan. There would be intense opposition to whatever they proposed, he said. And the one thing they had learned since they had been in town was that nothing failed quicker in Washington, D.C., than something that didn't have intense, vocal support. He had in mind Clinton's failed nominee for Attorney General Zoe Baird, but decided not to reopen that old wound. Lukewarm support against intense opposition, he asserted, would spell disaster.

They needed to remember, Sperling said, their proposal would only be their opening bid. It would be measured against plans expected to be offered by Republicans and others. How would they compare? The Clinton administration could become a nonplayer in its own major initiative if its plan did not attract intense support right away. The powerful, organized constituencies, such as senior citizens' groups and unions, wouldn't spend their money or political capital to support a bare-bones plan. And without active financial and other support, it could not survive a long, grueling fight.

Clinton was nodding.

Using the tentative numbers from the bare-bones package, Sperling posed a rhetorical question: Can you imagine, he asked, going before the American people and saying, Here's my great vision of health care? You voted for me in 1992; pass my plan and you'll only have to pay $1,000 out of your own pocket for limited health care? No one would fight for that, Sperling answered. If Clinton didn't adopt the full comprehensive plan, Sperling said, he would recommend that the president not go forward at all with health care. Instead, he should spend his time on welfare reform.

Clinton was now nodding furiously. The room erupted in applause. Mandy Grunwald said to Sperling, "You're on my side again!"

An open discussion followed, where everyone had a chance to voice reservations or preferences. None of Clinton's senior economic advisers endorsed the bare-bones Plan A, nor did they directly challenge the arguments for the comprehensive Plan B. Instead, the skeptics praised Plan B, qualified with escape hatches such as, "if the numbers work out," or, "so long as it doesn't divert resources from other things we want to do."

At the end of the meeting, Hillary Clinton raised the issue of trust. It was vital that all of those in the room be able to keep confidences. The president, she said passionately, believed in having inclusive meetings such as this, where lots of people could express their views to him and to each other. They must preserve the trust. Do not talk to reporters, she warned. The meeting ended about 9 P.M.

After midnight, Robert Pear, the health care reporter for *The New*

York Times, was calling people about the meeting. He already knew some details. Over the next several days, various accounts of the meeting appeared in the press. Some portrayed what had been a freewheeling debate as antagonistic; others described it as a decision meeting in which Clinton's enthusiasm was registered as anything from a tentative to a final decision for the comprehensive plan. *The Washington Post,* in its lead story on page one, Saturday, May 22, said: "Broad Plan on Health Approved; President Rejects Economic Advisers' Limited Proposal." The next day, Sunday, May 23, *The New York Times* news analysis was headlined, "A White House Fight, on Health Care, It Is Hillary Clinton Versus President's Economic Advisers."

Hillary was furious. Though the meeting had been somewhat mischaracterized in the media, the conflict was real. The economic advisers had deep reservations about health care—its scope, its cost, its timing. They or others on their behalf were leaking. She did not know who, but she voiced the gravest suspicions. "Are these people part of the administration or not?" she asked. "What side are they on?"

"These guys," Hillary told her husband, "are going to derail you." She reminded him that the economic team's limited view of reform was not what they had come to Washington to achieve. "You didn't get elected to do Wall Street economics," she said.

Clinton was also irate, focusing on the leaks. He forbade future health care meetings with so many people in the room. The leaks about possible new taxes on the health care plan could jeopardize his economic plan. Magaziner thought that some leaks were intentionally designed to scuttle health reform, and he considered them pernicious.

He visited Clinton in the White House residence. "Why would somebody do that?" Clinton asked. He seemed despondent.

But Hillary kept at it. On Wednesday, May 26, she reminded a union that represented hospital and nursing home workers of the demons. She lashed out at the "price gouging, cost shifting and unconscionable profiteering" in the health care industry. "We have to be willing to take on every special-interest group," she said.

23

BOREN HAD RUN HIS PLAN by his old friend and Yale classmate David R. Gergen, 51, a former speechwriter and communications director from the Nixon, Ford, and Reagan administrations. Gergen now wrote for *U.S. News & World Report* and was the conservative half of a popular weekly duet with liberal Mark Shields on public television's "The MacNeil/Lehrer NewsHour."

A tall, balding figure of relaxed humor and strong ambition, Gergen was not abrasive. Though he had a Harvard law degree, he was temperamentally not an advocate. His public commentaries were cast in friendly, hopeful tones, and his private responses often evoked empathy. "I see your point," he often said. "Your point is well taken." He had mastered such remarks and knew how to strike a tone of civility, implying his own views were the same or certainly not so different. Like Clinton himself, Gergen had learned that tentative but clear solicitousness could substitute for actual agreement. Gergen also loved presidents, the Washington game, and spinning out his inside version of events.

On Friday, May 21, the day after Boren's plan had been announced, Gergen gave it his blessing on "The MacNeil/Lehrer NewsHour." In his typically temperate style, however, Gergen's criticism of Clinton was gentle. "I'm glad to see the president out fighting," Gergen said in his deep, measured cadences. "Unfortunately, I think he's on the wrong side of the fight. . . . He is mostly now fighting with the moderates and conservatives in the [Democratic] Party. . . . David Boren is the new kind of Democrat.

"Politically that is exactly the wrong place for him to be in this country. He ought to be on the side of moderates fighting off the left side of this party." Gergen added cautious encouragement for Clinton. "I think the man still can succeed. And I find people around the country are getting really worried about a broken presidency."

Despite Gergen's support and some tentative support from two other senators, including Democrat Bob Kerrey of Nebraska, Boren's plan had no other vote on the Finance Committee, so its shelflife was only about 48 hours. Boren still had leverage, however: No plan would get out of the Finance Committee without his vote.

UNKNOWN TO GERGEN, Clinton had been looking for a new communications director, someone with seniority and experience who would soothe the Washington establishment that seemed to have risen up against him. "I can't get a break," Clinton said repeatedly. Stephanopoulos clearly had too much to do. Each day Stephanopoulos would be pulled out of crucial meetings or discussions with Clinton to prepare or give his briefings, or return reporters' phone calls. At the same time, his dealings with the press were repeatedly shortchanged. Both Clinton and he were getting killed in the press in part because Stephanopoulos never had time for the reporters. He and Clinton had agreed it was not the right job for him.

Stephanopoulos was willing to get out of the line of fire. One of the problems with the job, and one of the little secrets, was that a number of fights he picked with the press were on direct orders from Hillary. Conscious of media relations, she had the view that reporters shouldn't be allowed to get away with anything. The First Lady and her close friend, New York attorney Susan Thomases, had from the first day of the administration wanted to move the press operation physically out of the White House West Wing into the Old Executive Office Building. The idea, to get reporters further away, made a certain amount of sense —except that reporters had become used to traveling within the Oval Office orbit. Instead, they denied reporters direct access to Stephanopoulos's office, allowing admission by appointment only. Reporters were enraged. Shortly afterward, Stephanopoulos suggested lifting the ban altogether, but Hillary wouldn't hear of it.

Over lunch months earlier, Gergen and McLarty had had a lengthy discussion. Gergen talked as a student of the presidency and Washington. Boren had privately been urging McLarty to hire a centrist at the White House to help Clinton with his communications and correct the impression that he had moved to the left. Boren had even suggested his former classmate Gergen. McLarty liked the idea and recommended that the president hire Gergen for the communications job. He received approval from Clinton and the job was confidentially offered to Gergen on Tuesday, May 25.

After working for three Republican presidents, Gergen realized that to sign on suddenly as spokesman for a Democrat would be a big personal risk. He consulted some of his closest friends. Most advised against it. He would face difficult questions. What did he believe? Whose side was he on? How could the spokesman for Reaganomics become the spokesman for the president who wanted to demolish the legacy?

Gergen spoke to Alan Greenspan, a friend of two decades going back to the Ford administration. As a friend, Greenspan said, he would recommend that Gergen say no to the job offer. But speaking in the interests of the country, Greenspan said, he would recommend yes. These were volatile times, and there was too often a sense that children were running the White House.

REPRESENTATIVE DAVE McCURDY, a 43-year-old Oklahoma Democrat, had considered running for president in 1992. Politically ambitious, athletic, and boyishly handsome, McCurdy could have passed for a student council president if not for the beginnings of gray in his thick head of hair. When he chose to sit out the 1992 race, he threw his support to Clinton early. McCurdy had been vice chairman of the Democratic Leadership Council (DLC) and saw Clinton as the leader of a conservative-moderate coalition from the South and West. This group held the balance of power in Congress and in McCurdy's opinion represented future national leadership.

If no one else did, McCurdy congratulated himself on the selfless work he had put into Clinton's campaign. In early 1992, during the grimmest days of Gennifer Flowers and the draft stories, Stephanopoulos had called him. "We're in deep shit," Stephanopoulos had said. "This is bad, we need help. Can you do something?" McCurdy, a pro-defense Democrat on the House Armed Services Committee and a captain in the Air Force Reserve, agreed to help. "Here's what we're saying," Stephanopoulos said, outlining the campaign's spin on the potentially calamitous stories. Dutifully, McCurdy walked the New

Hampshire snows, visiting VFW halls and small towns. He eventually campaigned in 37 states for Clinton. He had a prominent role at the Democratic Convention, seconding Clinton's nomination.

One night in November 1992 at a party given by longtime Democratic Party fundraiser Pamela Harriman, McCurdy had warned the president-elect that he was spending too much time during the transition consulting with the congressional leadership and could soon become their captive. Clinton had to be careful about hooking up a life-support system to the brain-dead Congress, McCurdy said. It would be a mistake to be so closely identified with the leadership, despite what Stephanopoulos and his crew were advising. Bob Byrd and Tom Foley would not make Clinton a successful president.

They controlled the institution, Clinton responded. He would have to deal with them.

McCurdy lobbied to be chosen as Clinton's Defense Secretary but was passed over. He grew more disillusioned with Clinton in the early months of the administration. McCurdy was convinced the government was now like General Motors and IBM—old and stale—and it didn't seem to him that Clinton was changing or reshaping it. When it came time to take sides on Clinton's economic plan, McCurdy invited Howard Paster to address a group of 60 House Democrats called the "Mainstream Forum." The group, which McCurdy had established in 1990, included a large number of freshmen and conservative Democrats not enamored of the House leadership. Scheduled for about an hour, the meeting lasted a tense two and a half. The group wanted more spending cuts, fewer taxes, and significant cuts in entitlements. Though he was addressing a group of potential anti-leadership renegades, Paster repeatedly pointed out that spending cuts were difficult and cuts proposed by one member were other members' pet projects. Paster knew he was going to have to go where the most votes were in the House, and that was still to the left. His strategy was simple: get 218 votes—the bare majority in the 435-member House.

On May 17, McCurdy went public and charged Clinton with betraying his campaign principles with an economic plan that had too many taxes and too few spending cuts. McCurdy told his old friend Mack McLarty—he also knew McLarty through Oklahoma gas and oil connections—that he was going to vote against the plan.

PASTER WAS ALMOST WHITE with nervousness. Clinton had responded and made his sales calls. He immediately wanted more names to call on the phone or to invite to the White House. At one point, Paster came out of the Oval Office after talking to Clinton. "He likes this," Paster said in wonder. "He thinks this is fun."

In the final week before the House vote, after a large meeting at the White House, Clinton and McCurdy spoke privately.

"I have learned something in my time in Washington," Clinton said.

"What's that, Mr. President?" McCurdy inquired.

"The painful lesson," Clinton said, "is that you define yourself by who you fight, and on this one I've been fighting the wrong folks."

McCurdy was delighted to see the apparent realization, but said he still had profound problems with the economic plan. He realized that the White House strategy was not to deal with the moderates like himself as a bloc, but to peel them off one by one, adding them to the base of liberal Democrats to garner just enough votes for a majority.

The morning of the scheduled House vote, Thursday, May 27, Clinton called McCurdy, still hoping to win him over. What are your concerns? Clinton asked.

McCurdy said he still could not see voting for it. The administration was assembling the wrong coalition, sending the wrong signals, and planning to set up an unwieldy bureaucracy for the new BTU tax. McCurdy said he wanted more deficit reduction and more entitlement cuts.

Clinton said that the entitlement cuts would come with his health care reform package.

McCurdy said he was still going to vote against it.

"Have you announced?" Clinton asked.

No, McCurdy said.

"Well, don't," the president requested. They would review McCurdy's main objections—the energy tax, more spending cuts, and entitlement caps—in the White House. "Let me get back to you," Clinton said.

McCurdy held off announcing. In midafternoon, Clinton called again, saying McCurdy should talk to Bentsen about the BTU tax and talk to Rubin or Altman about the other matters. They would work it out.

"It's too late," McCurdy replied. "I'm sorry. We should have had these negotiations earlier."

After making more phone calls, Clinton spoke with McLarty. "Mack," he said, "we just don't have the votes."

Within an hour, McCurdy was summoned to the office of Representative Charles W. Stenholm of Texas, a leader of the conservative Democrats in the House and one of the so-called Boll Weevil Democrats who had supported Reagan's tax cuts in 1981. Stenholm had just spoken with Clinton. "They want a deal, and they want you to come over and we'll all talk," Stenholm told McCurdy.

When McCurdy arrived, about ten fence-sitting Democrats were gathered in Stenholm's office. All agreed on one point: The White House had displayed the worst political management any of them had seen. Several walked out of the meeting, saying they could not trust the outcome.

The group talked to Bentsen and urged cutting the BTU energy tax. They then spoke with Senator Breaux on the speakerphone. Breaux had talked with McLarty, he said, who had promised to scuttle the BTU tax. House rules did not allow amendments to the bill, but the Senate did. The differences could then be worked out later in conference. He promised the Senate would amend the plan to make sure the tax ended up on the cutting-room floor. "Just send it over," Breaux said, "and we will fix it."

McCurdy said it was madness. The White House wanted the House members to walk the plank and vote for the unpopular BTU tax, only then to drop it in the Senate. The Senate would get credit for its elimination while the House Democrats would be seen as energy-tax supporters. This last-minute panic was precisely the wrong way to change government.

McCurdy was summoned suddenly to take a phone call from McLarty in the private back room of Stenholm's office. "Dave," the chief of staff said, "we've got to have this vote. This will kill the president. You've got to vote for this." There were four other votes that Paster was supposed to secure, but he had failed. It now turned on McLarty's oil-and-gas DLC crowd.

"Mack," McCurdy replied, "I can't believe it. This is the worst show I've ever seen. You just don't do this to people."

"Dave," McLarty pleaded, "I know it. But look, the president gets it. *He finally gets it.*"

McCurdy and McLarty had spoken previously about the war for Clinton's soul, and one of the schisms in the White House: McLarty with his ties to the moderates versus Stephanopoulos and his ties to the consultants and liberals. The phrase "finally gets it" had vast implications.

McLarty said he had won out.

You mean? McCurdy probed, trying to make sense of McLarty's message.

"Goddamnit," McLarty said again, "he gets it. He finally understands." McLarty said that Clinton realized that McCurdy and the centrist Democrats were the ones to deal with, Clinton's real political base, his real friends.

McCurdy was in agony.

McLarty made the pitch as personal as possible. If McCurdy voted against the president, he would also be undercutting McLarty. The war had been won and McLarty had to deliver. McLarty needed the vote as much as Clinton.

"Look," McCurdy finally said, "when it goes to the Senate, he'll take the BTU tax out and cut it significantly?"

Yes, the chief of staff replied. Breaux's effective veto on the Finance Committee had, for practical purposes, decided that issue.

"Deeper cuts?" McCurdy asked skeptically.

Yes.

"Entitlement caps or cuts?"

Yes.

"You're going to change the White House operation?"

Yes. "You'll see that tomorrow," McLarty promised. "We're going to make the changes."

That likely meant Stephanopoulos, McCurdy concluded.

McCurdy had one more request. The White House had to work with McCurdy's fellow Oklahoman, David Boren. He was acting in good faith and was serious about deficit reduction, McCurdy claimed. "You just can't stiff him," McCurdy said. "You're going to need him over there."

McLarty said he was on the case.

Okay, McCurdy said, he would vote yes, walk the plank.

The bells in the House were ringing, signaling that members had only 15 minutes to vote. The noise filled the House with an unnerving urgency.

Stepping out into Stenholm's main office, McCurdy reported the gist of McLarty's promises. Most of the congressmen wouldn't buy. Three, however, agreed to vote yes with McCurdy: Representatives W. J. "Billy" Tauzin, a classic Louisiana pol in his seventh term; John Tanner, a Tennessee banker and lawyer in his third term; and Jay Inslee, a freshman from Washington. The four went to the House Chamber floor, where they cornered Majority Leader Gephardt.

"Mr. Leader," McCurdy said, "you're not going to believe this one, but here's what they've agreed to to get this bloc." They walked with Gephardt off the floor into the Rayburn Room. McCurdy outlined the details: BTU out, spending and entitlement cuts, and a new White House operation.

"You're kidding me," Gephardt said.

It had come straight from McLarty, McCurdy assured him.

"They didn't have the votes," Gephardt said, fathoming the desperation. "They were dead in the water."

"I don't want you to be surprised," McCurdy added.

"Well, I'm going to go check," Gephardt said. He went out, called the White House, and returned.

"Okay," Gephardt said, nodding. Furious with the White House operation, he offered a few expletive-ridden comments of his own about the amateur show down there.

That night, 432 of the 435 voting members of the House were present, meaning 217 votes were needed to win. Clinton was stuck at 215 in favor of his plan, 2 votes short. McCurdy and the other three walked in and cast 4 successive votes for the plan.

In the White House, Clinton, Gore, and McLarty were watching together on a television set as the vote was taken. Clinton squinted at the small numbers at the bottom of the screen.

"We have lost this!" the president exclaimed with an air of dejection and certainty.

"No, Mr. President," Gore insisted, "we've won!"

McLarty was totally confused. He had known since kindergarten that Clinton was good at math. But Gore, the former congressman and senator, was the real expert on Congress. They quickly looked and realized that they had indeed gone over the top. McCurdy—and McLarty—had saved the day.

The final tally was 219 to 213.

Paster did not know if McLarty really believed that Clinton was this centrist New Democrat or had been bullshitting McCurdy to muster the votes. But Paster was convinced that Clinton didn't look on himself the way McLarty had described him. Yet at least McLarty had delivered. Paster offered to resign. "You might have to satisfy these people," he told McLarty.

The chief of staff said no.

It was a standing offer, Paster replied. Any time McLarty needed a head or a body to throw over the side, he was available.

VICE PRESIDENT GORE spoke with David Gergen that night. Gore had been designated Gergen's handler to close the deal so Gergen would come on as communications director as soon as possible.

Gergen told Gore that he didn't want to be communications director. He had done that before. The post would put him out front too much. He also didn't want to start off on the wrong foot, and that meant *not* replacing Stephanopoulos. It would not be fair to Stephanopoulos, he said, offering a selfless rationale.

Gore pressed, but Gergen wouldn't go along. They talked about other possible roles and titles. Gergen wanted something broader, more policy, closer to the center. Gore and Gergen went back and forth on the phone. At one point it seemed that the deal was on the verge of collapsing.

McLarty asked Gergen over to his house late that night. McLarty complained that he had not been able to organize the White House staff the way he wanted in the beginning. Bringing in Gergen would be a breakthrough. Couldn't they work something out? McLarty said he needed help. They reached Clinton by phone. Discussion turned on making Gergen the fifth member of an inner circle of five: Clinton, Gore, Hillary, McLarty, and himself. Gergen assumed it would be an inner circle of six and include Stephanopoulos. Clinton and McLarty continued with a late-night full-court press that did not resolve the issue.

On a helicopter ride to Philadelphia the next morning, Friday, May 28, Clinton called Dave McCurdy. The president said he knew how extremely difficult the vote had been, but they wouldn't have won without McCurdy and the others. Changes were going to be made and McCurdy would not be disappointed, Clinton said.

Clinton also called David Boren to extend an olive branch. He said he knew that the Finance Committee and the Senate were going to change the plan, and they needed to cooperate on those changes, the president said. He added that he probably had been too fast off the mark rejecting the Boren-Danforth compromise. Boren took the remarks as something of an apology, but also as Clinton's acknowledgment that he needed Boren's all-important vote in the Finance Committee.

Gergen was wary, not yet fully on board. He had been burned by presidents, having spent two years defending Nixon on Watergate. Raymond K. Price, Nixon's chief speechwriter and Gergen's boss during Watergate, had once told Gergen that he had long ago realized Nixon had a darker side. Price said it was natural for someone in public life to have this darker side and that one job of his staff was to guard against it. Gergen had never settled his questions about the darker side of public figures. Did they all have such a side? How far should the staff go to protect a politician?

He nonetheless was a student of power, and he asked for a one-on-one meeting with Hillary. Friday evening, Gergen had gone home for dinner, and since McLarty was in Hope, Arkansas, hometown to both Clinton and himself, delivering a commencement address, his deputy Roy Neel was sent out to fetch Gergen. About 10 P.M. Neel took Gergen up to the second-floor residence of the White House. Hillary was waiting up for her husband to return from Philadelphia. Gergen wondered if Neel was going to stay with them and monitor the conversation. If he stayed, Gergen thought, this was one kind of place; if he left, it would suggest it was another. Neel left—an important symbolic gesture to Gergen.

Hillary had known Gergen from the annual Renaissance Weekends. She had discussed the possibility that Gergen would join the staff with her husband and with McLarty, and she approved of the idea. She thought that Gergen was just waiting for Clinton, so they sat down to talk.

Gergen said that he had come to admire her husband over the years and liked him very much. He also shared the president's unease about the country. In conversations with Gore and McLarty, Gergen said, he had been told the White House wanted help with their press problem and whether anything could be done quickly to solve it. What was her thinking on that? he asked.

As negative and unfair as some of the press had been, she said, she was open to changing their approach to the press, opening the door a little wider and increasing access to Stephanopoulos's office. They were planning a big barbecue for the press and would extend dinner invitations to lots of journalists, she added.

Gergen was relieved, suspecting her attitude on the issue was central if not decisive. He turned to the bigger question. The general public perception, he said, was that the president was the moderate and his wife was the liberal, that she exercised a veto every time he tried to move to the center, producing a herky-jerky style of governing. If he came to the staff as a moderate voice, Gergen asked, would he be slamming into her?

Hillary said she had been misunderstood on a lot of these issues. In Arkansas, her work had been very mainstream—volunteer hospital work, the church. She reminded him that she had been a corporate lawyer with the Rose law firm. "At heart I'm a pragmatist," she said. Bill, she said, had been elected on a lot of these New Democrat ideas, and they were essential to his future goals. The proposed economic plan was not what Bill came to Washington to do, she said, but since they needed lower interest rates, they had to please Wall Street and the bond traders.

As they talked about the press and her ideology, she turned to what she said she considered a main issue. The White House had to get itself better organized. They weren't communicating effectively and they didn't know how to handle the attacks that had inevitably descended on them. They were overloaded, too—they had had more mail in three months than Bush had in a year. A lot of the people who had come right from the campaign were exhausted, their reflexes slow. They weren't getting the proper information or handling problems well. The stimulus package had been a disaster, she said. "We came and trusted the old hands in Washington and got our heads handed to us," she added to Gergen, the archetypal old Washington hand of his generation. She conveyed her deep frustrations about Washington. On health care, Hillary said, it was delay, delay, at every turn. They needed help. By and large Gergen found her encouraging.

About 11 p.m. Clinton returned from Philadelphia and joined Hillary and Gergen. The three of them talked for about 15 minutes, then Hillary left the two of them to talk alone. Gergen found the president wrung out, disenchanted, a little disoriented. He poured out his own sense of disappointment about Washington and Washington people, who he felt had misled him on disasters such as the stimulus package failure. He had followed Washington advice blindly. With the stimulus killed, health care delayed, his investments slashed, and the middle-class tax cut abandoned, all that remained of his economic plan seemed to be deficit reduction. The top Democrats on the Hill seemed to get what they wanted. He didn't. The media would not give him a break. Clinton said he didn't know where to turn within Washington.

Gergen noted that Clinton didn't have anyone on his staff who had much experience with the Washington press, a distinctive group that needed much care and attention.

How do you work your way through the system? How does this Washington culture work? How could he crack the code? Clinton asked.

The press, like any other group, needed to be handled, Gergen explained. He also repeated his belief that Clinton was fighting the wrong wing of his party. The Borens and McCurdys were his real friends and natural allies.

Clinton said he agreed. He had mispositioned himself politically, he said. He also needed Republicans with him. The folks on the street, Clinton said, were saying, wait a minute, there's a lot of pain here— more taxes, spending cuts, austerity. What was left? Clinton asked. A Wall Street plan that helped bondholders, he said. He was carrying the load for the financial markets in order to revive the economy. As a result, he was paying a heavy price politically, getting slammed publicly. What the hell am I doing? he asked. For two and a half hours, Clinton pressed Gergen hard. He did not know where to turn.

. . .

CLINTON AND THE OTHERS he had spoken to seemed strangely eager to close the deal. Gergen thought it made sense to wait another week and give them all time to think about it, but the White House attitude seemed to be that the decision had to be announced that Saturday. He suspected that they were afraid that news of the move would leak to the press and diminish the impact of the announcement. They seemed to expect that the force of the announcement alone was going to make a difference for them, but Gergen wasn't convinced.

Nonetheless, he had to make a decision, and Gergen could not resist. But he knew that his precise role and his precise title were important. He extracted a pledge that his role would be as broad as he wanted. He would be in on everything; his portfolio would include every meeting, issue, and decision on economic and domestic policy, foreign policy, and politics. His title would *not* be communications director or have anything directly to do with communications. At 2:30 A.M., Gergen left the White House.

GORE AND MCLARTY had prepared Stephanopoulos for what was happening. It was the first Stephanopoulos had heard that the new man would be Gergen, and as he understood it, Gergen was to be the new communications director.

Clinton finally talked with Stephanopoulos. Bringing Gergen to the White House would get them good press, Clinton explained. Gergen knew the media and knew Washington cold. He represented the establishment that they needed to understand. The president said that Gergen was pressing for a broader portfolio, and to accommodate him they had worked something out, though they had kept the talk fairly vague. Stephanopoulos would move to personal and political policy adviser— what he did best, Clinton said. Stephanopoulos was still left with the impression Gergen was coming in to take over the communications operation.

About 6:15 A.M. on Saturday, Gore was sitting before the computer in the office of Mark Gearan, the other White House deputy chief of staff. Gore, who had once been a reporter for the Nashville *Tennessean*, was personally pounding out the press release announcing Gergen's appointment. The story was leaking and they had to get it out fast.

"C-O-U-N-S-E-L-O-R," the vice president typed for Gergen's job description.

"Counselor?" Gearan asked. "What's that?"

"That's his title," Gore replied.

Gearan was shocked. That was contrary to everything he had heard. He too was under the impression that Gergen was coming in to handle communications. With the announcement to be made in about an hour, Gearan was worried. The Stephanopoulos-Gergen contrast could only make Stephanopoulos look bad. Gergen won on height, weight, age, and maturity.

"Half your battle is body language," Gearan advised Stephanopoulos. Take it, smile, stand up straight.

Early-morning word spread among the staff. Press Secretary Dee Dee Myers cried. It was hard to believe that one of the people who had orchestrated the selling of Reaganomics would be joining them. What about Stephanopoulos? several asked. Was this the old replacing the young? Were the young out?

Clinton noted that a number of them had been advocating such a move. "I'll put George right up close to me," Clinton reassured them.

Before the public announcement, some of the staff met with Gergen to brainstorm questions that reporters might ask him. Dee Dee Myers posed a hypothetical question. "What are you doing here?" she asked. "You're the engineer and the spokesman for what Clinton ran against and was elected on." She continued emotionally for half a minute, pouring out her own anger and resentment, framed as a reporter's inquiry. Gergen said only that it was a good shot.

At 7:30 A.M., Clinton appeared with Gergen, McLarty, and Stephanopoulos in the Rose Garden. Clinton referred to it as "Mack McLarty's invitation to join the White House team . . . it was really his idea. I want to give him credit for it; I wish it had been mine, but it wasn't." Clinton sounded the theme of bipartisanship. He announced that Stephanopoulos was moving from communications director to general policy adviser. "One of the reasons for this move is that I have needed the kind of contact and support that I received from George in the campaign, that I think was absolutely essential to the victory that was secured."

Stephanopoulos had been trying to follow Gearan's advice to look chipper. But just at that moment, he looked down and the cameras snapped, capturing the picture that ran in many newspapers.

Though Gergen was not replacing Stephanopoulos, it couldn't help appearing that way to many reporters. The story was irresistible: An upstart kid, heady with power, getting his due from a veteran of three Republican administrations. One news account mentioned Stephanopoulos's new relationship with the actress Jennifer Grey and said he had dropped his longtime girlfriend for the starlet. "How can they say that?"

Stephanopoulos said after reading the account. "She dropped me!" As the press beat him up, he tried to look upon the events as a Washington ritual—The Humiliation. He'd seen Clinton take countless clubbings from the national press. But no matter how many he had seen up close, taking the punches yourself was different.

On Sunday, May 30, Paul Begala appeared on CBS's "Face the Nation," and the questions quickly turned to how the salesman of Reaganomics and tax cuts could now sell Clintonomics and tax increases.

"He believes in a Reagan legacy that was good," Begala replied, almost gasping for air, but dutifully sputtering some of Gergen's arguments. Midway into his reply, Begala paused and thought to himself— always a dangerous practice on live, national television. What's left of my soul? he wondered to himself. Then, instead of giving Gergen's answer, he shifted. "Reaganomics drove this country not just in the ditch, but off a cliff," he said with proud defiance. He knew the message.

OVER THAT MEMORIAL DAY WEEKEND, Begala spent a good deal of time with Clinton, as the president spoke at West Point on Saturday for a commencement address, at the Vietnam Memorial on Monday, and in Milwaukee on Tuesday. As they flew together, Clinton told Begala he had needed help in selling his economic plan. "You gave me a week's worth of strategy and I needed three months," the president said. He had used the line before in public.

"We gave you a political strategy, but you walked away from it," Begala said.

"That's bullshit, Paulie," Clinton said. "You know we were not coordinated and I didn't have a political strategy."

"You walked away from emphasizing the tax on the rich," Begala said. Maybe Clinton should propose additional tax hikes on the rich, even more than he had already proposed. They needed a fight, Begala said. Clinton had done too good a sales job on the rich and the liberals, who weren't resisting enough. To Begala, liberals were often synonymous with the elites of the Democratic Party. They had to engender high-income opposition and liberal opposition. People needed to hear the rich squealing.

Clinton stared at his political adviser. "No," he said emphatically. In the Milwaukee speech Clinton was trying to lay out some general principles, not specifics. Clinton did confide that he was deeply unhappy with his economic plan. "I know this thing is a turkey," the president said.

Begala concluded that Clinton probably liked not having an overall coordinator in the White House. That way, Clinton remained the only one who knew everything, president not just in name but in fact. Begala had to acknowledge to himself that he too in a way liked this arrangement. He could parachute in at will or respond to the summons for help. He had to deal only with the other consultants or friends like Stephanopoulos who spoke his language. They then dealt directly with Clinton, with no gatekeeper in the way.

In darker moments, Begala and Carville wondered whether the enterprise could succeed as long as Mack McLarty was in power. McLarty was a perfectly nice man, but not a leader, not an instigator. He had never come up with a single idea, at least not until bringing in Gergen.

24

GERGEN COULD NOT HAVE JOINED the Clinton White House at a more frantic or desperate time. Having squeaked by in the House, Clinton's economic plan faced an even tougher fight in the Senate. The president's approval ratings were sinking. And personally, Gergen had to tread lightly, knowing a lot of White House staffers resented his very presence.

Gergen thought it important for Clinton to address the public perception of him as a compromiser. The president had to show that he would not run away from the next fight, that he was willing to take a stand. He even had to appear willing to lose a fight if it meant defending certain key principles. Clinton needed to articulate those principles that he would defend. That went to character, Gergen believed.

Having worked in three previous White Houses, Gergen knew that all presidencies had their quirks and intrigues and avenues of powers. But it was apparent to him at once that Clinton's White House was unique. There were three independent power centers: Clinton, Hillary, and Gore. Each of them had played a role in recruiting him. At any moment any one of the three could cut right across anyone else in the White House, including McLarty, or move into any piece of business.

. . .

BENTSEN WAS HAVING MORE and more problems with the all-fuels BTU tax, both its substance and the political handling of it. It could have been won in a snap if they had excluded manufacturers from the tax, but that would have drastically diminished the environmental benefits that Gore wanted. Now the National Association of Manufacturers, with its powerful lobbying office just two blocks from Treasury, had mounted a fierce attack. The oil companies had joined in funding studies at Louisiana universities that showed the results they wanted. Bentsen noted that the studies fell far short of the standard of disinterestedness and objectivity.

As Bentsen was trying to negotiate with both the Senate and House on the tax throughout the spring, he was frustrated to find the administration was not speaking with one voice. At one point, he learned that Howard Paster was making deals with Dan Rostenkowski in the House. Bentsen wanted to be tougher, but Paster and Rostenkowski were very close, too close, in Bentsen's view. One spring day, Clinton, Rostenkowski, and Paster had a cozy lunch on the president's patio without Bentsen. The Treasury Secretary, in front of Paster, finally lodged a protest with Clinton. Bentsen said that when he held firm with the members, they were simply going around him by dealing with Paster. Bentsen said he had to be the only one with authority to speak for the president to the Senate and House tax committees. The administration needed a unified approach. As often happened when others clashed in front of him, Clinton didn't respond.

Later, Paster complained to Clinton and McLarty about Bentsen's conditions. Dealing with Congress was a constant freewheeling enterprise of negotiating over pork and local pet projects, delivering small favors, adjusting federal spending timetables, and he had to have some latitude to deal. Hundreds of minor matters were at stake that meant votes. "I won't be able to do my job if that's the case," he said. He apologized for causing trouble with the cabinet, but insisted his channel to Rostenkowski and dozens of others was crucial to Clinton. Soon after, McLarty told Paster that he would have to work with Bentsen, with Roger Altman acting as an intermediary.

Gore later told Paster he was right about negotiating the small things, that it was simply unrealistic to expect Bentsen to sign off on every last one. "Bentsen wants his ring kissed," Paster said. Negative references to Paster from anonymous Treasury officials began appearing in the media. "That shit's got to stop," Paster told Altman. It didn't.

. . .

ON JUNE 6, McLarty hastily called Bentsen, Panetta, and Tyson to his office for a late Sunday-afternoon meeting. Prospects for the economic plan in the Senate Finance Committee were bleak. The main hangup was the BTU tax. Although McLarty had promised Dave McCurdy and other House members that the Senate would scrap the tax, it was still officially on the table. Boren was doing his best to kill it once and for all, wielding his Finance Committee vote as a threat to keep the bill from reaching the Senate floor. Bentsen was pressing to exempt manufacturers from the tax.

Tyson said that from an economic point of view, there was no reason to retain the tax. "We really have undermined it," she said. In the congressional negotiations, so many exceptions and exemptions had been given away—for aluminum, the airlines and other industries—that the whole principle of a broad energy tax had been subverted. The economists had fought these exemptions, but fruitlessly. Now the administration was effectively saying, We'll tax energy unless you use a lot of it.

Tyson also pointed out that the tax, in its present form, would favor certain industries over others, creating distortions in the market. Collection of the tax would also pose monumental problems. Finally, instead of raising $72 billion over five years as originally planned, it would now raise half that much. It had been gutted.

McLarty and the others each in his own way pooh-poohed her economic reasoning. For political reasons, they said, they had to retain the tax. Lots of House members had voted for the BTU energy tax because they had been told the White House would not abandon it. McLarty did not mention that at least a few, such as McCurdy, had voted for the plan because they were told the White House *would* abandon it.

OVER THE LAST SEVERAL MONTHS Moynihan had grown increasingly disturbed about the all-fuels BTU tax. The concept—taxing pollution—had sounded good, but in practice, the administration had agreed to lower the rate on coal, erasing much of the environmental benefit. With all the tinkering to satisfy special interests, the tax had grown so complicated that it would be an invitation to evasion. By one staff estimate the BTU tax would add volumes to the U.S. Tax Code.

Paster had set up a meeting for 5:30 P.M., Monday, June 7, for Senators Mitchell and Moynihan to meet with Clinton in the Oval Office. Before the meeting, Clinton told reporters that henceforth he was going to speak only about general "principles" in the economic plan and would leave the details to others. "Keep in mind, the main objective is to keep interest rates down, keep the growth going," Clinton said. "This thing is working."

In the Oval Office, Mitchell and Moynihan sat on the same couch, with their backs to Clinton's secretary's office. Clinton and Gore sat in the chairs; Bentsen, McLarty, and Panetta sat on the other couch; Stephanopoulos and Paster stayed in the back as staff. It was Gergen's first official full day on the job. Stephanopoulos thought that for a moment Gergen didn't know where to place himself. As counselor he was not just staff, yet he was not a principal. Gergen pulled up a chair to the back of the outer rim of the circle, straight across from Clinton and Gore. Gergen had already talked with Moynihan, who was on his maiden voyage as Finance chairman. It was also important that Moynihan, who would be chairman for a long time, have a success.

Moynihan had found that every time he suggested a modification to Clinton's economic plan, the White House would defensively reject it. He also wanted to be a good soldier for the White House. So he decided not to attack the BTU tax head on. Instead, he told Clinton he needed some guidance on whether to continue to press for the tax in the Finance Committee. He outlined the problems, most notably Boren's intransigence. "Mr. President," Moynihan suggested, "don't decide now. Take 24 hours to let me know."

What did Moynihan think? Clinton inquired.

"I don't think I can get it through my committee," Moynihan said. Senator Breaux, he added, would accept some kind of gasoline-tax increase instead, but Moynihan said he was aware that Clinton had opposed a gas tax in the campaign.

"Oh, I wasn't opposed to a gasoline tax," Clinton said, reframing his position a little. "I was opposed to the size." Tsongas, he said, had wanted too large a gasoline tax.

Mitchell was more direct. The Senate Finance Committee would not approve his economic plan with a BTU tax in it. Some had suggested an alternative strategy of bypassing the committee and going to the floor directly. "I think that would be *unwise,*" Mitchell said, invoking one of his favorite words, his gentlemanly way of saying not a chance. If they couldn't carry a bill in committee, it was unlikely that they could sustain it on the floor, and in any event he didn't think it would be a good practice.

"Why can't we go to the Senate floor?" Gore asked.

Circumventing a major committee, Mitchell said, was theoretically possible but it was untested in his time. It would be a big chance. Still, if it got to the floor, he repeated, he didn't think they could get the votes.

Moynihan, who didn't want his committee relegated to the sidelines, added that going around the Finance Committee would seem tricky and undemocratic.

Gore, who had served eight years in the Senate, would not hear of such quick capitulation. He pushed the possibility for ten minutes, refusing to let it go. Part of the administration's mandate was environmental reform, he said, and energy-tax reform could not be dismissed so easily. He was anguished.

Moynihan reminded them that the BTU tax, which had already passed the House, would eventually be in the conference between the Senate and House later in the summer, no matter what the Senate did. If the Senate-House conference included the BTU tax, the plan containing it would go right back to the Senate floor for a final vote, not to his committee. So, as a practical matter, they didn't need his committee or the Senate to pass the BTU tax in this round for it to survive.

Gore persisted. He wanted it passed in the Senate, realizing that if it weren't, that would effectively kill the BTU tax in conference. In his own mind he compared it to drawing to an inside straight, thinking that sometimes you had to gamble. The son of Washington could recall that his father, Senator Gore, Sr., had virtually written key bills from the floor as a member of the Finance Committee when Russell Long had been the chairman decades ago. Gore didn't mention this to the others.

Mitchell and Moynihan carried their argument one step further. A parliamentary maneuver to retain the BTU tax could jeopardize the entire economic plan. Mitchell said he was very reluctant to depart from regular practice. He recalled the considerable problems that had arisen on the stimulus package because of procedural maneuvers by Senator Byrd. Mitchell didn't want to get entangled in the rules.

Bentsen nodded along in total agreement as Mitchell spoke. Mitchell quietly persisted, arguing that "common sense" dictated compromise. Carrying it to the floor would mean suffering a defeat there.

Stephanopoulos thought Gore at times had a tin ear, and was as relieved as anyone when the vice president finally let up.

Mr. President, Mitchell suggested, why not give them authority to go back and negotiate through the Finance Committee the best economic package possible that would adhere to the president's major principles? He carefully added that he could not predict with certainty the outcome, but he felt it would be agreeable to the president, though it would not contain a BTU tax.

"The point here," Stephanopoulos said, walking up, placing his hands on the back of the couch, "is that if we are going to change on the BTU tax, we have to do it soon." A quick decision to fold would make it look voluntary, he added. The longer they waited before folding, the more it would look like forced surrender. In other words, how it died would be important.

Mitchell and Moynihan nodded.

Clinton said he would get back to them. They all agreed to say publicly that the BTU tax was still in the administration's plan.

Stephanopoulos left feeling the BTU tax was dead. Congressional messages didn't come much clearer. Clinton had no choice. The senators had not been making arguments so much as presenting reality.

Lawrence O'Donnell, Moynihan's Finance Committee staff director, later spoke with Mandy Grunwald. "Why have Gore in the room?" he asked.

"It served a useful purpose," Grunwald said. "That way Clinton and the others wouldn't have to convince Gore they can't do it." Mitchell and Moynihan had done the heavy lifting.

The next day, Moynihan and his staff tried to find out what Clinton had decided. Reporters were calling all day saying it looked like the White House was going to cave. But Moynihan could not get this confirmed by the White House. Even McLarty was saying the BTU hadn't been dropped. Moynihan felt it was a waste of time to talk to Clinton's chief of staff. He even seemed to glad-hand over the telephone instead of getting straight to business. At one point, while they were in the middle of debating the survival of the administration, McLarty had tried to ingratiate himself with one of Moynihan's aides by announcing that someone Moynihan had routinely recommended for a midlevel government job had been given the post. At heart, Moynihan concluded, McLarty still acted at times as if he were running the Little Rock Ford dealership, trying to make a sale by throwing in free floormats.

About 6:15 P.M., O'Donnell was on the phone with McLarty to check again. The rumors were flying. Was the BTU tax dead?

"No," McLarty said. "No one is saying that."

O'Donnell hung up the phone to watch Bentsen on "The MacNeil/Lehrer NewsHour."

On the show he was naturally asked about the administration's energy tax. "It will not be a so-called BTU tax," Bentsen said unequivocally.

O'Donnell choked and felt a wave of embarrassment for everyone.

When Gore heard the news, he thought Bentsen had made a mistake and had misinterpreted the state of play. "Why did he do that?" Clinton asked his vice president. Gore didn't know. Clinton was momentarily a little angry. But what could they do? Repudiate Bentsen? Some things were just done and could not be called back.

Bentsen had not made a mistake. His experience in the Senate told him that the BTU tax was already chucked. That was the way it was.

He hadn't felt a need to consult with anyone, even the president, so he had gone ahead on his own. It was not only a matter of his authority. It was a matter of his responsibility.

Gore was depressed. The chance for a major environmental revolution had been lost. Panetta visited him in his office at one point to try to cheer him up.

"We've lost this issue," the vice president said in total dejection. He believed that the hard political choices had to be made and enacted into law during the first year, and that meant the BTU tax could be gone for good. He had virtually designed the tax and spearheaded the fight.

"This is just one of many battles," Panetta said. The larger issue of energy conservation was still there. They would be back to fight. It took some time for Gore to realize that it had been a mercy killing.

Clinton's only response to McLarty was to say how bad he felt for Gore. The "bold" ideas of six months earlier had succumbed to political necessity.

Paster had some difficulty with the House members who had voted for the BTU tax. "We wanted this BTU tax," Paster said more than once, trying to explain. "There was this little problem with the votes. . . ." As he lobbied House members on other issues, they frequently ended the conversation with a sarcastic question, "Are you going to give it away in the Senate?"

CLINTON STILL HAD A BIG PROBLEM with his relations with the press. Since the death of the stimulus plan, through the travel office and haircut snafus, the media had been churning out negative stories and assessments of his presidency. Clinton still needed a replacement for Stephanopoulos, someone with an easygoing manner who could also assure reporters that the White House was no crackpot organization. As the consultants had recommended in April, he decided to name Mark Gearan to the post. A graduate of Harvard College and Georgetown Law School, Gearan had served Clinton as executive director of the Democratic Governor's Association in 1990 and managed Gore's vice-presidential campaign.

At 36, Gearan was just a few years older than Stephanopoulos, but in contrast to Stephanopoulos's dapper, youthful clothes, Gearan wore banker's pinstripes, gray or conservative blue. When Clinton officially appointed Gearan to the post, he gave his aide a word of advice about his own image. "You have got to be older and boring," the president said.

. . .

AFTER THE INITIAL HUMILIATION, Stephanopoulos felt liberated in his new job. His move from communications director to Clinton's special assistant allowed him to focus on policy, strategy, and day-to-day decisions. His task was to bring a sense of discipline and order to Clinton's work, to help anticipate how policies and pronouncements would go over with the public—in short, to sort out what was important, what wasn't. Stephanopoulos felt the job was a promotion: He now spent more time with the president than probably any other aide, following the president's schedule from morning to night. His office was next to Clinton's. He was no longer on the frontlines with the media, but in the general's tent, where the decisions were endlessly debated, and eventually made.

Although parts of Clinton's day were unfathomable blanks—he rarely was sure when Clinton awoke or went to bed—he otherwise kept a bead on the president full time. Stephanopoulos usually arrived at his White House office at 6:30 A.M. and checked the little electronic videoscreen on his desk that told the president's location. In the morning it normally showed Clinton in the second-floor residence of the White House. Then, roughly between about 6:30 and about 7:15 A.M., depending on the day, the device beeped, signaling that POTUS (President of the United States) was moving. Next, it said South Grounds; Clinton was going out to jog. Then, Out Locally. Again depending on the day, some time between 7:30 and 8:30 it beeped again, showing that Clinton had returned.

Usually, Clinton showered and dressed immediately. Sometimes he stopped at the Oval Office in his sweatclothes to look at the newspapers, check his in-box, or make a phone call. If Clinton had brought along a jogging mate, he might show the guest the Oval Office. Stephanopoulos might then steal 30 seconds to review with Clinton something that happened overnight. Stephanopoulos, an exercise addict himself, saw that Clinton was right on the edge of addiction to his running. He ran three to five days a week. Missing a single day was okay, but if he missed two, Stephanopoulos could see the effect of increased irritability.

After a national security briefing in the morning, Clinton generally attended a policy meeting or a ceremony. The staff was trying (and for the most part failing) to build in two to four hours a day of free time for Clinton to read or make phone calls. At night the president attended a social event, or a working or family dinner. Then he would flit among the kitchen, his bedroom, the living room, the family room, and the office in the residence. Little piles of paper that he was reading would accumulate. He would watch some TV, call people, or get into long late-night conversations with a visitor, known or unknown to Stephanopoulos.

In the mornings, Stephanopoulos still sat in on the senior staff meetings reviewing the White House news summary, a photocopied encapsulation of the daily network news items and major print articles. On a personal copy for Clinton, Stephanopoulos highlighted items of special importance; boiling down the news helped the president notice the most important items. For months now, Stephanopoulos always made sure he found the summary of the bond market's activity, particularly the benchmark 30-year bond rate. In mid-June, the long bond was still hovering around 6.8 percent—the same, despite some ups and downs, as it had been after the economic plan was unveiled in February. Stephanopoulos had spent 31 years of his life oblivious to the bond market, and now he was tracking it like some Wall Street wizard. Its movement, he knew, was interconnected with daily White House business. How was the bond market? Clinton and others asked frequently during the day. It had become a barometer of their political fortunes.

Stephanopoulos had watched Clinton chafe and occasionally explode at the notion that his administration was at the mercy of this traditionally Republican market. Clinton realized that in the perverse world of Wall Street, the bond traders were betting on a weak economy as much as on deficit reduction, since either a recession or deficit reduction increased the chances of lower interest rates. Several times in private, Clinton had remarked bitterly on the irony that getting economic growth just didn't matter any more. Once in the noose of the bond market, Stephanopoulos felt, they couldn't struggle free. If they gave up on deficit reduction and interest rates shot up, they would be seen as failing. The only spur was coming from the low interest rates and refinancing of loans, which provided consumers with more money to spend. To choke off that source of stimulation might bring on a recession.

The future didn't look much brighter. As the deficit reduction—and the accompanying contraction of the economy—took hold the next year, what would happen? Stephanopoulos had heard Clinton express profound worries. The best the economic team could answer was that if interest rates and inflation stayed low, they might see some solid growth in 1995. Then again, there was no guarantee.

Clinton was having more and more private outbursts about his people, particularly Bentsen and Panetta. The president, Stephanopoulos felt, had come to see that in picking these Washington hands fixated on a deficit reduction agenda, he had in effect also chosen his economic policy. Clinton raged about his "Wall Street" advisers who, he said in moments of ire, didn't care about his campaign promises or share his vision. He returned several times to the last-minute decision in February to drop welfare reform at Bentsen's urging. Clinton blamed Bentsen for that, but also was angry with himself for abandoning a cherished reform in his haste to meet the initial deficit reduction target he now considered arbitrary.

Stephanopoulos couldn't pretend to discern the real Clinton. Clinton was uncomfortable with unanimity of opinion from his advisers, and he often liked contradictory things. For instance, he could erupt over the slashing of his investments, but he could also see the appeal in cutting federal spending, agreeing there was vast waste and stupidity in government. By calling for more spending cuts, Stephanopoulos felt, Clinton had even helped fuel the mania that had devoured his investments. So it went: One moment he wanted more costly investments, the next moment more cuts. Stephanopoulos referred to the conflict as the "unbridgeable chasm" in Clinton and in the economic plan: the investment, populist, soak-the-rich side versus the deficit reduction, slash-the-spending side. Clinton's conflict, rather than being resolved, seemed only to be deepening with time.

Stephanopoulos also felt that the current deficit reduction drumbeat resulted from the public perception that government wasted money. All government spending—not just executive perks and outdated programs, but the investments that would actually help in the long term—was suspect and lumped together in the public mind as profligacy. Stephanopoulos concluded that the administration's biggest failure was not to have drawn a clearer distinction between investments and spending. This failure accounted in part for Clinton's inability to strike a sharp public persona.

Policy depended on message, Stephanopoulos believed. The administration had lost the stimulus package, he felt, because they had lost the message war. They would not pass their economic plan, or anything else, unless they beat Bob Dole on message. The additional problem now was that they had also to beat David Boren on message. Already, people didn't know whether to believe Clinton or Dole; now a fellow Democrat was saying Clinton had betrayed his campaign and caved to the left.

In fact, there were problems everywhere now, with seemingly every major plank of Clinton's agenda. His investments had been scuttled; health care reform was on hold; Boren was leading an insurrection for more deficit reduction; the middle-class tax cut had been abandoned, the populist themes downplayed; the stimulus package had been strangled in the crib; economic growth was foundering at less than 2 percent; and entitlement spending was still climbing. Change was not occurring.

25

STAN GREENBERG WAS ANGUISHED. By Tuesday, June 8, he had received his latest poll. Various public surveys had shown Clinton's popularity declining and disenchantment with his plan growing. But Greenberg's numbers, which he guarded scrupulously to keep them from the media, showed something new, grimmer.

Greenberg had asked the respondents how Clinton was doing as president. Most surveys polled for a general approval or disapproval response, but Greenberg felt his were more sensitive, offering four categories: excellent, good, fair, or poor. A full 70 percent rated Clinton's performance in the two lower categories of fair and poor, while a paltry 28 percent chose the excellent or good category.

Is the country going in the right direction or the wrong direction? his survey also asked. Sixty-six percent said the country was headed in the wrong direction; only 22 percent said the right direction.

Greenberg wanted to shake up his client. Clinton and his advisers were muddling along, supporting and affirming contradictory aspects of the economic message. The president had to choose a single course of action and follow it. Greenberg wrote a memo from all four of the consultants to lay out these choices and force decisions. He checked and revised it with them before sending it to Clinton.

The memo, entitled "Strategic Rethinking," ran seven pages. "The administration is internally divided on key strategic choices," it said, "producing a fairly discordant result." It laid out four key areas of disagreement where choices were needed, describing the choices in somewhat loaded terms. Should Clinton:

- emphasize deficit reduction in order to win over Senate moderates, or economic growth to appeal to the middle class;
- put forward a Wall Street message that would "not spook the business world," or a populist message that would dispel the erroneous notion that the middle class was being taxed under his plan;
- pursue a "legislative focus" according to Congress's agenda, or a "real-world focus" to develop a broader message strategy for influencing Congress through public opinion;
- define himself as a "social liberal," who works on issues such as gay rights, abortion and quotas, or as a "new kind of Democrat," who focuses on middle-class values, rewarding work, and responsibility?

In all four cases, not surprisingly, Greenberg argued for the latter option: a growth message with populist rhetoric, a real-world strategy, and a New Democrat image—the elements that had won Clinton the election.

It was the first of these memos that Gergen had received. He was a little astonished. The consultants, he felt, were more or less calling for a message of class warfare.

As congressmen returned from their recess, Clinton heard more and more that their constituents weren't buying his line on the economic plan. "Nobody knows we have any spending cuts," Clinton complained. "We've got the worst of all worlds. We've gotten all this deficit reduction. We've made all the hard, painful choices, and nobody even noticed."

GERGEN BELIEVED that the Fed chairman should communicate regularly with the White House. After assuming his White House duties, he spoke again with Greenspan. Could Greenspan come over to the White House and speak with the president? Gergen asked. Give the economic outlook? Kind of cheer him up? There was much at stake, and the pressure on Clinton to emphasize investments, or health care and other issues, potentially at the expense of deficit reduction, was intense.

Greenspan agreed. He was mindful of the independent surveys by both *Time* and *Newsweek* at the end of May showing that only 36 percent approved of Clinton's performance as president—the lowest of any president during his first four months in office—while about 50 percent disapproved. The meeting was set for Wednesday, June 9.

Before the meeting, Rubin, Tyson, and Gergen briefed Clinton. Greenspan was protective of his independence, they reminded the president, and Clinton should not push him on interest rates. The Bush administration had tried, unsuccessfully and disastrously; Gergen was convinced that Nick Brady's jawboning of the Fed had backfired, keeping interest rates higher than they would have been otherwise. Even to inquire about the Fed's intentions could be considered out of bounds.

Greenspan arrived and began on an upbeat note. He said that the long-term economic outlook was the best and most balanced he had seen in 40 years. Given these great prospects, the chairman said, the president was doing the right thing in pushing his deficit reduction plan. Though he reminded Clinton he was not endorsing the specifics, some of which he might do differently, the political capital that was being expended on behalf of the plan was well worth it. That was what political capital was for. What the president had done took real political courage, Greenspan said. The magic bullet was to keep those long-term interest rates down, Greenspan added. So far, that strategy was working. Sounding like the administration's deficit hawks, Greenspan said there was no alternative.

Greenspan added a note of caution. The inflation numbers weren't behaving well, he said. He turned to Tyson. Of course, he said, it would all depend on what she told him the next day, when the May inflation data would be available. Although the figures would not be released publicly until the following week, both Tyson and Greenspan expected that the new data would allay inflation fears. It looked as though inflation would be only .1 percent for May.

Greenspan outlined the authority his committee had given him three weeks earlier to raise rates. "If I have to do something, it will be very mild," he said. "It will be to get rid of inflation expectations." He hoped not to have to raise short-term rates, but—and this point was critical—if he did, it would signal the markets that the Fed was determined to contain inflation. That signal might actually keep *long-term* rates down.

Clinton made it clear that he fully understood the seeming paradox of raising short-term rates to keep long-term rates low. Largely because of the inflation expectations, the 30-year long-term rates were up around 7 percent, while short-term rates sat at 3 percent.

Greenspan enjoyed wearing his professorial hat. He could teach these Democrats, he felt, where he hadn't been able to teach the Republicans like Bush and Brady. Brady couldn't get to first base. To underscore his point, Greenspan reiterated that the low long-term rates were making the current economy viable. They had to keep their eye on that. It would not always be so. Clinton had to understand that if the long-term interest rates went up now, the housing markets would crash and the recovery would disappear. He would have not just a recession, but worse. The key, Greenspan continued, was to resolve the budget and pass the economic plan. Health care reform should be stretched out, Greenspan said.

Clinton spoke at some length about his commitment to deficit reduction and getting his program passed. He spoke with such fervor and knowledge that Greenspan concluded that unless this guy was the greatest actor ever, the president was a believer.

Clinton was doing a great job, Greenspan said again. The plan was working on schedule. The economy was going to be in good shape after they got this done.

The next day, Greenberg gave Clinton a memo with his latest poll numbers. He declared it to be the bottom of the slide.

Bob Rubin, Gene Sperling, and others on the White House staff were being bombarded by members of Congress, and the cry was always the same: More deficit reduction. One day an experienced liberal Democrat from Michigan dragged the two of them into his office. Please, he beseeched, deficit reduction, deficit reduction, deficit reduction. That was all he needed, he said. His constituents believed they were going to be hit hard with increases in income taxes and the energy tax. He needed help convincing his constituents this was a deficit reduction bill, not a tax bill.

At one point several experienced Democrats were invited to a political meeting in the White House Ward Room to give advice. Attending were Jody Powell, former President Jimmy Carter's press secretary; Tony Coehlo, the former number-two Democrat in the House; and Geoff Garin, a Democratic political consultant. All three said deficit reduction was the only message for Clinton. The people were clamoring for it.

Like Stan Greenberg, Rubin was aware that the administration needed to straighten out its message of economic growth and deficit reduction. He asked Sperling to prepare a memo that might go to the president, outlining the arguments both for and against the two possible approaches. Sperling completed it June 11 and sent it initially to Gergen, Stephanopoulos, and several others in the White House.

"There has been some difference in opinion among White House staff and advisors as to what our message should be over the next few weeks," the six-page memo began in dramatic understatement. Sperling seemed to make painstaking efforts not to imply that any argument might be wrong or any strategy ill-advised. Capable of seeing several sides of the issue, he agreed that "People are using the deficit to symbolize the desire for jobs and economic growth," and added that trying to prove "that we are champion deficit-cutters . . . is an argument within a framework that we cannot inherently win." Yet he also argued that "The national media may limit the parameters of this debate to a choice between 'a tax plan' or a 'deficit reduction plan,' " and that, given that choice, passing a "deficit reduction plan" was the only way to win.

In contrast to Greenberg's clear positions, Sperling offered a tight-rope-walk recommendation: A broad growth-and-investment message was right because it was on Democratic turf and looked beyond the "mood of the day—or even the mood of the month—in Congress." It was wrong, however, because "deficit reduction is . . . what many of our Hill supporters want for political cover, and it is the message we most need to communicate to pass our reconciliation bill." His final recommendation was four different messages of deficit reduction, getting our house in order, spending cuts, and progressive taxes.

Sperling also briefly took up the rift on "populism and progressivity." "I do not think, however, that this difference is an irreconcilable one . . . ," he wrote. "This can usually be dealt with on a case-by-case examination of the language used with the relevant parties all reviewing the text."

BOREN WAS NOT GIVING UP on his hopes for a bipartisan plan. He urged McLarty to have Clinton call Senator Danforth, the Republican moderate who recently announced he would not seek reelection. Also a member of the Finance Committee, Danforth had joined Boren in his unsuccessful alternative economic plan. Boren saw Danforth as the path to bipartisan support.

Monday night, June 14, at 10:35, Danforth was sitting at his kitchen table, writing an Op-Ed piece on a laptop computer borrowed from his office. He was struggling with the unfamiliar machine when Clinton called.

On a standard form with the presidential seal and the heading, "Presidential Phone Call," Clinton filled in the time and the date of the call in the designated spaces at the top. How can we get your support? the president asked. Was there any possibility?

Danforth said he didn't think so. Clinton began taking notes. Danforth said the plan was wrong in his view. He strongly opposed it. At a time when Republicans were split on a range of issues, Danforth felt, Clinton had found the one that united all Republicans: economics.

What should we do? Clinton inquired.

Danforth noted his objections to the plan's taxes and what he saw as a failure to make meaningful spending cuts. His core objection, he said, was the failure to stop the growth of entitlements. Maybe it was gratuitous to say since he was leaving politics, Danforth added, but adopting a truly bold position on entitlements meant the president had to be willing to lose and risk failure.

To Danforth's surprise, Clinton said he agreed. "We should do something about retirement," Clinton added, referring to the cost-of-living allowance increases on Social Security and other federal programs.

"I don't know whether you can do that politically," Danforth responded, but agreed the president should be trying.

Clinton continued philosophically. For 15 minutes, the two settled into a relaxed conversation about what really needed to be done. Danforth was used to calls from President Reagan reading from index cards or pro forma calls from President Bush. Though Clinton was obviously testing for a soft spot, the president seemed willing to engage in an exploratory give-and-take about real problems. It was not a sales call.

When the conversation was over, the screen on Danforth's computer had gone blank. He had lost the draft of his article, "A Presidential Nomination? Forget It. Nominees Are Routinely Subject to a Public Thrashing."

Clinton passed his notes on to McLarty. "Mack, I can explain," Clinton wrote at the top.

MITCHELL HEARD ABOUT Clinton's call to Danforth, and the majority leader notified Paster. Danforth was apparently spreading word that the president seemed agreeable to more entitlement cuts. A useless exercise, Mitchell told Paster. The Republicans had expressed themselves very clearly that they were not going to compromise. "It's a waste of time."

Paster was livid. He had no idea. Ten days away from the Senate vote, Paster was trying desperately to keep the Democrats in line. Just a week earlier, Bentsen had slipped the BTU tax out from under him, and now Clinton himself was suggesting more entitlement cuts, bedrock stuff with liberal Democrats. The president's call, made without his knowledge, was not just embarrassing, it was a threat to all their progress.

"At least give me the courtesy of letting me know," Paster raged at McLarty. Paster once again was reminded that McLarty simply did not understand congressional politics. If the administration tinkered with the plan to win over Republicans, they would lose many Democrats, who reacted badly to things like Medicare cuts. The liberal Democrats were Clinton's most loyal supporters, and they could not be taken for granted. You may get Jack Danforth, Paster told McLarty sharply, but you'll lose George Mitchell.

Paster was furious to learn that Boren had made the suggestion that Clinton call Danforth. How could they do this without consulting Mitchell? He was Clinton's best ally in the Senate. It was outrageous. It was silly. Who had done more to help Bill Clinton, David Boren or George Mitchell? The answer wasn't difficult. Paster almost lectured McLarty: it was not a game in which they could gain Republicans and not lose Democrats. The president needed to know that. Paster had to go back to the congressional Democrats and unwind what Clinton had said to Danforth. He tried to assure them that it had been nothing more than Clinton having one of his chats, which might have been subject to misinterpretation.

For Paster, the phone call was the last straw, more than a humiliating experience. The episode symbolized a bigger problem, a major obstacle to the president's success—McLarty himself. Fundamentally, Paster believed McLarty had too little control of the White House operation.

Paster found working with McLarty maddening. McLarty was always cutting deals with Boren and McCurdy behind Paster's back. Personally, the man was obsessed with his press coverage. Once, when Paster mentioned to McLarty that *Newsweek* had called him about a profile of the chief of staff, McLarty had Paster return the call right there and then, in McLarty's own office, where he could hear Paster's end of the conversation. McLarty also always seemed to need an entourage. Paster felt that McLarty, a former CEO, was just not temperamentally suited to being a staff person.

Things got so bad that at one point Paster went to see Warren Christopher. Since Christopher had helped Paster get his job in the administration, he wanted Christopher to know that he didn't think he would last. It was not just the hours, not just the pressure, not just the pace. He loved Clinton, he explained. But out it came. Something had to be done about McLarty, Paster said. The ever careful Christopher indicated that he didn't disagree. But he didn't actually say that, and did not offer what, if anything, he or anyone could do about it.

Paster prided himself on being someone, as his former employer Senator Birch Bayh once said, who would tell the boss when his zipper was down. Paster finally told the president directly that McLarty was hurting him. Clinton's response was perfectly smooth, Paster felt, indicating with his tone and body language that he understood, but avoiding any actual words that would prove it or might offend McLarty, if he were ever to hear them repeated.

26

FOR CLINTON, the Senate vote was now a matter of practical politics. The question was not what he wanted but what he couldn't accept, and that was just one thing: defeat of the package. Almost any terms would be acceptable, so long as some version of the plan passed. Details no longer mattered. And since every Democrat on the Finance Committee had an effective veto, the fate of the program was out of his hands.

Much of insider Washington was still watching to see if Pat Moynihan could lead the Finance Committee. In contrast to Bentsen's back-scratching approach, Moynihan's professorial style didn't always lend itself to the tricky negotiations of committee work. Moynihan now regretted that he had been too junior to complain years earlier when the committee had been expanded to include another oil-and-gas state senator, a newcomer named David Boren. Though Moynihan and Boren had offices on the same corridor of the old Russell Senate Office Building and talked frequently, they had little in common.

The negotiation with Boren, kept tightly confidential, received the highest-level attention: McLarty from the White House; Bentsen, the former Finance chairman; and chiefly Mitchell, the majority leader and a committee member. Moynihan, left out, could only ridicule the "good-old-boy" relationship among Southerners McLarty, Bentsen, and Boren.

Working out of Mitchell's leadership office and over the phone, the group heard Boren lay out his position: Fewer taxes, with more entitlement and spending cuts. They worked out a compromise plan that would replace about $80 billion of taxes in the House plan with more cuts. At a closed session of the Finance Committee, Mitchell presented this plan as his own, knowing secretly that Boren would support it.

Mitchell's proposal, however, met with new resistance. Jay Rockefeller and others protested the Medicare cuts. Around the conference table in his brightly lit suite on the second floor of the Capitol, Mitchell had several meetings trying to find a middle ground. Boren on one side pushed for more; a larger group on the other side did not want further entitlement cuts. They yelled at each other and there was the usual posturing. From experience Mitchell found it more effective to discuss the matter with each individual.

He called Boren to say that he was going to have to cede back $5 billion of the cuts. Would Boren stay aboard? he wanted to know. Boren said he would. Soon Mitchell came back to Boren with another trim, insisting he was having problems. It seemed to Boren that Mitchell was making a good-faith effort, and there was no reason to make enemies at this point with the majority leader. Boren also realized that Mitchell or the Finance Committee could, if desperate, find some way to go around him. If he pressed too hard, he could lose. So Boren acquiesced, promising to vote the plan out of committee. He took satisfaction in knowing he had forced through about $20 billion in additional Medicare reductions. With the BTU tax dead, the Finance Committee was proposing a gasoline tax that would raise some $20 billion. Boren stopped short of pledging to vote for the plan on the Senate floor later in the month.

On June 16, after five days of negotiations, the Finance Committee Democrats agreed to the compromise plan. It passed the next day before the full committee in a straight party-line vote, all 11 Democrats for it, all 9 Republicans against. Headlines heralded the new Senate kingpin—Pat Moynihan.

GRUNWALD FELT that Clinton was talking too much to the media about the logistics of the legislative process, comments that weren't going to excite anyone. She also felt the president could not just communicate with what she sarcastically called "the Boren gang." Too often, Clinton would finish a discussion or a negotiating session with the conservatives and then recite the conversation back to the TV cameras. "The economic message cannot be what you say to the last six conservatives on the Senate Finance Committee," Grunwald said at one point.

That same day, at 12:40 P.M. in the Old Family Dining Room of the White House, Clinton made a public pitch for his plan and briefly answered questions from reporters. Asked about the energy tax, Clinton fell into his old routine: "You know the Senate is going to change the energy tax, but if they have enough deficit reduction and they go to the conference committee, I think that they will come out ultimately with a bill that I'll feel good about." It was the sort of statement that was driving Grunwald crazy—all process and no vision.

Later that afternoon, at 5 P.M., Grunwald came to the White House and played a five-minute videotape for a group of senior advisers designed to illustrate her point. First were a series of short newsclips of Clinton from the campaign. In the clips, Clinton was standing forcefully and confidently, exuding a passion and vigor. His voice was clear, his words crisp. He spoke with energy and commitment about how he would help the middle class, offering a broad, lofty message of hope and change.

Then the video showed a series of snippets of Clinton as president over the last few months taken from TV news broadcasts. Gloomy and poorly lit, with fuzzy sound, the shots showed the president seated at a table in the Cabinet Room or in other lethargic poses. His eyes gazed downward. He answered reporters' questions offhandedly, rambling on about the uninspiring details of the legislative process, committees, and narrow votes. He used Washington jargon terms like "reconciliation." Begala, watching the tape, imagined that people who saw the news that night must have thought, "What, did he have a fight with Gore?"

Gergen was struck by the vivid contrast of both style and substance. He agreed that Clinton was focused too much on the process, not enough on the overall message and vision. Afterwards, as a small cosmetic correction, they started moving Clinton's public appearances for the summer outside to the White House Rose Garden.

OVER THE NEXT SEVERAL DAYS, Clinton actively campaigned for his plan, which was scheduled to come up for a Senate vote in the next week. On June 17, he held the first prime-time press conference of his presidency. A reporter asked him whether the budget deficit wouldn't start creeping back up after the fifth year of the plan. "That is true," he said, "but why is that? That is because primarily of the projected exploding costs in medical care . . . we cannot get the deficit down to zero, which is where it ought to be, until we do something about health care costs, which is why the next big piece of this administration's work is to provide a comprehensive health care plan." This plan was only the beginning.

On Saturday, June 19, Clinton visited Boston and Mitchell's home state of Maine. At a rally in Portland, Clinton bubbled with praise for the senator, calling him a "genuine national treasure," and thanked him specifically at five different points in his speech. He praised the Senate for passing a campaign finance reform bill, "thanks to Senator Mitchell." He congratulated the Finance Committee for approving the economic plan, "thanks to the leadership of . . . Senator Mitchell." And he promised passage of the plan, adding, "thanks in no small measure to George Mitchell."

THERE WAS ALMOST no discussion of economics now, little or no economic theory behind the arguments, Sperling felt. Republicans were arguing that new taxes would hurt the economy while spending cuts wouldn't, a statement few economists would support. If anything, economists believed, taking a dollar of spending from the economy would cause more contraction than another dollar of taxation. But economic arguments didn't matter. It was all politics.

Sperling spent the weekend trying to nail Bob Dole. Sperling was aware that some in the White House felt that the campaign mentality was too pervasive, that the consultants were too influential. But Sperling believed just the reverse was true. The White House needed more politics, not less. On the stimulus package they had been killed because he and Stephanopoulos and others had been working on pure policy when they should have been fighting and playing hardball politics.

Having crushed the stimulus, Dole was now blasting away at the economic plan. He was the Republican heavyweight who had to be knocked out. Sperling went on the offensive. He and the White House research office obtained quotes and data from the *Congressional Record* and elsewhere to point up Dole's inconsistencies. He wrote up a hit memo for Stephanopoulos, Gergen, and Gearan, and distributed extra copies to the CBS Sunday news show "Face the Nation" and other reporters.

Over the next couple of days, Sperling judged his efforts a success. On "Face the Nation," Bob Schieffer, saying that he had talked to the White House, asked Dole two questions straight from Sperling's material. Dole had accused the White House of using devious accounting practices to arrive at its deficit reduction figures. Schieffer noted, as Sperling had pointed out, that during the 1990 budget deal, Dole had used similar practices. *The Washington Post* also used the information in an editorial chiding Dole for hypocrisy entitled, "Mr. Dole Knows Better." Sperling felt it was a perfect example of how the White House ought to operate—put Dole on the defensive.

. . .

PASTER REMAINED under the gun. He still hadn't lined up enough Democrats to ensure the plan's passage. He was calling senators constantly. He took them to dinner. Every day he or Panetta or Bentsen or Gore or Clinton would talk to another senator and try to secure another vote.

Working with a list of the 56 Democratic senators, Paster attempted to get a vote count. He revised his lists, seeking the latest up-to-the-minute headcount. The vote was dicey, looking increasingly unpopular, and he knew they couldn't take people for granted. With not a single Republican vote, he could lose no more than six Democrats. But on Paster's list, over the last week, 19 Democrats had voiced one reservation or another. At this late date, Paster felt, such a high number of doubters was ominous.

BOREN STILL HADN'T committed to voting for the plan in the full Senate. After the plan had emerged from the Finance Committee, senators were attaching various amendments that Boren didn't like. He planned to vote against it.

By Mitchell's count, he needed one more vote. Desperate to ensure the bill's passage, he called Boren. Please, he beseeched, at least let the process go forward. A vote for the plan would only send it to the Senate-House conference.

Boren weighed Mitchell's request and agreed. Even though he didn't feel an obligation, he would vote for it, allowing it to go to conference. He made it clear that more than anything else, his vote was a personal favor to Mitchell, who he felt had played fair. He was not promising to vote for the final compromise that would come out of the conference with the House.

That Thursday, June 24, the plan came to a vote on the Senate floor. Boren kept his promise and cast his vote in favor, making it a tie. With two senators absent, the vote was 49 to 49. At 3 A.M., Vice President Gore cast the tie-breaker, and the bill passed, 50 to 49. At the White House, the real hero was George Mitchell.

UP IN HIS SECOND-FLOOR West Wing office, Bob Rubin felt the isolation. Though he was coordinator of economic policy, he was not naturally in the flow of business. It had been more difficult to reach out to people than he had anticipated. He had to make the phone calls to people or invite them up. He was not that involved in the legislative strategy which had overwhelmed the White House. Aghast that Democrats would abandon their own party's president, he was not comfortable or skilled at working with Congress. Still, he felt the administration had avoided the internal warfare of the Bush administration. And despite the various pressures on Clinton, Rubin had been arguing that there was not a significant rift between the populist political consultants and the economic policy team.

About 10:30 on the morning after the Senate's 3 A.M. vote, Sperling and Rubin were in Rubin's office when Carville and Begala showed up unexpectedly. They had no appointment; they wanted to talk.

"Nick," Carville said, greeting Rubin. He had started calling Rubin "Nick" after Bush's Treasury Secretary Nicholas Brady. Like Brady, Rubin had remarked publicly that all was okay in the United States, at least compared to the economic conditions in Japan and West Germany. "I've arranged a speech for you in Baton Rouge," Carville joked, "and you can come down and tell them how bad it is in Germany."

Rubin laughed. He told them that he had just been saying the day before that the whole administration was working together, that there was no contention with the political side.

"There is a big schism," Begala contradicted. That was why they had stopped by.

Rubin squinted, sat down, and asked what was going on.

The two consultants said they couldn't get enough information about the investments in the economic plan. They needed the information to craft Clinton's political message. Investments needed higher billing, Begala told Rubin. "There's too much deficit reduction emphasis. We've got to do investments," he said.

Sperling had been trying to work up the details on investment programs and the amounts of money that would go to each one. In truth, they were meager compared to the dramatic investment increase Clinton had envisioned months ago, with many specifics still to be worked out by various congressional committees.

Rubin had to run out to a meeting. Carville and Begala said they would await his return. This was important, Carville said, calmly picking up a newspaper in a display of conspicuous patience.

When Rubin returned, Carville and Begala broadened their complaint. "We can't shy away from the populist rhetoric," Begala said. Clinton was being too soft on the rich.

Rubin, the multimillionaire, said frankly that he hated it when Clinton used the word "rich." They should use some other phrase, he suggested, like "the well-to-do" or "people who have done well." He used the word "progressivity" to describe increasing taxes on the well-to-do. The language was important. Rubin added that he had not heard a single person who had done well complain that their taxes were going to go up by as much as a third.

The two consultants nodded, seeming to agree.

"And you can't say, we're going to *make* the rich pay more taxes," Rubin said, warming to his defense. "That sounds like it's coming out of the barrel of a gun. You've got to say, we will *ask* the well-to-do to pay their share."

Begala shrugged. That was okay, but the tax system was not voluntary. If they didn't pay their taxes, they would just go to jail.

"Look," Rubin said impatiently, "they're running the economy and they make the decisions about the economy. And so if you attack them, you wind up hurting the economy and wind up hurting the president." This was not merely a matter of where to position the president politically, Rubin said, but a decision with serious practical consequences. The language should not demonize them, he said.

"Fuck them," Begala said.

Carville jumped in. The administration shouldn't be cowed by the mauling it had taken on the stimulus package. The political message they now wanted to convey was simple: Emphasize the taxes on the rich and the new investments. "The problem here," he continued, "is you're withholding the data on the investments and we can't go make the case. You're trying to play games. You don't want us to talk about the investments. That's chickenshit."

Sperling took the charge personally. Soon he and Carville were shouting at each other. It degenerated into a screaming fight. Sperling reminded them that he had been working day and night, working harder than anybody else. How could Carville say something like that?

"Let me say what we're accusing you of," Carville answered. "We're accusing you of withholding the information from us on the investments." Carville said he had a practical problem. "Look," he said, his words racing together, "these people are calling me to go out for whatever reason to do some of these talk shows. I ain't doing 'em because you all got to tell me what to say. I can't go on 'Meet the Press' without a message. And the only thing I get is deficit reduction stuff, and no one ever told me this was the message. And for better or for worse, and whether you guys like it or not, I have been dubbed as kind of a spokesperson for the administration. I'm going to decline this shit until we get a strategy on what to say."

They didn't have the answers, Rubin and Sperling replied. Sperling concluded that the consultants—first Grunwald, and now Carville and Begala—were battering him because they felt out of the loop, not in control of the documents and paper that drove the system. He also felt that they were, no doubt, frustrated that they had to deal with him, a former junior staffer on the campaign. But he saw that the economic team felt the same way. They knew that the consultants had these confidential memos flying in to the president and the First Lady. Both sides thought the other side had the advantage.

"You've got to defer to us on political judgments," Carville said finally, getting to the heart of his problem.

Sperling said that he wanted to attend the political briefing they regularly gave the president.

No, Carville and Begala said, they were exclusively political.

"You can come to the economic briefings," Rubin noted.

The discussion again degenerated into a heated shouting match. Where were the divisions between political and economic advice? Who was trespassing on whose territory?

"You're giving Clinton political advice when you call for everything to be deficit reduction!" Carville said.

The consultants, Rubin shot back, were giving what amounted to economic advice when they instructed administration officials to emphasize investments. The political message echoed throughout the business community, Congress, everywhere. Begala took it as a "so's-your-mother" reply.

The four finally cooled down. They agreed that they would try to work it out, ending the acrimonious morning on a comrades-in-the-foxhole note. Carville thought Rubin was a good man, and thanked "Nick" as he left.

As COMMUNICATIONS DIRECTOR, Mark Gearan had to try to get a handle on the president's crazy schedule. The economic plan needed the president's full attention, but his schedule was overloaded. Gearan constructed charts listing three categories of planned events or issues: those involving the president; those involving the White House; and those involving a cabinet department or another agency. For each category, he drew up a "thermometer." The thermometer's reading measured how many of these events were scheduled for each month on such page-one issues as the economic plan or health care. The busier the schedule, the hotter the temperature. For most of June and July, Gearan noted, the readings were radioactive. They were headed for a disaster. The president had to clear the decks of peripheral issues and deal only with those that were central.

On June 25, the consultants wrote another memo to the president, called "Positioning for Conference." It also recommended a "clear the decks" strategy similar to what Gearan was urging. With the conference between the House and Senate coming up, there was not even a sliver of room for the sorts of side issues that had distracted Clinton throughout the spring.

NEAR THE END OF JUNE, at a meeting of the consultants, Stan Greenberg said that he had tested the message of economic growth and investments against the message of deficit reduction. The two messages were equally popular, he said. The deficit reduction message, however, was much cleaner and easier. "I was wrong," he said. Greenberg, too, had become a pod person.

Greenberg added an important distinction. His polling still showed that deficit reduction could not be presented as an end in itself. It had to be seen as part of "putting our house in order," a general feeling that Clinton was trying to clean up the government and the economy. This, he felt, should be the new message.

27

O<small>N</small> F<small>RIDAY</small>, J<small>ULY</small> 2, Greenberg distributed a four-page memo, marked *"CONFIDENTIAL,"* from Begala, Carville, Grunwald, and himself. It was stamped like a sensitive CIA document, intentionally lending an aura of importance. Eleven copies were printed. Each of the first six was addressed to the person by name, with its own number, so that each might be more easily accounted for, or a leak more easily traced:

> To: President Bill Clinton (1)
> Vice President Al Gore (2)
> Hillary Rodham Clinton (3)
> Mack McLarty (4)
> George Stephanopoulos (5)
> David Gergen (6)

The four consultants who wrote the memo received copies 7 through 10. There was one extra. The consultants intended to ring the fire alarm. They began:

"We do not exaggerate when we say that our current course, advanced by our economic team and Congressional leaders, threatens to sink your popularity further and weaken your presidency." Few sentences could have received more attention in the White House.

"However," the consultants continued, offering hope and a remedy, "we believe if you act boldly, there is an opportunity here to remake your presidency. The current conference debate centers exclusively on taxes—as the primary difference between the House and Senate bills. That course will turn your economic plan, again, into a 'tax plan' and Bill Clinton into somebody who cares about little more than taxes. We cannot afford this dangerous strategy."

The memo said that Clinton had three options: a compromise between the House-passed BTU tax and the Senate-passed gas tax, finally set at 4.3 cents a gallon; the gas tax not to exceed a nickel; and dropping the BTU and gas tax entirely—called the "bold zero option," an obvious jab at Gore and his insistence on a "bold" BTU energy tax.

The consultants strongly recommended the "bold zero option," so that no new taxes would fall on the middle class. They argued that it would show the president in touch with people's fears and able to shift course and lead. Polling showed that approval of Clinton's performance on the economy had recently slipped 4 points, and his overall approval rating was at 45 percent. "There is no momentum," the memo said, stating that the "bold zero option" would set a new and clear course.

Attached was a thick packet of specific polling data and charts. Greenberg had tested the three options in a poll. On the "bold zero option," he had asked the following question to a large sample: "President Clinton may announce important changes in his economic plan in order to address the slow economy, which he believes is not creating jobs fast enough. This is the proposal. First, eliminate any new taxes on the middle class in order to boost consumer confidence. That means completely eliminating the energy tax. All new taxes will be paid by people making over $140,000. People earning under $30,000 will get tax relief. Second, Clinton will reduce slightly the deficit reduction goal from $500 billion to $480 billion over five years in order to fund new incentives to create jobs." (Of course, the $20 billion reduction was going to do nothing of the kind; it simply occurred because the gas or energy tax would be dropped.) "The plan will allow tax incentives to small business and technology companies to create jobs once the House and Senate pass his revised economic plan within a month." For this somewhat skewed proposition, 63 percent expressed support and only 28 percent opposition.

Greenberg spoke to Hillary and urged a meeting. He believed the senior White House staff wouldn't want to deal with the recommendation. They would see it as too much of an intrusion on the day-to-day operations.

It was not a good time for the economy. The basic numbers were lousy—on overall economic growth (a meager 0.7 percent for the first three months of 1993, compared to 4.7 percent for the last three months of 1992) and on unemployment (up to 7 percent, the first rise during Clinton's presidency). Clinton's approval rating had shot up 11 percent the previous week only because he had launched a massive Tomahawk missile attack on the Iraqi intelligence headquarters in retaliation for an alleged Iraqi plan to kill former President Bush. This was precisely what the election had *not* been about. He needed approval for his economic policies. He was hoping that the prospect of his plan passing would boost the economy. As sluggishness prevailed, he peppered his economic advisers regularly with the simple question, "When is it going to work?" No one knew.

Hillary spoke with McLarty. It was panic time. They had barely survived the House and Senate the first time. How were they going to get it passed on the final vote? What was the plan? They had to get organized to sell it, and she had some of her own ideas. McLarty called a meeting with the president and Hillary for the next day, Saturday, July 3, at 5 P.M. A dozen of the president's key advisers were to attend.

The meeting was to be held in the White House solarium, a sun parlor or summer room with bays of glass windows on three sides, perched on top of the White House. Calvin Coolidge's wife had called a smaller version of the room the "sky parlor," and President Nixon had called it the California Room. During the 1992 transition, President Reagan had told Clinton that the solarium was his favorite White House room. He had recovered there from his bullet wound after the 1981 assassination attempt, Reagan had explained. For Clinton and his longtime advisers, the room most resembled the informality of the basement of the Arkansas Governor's Mansion. A kitchenette and a large, PTA-sized coffeepot substituted for servants. Fritos, the favorite junk food from the Governor's Mansion basement a year before, were set around.

Upon coming to the White House, Hillary had noted how faded the furnishings were up there, so she had had it redecorated. It was so pretty now and she wanted every possible meeting held there. The Clintons also liked the solarium as a way to limit attendance. In the White House, dozens of staffers had all-access passes, and some would come in and sit down in the Roosevelt Room or Cabinet Room meetings. No one would know who had invited them or whether they had been invited at all. Several became experts at attending any meeting that included the president or Hillary. So a few weeks earlier, the important political meetings had been moved to the solarium because those admitted had to be on a special list prepared for each meeting.

The meeting included all four political consultants—Grunwald, Greenberg, Carville, Begala—and most of the key administration officials: Gore, McLarty, Rubin, Panetta, Stephanopoulos, Paster, Gearan, as well as a representative from Treasury and two of Mrs. Clinton's aides, including her chief of staff, Margaret A. Williams. Sperling was told he was not invited because only one person from each department or area was to be present. It was one of the few times he had been specifically excluded from a big meeting, and he was upset.

Bentsen, Altman, and Gergen were absent because they had gone to Tokyo for the annual economic summit of the leaders of the seven major industrial nations. Clinton planned to leave the next day. In Japan, he would have an opportunity to showcase both his economic gameplan and himself in an international forum. This was the last chance to confer before Tokyo, his longest and most serious foreign trip so far.

Clinton took a seat he liked in a chair with an ottoman that was set to the right of the door as the advisers walked up a ramp to the solarium. Everyone took seats on the sofas and chairs around the room. Clinton propped his feet up on the ottoman. Calmly, he said he wanted to focus on the next stage of passing the plan. They had to deal with the consultants' recommendation that all energy and gas taxes be dropped —the "bold zero option"—which would reduce the overall deficit reduction target from $500 to $480 billion. They also needed to address the festering problems arising from the continuing lack of coordination between the economic policy and the political message. They had to get so they were all saying the same thing, he said.

Stephanopoulos said he was concerned that they weren't getting closure on the final administration position on key issues, especially on the energy tax. He wanted, once and for all, to settle on something simple and clear. He preferred the 4.3 cents a gallon approved in the Senate version of the bill or something close to it, so they could say the tax was no more than a nickel. He agreed they had to avoid another month in which it would appear the administration was trying to raise taxes while everybody else was trying to lower them. They would be hurt if the entire conference period were about taxes. "There is blood all over the floor already," Stephanopoulos said.

Gore disagreed. They had to keep their flexibility, the vice president said. They might want to go higher on the gasoline tax. The energy tax was a point of principle for the administration, he said, and they should let the process unfold in the Congress. His body language showed he was churning. He coiled and uncoiled muscles, shifting in his seat, his jaw working intensely, his face almost stricken at times. With graphic, pained sincerity, he rolled out the most powerful argument—one that hit the nerves of the others. President Clinton could be attacked on character if he dropped it, Gore said, emphatically and emotionally.

Stephanopoulos could not openly challenge the vice president. But he knew that only votes mattered now. The margins in Congress were so thin they couldn't afford to make any alteration in the package without knowing the precise effect on the vote. The only reason to move was to win over votes or avoid losing them.

Rubin, in outlining the expected congressional timetable for the House-Senate reconciliation conference, noted that this upcoming vote was the Super Bowl. All were aware of the heated dissension over the basic questions: how to describe the economic plan, how much to emphasize deficit reduction versus other campaign or populist themes. The issue before them was somewhat simple: where did economics end and politics take over? Or where did politics end and economics take over? At times the two forces seemed to be pulling in different directions. Personally, Rubin said, he felt they could all agree and work from the same page. They had been hurt, he added, because they hadn't sufficiently explained that the bill was not just a budget bill but a total economic recovery plan.

Clinton said the problem was graver. They lacked a long-term strategy. On the initial vote, the plan had just barely passed both houses. Now they hadn't planned for the endgame. Lots of opinions were being voiced on television and in the newspapers that the administration had lost its momentum, that few people understood the plan. He had been forced on the defensive. He realized he sounded defensive, and he didn't like it.

The president turned to Stan Greenberg to explain his latest findings. Focus groups and polls showed additional bad news, Greenberg said. At the latest focus groups he had asked people to write down three things they knew about Clinton's plan. This was an open-ended question, asked with no prior discussion. The answers showed, he said, that people knew nothing except that the plan included taxes. They didn't know about the deficit reduction; they didn't know that most of the taxes would fall on the wealthy; they didn't know about the new investments.

"We have a very short period of time. This penultimate period leading up to the enactment of the budget is going to be what people remember," he said. "And if we don't communicate something serious and focused in the period, we're going to be left with what our detractors have used to characterize our plan." Greenberg recalled what happened to George Bush when he reneged on his "Read my lips" pledge in the 1990 budget deal and raised taxes. "That seared in people's consciousness." Bush had broken his promise, and people believed to that day he had raised heavy taxes on the middle class. In fact, the only tax in the 1990 budget deal affecting the middle class was a gas tax of precisely 5 cents. But that didn't matter. People remembered the broken promise. "Don't assume what they hear will then simply fade into history. It did not happen with George Bush. It remained a vivid recollection. And what we do in the next two months will remain in people's consciousness through our administration."

What Greenberg was saying was not lost on anyone: This decision would have lasting repercussions for Clinton's 1996 reelection, where broken promises were sure to be an issue. Greenberg added, "We need to know what people are going to be left with the day after this vote. Don't assume we can fix it in August."

Howard Paster was in a slow burn as he listened to Greenberg. He hated these meetings. It was outrageous that the outside consultants were providing the president with major policy option papers in confidential memos that Paster often never saw or saw only too late. If lobbyists with business clients had this kind of relationship with the president, it would be a giant scandal. The consultants had clients, some businesses, some politicians like Senator Moynihan, who paid big fees for their work. Paster wasn't sure the political consultants were that different from other outside businesses. He resented their influence and was sure they presented Clinton with a potentially serious liability. Valuable inside information and conflicts abounded. Just as bad, the consultants were trying to remake policy because the poll numbers were down. Paster gravely doubted the wisdom of running a perpetual political campaign from the White House. Good, sound policy would be followed by good poll numbers in the long run, he believed. This lurching from one policy to the next would be stupid. Paster decided to speak up.

There was a looming practical problem, he said. They didn't have the votes in Congress. They would be hard to find. The game now was a matter of working with a handful of congressmen and senators. "Let's just get the thing passed," he said in some frustration. After its passage they could go out and explain to people what the plan was.

"They won't care in August," Greenberg said.

"I need all the chips that are available," Paster said, indicating that their backs were to the wall. He needed to be able to deal with other parts of the package. The Black Caucus, for example, or other groups on the Hill wanted certain things. He, in turn, needed the energy tax and all other issues open so he would have bargaining chips. "Don't bargain them away here. Let me have maximum latitude," he said.

Greenberg repeated that the economic plan was being perceived as a tax package, not as a broad economic recovery plan. Though some weeks earlier he had thought deficit reduction was an acceptable message, he was now convinced it had failed. The Republicans had defined the debate, portraying Clinton as a tax-and-spend Democrat. When people thought about the deficit, Greenberg explained, they thought about taxes, and when they thought about taxes, they thought the taxes were going to fall on the middle class. The focus groups demonstrated a hunger for information on the positive parts of the program—the investments in kids, tax credits for the poor—and the administration was not talking about them. Overall, Greenberg said, in the last six months the public had lost track of the purpose of the economic plan— the investments, tax fairness, and getting our house in order. The only way he saw to recapture the public was a bold, clear move such as dropping the energy tax.

"This isn't an election!" Paster blurted out. "The Senate breaks its ass to get a 4.3-cent-a-gallon tax passed, and we can't just abandon it *or* them."

Mandy Grunwald seized on Paster's focus on Congress. She repeated her belief that the president's popularity first had to be improved, and then Congress could be moved by a popular president. Killing off the gasoline tax would raise his popularity and improve the administration's bargaining position. Why take all this risk for only $20 billion?

Begala said he agreed with Greenberg and Grunwald. With the all-fuels BTU dead, the $20 billion expected from the gas tax was paltry. Begala had asked Sperling to examine some alternatives. An additional 1 percent hike in the income tax on the rich and corporations, for example, could raise the same $20 billion. Elimination of the gasoline-tax increase would mean there would be absolutely no middle-class tax increase, and signal a return to the successful and popular middle-class theme of the campaign.

Panetta seemed initially intrigued and started doing some calculations. But he soon realized it wouldn't work. No way, he said. Moynihan in the Senate and Rostenkowski in the House would *never* agree to a "zero option," period. The zero option was no option. Gore and Paster indicated they agreed.

Begala said they could just cut $20 billion from somewhere else. "Get your green-eyeshade people to come up with a way to replace it," he said to Panetta.

"Shit," Panetta replied, "we've been working this damn package for six months. You don't expect that we're just suddenly going to find $20 billion some place?"

"Well, I'm sure they can do it," Begala said. "Goddamnit, you have these propeller heads stacked up like cordwood over there. They can find it," he added eventually.

No, Panetta said. Any replacement would create a whole new set of problems, probably greater problems. Moving one piece in the plan would upset the rest. "If it was easy," the budget director said convincingly, "we would have found the $20 billion."

Gore, still smarting from the sacrifice of his BTU tax, seemed ready to bolt out of his seat. Environmental policy reform was still foremost in his mind. With renewed and almost excruciating sincerity, he said that they could not cave.

The House Democrats, including a wide spectrum of liberals and conservatives, were moving on their own toward dropping the energy tax altogether, Begala said.

True, said Stephanopoulos. But the administration, he said, was in the final tunnel. They just needed a final decision. Both the Senate and House members in the conference wanted to know the administration position. A nickel gas tax had a little magic to it, sounded small, and would help moderate the charge of extravagant tax proposals.

Begala persisted. Then go to $480 billion in deficit reduction for the five years. The deficit reduction number, whatever it was, was a classic insider issue that only the propeller heads cared about. "My mother doesn't care," Begala said, holding her up as an example of the perfect average person.

Rubin reminded them of the optimistic days in January when Bentsen had mentioned the energy tax on TV, and the bond market had immediately rallied, driving down interest rates. He was pretty sure that the index of White House seriousness for Wall Street was the inclusion of some form of energy tax, some form of spreading the sacrifice. Carefully noting that neither the energy tax nor the whole plan itself was exclusively responsible for the interest-rate drop, he said that the rate drop was probably the best thing the administration had going for it. It was helping the economy. The credibility of the package was holding. If they simply dropped all energy taxes because of short-term adverse political reaction, the question would become what else was going to slip out of the package. In fact, Bentsen, who was not there, felt strongly about increasing the gas tax by a penny or two more because 4.3 cents a gallon was too small.

What about $496 billion? someone asked. Or what about the $480 billion tested by Greenberg?

Rubin said that he thought they could not drop below $490 billion. Anything in the 490s sounded like 500, but $480 billion would tamper with the confidence of the bond market. Below that would be a clear negative.

The president, Panetta said, had shown tough leadership on the economic plan. Mr. President, the budget director said to Clinton, you knew that from the beginning. Once the plan was passed, the president could move on to the other issues he found important and easier to sell publicly. Panetta reminded them that the initial budget resolution had been passed in record time, and they were onto reconciliation in record time. The administration was in a good position and this was no time to pull the plug.

At one point Clinton made a crack about how this was the process that was driving him nuts.

Panetta gave one of his bright, intense laughs. They had to win, the budget director said. The president had set a path and he could not waver. A defeat of this plan could not be repaired with speeches or message revision, by reverting to old campaign themes, or by thrashing the establishment.

"The economic people don't have any respect for the political people," Begala said. "At least when we talk we know what the fuck we're saying. You can't give out this technopolicy babble." Bond market talk was precisely the wrong message; it soared above the lives of real people. "When we propose something," Begala said in his intense, loud voice, "the response from the economic team is, 'We are men of great substance and above politics.' "

Begala's hands and arms were flailing as he spoke. "The idea that the long-range benefits in this economic plan will propel it to passage is bullshit," he said, addressing the economic team. "You think the merits will gain passage?" he asked. "They won't. We have to sell this. We have to make our case to the people."

Greenberg said that because no one agreed on the purpose of the economic plan, they had been unable to communicate a clear, specific message. The plan did a variety of things, which the president thought was good policy, but it had led to a fractured message. They had not forced themselves to reach a common agreement. They had accepted their differences, which had produced the mixed messages, varying with each administration spokesperson.

Too many of them were going on television and still talking pain and sacrifice, Begala added. "If I see one more administration person on TV looking like he just sucked a lemon, I'm going to recommend he be shot." He cited a recent television appearance by Bob Reich as a good example of the upbeat message. It had been in the newspapers that Reich had just lost some internal battle for more worker-training funds. But on television Reich had emphasized the benefits of the smaller increase. "If you saw it on TV," Begala said, "you would have thought he'd won." Rubin was speaking to the bond market, Paster and Panetta to the Congress, and Bentsen to the Federal Reserve, Begala said. "But we have left off the people who elected Bill Clinton president."

Rubin and Panetta balked. The bond market talk might appear removed, Panetta said, reminding them for the umpteenth time that low interest rates allowed real people to borrow money or refinance mortgages at lower rates, giving them more money to spend on other things. The long-term repair to the economy, getting investment up, improving the standard of living were all tied to deficit reduction.

Panetta looked out the large panels of windows. A summer thunderstorm was brewing. He was awed as it built, black and gray clouds approaching, then the rain and wind, and finally the storm itself passing through. He had watched, from a much greater distance, other presidents go through similar turmoil as they navigated some rough political shoals, while the political advisers were warning a president off the hard, momentarily unpopular course, deeply and rightly concerned about lasting damage. This marked an important moment for Clinton, Panetta felt. The political consultants were trying so hard to spin him away from the deficit reduction to a more populist presentation. The intensity of the debate itself seemed to bring Clinton suddenly to a transition. Normally during a political campaign when the consultants, pollsters, and media advisers spoke with such a unified and loud voice, they would virtually dictate the decision. Panetta suspected that this debate was a turning point for Clinton, deciding whether the same campaign orientation would control his presidency.

Damnit, Carville finally interjected. "There's too much self-flagellation here," he said. "We're always running around saying *we* screwed up the 1980s. Well, the 'we' is Ronald Reagan and George Bush, not *us*." Clinton was attacking the deficit, the Reagan-Bush disease. You've got to tell me why this Clinton plan is different and important, Carville said. If you tell me that this is the right thing to do because my kids are going to be better off, fine. Even if the gasoline tax will cost people $49 a year, if you can show that people will pay less on their house, then goddamnit we can do this. The question is what is the payoff for that $49? A whole better life and future, he said, reciting a list of improvements in college loans, and tax breaks for the poor and small businesses.

Carville then rather suddenly indicated his preference for the nickel gas tax, breaking ranks with his fellow consultants and their recommended "bold zero option." They probably needed to keep the $500 billion in deficit reduction, he said. "We have to stick with something," he said. There had been too much slipping and sliding. If the president changed, everyone knew what the news would be. After promising and then backing off a middle-class tax cut, President Clinton was now promising and backing off a middle-class tax *increase*. The result would be no change from the candidate of change. Clinton could not flip-flop. "Just draw the line in the sand."

The message coming out was too dreary, Carville said, shaking his head in profound defeat and disappointment. "We've lost our message of hope and optimism," he said sullenly. "Every time I read a fucking newspaper, I'm hearing about our deficit reduction plan." Do an experiment, he said. Take one month of newspapers. Go from June 3 to July 3 and find me a reason anyone would be for this plan. He had been in Florida and picked up a newspaper in which the president's own people were saying the plan was not perfect, that it was missing this and that, too much of something, too little of something else. That was what people were responding to, he said. All this entered the information chain and was recycled. No wonder the polls showed so little support for the president's plan. "We aren't telling anybody anything good," Carville said, a fierce, almost ugly look of certainty and determination on his face. "Why would anyone believe it's good?"

Carville turned to a solution. "My daddy used to say when we were kids, whatever we had was the *best*. The *best*. We had the best house, the best clothes, we lived in the best town, we lived in the best homes, we had the best school. I had the best sisters. Louisiana had the *best* soil to grow things. That was what my dad used to say. What we have to start to do with this plan is say that it's the *best*. It's the *best* thing for the economy. The *best* thing for jobs. The *best* thing for interest rates. And be really full-throated about it."

The debate, Carville said, had to be recast, so that people were either for or against the plan. They had to get beyond the particulars. The answer was to say the whole plan was the change they needed and was going to be good for the economy, the *best* for the economy. "And if you're against it, you're being against the economy.

"We have to believe in this," he said. "We'll die if we don't get clarity on it, and I don't want to hear anybody saying you like it but you wish you had something else. This is the best. Why don't we just go out and say it's the best?"

As if at a revival meeting, a number of people seemed to mutter yes, I do, or we do. One of the strongest amens came from Hillary. "James is right," she said firmly.

But it wasn't being done, someone said. The president was having one set of meetings with his economic team and separate meetings with his political advisers. The strands were not being tied together.

Panetta felt that Carville had sliced through some of the clutter. Though Carville, like the others, saw the advantage of putting off the pain, he seemed to realize there was nothing worse than a politician trying to hide something. It was a simple but inspired message.

Greenberg presented some poll data from other pollsters to reenforce Carville's overall point. Since February, support for taxes had dropped, as had belief in the fairness of the Clinton plan. But the biggest drop— 20 points—was on the question whether the plan was good for the economy. "If we don't say that we believe this is good for the economy, why should the American people believe that?" Greenberg asked.

Others joined in. Much criticism focused on the lack of coordination, seeming to imply that McLarty as chief of staff was supposed to bring policy and message together but had failed. McLarty wasn't directly attacked; the criticism was veiled. McLarty said little but was taking extensive notes. He realized he was being faulted, and to several others he seemed chastened. Some of the criticism also seemed directed at the president for failing to choose among the competing personalities and ideas. For nearly an hour and a half, everyone had been banging hard on each other about the gasoline tax, the political message, the bond market, the overall strategy. Someone asked if they were going to apply the lessons they should have learned from the failure of the stimulus package in April. That triggered more debate about what lessons applied and created more undertow about who had screwed that up.

Stephanopoulos thought their position was precarious. The Chinese Taoists said all great wars are lost in the middle. And it seemed too possible. Six months in and they were still improvising.

Gore then tried to wrap up the meeting as was his habit with a message of unity and optimism, saying that it had been a good meeting, a lot had been accomplished.

"No," Stephanopoulos said, "we have not reached closure on these things." What was the position on the gas tax?

No one, including Clinton, had an immediate answer. The president had heard strong arguments for all three options: Greenberg, Grunwald, and Begala strongly for no gas tax; Stephanopoulos and now Carville for the nickel tax; and Gore and Paster most strongly for keeping negotiations open. It was agreed that Gore and Paster would talk to the congressional leadership.

Stephanopoulos, having peeled off Carville to his position, tried to attack the other options. Either might be a better long-term policy, but that didn't matter now. They were in a life-or-death situation. "We have to *win*," he said. Changing public opinion, as if that could be done in several weeks, didn't matter. It could have mattered in February, March, or April, but this was July. "And it is all a matter of what's going to move these individuals," he said.

. . .

HILLARY CLINTON had been relatively quiet throughout most of the meeting. She often held back during large meetings to get a sense of the discussion and the various positions. Her role as First Lady was somewhat strange, she realized, and she knew that some people liked it and some didn't. She considered herself a peer of her husband's advisers—not set apart, not omnipresent, but a full participant.

Over the last months she had reached some conclusions. The burden of carrying out the administration policies was too much on her husband, she felt. He was the chief congressional lobbyist, the chief message person, the policy designer, the spokesman—he carried out all the functions. Too many senior people in the administration and on the staff were stopping short of full preparation. The president invited this slacking off in some ways. Because he wanted to hear all the points of view and was very hands-on, lots of them would just take problems to him in midstream, knowing he would have thought about it and would have ideas and questions they might not have considered. Issues and work often landed in his office prematurely. Hillary's body language began to signal her frustration.

"This isn't working," she said finally, her voice sharp and direct, "and we're not selling the plan, nobody knows what's out there." To those less familiar with her style, it seemed she was popping off. Those from the campaign were almost certain her anger was calculated and purposeful. "Six months into it," she said in bewilderment, "the American people know nothing about it?" All of them were there to help the president communicate his policies and philosophy, and yet the country knew nothing. "He's out there every day," she said, referring to her husband.

Carville could see that she was at the end of her rope. They had been talking privately and both had commented on the low quality of work coming out of the White House staff. She had privately told him the meeting was going to be about having a plan and an overall strategy, not about settling on a nickel or 7 cents or 4 cents in gas tax.

"This is unacceptable and unfair to Bill," Hillary added, in a lawyerly closing statement. "It's not right to dump it all on him." She pointed to some of the economic team and said, "You're not serving him well by not knowing what they are doing," and directed her attention to the consultants. "And they have to know what you're doing." Then pointing again to the economic people, she said, "You do wonderful policy, but you don't think enough about how to explain it . . . every time you make a policy decision, you've got to figure out how to explain it."

She addressed both the political and economic policy groups. "You people need a process to talk to each other," she said.

She said that on the health care task force, they were always thinking about the link between policy and message. "You all have to figure this out," she summarized. "It's not Bill's job. This has to be coordinated." They were not organized to present it. She said with biting sarcasm that she spent more time deciding on a Friday-night movie than they had spent devising a strategy. "I can't believe that we're not capable of coordinating this among ourselves," she said. Quit talking about it, she said. Put something down on paper saying where we are going and what Bill's going to say, what each of us is going to say and do.

"First, we need a War Room to coordinate this," she said, all but dictating that command and communication authority be invested in one group that would work out of one room, similar to the campaign war room Carville and Stephanopoulos had run in Little Rock. She believed that the White House was dysfunctional in its use of physical space. For three months, she said, she had done a lot of work to get a War Room together for health care. Her team had been physically separated, making it impossible to coordinate. Getting the phones and office space had been a huge undertaking, but people with comparable functions had to be grouped together the way they had in the campaign. She volunteered her room. "Take the War Room and do something with it," she said.

Her husband had become, she said, the "mechanic-in-chief," put in the position of tinkering instead of being the president who had a moral voice, who had a vision, who was going to lead them on this journey. The economic plan wasn't about budgets and numbers, she said. It was a values document, she said. It was to help working people and small businesses, the effort to begin to reverse the greedy 1980s. That's what he should be talking about, she added. "I want to see a plan." She wanted everybody involved. "As we develop these policies, we have to decide how to explain them."

As had happened many times before, her anger ignited his. As Clinton had listened to Carville's message prescription and Hillary's critique, their state of unpreparedness became all too evident. Nothing was ready. Clinton rose to his feet. He was seething, and he just started yelling. He picked up where Hillary had left off, reenforcing her points.

Stephanopoulos almost tuned out. He had seen and experienced Clinton's temper tantrums so many times before. Others called them "purple fits" or "earthquakes." Stephanopoulos simply called it "the wave," an overpowering, prolonged rage that would shock an outsider, and often was way out of proportion to what caused it. He couldn't listen to the precise words, which really didn't matter anyway. The words were also best unremembered. The point was simple: They had to move, get something done.

"I'm leaving and I'm going to Tokyo," Clinton yelled. He turned to McLarty and Gore. "Mack and Al, you two, I want it solved. I want it done before I get home." He didn't resist adding some instructions. "I want you to meet on this and I want you to meet every day. Don't wait for me to get back from Tokyo."

There were lots of mumbled "yes sirs." The order was clear. The sudden silence meant the meeting was over. Clinton didn't storm out. The wave had passed. But his peremptory, almost bitter rebuke sent the others out down the solarium ramp somewhat battered. Though his eruption carried the emotional punch, it paled compared to Hillary's withering analysis. There was no denying the critique—most pointedly, a scalding indictment of McLarty. At crucial moments like this, Hillary was often the *de facto* chief of staff.

PASTER AGREED with the criticism of McLarty. But Paster was, once again, amazed at Clinton's willingness to allow these extended debates where they essentially talked to death the inevitable. Clinton was always trying to pick out a new course, move the debate or the policy slightly. The dynamic had a pattern. Clinton, unaccepting of the conventional wisdom, especially about Congress, would test the edges of what was possible, stretching the boundaries of the Washington and congressional playing field. Clinton wanted to have an outsider administration, adeptly playing the insider game.

In the hall outside, Stephanopoulos and Greenberg walked together. It looked like agreement on the nickel gas tax, Greenberg said.

"We don't have closure," Stephanopoulos said pessimistically. He was upset. "Gore still has room to lobby this issue and take it further."

Gore was being humored, Greenberg said. He would talk to the leadership and they would tell him it would stay at 4.3 cents.

No, Stephanopoulos said gloomily. Clinton had not actually said that this was the decision. Gore still had maneuvering room. His appointment to work with McLarty on the plan would certainly keep the debate alive. Worse, Stephanopoulos said, they certainly didn't have a consensus on what the message was or even what the essence of this economic plan was.

Greenberg realized that Stephanopoulos had much more experience and knew how to read both White House meetings and Clinton.

Stephanopoulos also spoke to Carville. Carville said that the business about the gas tax seemed to be all futility. Eliminating it altogether in the bold zero option, or increasing it as Gore seemed to want, was just bullshit. "Why are we agonizing over something that we know is already done?"

Stephanopoulos wondered the same thing himself.

For Panetta and some of the others, the meeting was highly unusual for the Clinton White House: Clinton had actually delegated a major responsibility of his presidency to other people.

Carville and Begala talked afterward, agreeing that they had never seen Clinton quite so angry at his advisers. If they didn't fix this situation, they felt it possible that Clinton would fire the two of them, or all the consultants, or even the White House staff and cabinet. They also saw that the bleeding caused by the divisions in the administration, reflecting the divisions within Clinton, had to be stopped. They had ten days before Clinton was scheduled to return.

By staying back in Washington, McLarty was seen as even further removed from the center of the Clinton presidency. Not to accompany the president only fed the widely repeated rap that he was out of it.

Carville went to see him later. "You know, Mack," Carville said, "you're an unusual person. If the president came to you and said you need to go back to Little Rock, this thing is not working out, you could pack your bags and go back and you would think about it for two days and you would go on with your life. But the truth of the matter is, if we don't get this fucking thing done, we all ought to go back." McLarty said he agreed.

28

O~N JULY~ 7, the consultants visited the White House to see McLarty, Rubin, and Paster. Mandy Grunwald was determined to get McLarty and Rubin to see that the all-consuming focus on Congress was part of the problem. It was as if the senior staff consisted of half a dozen Howard Pasters. As a result, the communications strategy was built around the relationship between the White House and the Congress. That was what they thought about, and that was what they were talking about. Grunwald told them in her direct manner that they had lost the sense of the journey, of the story, that had been outlined after Camp David. They had lost the vital message that the plan was good for the middle class. The only way to prove that was to show that the rich were paying for most of it. "We've got to talk about this," she said.

Rubin interrupted her. "I talk about progressivity all of the time in my speeches," Rubin explained. He had had this argument before. "But we can't demonize the people who have done well in this country."

Grunwald erupted. "People don't understand fuck-all about progressivity," she said. Rubin's friends from New York City all knew what the term meant, but real people did not. "We have to say we are taxing the rich. R-I-C-H. That's a four-letter word people understand." The president had to name exactly the income groups that would pay the most, to make clear that nearly all the taxes were coming from those who made more than $140,000 a year. People could then hear that and say, Hey, that's not me, she said. That was the only way to convince them. The point had to be delivered confrontationally and with specifics. To say the middle class would pay little meant nothing.

Rubin said he didn't have any problem with using the specific numbers if that would help.

They all agreed that the president had decreed that they had to appoint a chief coordinator and message czar, as Carville had been in the presidential campaign. Carville, though, was occupied with speaking engagements, other political consulting work, and a book he was writing with Mary Matalin. Begala didn't want the job. The group talked about recruiting a Washington lawyer from outside the administration for this one-time task.

"How about Roger Altman?" Paster suggested instead. They needed a policy person. In his opinion, Altman had served as the perfect intermediary with Bentsen—less sensitive about protocol and more attuned to White House political needs.

The consultants paused. "Perfect," Begala replied. Putting a policy person in charge of message might work if they had the right policy person, and Altman seemed to have a good ear for politics.

They would also assign senior staffers from all departments and White House offices to the team. A War Room would have to be set up, too, but it would have to be called something different. "War Room" was too reminiscent of the presidential campaign and politics. This was a vast economic recovery plan, and they had to evoke the goal of helping the country, not winning an election.

On Thursday, July 8, the four consultants delivered a single-page memo to McLarty. Its title: "Proposal for Coordinating Strategy and Message."

"We propose the following structure to integrate strategy, politics, policy and communications.

"1. THE ESTABLISHMENT OF A BOILER ROOM. We need a central location to bring together, physically, representatives of the key players in the reconciliation conference strategy. We suggest Room 180 of the Old Executive Office Building be turned into a boiler room, which we'd call THE PIT (after the name given to the center of action at a stock exchange). This is not the campaign, so anyone who calls this place the 'War Room' will be fined $10, with the proceeds going to the Children's Defense Fund.

"2. EACH KEY DEPARTMENT MUST ASSIGN A SENIOR PERSON TO THE PIT FOR THE DURATION. We suggest the following All-Star lineup." Included were Sperling and ten others from the agencies and sections of the White House. "This group could be chaired by Roger Altman.

"3. ALL KEY PRINCIPALS SHOULD START THE DAY WITH A MORNING MEETING. To ensure coordination at the highest levels, the Vice President and the Chief of Staff should meet each morning with Bentsen, Rubin, Panetta, Paster, Stephanopoulos, Gergen, Altman, [Staff Secretary John] Podesta, and one of the political consultants.

"4. THE PIT SHOULD BE UP AND RUNNING BY THE TIME THE PRESIDENT RETURNS FROM TOKYO. In addition, the Pit Crew will present to the President, on his arrival, a plan. . . ."

Gore and McLarty approved.

The crew of aides commandeered Hillary's health care war room. She said that if the economic plan didn't pass, the heath care proposal, whatever its contents, would be dead-on-arrival in the Congress.

Jeff Eller, a senior communications aide who was running the health operation in the room, was less than happy. "When did you guys figure out that they were going to vote on the fucking budget?" Eller screamed in the hall when informed that his room had been seized. The new team could only offer apologies. Even though the battle over the economic plan was technically not a campaign, the new headquarters quickly became known as the War Room.

McLARTY REACHED Altman in Tokyo to tell him he had been tapped to run the new War Room. Altman was happy to get the job. He knew that the War Room was being created because the economic plan was in deep trouble. The administration, he felt, had lost the battle for public opinion on the tax-and-spend accusations by the Republicans. He believed in the financial markets strategy to lower interest rates. The strategy was not an appeal to 25 people in suspenders on Wall Street, he felt, but to real people who would pay less in interest. Yet that message had not been delivered with the necessary clarity. Gergen's arrival was supposed to turn around Clinton's image, but apparently it had failed. Clinton seemed to have lost his populist mantle. Why? Altman wondered.

Altman believed that Republicans played hardball and Democrats played softball, that Clinton himself was soft and that Hillary was hard. Getting the plan passed would require playing hard, and he was willing. This was not a simple task, not to ride a winner home to victory but to turn a loser into a winner.

For his new assignment, Altman sought advice from the king of war rooms, James Carville. "You've got to make a Roger Altman war room and not a James Carville war room," Carville advised. "Part of it is the president knowing that it's there, and 75 percent of the battle is probably that the president and the First Lady know that there is somebody defending them."

ON JULY 14, Clinton returned from Asia. The Tokyo summit had been a big hit, and he had received substantial credit in the international community for starting to get America's economic act together. Seeming reinvigorated, Clinton said he was ready to nail the economic plan and get it passed. His staff presented him with a two-inch-thick binder of memos. Included was a four-page summary that Begala had written, an elaboration on Carville's speech about declaring the economic plan the best. The memo began in the center of the page, like the headline on a newspaper extra:

HALLELUJAH!
Change is Coming

"In those four words we convey the two central concepts we need to communicate to the American people: This is good, and this is change."

The memo said that Clinton's plan would allow the economy to grow "by finally paying down the deficit." In fact, the plan would only reduce the growth of the deficit, which would still be $200 billion each year. As the Republicans reminded everyone, the total national debt would still increase by about $1 trillion over Clinton's first term.

"This plan will create JOBS—8 million of them," the memo said. In fact, the economy would create those jobs and the economic plan would have little direct impact.

In its conclusion, Begala's memo offered instructions to all administration members. "Anytime you're asked about a specific in the economic plan, look for ways to bring it back to the general points that this is good for the country, and this is real change.

"Finally, never forget that the optimism, energy, enthusiasm you project is vital. Even your most cynical critics will walk away impressed with your COMMITMENT. And that's half the battle. Your body language, attitude and confidence will be infectious. If you become a merchant of pain, you'll find that the middle class isn't buying—they already have enough, thank you.

"Now go forth and spread the good news."

Begala was not fully comfortable with the simplistic, happy-talk memo. He realized, somewhat painfully, that he had become a salesman for a plan that neither he nor Clinton really believed in. He spoke with

Clinton and said that the whole administration and its supporters all had to rally around the plan. If they couldn't convince themselves, Begala said, they couldn't convince the public and Congress. The first step had to be for them to get their own religion. The hallelujah motif would have to be pushed hard, with sermons and an evangelical approach. Heretical attitudes, negative body language, and private, snide comments could undercut the effort.

Also, it had to start at the top. "You're not allowed to criticize it anymore," Begala told the president.

"You're right," Clinton said, laughing.

Begala told a joke to demonstrate the importance of Clinton's own state of mind: Oral Roberts, the faith healer, dies and goes to heaven. Greeting him, St. Peter, the gatekeeper, asks, "Are you Oral Roberts the faith healer?" Roberts says yes. "There's someone I want you to meet," St. Peter says, and takes him to Jesus. "Oh, you're Oral Roberts the faith healer?" Jesus asks. "There's someone I want you to meet." Jesus takes him to God, the Father. "Oh, you're Oral Roberts the faith healer?" God asks. "Yes, I am." God reaches up to His shoulder and says, "I've got this pain here . . ."

We need to believe in our own faith and its power, Begala said.

Stephanopoulos saw that Clinton had to internalize Carville's message that the plan was the "best." "I've got to make my economic policies popular," Clinton told his advisers at one point. "I've got to go out and say that this is the right thing to do. And I have to say that I believe in it."

Sperling had stayed up almost three days straight to compile a spokesman's bible, a half-inch-thick document of graphs, tables, pie charts, quotes, and lengthy arguments totaling 86 pages. It was the manual for all-out political war, the kind of extreme effort they wanted.

"Gene," Altman said in some wonder when he saw it, "what a marvelous book! I can't believe you did this wonderful thing in just three days."

That Friday, Clinton wrote Altman a note, saying he was impressed with the outline of the plan and the setup of the new war room. Almost as if trying to bring himself to the point of determined self-conviction, Clinton closed the note with motto, "Let's go do it!"

ALTMAN CALLED LAURA TYSON. She agreed to supply a representative from the Council of Economic Advisers to the War Room. Her one hesitation was that she didn't want the Council to be part of a spin organization. Her audience was not the general public, but experts and economic professionals. If they detected a political twist in the Council's work, Clinton and the whole administration would pay a price in credibility that would outweigh any short-term gain. For instance, she insisted that the team agree to attribute the job growth of 8 million to the economy, not to Clinton's plan. Virtually all economists agreed that the 8 million jobs were going to be created, no matter what the impact of the plan.

Tyson had been studying the numbers in the five-year deficit reduction plan. She and the budget office had been careful to backload most of the actual reduction in the last years, to put off the pain. The exception was 1996. For election-year purposes, they didn't want a big drag on the economy. Since this arrangement was made clear in the public budget documents and not concealed, it was considered acceptable for the Council.

But since the stimulus package had been killed and Congress was in the mood to reduce the deficit more, the reduction in the years 1993 and 1994 had doubled. In the short run, they had effectively wound up with an anti-stimulus package in a weak economy. Tyson and her deputies, Alan Blinder and Joseph Stiglitz, a senior Stanford economist, wrote a two-and-a-quarter-page memo for the president on July 15. Clinton received it the next day.

The memo said there was another side to the deficit reduction coin, namely, that the president's program might contain *too much* deficit reduction, particularly in the current and following year. The contractionary impact of cutting spending and raising taxes in a weak economy could have a significant adverse impact. The memo added that since the introduction of the president's plan five months ago, two things had happened: The economy had worsened, with annual growth expected to be just 2.2 percent instead of the 3 percent of their earlier forecasts; and Congress had imposed more deficit reduction than the president's plan, while front-loading more cuts and taxes into the early years.

The numbers were important. Initially, Clinton's plan called for deficit reduction in the years 1993 and 1994 of only $26 billion. Since the defeat of the stimulus package and other changes by Congress, however, the plan would cut twice as much, $53 billion, in the same two years. Though a relatively tiny percentage of GDP, the change, especially with growth already slow, could tilt the economy in the wrong direction.

The memo offered Clinton two possible responses. He could try to change the timing of the cuts and taxes while preserving the five-year goal of $500 billion. Or he could reduce the overall five-year goal. Either way, the memo suggested, he should consider eliminating the retroactivity of the income-tax increases. In its current form, the plan called for making the tax increase effective as early as January 1, 1993, regardless of when the bill was signed into law. Eliminating six months of retroactivity would save people about $9 billion in taxes, giving them that much more to spend and providing the economy a short-term lift. Another option for changing the timing of the tax bite, the memo proposed, would be to phase in the gas tax in a way that none of it would take effect the first year. It was also possible to delay every tax increase for six months, or delay the middle-class or gas-tax increase for a year. The result would be to slip $10 billion to $20 billion on the overall $500 billion deficit target.

Though the memo didn't say it directly, it warned indirectly that the president's plan might trigger a recession. The economic situation Clinton was facing paralleled the one President Bush had faced in 1990, when a $500 billion deficit reduction plan was passed as the economy was sliding into recession. No one had to remind Clinton what happened to the economy, or to Bush.

The Council's July 15 memo was the collective professional opinion of the president's economists, among the best in the field. It would be madness to ignore the warning. Besides, Paster reported that a number of liberal Democrats were also saying that the plan might contain too much deficit reduction. Tyson had been going around the Congress floating the idea that maybe they had gone too far. She realized, however, that in all probability Congress was locked into its figure. One senator said that if the plan contained even one dollar less than $500 billion, he would vote against it.

Clinton called his economic team to a meeting in the Oval Office. Included were Gore, Bentsen, Panetta, Tyson, Rubin, Stephanopoulos, and Gergen, as well as Grunwald and Begala. In his six weeks at the White House, Gergen had come to support Tyson and her council, basically because he didn't like tax increases and they were proposing ways to defer, minimize, or readjust the tax bite.

Tyson said she knew they probably couldn't do anything about it, but the president needed to know.

Rubin said he agreed that the economy was not doing well and that minimizing the contractionary impact of the plan was a legitimate concern. They should discuss the issue.

The others indicated that they saw the need to discuss it but felt there was little they could do now that they had reached the endgame. House and Senate plans had been passed and were about to be reconciled in conference. To throw in new ideas could wreak havoc.

As it was, the gasoline-tax debate was still dragging on, and it wasn't clear what was going to happen. By indecision, Clinton was letting the conference come up with a number. He had not come out firmly for the nickel gasoline tax, nor had he proposed dropping the tax altogether as suggested by the consultants' "bold zero option." Charles Stenholm of Texas, whom Clinton considered a great vote counter, was also urging that the gas tax be dropped. Stenholm had argued that such a move would kill the Republicans because they would not be able to say the Clinton plan had middle-class taxes. But it was the eleventh hour, and Clinton was not sure what to do.

"It's too late," Begala said of the proposal to reduce the $500 billion target. "We can't come off it." He had been converted.

Grunwald, who also had preferred dropping the gas tax entirely, now agreed that the option to defer all of it to the last three years was too cute. A no-pain-now, more-pain-later plan would sound too much like "Slick Willie" of Arkansas.

Tyson didn't back down. Her job was to alert them to a problem, and this one was real. At one point, she suggested a technical tax adjustment of several billion dollars. During the discussion of this small matter, she handed Rubin a note, saying in effect that she assumed the adjustment would go over fine with the bond market. "Definitely not," Rubin scribbled back.

Clinton floated a solution. "If it doesn't work and we fall into recession," he said, "we'll have to stimulate by lowering taxes." Someone noticed the blood run out Rubin's face. Nothing could blow the deficit reduction plan sky high like lowering taxes. Clinton seemed a little angry, noting the process was out of his hands, but indicated he wanted to meet further on the issue. They had to keep tabs on it, he said.

Stephanopoulos had one reaction: Nothing mattered except votes.

THE WAR ROOM was helping. Its mere presence made many in the administration feel that they were speaking with one voice, had their act together, and could engage in a tough fight. Altman played coach, trying not to get involved too much in the others' jobs. He gave pep talks and praised the work of his crack staff. At one point, Senator Breaux publicly proposed scaling back the deficit reduction package to $400 billion instead of $500. Altman raced enthusiastically into the War Room. Let's respond! he declared.

There was total silence.

"Don't you see?" Sperling said. "We don't need to respond. What Breaux said helps us. It proves that we're the tough ones."

Others agreed. The room was full of deficit hawks.

"Bad idea," Altman said, folding his arms before the room full of newly converted deficit hawks. "Bad idea, you're right."

ALAN GREENSPAN TESTIFIED before a House Banking subcommittee on July 20. Over the last six months, in his congressional testimony and in his private exchanges with Clinton, Greenspan's tweezer-chosen words had been critical, if not decisive, in launching the financial markets strategy. Now, with the rumblings of dropping the gas tax and Breaux's suggestion to jump back to $400 billion of deficit reduction, there was a real danger of backsliding. Greenspan was anxious to voice his opinion.

"If you appear to be backing off, I think the markets would react, appropriately, negatively," Greenspan said, shunning his usual public smoke-signal circumlocutions. He urged that Congress stick to the $500 billion target. It was a message to the White House as well. Whether Greenspan was right or not, his public declaration made the $500 billion the benchmark of credibility in the financial markets. Clinton's hands were tied.

THE ADMINISTRATION'S BATTLE PLAN included a visit by Clinton to the House Democrats to give a talk and shore up their support. House Speaker Foley had told the White House congressional relations staff that Clinton should stay away, that a visit wouldn't work. But Gephardt passed the word through back channels that Clinton should come. The more they heard Clinton, the better off they would be, he had contended. Clinton agreed to visit Capitol Hill, Tuesday, July 20. The day marked a special anniversary for Clinton. Thirty years ago, on July 20, 1963, Clinton, at age 16, had visited the White House and shaken hands with President Kennedy, an event that had been captured in a photograph published widely during the campaign. July 20 also marked the close of Clinton's first six months in office.

Begala had written a draft of the speech and filled it with slash-and-burn rhetoric. "We must protect older Americans from the Draconian cuts in Social Security, Medicare and veterans benefits the Republicans have proposed . . ." the draft said. "I will not agree to a penny more than the level of Medicare reductions already approved by the Senate, and I hope we can do better."

But when Clinton spoke, he toned it down: "We have to recognize that there is a limit to how much, particularly in this reconciliation process, we can cut beyond where we are without hurting the elderly, the working poor, and the middle class. . . . I do not believe we should cut Medicare more." Clinton smoothed the edges, thanking the congressmen, but retaining some of Begala's fiery language. Representative Jack Brooks of Texas, a 30-year House veteran, gave Clinton a hug afterwards. Back at the White House, Clinton visited the new War Room to rally his troops personally. Then he did separate, half-hour satellite television interviews with journalists first from Wisconsin and then Louisiana, both states with wavering senators.

At 9 P.M. that night, Clinton went on the "Larry King Live" television show from the White House library. Originally scheduled for an hour, he agreed during a commercial break to stay on a half hour more. In the meantime, McLarty had received a phone call, and he urged King to cancel the last half hour. Neither King nor Clinton understood why, and Clinton asked McLarty what was going on.

The call had informed McLarty that Vincent Foster, the deputy White House counsel who had grown up in Arkansas with Clinton and McLarty, had shot and killed himself in a Virginia park. Almost at once, the tall Clinton and the much shorter McLarty left the White House with their arms draped over each other's shoulders. They headed out to visit Foster's widow at her Georgetown townhouse.

The next day, Clinton addressed the White House staff about Foster's suicide. "No one can ever know why this happened. Even if you had a whole set of objective reasons, that wouldn't be why it happened, because you could get a different, bigger, more burdensome set of objective reasons that are on someone else even in this room. So what happened was a mystery about something inside of him. And I hope all of you will always understand that." Two days later Clinton said more. "I don't think there is anything more to know. His family, his friends, his co-workers, we've been up really late two nights in a row now, remembering and crying and laughing and talking about him. I don't think there is anything else."

Privately, Clinton told several others that Hillary, who had been exceptionally close to Foster, was "destroyed" by the suicide.

ON JULY 21, Greenberg and Carville visited a Chicago suburb out by O'Hare Airport for four hours of intensive listening to "real" people. They had begun research on a secret project for Clinton called "The Presidential Project," a comprehensive study of how people viewed the

Clinton presidency and why they weren't connecting with him or his economic plan. The Democratic National Committee financed the research. In the standard focus group, first ten women, and then ten men answered questions and participated in separate two-hour open discussions run by a moderator. Both groups consisted of noncollege graduates who had either supported Clinton with reservations or supported Perot. These voters had been selected because Greenberg and Carville had concluded that they would likely decide the 1996 election. For the four hours, the two men peered through the one-way glass and listened.

Among other things, Greenberg was looking for the index by which people measured Clinton, the first post–Cold War president. During the Cold War, managing and dominating the relationship with the Soviet Union had been the way Kennedy, Nixon, and Reagan had created a moral imperative around their presidencies. Controlling that relationship with the Soviet Union had been the threshold test that voters had used to judge their presidents.

As Greenberg listened to the focus group, he was struck by what people didn't mention. They were not discussing foreign affairs or military matters or Clinton as commander in chief. But neither were they talking about taxes or even the specific contents of Clinton's economic plan. They did show curiosity about the drama going on in Washington as the kind of basic, ageless struggle between a new president and the Congress, between the young outsider and the old insiders. Often in tones of resignation, many said that Congress would no doubt win once again. Congress was a negative force that dominated and broke presidents. Carter had been broken; so had Bush. Maybe Clinton would be next, one of the people behind the glass indicated.

Sitting there in the dark, Greenberg had a sudden revelation. "James," he said, turning to Carville, "this is a threshold issue." Congress was the new Soviet Union, the primary threat for a president and a relationship to manage and dominate. Clinton was being tested and measured by his ability to master the congressional forces arrayed against him. It immediately clicked for Carville, too.

At once they began polling larger numbers of people. One key question: What personal characteristic and strength is most important for a president to lead the country today: (1) to handle relations with other countries and protect American security; or (2) to handle Congress and get things done to address the country's problems? Only 23 percent picked managing affairs abroad, while 63 percent picked managing Congress. However, to a question about which presidential style they preferred a president to use in dealing with Congress, 53 percent selected working with the congressional leaders, while only 35 percent selected challenging the legislative branch for doing nothing and attempting to mobilize the public to pressure Congress.

The conclusion was very clear to the two consultants: The public wanted a president to master but not overwhelm Congress. To extend the analogy with the Soviet Union, they wanted containment and peaceful coexistence, not conventional war, and certainly not thermonuclear war. They wanted an end to gridlock.

TYSON WAS GROWING TIRED of the constant refrain about the bond market. In reality, she realized, the "bond market" was an abstraction, a nonexistent entity. There were thousands of traders, buyers and sellers of bonds worldwide, who never did the same thing, never acted in concert. If they did, after all, there would be no market: Bond sellers would find no buyers, or buyers would find no sellers.

Yet to many, particularly Bentsen, she realized, the bond market had become the new god. Greenspan had said publicly and privately that the deficit reduction plan was one of the reasons for the favorable decline in interest rates. He had been precise, specifying it was but one of the reasons. Yet by the time Greenspan's statements filtered through Bentsen—the two met each week—and reached the White House table and the president's ears, the deficit reduction plan was the *only* reason bond market rates were down. Tyson couldn't tell whether Bentsen really believed that or was just saying it for emphasis, but a lot of nuance was being lost. At times, she felt, it bordered on distortion.

For months she had tried to be the voice of uncertainty. She had told Clinton that no theory could explain how much or when the interest rates would move. She had brought articles underscoring the point to the table for the president to see. She was also unsure how much additional consumer spending and investment the lower rates would bring.

The argument about the bond market that Bentsen and now the president were making disturbed Tyson. Some economic models suggested that each year-long drop in the long rate of 1 percent would trigger new refinancing and loans, freeing up $100 billion of stimulus for the economy. But Tyson and Blinder had both talked to Greenspan about that $100 billion number. Greenspan had said he wouldn't use the number. Certainly some stimulus resulted from a 1 percent rate drop, he said, but probably closer to only $50 billion or $75 billion. The whole notion was riddled with imprecision. Tyson had studied the issue closely and tried to get the War Room to take the $100 billion number out of its official message. How about coming down to $75 billion? she had suggested. That figure would be much more sound. They replied that they and Clinton had already used the $100 billion number. It would stay.

Tyson worried that since the administration was in the grip of the bond market, it was beginning to appear that lower interest rates were all the administration had achieved. Unfortunately, she realized, it was difficult, if not impossible, for the public to understand the connections between Clinton's program, lower deficits, lower interest rates, more investments, higher productivity, and a better standard of living. As Alan Blinder liked to say, it just didn't fit on a bumper sticker. She, too, had heard Clinton label his plan a "turkey."

On July 21, she, Blinder, and Stiglitz sent a three-page memo to the economic team following up on their argument that the plan might have too much deficit reduction. "This document represents groupthink," the memo said, noting that no one of them endorsed all the ideas or options. It said a shift of some $20 billion within the budget was possible. "A meeting on this subject seems imperative and soon."

The next day, at 4:45 P.M., Rubin convened the senior members of the economic team, now called the reconciliation team, in Room 324 on the third floor of the Old Executive Office Building. Clinton was not there. Rubin always ran meetings with a velvet glove, gentle and guiding. This one he ran with no glove, turning it over to Tyson.

She laid some numbers on the table. Perhaps the total deficit reduction target should be something like $480 billion, instead of $500 billion, she suggested. The $480 could be achieved by altering the timing on the income or gasoline taxes. She reviewed some specific options. At one point she suggested a move that would alter the tax bite by about $5 billion.

Bentsen, his unhappiness apparent beneath his restrained gentlemanliness, said he was not keen on fiddling with it at all. He chastised Tyson for even suggesting that they tinker with the deficit reduction goals. It was almost as if she were guilty of blasphemy. Negotiations with Congress were at their most fragile stage. Even public disclosure of this discussion could have ramifications. One little change could start an unraveling or make it appear that they were losing confidence in their package. Her suggestion would destabilize the bond market, Bentsen said.

"Oh, come on!" Tyson said. "You don't think the bond market is going to react that way to $5 billion? Please." The sum could not possibly be enough to matter, and the option simply to shift some of the reduction to the latter years would even preserve the $500 billion number. There was no theory of economics or psychology or politics to support Bentsen's view. "That is ridiculous," she said.

"I disagree," Bentsen said coldly.

Tyson was exasperated. Hocus-pocus was ruling the day. She felt she was merely making the case for caution, wanting to protect the plan and protect the president. Bentsen, in contrast, was so certain of himself, so rigid.

Panetta didn't want anything to throw them off track or undercut the momentum. They had to wrap up the son of a bitch they had been struggling with for half a year. They could not be diverted, he said. Once the package was passed, they could on their own speed up spending of about $5 billion. It had been tried in the Bush administration unsatisfactorily, but they could give it a shot. Also another $5 billion was going to the Midwest in relief because of extensive flooding. So that would add up to $10 billion in stimulus.

They all agreed. The group also pledged not to say anything publicly as they pushed on to the main battle. They had to prove the administration's courage and not flinch from real deficit reduction now.

Panetta was developing more and more sympathy for Clinton. The concerns of the consultants were legitimate and real; so were Tyson's; so were those of most others. Legitimate concerns were everywhere. The president was getting it from all sides, strapped down by a little thread here and a little thread there, like Jonathan Swift's shipwrecked Gulliver, immobilized by the Lilliputians.

29

BENTSEN WAS LEANING ON BOREN, his longtime friend and ally, about the upcoming final vote. The bond market was already responding favorably in anticipation of passage, he reminded Boren, and failure would drive up interest rates.

Boren called a few friends in New York. Skull and Bones, his secret society at Yale, had extensive Wall Street connections. Boren asked if Bentsen's argument was accurate. He maintained his friends said no.

The White House wheeled out some other administration big guns. Secretary of State Warren Christopher called Boren and said a defeat would harm the president in the international community, particularly with the seven leading industrial nations. Attorney General Janet Reno, whom Boren had publicly praised, even made a run at him.

Then McLarty called Boren to say the president wanted to see him and talk about it.

"Mack," Boren warned, "I'm not a very good prospect." Boren had been left off the conference committee, and had no control over the bill that would be up for the final vote.

"We can't lose anybody we had before," McLarty said.

"Mack, you lost me before it ever went to conference. But I just let you go to conference in hopes it might get better. It's gotten worse, and I can't be for it."

McLarty insisted that Boren come see Clinton on Saturday, July 24.

When Boren arrived at the White House, he was greeted in the Oval Office by Clinton, Gore, McLarty, Gergen, and Stephanopoulos.

For some time, Boren had been trying to get Stephanopoulos to speak to Boren's summer interns. Boren had dozens of interns each year and treated the program with the utmost seriousness and personal attention, calling in chits all over town to get the most high-profile speakers the capital could offer. Stephanopoulos had never answered his request.

"Guess what?" Stephanopoulos said. "I'm going to see your interns next week." Boren thanked him, and Stephanopoulos left.

Clinton, dressed casually, sat in his high-backed armchair. Boren, wearing a blue blazer, took the seat in the other chair. For perhaps the first time in the Clinton administration, someone other than a visiting head of state or ranking or honored visitor had taken the seat normally reserved for the vice president. No one said anything, and Gore joined McLarty and Gergen on the sofas.

Clinton began by saying how appreciative he was of Boren's efforts on behalf of Joycelyn Elders, his nominee for Surgeon General, and of Boren's support for the national service bill. The two engaged in a lengthy review of those matters.

We're going to have to get to the subject at hand, McLarty finally interrupted.

Why? Boren tried to joke. They were having such a nice conversation on all these things they agreed about.

Tell me where you are on this, Clinton solicited, referring to the upcoming vote.

Boren said he remained unconvinced at that point that the bill was a good thing. He said Clinton was effectively repeating Bush's mistake, raising taxes too much. Clinton wasn't controlling entitlements and wasn't going to lower the deficit enough, he added, and people would feel angrier than ever. Boren didn't think there was a strong enough ratio of spending cuts to tax increases in the plan. "You can stand up in the back of a pickup and defend tax increases if you've really cut spending," he said, but Clinton hadn't.

Warming to the opportunity, Boren gave a version of his speech about the "twentysomething" generation that was going to be screwed by the explosive entitlement costs. Too much spending on Social Security and Medicare was going to those who didn't need the benefits. "Welfare for the wealthy," Boren called it. "All of us are adult enough to know here we'll never get spending under control until we means-test," Boren, referring to the proposal to assess whether those receiving federal money had substantial income or wealth. "Let's start it."

"We've got to do it in health care," Clinton said.

Boren cautioned that the president should seize the opportunity now when he had the leverage. "Mr. President," he said, "you may never get all of health care. It's not going to pass in one fell swoop. This is going to be another decade-long struggle." They could get some savings from health care right away.

Gore interjected that the American Association of Retired Persons and other senior citizens' groups were now on the reservation for the economic plan, and slashing Medicare and Social Security any more would mean losing them.

But at what price are they on the reservation? Boren asked. That was what bothered him.

Well, Gore asked, what did Boren want changed in the plan in order to secure his vote?

Like a little list? Boren asked.

Yeah, Gore said.

Boren said he didn't have a little list. Raising the gas tax a nickel or cutting it a nickel or anything like that wouldn't do it, he said. He had given his list to Moynihan like everybody else back in the Finance Committee. It was over and done with, and Boren likened himself to a free agent in baseball. "I have the luxury of standing back here and looking at this," Boren said. His test would be simple: Would it work? If not, it didn't serve the national interest.

Gore said he was optimistic for the first time, hearing Boren say he would make his decision based on the national interest.

That should not make you optimistic, Boren shot back. "There's nothing you can do for me or to me that will influence my decision on this matter," he added. "I'm going to make it on the basis of what I think is right or wrong."

Nobody responded for a moment. Clinton then stepped in. Why didn't Boren think it was in the national interest? he asked.

It wasn't bipartisan, Boren answered. To be successful in this country, it had been demonstrated over and over, an effort had to be bipartisan. Clinton had even said so himself, Boren pointed out. Even most optimists, Boren said, thought they were still not even halfway there.

We all want bipartisanship, Gore said.

You'll forgive me for being skeptical about that, Boren snapped at Gore. Four of the five of them in the room, he said, excepting Gergen, had been next door in the Cabinet Room two or three months before, at the May 6 meeting of the Senate Finance Committee Democrats. They were asked to raise their hands, Boren reminded, to promise not to even talk to Republicans. So they could forgive him for being skeptical about the commitment at the White House to bipartisanship, Boren repeated caustically.

He then grew even testier. While he was at it, he said, he wanted to clear the decks of everything. The past was not going to influence his vote, and if any further entitlement constraints could be put in at the last minute, he would consider voting for the bill. But he had his grievances. The administration had known where he was going to be and nonetheless had implied publicly that they still might get his vote.

No one pointed out that Boren had himself just said they still might get it with a new entitlement constraint.

In a low roar, Boren continued. Immediately after his May 20 press conference he was branded as someone who cared more about oil than people because of where he happened to be from. That, he said, was an insult not only to him but to everybody he represented, as if they couldn't be patriotic in their part of the country. The same hadn't been said about Sam Nunn of Georgia, or any of the other Democratic senators who voted against the plan—who, unlike himself, didn't even vote to send it to conference. Boren reminded them that he had handled the campaign finance bill, Dr. Elders, and the national service bill. He supported the North American Free Trade Agreement. "I'm not an enemy. Why am I treated like one?"

The president looked down. "David," Clinton said, "it's more like what you wanted. So it's going to be easier to vote for it than the one you voted for in June. You said you weren't going to be the person to bring this down. And it is not fair for you to say we're treating you like an enemy." Boren's own plan didn't get any other votes, the president reminded him.

Gore had one more card to play. He laid it on the table heavily. A no vote would destroy the presidency of Bill Clinton, Gore said.

It really will damage my ability to govern, Clinton echoed.

How could Boren do this? Gore asked. Surely he did not want to be responsible for bringing down the president?

No, Boren said, and he wouldn't be. It wouldn't be the end of the world. They were all thinking too short term. What would bring down the president, he said, would be if in three years his economic plan didn't work and people complained that all these taxes were raised but the deficit hadn't come down and entitlements hadn't been controlled. Boren said that Clinton's argument was that if Boren thought Clinton was marching off a cliff, he should help him by marching off the cliff too. He was arguing no, that he should try to stop Clinton from going over the cliff, even if he didn't want to be stopped.

Clinton and the others insisted the plan would work. They argued that Boren's failure to support it would undercut his credibility. It was the best plan they could get, they said. They couldn't get any Republicans to help them.

They could have, Boren countered, back in May, and even later. Three Republicans on the Finance Committee had signaled they would go along with a compromise. Boren said there was no way the Republicans could have refused an invitation to sit down and work on this.

Clinton said there really was no Republican alternative. It was this plan or nothing. And doing nothing would shake confidence and rattle the financial markets.

Boren said they should spend their time on people more likely to support the plan. He claimed he wanted to tell them that up front, as a friend. He didn't want to mislead them. They all knew who was apt to change his mind at the last minute and who wasn't—and Boren wasn't. The hour-and-15-minute meeting ended on a cordial note.

Clinton had always admired the way Boren had played politics in Oklahoma, but found this behavior bizarre. If Boren voted for the plan, no one would lay a hand on him in Oklahoma. The president realized one other practical consequence. Not only would this make the vote impossibly tight in the Senate, but Boren's desertion would take away the cover of the key Democratic House members from Oklahoma like Dave McCurdy, making the prospects in the House also dangerously tight. Clinton could not avoid a painful conclusion: Despite his hefty denials, Boren might just want to be the one to bring the plan to its knees.

GERGEN HAD JOINED the White House preaching bipartisanship, and here he saw the administration unable to hold even conservative Democrats like Boren. Clinton was fighting with Boren instead of the left wing of the Democratic Party. The left was where Gergen felt the fights should be waged. That would give them a chance to pick up some Republicans. The root of the problem, Gergen believed, was the decision to lock themselves into working with the Democratic congressional leadership.

The next day, Gergen called Boren at home to see if there was any chance left to get his vote.

Well, Boren asked, how would you describe the meeting?

"Sobering," Gergen said.

Then, Boren said, he wasn't misunderstood. He had clearly made up his mind. There would be other days, and he wasn't going to let this decide his attitude toward the administration or president. He hung up.

Boren concluded that Clinton didn't understand. He attributed the push away from bipartisanship to the influence of Gore, a former House and Senate member, and Stephanopoulos, a former House aide. Most important, Boren was not sure, given the mixed signals from Clinton's staff and from Clinton himself, that he knew what Clinton really believed. The struggle for Clinton's soul and for control of his administration was continuing, and Boren wondered how it would turn out.

Clinton was resigned about Boren. "I'm never going to get him," the president complained to Stephanopoulos. Stephanopoulos felt that one of Clinton's defenses when he didn't get somebody to agree was to appropriate that person's arguments. Some of Boren's made terrible sense. "Oh, he's right!" Clinton said at one point soon after. There weren't enough spending cuts, he complained. They had not zeroed anything out completely—that would have been dramatic. There weren't enough entitlement cutbacks. Before it was over, Clinton was yelling at everybody else about Boren's points.

．

ON MONDAY, JULY 26, Clinton read an editorial in *The New York Times* headlined: "A Budget Worthy of Mr. Bush." "If the conferees who will meet this week to finish a budget stick to their present path, they'll likely hand President Clinton a package much like the one George Bush signed three years ago," the editorial said, referring to the 1990 budget deal that also had about $500 billion in deficit reduction over five years.

The editorial continued: "Mr. Clinton promised voters more than a rehash. He pledged to end the consumption frenzy of the 1980s by turning the federal budget toward investments in infrastructure, children and training. But Congress is veering in a different direction. Unless it turns around, and fast, Mr. Clinton's victory in getting a deficit-reduction package through Congress will be hollow.

"What about investment? Congress knocked tens of billions from discretionary spending that Mr. Clinton proposed . . . most of his plans to hike spending on worker training, education, mass transit and technological research will be slashed. He'll be lucky to save a third of his investment program.

"It won't be a budget that invests in the future and it won't be a victory for those who voted for an economic turnabout."

The editorial was raised with Altman at the War Room meeting that morning. The subject was delicate. Clinton himself had made some of the same points in his private tirades against the investment cuts. Carville and Begala had likewise blasted dire investment compromises.

In the War Room, Sperling said that the *Times* editorial was a bit off, that Clinton might get about half his investments. It was decided that

Sperling would make that point to Clinton later that morning. Sperling already had two other matters to bring to Clinton's attention, and would add the editorial as a third.

When Sperling arrived outside the Oval Office, Stephanopoulos warned him angrily, "You've got one minute!" Clinton's schedule was again chaos. He had to leave for speeches in Chicago.

Inside the Oval Office, Sperling said quickly, "Mr. President, I've got three things to tell you."

"Hey," the president said, "did you see that great *New York Times* editorial?"

Sperling paused briefly. "Mr. President, I've got two things to tell you."

LATER THAT MORNING, Clinton was on Air Force One heading for Chicago, thumbing through his briefing book and schedule for the one-day trip to help sell the economic plan. The book said that Mayor Richard M. Daley of Chicago had wanted to meet with Clinton, but the president's busy schedule had not permitted it.

"Who the hell could make such a dumb fucking mistake?" the president bellowed out. He raged on, noting the obvious: Mayor Daley was only the most important politician in Chicago, Chicago was only the most important city in Illinois, and Illinois was one of the most important states for 1996. In the confined spaces of the plane, Clinton stormed on and on. It was truly awful, on the edge of controlled violence. "Why are we not organized to do this?" Clinton screamed.

Gergen, watching the outburst, was stunned. He had never quite seen an adult, let alone a president, in such a rage. Interestingly, no one on the plane had an answer to Clinton's questions. It was a dumb mistake, and they weren't organized. But because of the diffusion of power within the White House and the administration, no one was held responsible. After the explosion, Clinton became calm and almost apologetic. A meeting with Daley in Clinton's hotel suite was arranged. The larger problem of political judgment and organization on his staff was forgotten.

At the Sheraton Chicago Hotel that afternoon, the president made a pitch for his plan, modifying his argument on the interest rates as Tyson had urged. "If we can keep interest rates down for over a year at this level, it is estimated from a low side of $50 billion to a high side of $100 billion will be released to be reinvested back into the economy to jump-start the economy again."

He was visibly impatient with the Congress. "The government needs to pass this budget and get on with the rest of the business," he said. "Hanging out there, debating it, dragging it out for weeks and weeks, will only make it worse. There comes a time when delay to get a slightly better decision is worse than action to get a pretty good decision. We have reached that time."

Near the end of his talk, a heckler interrupted him, shouting about gridlock and the Democratic-controlled Congress. "Why don't you take leadership?" the person shouted.

"Now wait a minute," Clinton snapped. "Whoa! . . . If they want to vote against me, fine; let's make a decision and go on to something else. Let's just move. I think that's the issue."

In a meeting with the Indiana media later that day, Clinton said, "Spending eight months or seven months doing nothing but this is not my idea of recreation. But we have lost control over our financial affairs. And this deficit is like a bone in our throat, and we have to take it out."

Late that night Clinton was told that they had found an apparent suicide note from the late Vince Foster. The note, torn into dozens of pieces, had been discovered belatedly in his briefcase, the White House said. Foster listed various distresses, including a bitter attack on Washington: "Here ruining people is considered sport."

UP ON CAPITOL HILL, Mitchell was meeting nearly every day with the House and Senate leaders dickering over the gas tax. "Six cents can pass the House," Gephardt reported. "Even 6½ cents. But 7 cents doesn't work."

From the Senate side, Mitchell said, "I don't know what can pass on the gas tax. Maybe a nickel."

Rostenkowski hated these gatherings. "I'm not going to a fucking meeting," he declared several times, but then he would show up claiming that his chief of staff had made him come. "We have to make a deal and go ahead," Rostenkowski declared. "We cannot let every single member have his finger in the soup. I walked over here with Mike Andrews [a Texas Democrat]. He was trying to tell me 31 members won't go for the gas tax. And I told him, 'So what?' " Rostenkowski added, "Only two things will sell this: help the president, and get home for August!"

. . .

GERGEN WAS CONCERNED about Clinton. The incident on the airplane was not isolated. Many mornings the president came into the office, seized on some bad news or leak to the press, and let loose for up to ten minutes. Once Clinton came into the Oval Office with a newspaper folded into quarters showing some story based on a leak from the White House. "What the fuck is this?" Clinton had shouted. Presidential flare-ups were common enough, but Clinton often would not let an incident go, roaring on for too long before calming down.

Gergen finally raised the issue with Stephanopoulos, who Gergen knew was the chief recipient of the blowups. Gergen described the incident on the airplane to Chicago as a serious example of Clinton's "morning vents." Stephanopoulos saw that Gergen was very upset, treating it like the end of the world.

"It's just not a big deal," Stephanopoulos said, suggesting that Gergen relax. It was a reflection of the weight of everything, day-to-day life, just the way things happened, and it was best to accept it, navigate around it. But it was clear to Gergen that Clinton was going through a lot of psychological anguish.

FINALLY, ON JULY 29, the House and Senate negotiators agreed on the modest 4.3-cent-a-gallon gas tax. Bentsen reported this to the White House. It was "pathetic," he said, but it was all they could get.

In some respects, Vice President Gore had lost the most. The ambitious, sweeping BTU tax, initially designed to shift fuel use from polluting coal and oil to natural gas, and improve the environment, had been whittled down to a piddling 4.3-cent gas tax, even less than the 5 cents in Bush's 1990 budget deal. But this was legislative warfare, Gore knew.

Gore saw that Clinton was too shaky and tentative in his public, let alone his private, pronouncements. The administration needed to go all out, and a tone of presidential ambivalence was reverberating through the administration and the Washington political establishment.

One day in the Oval Office, Clinton was lamenting to Gore, McLarty, and Paster over his dilemma, rambling on inconclusively about the endless compromises and delays on investments and health care that had left him with a Wall Street plan. Among Clinton's inner circle, some felt Gore was developing a way to talk bluntly with Clinton, to walk right up to the line that divided their offices and roles. Gore was careful of the line but not afraid of it. He generally prefaced his candid and frank advice by saying, "I hope I'm not offending you," or, "I hope I'm not taking advantage of our relationship."

As this particular conversation progressed, Clinton turned to Gore. "What can I do?" he asked the vice president.

"You can get with the goddamn program!" Gore answered tersely, his own exasperation boiling over.

Gore, McLarty, and Paster sucked in their breaths. No one, certainly not a vice president, was supposed to speak to the president that harshly. Had a fine line been traversed? Had he taken advantage of their delicate relationship? Had the junior partner been too abrupt with the senior partner?

Clinton paused a long time, the scene virtually stopping in freeze-frame. The president finally laughed. Mildly.

"Okay," Clinton said.

30

In the days following his meeting with Clinton, Boren read White House officials quoted as saying they still thought they might get his vote. Boren had agreed to go on the CBS Sunday-morning show "Face the Nation" on August 1 and decided he had better proclaim his unequivocal opposition. If he was the last and deciding vote, he didn't want to defeat the plan with a surprise no. Before the show, Bob Schieffer, the moderator, asked Boren if he should inquire on air whether Boren had made up his mind. "Yes, you ought to ask me. That'd be a good question," Boren said. Whether he was asked or not, Boren was going to find a way to say it anyway.

On the air Boren was asked. "I have made up my mind," he said. "I simply must vote against this plan."

At the White House, many, including Paster, were furious. For all Boren's talk about being the president's friend, they felt, no one had done more to undercut the plan. Now he had potentially destroyed it. Boren was a turncoat. His defection created an urgent practical problem: They needed to find another vote in the Senate to make it up. None of the remaining Democrats seemed willing to switch. "This really shouldn't be this hard," Clinton said to Gore at one point.

Clinton and Paster went to work on Senator Dennis DeConcini, an Arizona Democrat who had been tangled up in the Savings and Loan scandal as one of the Keating Five. DeConcini was running for reelection in 1994 in Arizona, a traditional Republican stronghold, and a vote for Clinton's plan could do him in. His position was so precarious that on the June vote Mitchell had confidentially released DeConcini, telling him it was okay to vote against the plan because Mitchell had secured Boren's vote.

Clinton spoke to DeConcini three times. "God, I need your vote," Clinton said. DeConcini found Clinton engaging and solicitous. One meeting, scheduled for 10 minutes, lasted 40. Clinton made it clear he was less than delighted with his own plan. DeConcini explained the political situation in Arizona.

"I don't want to kill you," Clinton said. "What can we do with this package?"

"I want to help you," the senator said. "I've just got to have some improvements."

"Dennis," Clinton said, "this is a tough job."

DeConcini sent his top aide, Gene Karp, to see Paster. Karp explained that the senator would vote with Clinton, but he needed an explanation for the voters back in Arizona. Paster had the distinct impression that DeConcini was going to vote for the plan no matter what improvements they came up with, and that it was just a matter of erecting an explanation for switching to satisfy the public back home. After a good deal of back and forth, Clinton agreed to sign two executive orders formally setting up a deficit reduction trust fund—another display device for what Rivlin had called a "display device." The economic plan was also altered by lowering slightly the number of people whose Social Security benefits would be taxed, a key issue in the retirement haven of Arizona.

After it was all arranged, DeConcini went to the White House and told Clinton he would vote with him. "I'm not going to let you fail," DeConcini told Clinton privately, but added, "If you pick up another vote and don't need me, I'd be happy *not* to vote for it."

EVEN WITH DECONCINI'S VOTE SIGNED and sealed, Clinton was still one vote short in the Senate, since Nebraska Senator Bob Kerrey, a supporter in June, was talking openly of switching. Worse, the House vote count was a big question mark. Clinton decided to make a final appeal in a nationally televised speech from the Oval Office. No more half measures.

The speech had to convince people his plan was not a tax plan. Republican attacks on the taxes had sunk in. Polls showed that a vast majority of the public, as high as 78 percent, believed that most of the new tax burden would fall on the middle class. In truth, 80 percent of the new taxes were going to be paid by those making $200,000 a year or more. Clinton had to try to turn around the public perception. Begala and two White House speechwriters worked several days on a draft.

Gergen read it. The second paragraph began: "It's been at least 30 years since a President has asked Americans to take personal responsibility for our country's future." This was a direct shot at Gergen's previous Republican bosses, Nixon, Ford, and Reagan, let alone Democrats Johnson and Carter. The speech was filled with hyperbole, attacks on "trickle-down" economics and other Clinton campaign themes. Gergen called the White House speechwriters, expressed his unhappiness, said it was wrong, and asked for a chance to weigh in.

On Tuesday, August 3, a meeting on the speech was scheduled in the Oval Office. Clinton had to deliver it at 8 P.M. Before the meeting, Gergen spent an hour drafting a new beginning and took two copies to the Oval Office where the meeting was already in progress.

Gergen waited a few minutes before speaking. "They've done a very good job," he said, "but I want to at least offer this," realizing that he might never have another chance to present his alternative. Since he had only two copies, he handed one to Clinton and kept the other copy for himself. Begala, Stephanopoulos, and the speechwriters had no idea what was on the paper. They sat and watched while Clinton and Gergen read.

Stephanopoulos thought Gergen's move was so obvious and clumsy as to be embarrassing. Clinton's campaign advisers had had an unwritten rule to consult each other fully before presenting Clinton with any new ideas or problems, so no one would be surprised in front of him. The ban on oneupmanship worked to everyone's advantage, Stephanopoulos believed.

Clinton said he liked the Gergen alternative, really liked it, and wanted it in the speech.

The meeting ended. Begala stalked Gergen down in Gergen's office, which had previously been the White House barbershop and for the moment was the only available room in the West Wing anywhere near the Oval Office.

What a chickenshit double-cross, Begala shouted, flying into a rage. "I'm going to work with you," Begala said. "I'm going to respect you, but I'm not going to trust you."

Gergen was dumbstruck. He tried to explain, insisting he had not intended to circumvent the speechwriting process or Begala. Gergen was at his most sympathetic and understanding, saying he now realized how it had appeared. It was his fault, he said, and he apologized. For over an hour the two men tried to iron out their relationship. Though the argument turned largely on procedure, the real differences the two had were over the nature of Clinton's presidency and his authentic voice. At the end, Begala finally said that over time they would work out a relationship of trust.

The speechwriting continued, as did the meetings. Begala had used the word "we" throughout. Clinton rebelled. It sounded too much like a royal "we," and he wanted to take each one out and replace it with "I."

"Mr. President," Begala suggested, "there are times when you've got to speak for the nation."

The "we" stayed in, as did the paragraph blasting presidents over 30 years for not asking Americans to take personal responsibility for the country's future. The speech had something for everyone, laced with populist themes—tax fairness, health care, and jobs. Borrowing a page from Perot, Clinton displayed and explained several charts. He also said that Wall Street had validated the plan by lowering interest rates and that many business leaders, Republicans and Democrats, supported it.

An overnight poll by CNN showed support for Clinton's plan had dropped after the Oval Office speech, and more people opposed it than supported it. Panic overtook the White House. Stan Greenberg's dial groups, focus groups, and polling showed a more positive response. For the first time, Greenberg released his private poll data, though even his numbers showed only a plurality favoring Clinton's plan, 48 percent to 41 percent.

TO GET THE LAST SENATE VOTE, Clinton had to turn to Bob Kerrey, his former opponent in the presidential primaries. Kerrey had in some ways been Clinton's main generational rival in the early phase of the Democratic primaries, when Kerrey momentarily attracted media attention as another new JFK. Kerrey seemed to have broad appeal in the post-Vietnam crosscurrents, fearless, restless, youthful. He had served in Vietnam, lost his right leg below the knee from a grenade, won the Congressional Medal of Honor, and later opposed the war. As a one-term bachelor governor of Nebraska, he had carried on a public relationship with Hollywood actress Debra Winger. Then in 1988 he was elected to the Senate, the first Medal of Honor winner to serve there since the Civil War. But Kerrey faltered in the New Hampshire primary. While Clinton had finished second with 25 percent, Kerrey had been a distant third with 11 percent. He then had bluntly attacked Clinton's lack of candor on the draft, saying that Bush would open Clinton up like a "soft peanut" in the general election.

Kerrey had seemed a natural pick for Clinton's running mate, but news leaked that Hillary would not hear of it—reports that Clinton denied less than convincingly. After Clinton's economic plan was unveiled, Kerrey said he opposed it because it didn't aggressively take on entitlement programs. Clinton had taken Kerrey out jogging on June 22, shortly before the first Senate vote. As a half-joke, Kerrey wore a large printed sign taped to his T-shirt: "HILLARY KNOWS BEST." Clinton had told Kerrey that if his plan didn't pass the Senate and get to conference, it would hurt him at the upcoming Tokyo economic summit. "I appreciate that there's a lot about it you don't like," Clinton said, noting that the plan could be improved in conference. "I hope you can give me a vote because I need it to go to the G-7 meeting." Kerrey had acquiesced and voted to send it to conference.

But the agreement had just been for the preliminary vote. Now Kerrey had to be courted all over again. It could not have been much worse for Clinton.

Stephanopoulos thought it was possible to write a book about the Clinton-Kerrey relationship. It was so complex, filled with feelings of love-hate and the rivalry, envy, and kinship almost of brothers. Clinton could get angry at Kerrey and the real Clinton would come out, inflamed and almost swinging mad. It was like fighting the Vietnam War all over again. That the economic plan hinged on Kerrey, Stephanopoulos concluded, was dangerous.

At one point, Clinton tried to put the best face on the situation, insisting that he and Kerrey always got along. He told the story about when they had both been governors in the late 1980s, and Kerrey had come up to Clinton at one of the governors' conferences and said that Clinton ought to run for president. "We're friends," Clinton said more than once.

Like Boren, Kerrey was reading and hearing that the White House expected his vote for the final reconciliation. Gore spoke with Kerrey and played on the friendship theme. Kerrey said he didn't want to be an FOB, a Friend of Bill's, and vote with the president merely out of loyalty. No, Kerrey said, he wanted to fight some battles together with Clinton and then, as a consequence of winning those battles, have a natural, evolving friendship based on shared interests. Becoming friends with a president, a commander in chief, was dangerous, Kerrey said. He was worried about being coopted.

Paster also spoke with Kerrey, who remained steadfast. "It's not a bold step," Kerrey said to Paster about the plan. "It's incremental bullshit. This is not the change presidency. If I vote no and bring this down, I'll be doing Bill Clinton a favor."

Thursday, August 5, was the day of the House vote and the day before the Senate vote. At about 8 A.M., Kerrey called Clinton at the White House. "Mr. President," Kerrey said, "I'm going to vote no."

Why? Clinton wanted to know.

Insisting that his decision was final and unchangeable, Kerrey dumped on the bill. The plan did not solve the entitlement problem, he repeated. It did not shift the country away from consumption to savings. The taxes could kick the country into recession. It wouldn't create jobs. It wouldn't achieve genuine recovery or solve the long-term economic problems. Clinton had a plan, he said, that wouldn't work. Nothing could be offered to change his mind, Kerrey said.

In response, Clinton's tone was visceral and personal. "If you want to bring this presidency down," the president said, "then go ahead! I was told that this was going to be the good thing to do, and I took on the most difficult problem the country faced and suddenly I'm regretting it. I wish I hadn't done it. All I'm doing is catching grief for doing what everybody knows is the most difficult problem we face."

Kerrey agreed. Clinton was absolutely right: It was the most difficult problem. But the final product didn't solve it.

Clinton said it was the best he could do after months and months of negotiations, endless compromises and deals. "Everybody said this is going to be the smart thing to do," Clinton said, his voice rising with fury and defeat. "I took this thing on head on and I gave a good-faith effort."

Kerrey said that no one could deny that about the effort, but it had failed.

"Now I find myself not able to get it across," Clinton answered. "Now maybe I ought to just pick it up and go back to Little Rock. Chuck it!"

"The Constitution gives you that option," Kerrey replied, "but I wouldn't take it."

Clinton again pleaded with Kerrey that he needed his vote. "My presidency's going to go down," he said sharply, by now shouting.

"I do not like the argument that I'm bringing the presidency down!" Kerrey shouted back, getting fed up.

Clinton shouted that the defeat would do precisely that. Kerrey could not flee from his responsibility.

"I really resent the argument that somehow I'm responsible for your presidency surviving," Kerrey bellowed.

"Fuck you," Clinton yelled.

Kerrey felt he always tried to be respectful of the commander in chief, but he also wanted to defend himself, and he continued shouting back.

Clinton pressed on two themes: He had to have Kerrey's vote. "I need it," he said at one point plaintively. He also said that if Kerrey denied him the vote, Kerrey would wreak national havoc.

"I've got the responsibility for me," Kerrey replied. "I've got my vote, my vote matters, I vote based upon what I believe is right, always have. I don't, particularly in big issues like this, like to shave it. And so that's where it is."

"Fine!" Clinton said brusquely. "Okay! If that's what you want, you go do it!" Both crushed their phones down.

Clinton was irate. "It's going to be a no," he told his advisers after the conversation.

GERGEN, who knew Kerrey from his work in journalism, was next to try his hand at winning over the senator.

"Can we talk?" Gergen asked Kerrey over the phone. "Would it help to talk?"

"Of course," Kerrey replied. "It never hurts to have a conversation." He proposed lunch that day.

"Fine, I'll come up," Gergen said.

"There's an American Cafe at Union Station," Kerrey said. Union Station, Washington's main railroad terminal, was just a few blocks from the Senate. Moynihan had advised Kerrey to go to the movies to help him relax and get away from the weight of the decision, since the media wouldn't let him alone, clustering thick around him now in the Senate hallways. Kerrey said he planned to catch a movie at the Union Station theater complex that afternoon. Did Gergen want to go to an afternoon flick? How about bringing Clinton along to the movies?

Gergen declined, but said he would be there for lunch.

Within the White House, Gergen had been criticized for not including Paster in some of his lobbying work in Congress, so Gergen asked Paster if he wanted to go. He did. As the two headed out to a car, they ran into McLarty, who asked where they were going. Gergen explained, but did not invite McLarty. The chief of staff felt he knew Kerrey pretty well, and if the vote on the economic plan was shattered, he would have to work with Kerrey in the future. And, of course, this was going to be the important encounter. McLarty invited himself along.

Because of a mix-up about the restaurant, it took the three senior White House advisers about 20 minutes to hook up with Kerrey at a different American Cafe, across the street from Union Station down Massachusetts Avenue. Paster felt they were like three Keystone Kops, not only because they couldn't seem to get the meeting place straight but because they had no agenda or plan about what to say to Kerrey.

Kerrey could see that the three were anxious, on a razor's edge. All three had the same question: What can we do to get you to vote yes?

Nothing, Kerrey said. But there was an opportunity to get Clinton on the moral high ground and say he was doing the right thing. He would have to return to the rhetoric of his February 17 speech. Kerrey said the problem was not just economic but moral. Talking as if the fight over the economic plan were over, Kerrey asked what was next for the White House.

Paster mentioned something about how they were going to move on to health care.

"No, no, no," Kerrey said loudly and dismissively, "I don't mean legislative strategy. I mean, what's this presidency about?"

The three from the White House tried to turn the conversation to the importance of Clinton's plan. Kerrey was on a higher road, and the three others huddled together and listened.

Being an American was a privilege, the junior senator from Nebraska pontificated. The basic entitlement was freedom, nothing beyond that. If the government wanted to give him something, he should say thank you. As a consequence of being a disabled veteran, he was now entitled to government benefits as if Moses or Thomas Jefferson had said it. But the whole entitlement mentality was screwing up kids who thought they could bumble along in school and still go to college, or business people who went broke but then wanted the government to bail them out. The country's strength had always been that people did *not* ask to be protected from the consequences of their own actions. People had to sacrifice. Clinton had won the Democratic nomination, Kerrey said, because he had figured that out. But his economic plan was a departure. There was too much divisive, soak-the-rich rhetoric.

McLarty told Kerrey he was right. The White House needed his influence, McLarty assured him. "You can be constructive," the chief of staff said. McLarty suggested that Kerrey not worry about tinkering with the details of the plan but that he share his meditations with Clinton. "You can help," McLarty said, "not to push the numbers back, but you can help us, and you should go talk to the president about these concerns."

Gergen loved to discuss the moral dimensions of politics. "Clinton believes this," Gergen told Kerrey. "He agrees with you."

All the entitlement programs strangling the government came from this corrosive give-to-me, help-me attitude, Kerrey said. Clinton needed to use his moral compass, which, although surely different from Kerrey's, was on many of these issues pointing the same way. Clinton needed to respect that others had different experiences. "I might be able to, as a consequence of those experiences," Kerrey said, "as with other people, provide some point of view that could be constructive, particularly in this case."

Yes, yes, they all said.

Kerrey reminded them that he had started a successful restaurant chain after his military service, and understood market forces and how to create jobs. Clinton's own experience had not taught him that the marketplace created jobs. In his head, Kerrey said, Clinton understood that, and he had people around him, like the three of them, who had experienced it; but Clinton didn't understand that in his gut.

"He needs to hear this," one of the three from the White House said. The other two agreed. Kerrey could help them. Regardless of how Kerrey voted, this needed to be heard. Please, they all urged, try to get down to the White House to see the president to say these things.

"You're the first guy we talked to who hasn't asked for something," Gergen said.

Kerrey realized that in a way he was asking for everything. Kerrey then went to see the movie *What's Love Got to Do with It*, with an old friend from Nebraska. Kerrey had asked his friend to spend this time with him to make sure he did not get trapped in the bowels of Washington, D.C., logic.

At the White House, Paster tried to arrange a meeting between Clinton and Kerrey. But Clinton had an even bigger problem. It was turning into the day of maximum peril—and not because of Kerrey's uncertainty.

31

EARLIER THAT MORNING, the day of the House vote, Altman began the War Room meeting a little late, about 8 A.M. The administration was in the midst of an all-out media blitz, concentrating on states such as Nebraska, Wisconsin, Arizona, and Texas that were heavy with swing votes. Gergen and Paster had gone through the comparisons of taxes in each congressional district and state. Altman pointed out that some were stunning. In predominantly poor areas, the earned-income-tax credit had a tremendous impact: Some districts contained up to ten times more poor people whose taxes would be lowered than wealthy people whose would be raised. This information was being fed to the local media, which were making much of it. In the wealthy districts, where the numbers showed more getting tax increases, the information was not released. Gergen and Paster said they wanted the research presented to Clinton.

Altman thought it was a little late in the game to show it to the president. He felt supremely frustrated. The White House had so badly misjudged the public mood. The public clearly wanted fewer taxes and more spending cuts, and a Clinton plan could have been crafted with that in mind in order to ride the wave of public opinion rather than swim against it. There was just very little strategic thinking at the White House, Altman concluded.

Clinton met with Altman later and reviewed the state-by-state and district-by-district comparisons. The president loved it and just couldn't stop looking through it. This was ammunition he could use.

Clinton took to the phones. Representative Bill Brewster, an Oklahoma Democrat who had voted for the plan in May, had just announced he was now voting against the plan and promptly left his office. The White House tried to reach Brewster, but he wasn't returning phone calls. Clinton tried himself, but incredibly, even the president couldn't get Brewster on the phone. Clinton realized that part of Brewster's defection was attributable to Boren, whose own switch had stripped away cover for his fellow Oklahomans.

Clinton called McCurdy and congratulated him. In the congressional softball match against the Republicans, McCurdy had struck out the first 12 batters and gotten two hits in a 13 to 1 rout. Now what about Brewster? the president asked. He won't return my damn phone calls.

McCurdy said he didn't know about Brewster. For his part, McCurdy said he was *not* going to vote for the plan either this time.

Clinton couldn't believe it. Why? The BTU tax was gone. The gas tax was much lower.

No serious entitlement cuts.

Clinton said McCurdy should trust him. Health care reform would lead to the cuts.

McCurdy had already met with Hillary on the health care package and had a good idea what it was going to look like. It would not reduce the deficit, he believed. He told Clinton he was skeptical.

Clinton was upset. Boren was screwing him with the Oklahoma Democrats.

McCurdy said he had made up his mind and was not going to change it this time no matter what. He next heard from McLarty, who seemed to realize he had used his chip in May and it just wasn't going to work again.

In the afternoon, the Democratic leadership sent down to the White House the latest detailed spreadsheets, the whip sheets that Clinton had been using for the last three days. They showed the number of committed yes votes in the top left-hand corner—only 180—far short of the magic number of 218. The spreadsheets listed the remaining names and how they might vote in five columns: leaning yes; undecided; leaning no; no; and no response.

Clinton stationed himself at his Oval Office desk, the spreadsheets in front of him. They had to concentrate on the 38 Democrats who had voted no in May. He ordered a full mobilization. Everyone and anyone was to call House members. Deals had to be made.

Earlier, Moynihan had demanded that Clinton scale back his planned elimination of the Puerto Rican tax credit. He had raised the specter of revolution in the Caribbean. He had also said that eliminating the tax would not only double unemployment in Puerto Rico, but could vastly increase immigration to New York, and that the increased welfare and other social service costs would outstrip the savings achieved from abolishing the tax. This was another argument that could not be made publicly.

Clinton earlier had invited three House members who were Puerto Rican down to the White House: Representatives Luis V. Gutierrez of Illinois, and Nydia Velazquez and Jose Serrano of New York. They adamantly opposed elimination of the tax credit. They said they were Clinton's best votes, which was true. They were with him on every vote, which was true again. They gave him solid majorities in their districts as did Puerto Rico—also true. They weren't pressing to have the tax credit fully preserved; they just didn't want to see it gutted entirely.

It was a real gimme, and Clinton had promised the three representatives to retain some of the tax credit. The three votes were secure.

MARTIN LANCASTER, a soft-spoken North Carolina Democratic congressman, had known Bill and Hillary Clinton on a first-name basis from years of attending the New Year's Renaissance Weekends. Lancaster, 50, had been raised on a tobacco farm, and had been asking Hillary about the reports that her health care task force would recommend a tobacco-tax increase. One report said the Clintons were going to seek a $2-a-pack tax hike. She said some cigarette tax was more than likely. Lancaster replied that it was only fair that other products that contributed to increased health care costs also be taxed, such as high-cholesterol foods, and certainly alcohol. That way the burden would not just fall on one region of the country. Hillary said she understood his point of view, but made no promises. Lancaster tried again several times but could not get any assurances.

As the final hours approached, Lancaster had not declared his position on the economic plan. Nor had another half dozen representatives from such tobacco states as Kentucky, South Carolina, Georgia, and Virginia. Though Lancaster did not have the proxies of all of them, he was effectively their spokesman. On the final day, he informed the White House that his vote for the economic plan depended on absolute assurance that Hillary's health care proposal wouldn't single out tobacco for additional taxation.

Hillary called him from her car phone that afternoon. She agreed to his terms. If the task force recommended a tobacco tax, she said, it would include some other tax as well. She could not state for the record what that tax would be, but she understood and agreed with the principle that one product and one region should not carry the new burden alone.

If that was the case, Lancaster said, he would be able to support the economic plan. He would inform the others in the loose tobacco caucus of the good news. He wanted a guarantee that he would be given advance notice of the details on health care taxation proposals. Hillary agreed.

In the Oval Office, Clinton called Lancaster, summoning him off the House floor to a telephone booth in the cloakroom. The president said he was calling specifically to reaffirm the deal that Hillary had made, and to thank Lancaster and the others for their support. Lancaster's Democrats in the House would vote for Clinton.*

THAT AFTERNOON, Senator DeConcini, who had announced the day before that he would switch and vote for the plan, called Altman. An editorial that day in the conservative *Arizona Republic,* the state's largest newspaper, attacked the deficit reduction trust fund, quoting Alice Rivlin's remark months earlier calling it a "display device" and a "gimmick." DeConcini was furious. He was not being given the political cover he had been promised and desperately needed. Rivlin's on-the-record words were undercutting him.

"We will correct that," Altman pledged. Rivlin immediately dispatched a letter to the *Republic* saying her words had been distorted. "I did use the word 'display,' but not as a criticism," she said, and her use of the word "gimmick" had been directed at an earlier Bush proposal. "Senator DeConcini's vote for the President's plan is a courageous decision," the deputy budget director said.

By late afternoon, Clinton had lost 7 previous yes votes in the House, but won back 6 no votes. But his tally stood only at 208.

Gore, very tense, came into the Oval Office. Bentsen, McLarty, Stephanopoulos, Altman, and he all crowded around the desk where Clinton stood. Gergen, his tie loosened, towered over the others. A half-filled plate of cookies sat on Clinton's desk.

---

* The next month, when the health care plan was unveiled, it recommended a cigarette tax of 75 cents a pack and a 1 percent tax on large businesses that chose not to join the proposed pools of insurance buyers called "alliances." Lancaster was furious and he called Howard Paster to charge double cross. He warned that the North Carolina congressional delegation, which had unanimously supported Clinton on the big votes, could no longer be counted on. He spoke later to Hillary, who told him that the administration had lived up to its pledge. "Tobacco has not been singled out," she said. The conversation was on the phone, and Lancaster wondered whether she made her assertion with a straight face. Hillary had not been specific, and she believed people often heard what they wanted to hear.

Given the uncertainty, should they get the leadership to put the vote off for a day? someone suggested.

Paster, who had joined the group, vehemently opposed a delay. So did Stephanopoulos, who argued that their position wouldn't get any stronger. A delay would be seen as conceding defeat. Better to roll for it.

It was bewildering to Clinton. How in the wide world were they all of a sudden having trouble passing this in the House when the House back in May had already voted for a more onerous version of the plan that included the BTU tax? The gas tax would be much less of a burden for the middle class. Clinton didn't understand. Too many House members had told him privately that they would not let it die, he said.

Stephanopoulos knew that the language of the House—"I won't let you down," or, "I won't let it die"—was not the same as a promise of a yes vote. These were very specific pledges and meant "I won't be the last one to vote no." There were many ways to keep the pledge without voting yes—voting no early, or waiting until the end to see if the plan was headed for defeat so that the congressman wouldn't be blamed personally.

Clinton said he felt he had enough real chits or promises and decided not to postpone the vote.

Then the subject of losing came up. They had to discuss contingencies, they all agreed.

Stephanopoulos was black with despair, standing off to the side. Paster was nervously pacing.

"Mr. President," Bentsen said, "if we lose, you've got to keep them in until they pass a budget."

Clinton asked how.

Bentsen said they would have to get the leadership to postpone the August recess, keep them in session, hold them in Washington, make them redo it right away. "You keep them here," Bentsen said sternly, gritting his teeth and throwing his whole body forward with his words. Members of congress had plans for the recess—engagements, speeches, vacations. Keeping them in would place an enormous amount of additional pressure on them. It was important for the president to show his absolute determination and toughness, the Treasury Secretary said.

"You will fight on for your principles," Gergen said. With such a move, Clinton could demonstrate that he was sticking to his principles and fighting for them.

Clinton realized that if they lost and let Congress go home, they might have to wait until October for passage. Nothing else would get done. A whole year would be wasted, all to fool around the edges of the economic plan.

"Yes, you're absolutely right," Clinton told Bentsen. "That's what we'll do." He said his decision was definite, adding that it could not leak that he had a contingency for defeat. Any public discussion that he had a defeat strategy could wreck it now, become self-fulfilling.

Brave words, Stephanopoulos felt, and tough talk. They would be able to act like they were keeping Congress in. For form's sake, Clinton would have to say Congress was staying. But either way it would be a giant delay of months. The impasse wouldn't be able to be resolved quickly.

Clinton's mind raced ahead, forming a strategy of what to do if they lost in the House. "We'll just drop the gas tax," he said, "and it'll pass the House."

"But it won't pass the Senate," Paster noted unhappily. The Senate would continue to insist on the gas tax.

Stephanopoulos realized that they would not solve an absolute crisis of government by dropping a 4.3-cent gas tax. It was not on the scale of the problem. The discussion, he concluded, was therapy.

Everything hung on a fragile yet-unrealized majority. The mood darkened more as alternatives were considered. Altman couldn't bear to stay in the room and watch. He realized the moment of maximum peril had arrived. He walked out to talk with some staffers in the halls.

Paster checked in with the House leaders. Their report was optimistic, but Paster wavered between confidence and pessimism, at one point almost hanging his head for about ten minutes.

Around 6 P.M., Clinton's count was still stuck at about 208. It wasn't moving; he wasn't getting any more votes. "I just don't see how we get there," Clinton said, staring over his reading glasses at the spreadsheet. "I just don't see how we break it."

Stephanopoulos went into a deeper panic. Though losing had always been possible, Clinton, the eternal optimist, never worried. Clinton had always said they had to win. That had been their motto throughout. Clinton had never even articulated the consequences of losing. As president, he couldn't admit the possibility. He might think it all day, but if he said it, if he breathed it, that might be a problem. They could discuss it around him, but he couldn't speak it. Now he just had.

Stephanopoulos looked over at Clinton. He could see that Clinton realized how little power he had. Once the clock signaling the vote started to tick, his whole presidency would be out of his hands. Was it possible that what had been so hard fought could slip away? Clinton leaned back and waited. For the first time, he seemed not to believe.

"This is the whole ballgame," Gore said, repeating a line he had been using for days.

. . .

RIGHT AT CLINTON'S DESK, Gore and Bentsen reached Texas Democrat Bill Sarpalius, who represented the 13th District of the Red River Valley. Sarpalius had voted against Clinton in May. Gore made the first pitch. "We need you," he said. "This is it."

Then Bentsen took the receiver. "I campaigned for you," Bentsen said sternly, holding the Oval Office rapt. "I've been down there for you. I have raised funds for you when you were behind and it looked like you were going to lose." Bentsen reminded Sarpalius that they had adjusted the budget to keep open a government helium plant in the congressman's district, which was virtually the helium capital of the world.

Clinton was chuckling, laughing at the Texas macho show. Bentsen was not finished. He was determined to lean on Sarpalius, 45, as heavily as he knew how. Bentsen was also determined to talk a lot tougher than either Gore or Clinton had. "I expect you to remember," Bentsen told Sarpalius. "I'm telling you you're going to vote for this." Sarpalius finally agreed to vote yes.

Bentsen had seen eight presidents at work and had never seen any of them so personally involved in the lobbying as Clinton. The president had stuck his neck out nearly as far as possible. Though admiring Clinton's grit, Bentsen felt Clinton had made it too desirable for congressmen to hold out, to appear to make up their minds in the endgame when they had maximum leverage. Clinton needed more discipline and should not keep paying off the holdouts. Punishing them sometimes by withholding plums for their districts or not inviting them to special events was preferable to always rewarding them.

STEPHANOPOULOS AND CARVILLE had their daily check-in call. "Do I have to come in for the vote tonight?" Carville asked. He had been out on the road and was dead tired.

"Are you shitting me?" Stephanopoulos said. "You'd better get your ass over here. Fuck, he'll be rat shit if you're not here."

"Why?"

"We don't have the votes," Stephanopoulos replied.

"Is this some kind of dark Greek shit you're pulling on me?"

"No," Stephanopoulos said. "I'm telling you we don't have the votes." Stephanopoulos was insisting for the sake of both Clinton and Carville. Carville couldn't be seen as completely divorced at a time like this, and he wouldn't want to be. And Clinton, if he lost, would have to have the right pitch when he went out to face the music. James was Clinton's tuning fork. He would be able to judge if something sounded right, or could come up with something himself. He would be useful, whether they won or lost.

Carville left for the White House at once. He had just been assuming it would work out. For the Democratic Party to let the plan go down would be a fantastic, colossal act of stupidity, one of the celebrated political blunders of all time. Clinton's case, summed up, was rather simple: Gridlock was over. A defeat would prove gridlock was undying.

Carville, wearing jeans and thick-soled tennis shoes, along with a dress shirt and a tie, arrived in the Oval Office. The mood was low and spooky. It felt like a hospital waiting room. He saw that Clinton's lips were contorted in that certain way that he knew showed the president's mind was churning. In their brief greeting, Carville desperately wanted to move the conversation off the patient. He told the president that he and Mary Matalin were engaged to be married. "But don't tell anyone," he said. It was a secret. Clinton was so distracted that the final denouement of one of the great 1992 campaign curiosities, the Carville-Matalin match, did not even register with him. Carville did not have a lot to do, and found a baseball bat and began posing in a batter's stance in front of Clinton's Oval Office desk. He smiled, waiting for the pitch.

Mandy Grunwald also received an all-hands-on-deck call. When she arrived at the White House, people were walking the halls. In the Oval Office, Clinton looked pale. On the phone he sounded like a machine gun.

Clinton was going crazy. "Get this person!" he instructed Betty Currie, his executive secretary, pointing to a name on the spreadsheet. After she made the call, he said, "Get this person!" again, referring to someone else. Stephanopoulos picked up the phone on Clinton's desk and dialed another number for him. At one point the flashing lights from the hold button indicated that five congressmen were waiting on separate lines. "Get this person!" Clinton said, as soon as he was done with a call.

With some congressmen, he argued. If his plan failed, he said, there would be no health care, no free trade agreement. "We don't get to do anything else. We diddle around," Clinton said. They had to get around the plan. "If we don't get this bone out of our throat, we can't do anything else," Clinton said. To the congressman on the other end of the line, that could mean absolutely anything he wanted. Assuming there was any sense of public service or any legislative goal, it had to strike a chord and jolt even the most cynical. It meant, "You're not going to do anything you got elected to do."

A frequent refrain from those undecided was that the plan could be better. "You tell me how," Clinton said to one. "You're going to put Dole in control of the budget process basically, and we'll fiddle around the edges of this. And we'll wind up with less tax on the wealthy, less break for the working people, and less deficit reduction."

The benefit to the working people was a key argument with other Democrats, and Clinton cited the larger number of people who would get tax relief compared to those who would pay more. "Reality is our friend," he said to many. He felt he had said the same thing to 30 or 40 of them. "This is the worst day. And it will get better. And April 15 will be the best day of all." On tax day, most people would be surprised to see that their taxes had not gone up.

Paster pushed Clinton to plead, to beg, to make it personal. "I need your vote, man," the president said to one.

Three freshmen, Eric Fingerhut, Ron Klink, and Don Johnson, were balking. Paster was working them. Stephanopoulos talked to Fingerhut, who was from Stephanopoulos's Cleveland district, then talked to Fingerhut's administrative assistant to work out the terms of a deal. All three freshmen wanted more deficit reduction from entitlement cuts and congressional hearings on wasteful pork projects.

Clinton spoke to Fingerhut directly. "If this goes down," the president said, "it will only get worse. This is the last best chance for serious deficit reduction." Clinton talked with the other two, closing the deal personally, promising to look for billions more in spending cuts. All three agreed to vote yes.

McLarty announced that Representative Ray Thornton, the Democrat from Little Rock and Clinton's own congressman, was definitely voting no. "He says he can't be with us," McLarty said. Many couldn't believe the chief of staff, since Thornton, a longtime friend of Clinton's, occupying one of the safest seats in Congress, had months earlier pledged his support and had even voted for the plan in May. Yet McLarty insisted, "No, no, I really think he's voting no."

"I made him the fucking president of Arkansas State!" the president thundered. The president indicated there was no way Thornton would ever get back in his good graces. "He doesn't have to vote no," Clinton said, realizing that Thornton had the easiest out. He only had to remind everyone that he was the president's congressman.

Paster shook his head quietly. Thornton's no should not have been a surprise. Several weeks earlier, Thornton had told McLarty that he couldn't vote for a plan that contained a gas tax. He had publicly promised his rural constituents he would oppose the plan and had even faxed McLarty a memo saying: "There should be no misunderstanding.

I cannot go back on my word to my constituents." Messages in politics were rarely that clear, but Paster noted to himself that McLarty, who had insisted on handling Thornton himself, just didn't get politics.

It was not a good night for McLarty. He was trying to broker a deal with one of McCurdy's cohorts, Billy Tauzin of Louisiana, but his efforts failed and Tauzin joined the opposition camp.

Clinton was still short several votes.

As 7 P.M. APPROACHED, David Bonior, the number-three House leader and chief whip, called Clinton. "You're going to be okay," Bonior said. "We've got the votes." They spoke for nearly 15 minutes. Paster whispered to Stephanopoulos, "He's calling because he wants the credit." It was a good sign. Clinton said he wasn't sure but indicated he felt better after the call. Some noted, however, that he didn't look better.

With some time yet before the voting began, Altman called a key undecided, Representative Marjorie Margolies-Mezvinsky of Pennsylvania, often called the "3-M Woman" because of her alliterative tongue-twister of a name. A first-term Democrat, she represented Pennsylvania's 13th District, a normally Republican district of affluent and Main Line suburban Philadelphia. "I know you know what the right thing is," Altman told her.

Her heart almost came through the phone, she was in such anguish. Margolies-Mezvinsky desperately didn't want to be asked to vote yes. It would be political suicide in her district, she told Altman. In the spring vote, she had confidentially promised Paster her vote if the White House was desperate. "I won't let it fail," she had told him then. "I'll vote last, but if you need me, you will have my vote." Paster didn't have to call it in then. After she had voted no, a would-be challenger for her seat had declined to run against her; but, she feared, a yes vote this time would unleash all kinds of opposition. She hoped and prayed that she would be spared and not called to support the president.

After the call, Altman told Paster that she was really shaky. They should not count on her.

About 8:35 P.M., Clinton talked to Margolies-Mezvinsky himself. He had the impression that it was she who had called. She wanted Clinton to come to her district personally sometime after the vote to run a forum on entitlement reform. Clinton said he would.

"I want you to know I'm going to be with you on this one," she said. Clinton grew teary. It was a shame that someone in such a vulnerable seat had to do this, while so many Democrats with safe seats were refusing. It looked good but too close to be sure.

At 9:55 P.M. the House voting began. The members had 15 minutes to vote. Clinton moved into his study to watch it on a small television. He stood with his hands in his pockets, his head down. Paster was on a phone with an open line to the House. Stephanopoulos sat in a big high-backed chair. McLarty put his elbows on the back of the chair, his cheeks puffed out, resting on his fists.

At first the formal voting seemed to move quickly. Just after 9:56, Clinton was behind 51 to 55. Four minutes later at 10:00, he had vaulted ahead, 179 to 156. He maintained his lead until time expired right at 10:11 P.M. Then, in an instant, the tiny screen showed he was behind, 211 to 212.

All the Republicans had cast their ballots, every one against Clinton. Now only 11 Democrats were left to vote. A customary grace period of several minutes was granted to those who held off voting until the very end. Within seconds, the vote deadlocked at 213 to 213.

Stephanopoulos reminded the group that close House votes were about physics: Momentum ruled. In the final minutes, the direction the vote was heading was often where it wound up. Near the point of victory, Stephanopoulos said, the last 5 or even 11 votes were rarely members who had directly promised support. They were more often of the type of Margolies-Mezvinsky's "I'm there if you absolutely need me." Stephanopoulos had never figured out precisely how close you had to get so you could credibly tell a member, "I need you," and call in the final handful of votes. On this vote the center of gravity seemed to be around 213. If they didn't get past that point, droves of Democrats could smell defeat and switch their votes. The whole thing could tumble back, and they could lose by 20 votes.

Bentsen and Altman went into the little alcove off the president's study. Altman leaned down on a glass-topped table, palms down. When he stood up, two sweaty palm imprints were left on the table.

On the House floor, McCurdy was standing in the back. He had promised that he would not cast his no vote early to avoid starting a possible stampede hurting Clinton. At the same time, he did not want to be the last vote to kill the plan, not number 217 or 218. A number of the last members were heading toward the well to vote, and McCurdy didn't want to be in that visible position. By the electronic device in the back, he voted no.

In the White House, the no vote flashed on the screen. Paster reported that it had been McCurdy's. Stephanopoulos concluded that McCurdy had timed his vote to maximize damage, right at the critical moment, right as the opposition was hoping to knock the momentum back. He concluded that McCurdy wanted to be the saboteur, start the dominos tumbling the other way. Stephanopoulos believed McCurdy was deliberately trying to kill the president. McCurdy was angry, jealous, self-righteous, and a coward. He had made a big mistake, Stephanopoulos felt.

For his part, Gergen had always felt that Clinton had erred in fighting with McCurdy while waltzing around with the liberals. This was McCurdy's way of saying he wasn't going to be taken for granted. The president was paying the price, Gergen thought.

It was 10:12 P.M. The vote was now 216 to 214. Four Democrats hadn't voted. Clinton needed two more.

Clinton stayed hunched over the small television set in his study. He had an unlit cigar between his lips that he was mouthing nervously. He was standing taut and moved back. Placing one hand on McLarty's shoulder and the other on Stephanopoulos's shoulder, he leaned toward the television. For a tense three minutes, the vote stayed exactly the same.

At 10:15 P.M., Margolies-Mezvinsky and Pat Williams of Montana finally filled out green cards, signifying a yes vote, and the count went over the top, to 218. The two remaining Democrats voted no for a 218–216 final tally. The House Chamber filled with wild cheering from the Democrats, while Republicans chanted, "Bye-bye Marjorie!"

Clinton grabbed his head with his fingers and thumbs, digging them in like a madman. He whooped and threw his arms around each of his aides, one at a time, giving each a bountiful Arkansas hug. The hugs and celebration were repeated for the White House photographer. Carville said he knew they would win just because they had to win.

Clinton said that Carville was the only one of them making top-tax-bracket money, and he would be the one paying the tax increase. The chickens of the big book contract and the $20,000-a-pop speeches were going to come home to roost. He would gladly pay it all, someone joked. Clinton bent Carville over his big Oval Office desk to pick his pocket. Mark Gearan had a chart with bar graphs showing the tax increase on the rich like Carville. About 20 of them posed around the desk with Clinton's hand in Carville's back pocket, the populist president fleecing the rich. Gearan held up the chart. Pictures were snapped.

Clinton finally released the wallet from Carville's back pocket. Some $80 in cash was inside. The president took it out and started throwing the $20 bills around the Oval Office, symbolically redistributing the wealth. A moment of maximum peril had passed, but only the first one.

Clinton had changed out of his tan summer suit into a dark suit for the television cameras in the Rose Garden. Using Hillary's words of the previous year, he said, "And we have just begun to fight."

32

Early Friday morning, Clinton reviewed the bidding. Paster had arranged for Kerrey to come to the White House. Stephanopoulos predicted there was now no way that Kerrey could vote against Clinton. He would be lynched by the House members who had walked the plank; they would not let one senator from their own party undercut them all. The only way Kerrey would do it, Stephanopoulos told Clinton, was if he were irrational, if he were suicidal like Libyan leader Muammar Qaddafi.

Clinton said that was precisely the problem.

About 8 A.M., the White House senior staff met. They discussed one of Kerrey's proposals: that Clinton set up an independent commission of Democrats and Republicans to make recommendations on spending cuts—with Kerrey as chairman. Kerrey had earlier indicated to Mitchell and Moynihan that he might support Clinton's plan in exchange for such a commission, and Mitchell and Moynihan had made it clear they would do just about anything for Kerrey's vote. One of Kerrey's requests for the commission was that its recommendations be automatically incorporated in Clinton's next budget. Everyone at the staff meeting agreed that such a stipulation would be preposterous. Clinton couldn't turn over part of his executive authority on the budget to a commission. Then again, they absolutely needed Kerrey's vote. Suddenly, Paster was called out of the meeting to take a call from Kerrey.

"I don't know how I can vote yes," Kerrey told Paster. He explained that he was sitting in a hideaway office in the Senate. "Don't argue with me that this is necessary to save the Clinton presidency," Kerrey said. He was more worried about the political consequences for his friends in the House and Senate who were up for reelection in 1994. "I don't want to be a tax-and-spend Democrat," he added. "I want smaller government."

Just come talk to the president, Paster pleaded.

"Cancel the meeting with the president," Kerrey said. "I'm not going to waste his time."

Paster tried to talk him down, arguing that Kerrey had an obligation to come, if only as a courtesy to his friend, the head of the party, the president. It would not be a pressure session. "If you come, I'll make it clear to him it is your intention to vote no."

Kerrey finally agreed.

Paster called Clinton to fill him in. Mellow was the only way to act with Kerrey, Paster suggested. The more Clinton argued, "Do this for me," the less likely he was to get Kerrey's vote. The president would have to convincingly present himself as the agent of change and say that his deficit reduction plan, though incremental, would advance, not destroy, the kind of revolutionary changes Kerrey wanted.

McLarty and Gergen strongly suggested that Clinton not talk about deals. Talk about your shared concerns, they suggested, the things you want to do together as partners in this great enterprise of saving the country. Keep it on the highest moral plane, the stuff of the early presidential campaign. Kerrey obviously wanted respect. He always talked in terms of respect, not friendship. He had a totally inflated view of his own importance and strength, and, unfortunately, his swing vote only magnified that self-perception.

Paster went to the West Lobby to wait for Kerrey. He didn't want anyone else even talking to the senator. When Kerrey arrived, Paster took him through a mazelike route into the office of Clinton's secretary and around back through the colonnade, avoiding the press room, and then up to the residence. Paster told Kerrey he would have his car moved around the side to the road between the White House and the Old Executive Office Building so he could avoid the press on the way out.

Clinton welcomed Kerrey in the second-floor residence, and they went out to the Truman balcony. It was about 9 A.M. A heavy rain was falling out over the Mall and the Washington Monument. The two men seated themselves in rocking chairs and drank coffee. Clinton, dressed in a suit, leaned back and pulled his feet up on the bottom rung of the rocker. He seemed calm.

Clinton said he too had moral concerns about the direction of the country—kids, schools, the economy. He said he had his own dreams for the country. But Washington had surprised him, he said. "It's more treacherous," Clinton said. It was more difficult to finish projects than he expected. He said he felt more isolated in the White House than he ever anticipated. It was harder to stay in touch with the outside world. He couldn't see some possibilities or options, he realized, because of his isolation.

Kerrey finally said that he thought he should tell the president how he felt about this final reconciliation bill. The process had gotten off track, Kerrey said.

Clinton said that he certainly would have liked the final bill to have been different. It was not the best.

"We're down wallowing in—debating what is in all honesty a relatively small proposal," Kerrey said. "It's not big enough to excite." Kerrey said that the plan must have appeared monstrously big to the president when he put it together at the beginning of the year. The power of Clinton's February 17 speech was that it *looked* as though Clinton was willing to risk his political career on a big plan. But the final product was too small. Kerrey said that the decision to go with a small 4.3-cents-a-gallon gas tax instead of 7 cents was particularly upsetting.

Clinton pointed out how hard he had tried for the larger BTU tax or a larger gas tax, but the main taxes were now on the rich.

"I don't like the soak-the-rich rhetoric," Kerrey added.

Clinton tried to work the problem from a side angle, to draw them back to the idealism of the campaign and to recapture the rhetoric of sacrifice. He appealed to the high-mindedness of their work, their dreams, steering the topic away from his immediate desperation and the absolute need for Kerrey's vote.

"I'm still a no, Mr. President," Kerrey said at the end.

Clinton said he was sorry, disappointed.

Kerrey stopped by Gergen's small office downstairs. The meeting with the president had been respectful this time, Kerrey said. He repeated his belief that they had to teach people in this country to say no. "You've got to go out and tell people no to this, no to that," he explained, "and you guys aren't willing to do this. You've got no guts. How the hell can I vote for a program that's not going to go anywhere?" The big problems were not being tackled, he still felt. "I'm going to vote no."

Afterwards, Clinton reported that he felt he had made some progress. He felt he might have penetrated Kerrey's cosmic zone, but, he mused, who could tell? Though Kerrey was talking no, as a practical matter they could not be sure, and they certainly couldn't act as if it were over. Kerrey was unpredictable, still in his dream world.

KERREY WAS CONCERNED about the way Clinton's plan was playing back in Nebraska. There his constituents viewed it as a tax bill, not a deficit reduction bill. Listeners of Rush Limbaugh's radio show and others were calling Kerrey's office, overwhelmingly opposing the plan. Some of Kerrey's wealthy friends had embarrassed him with their professed hardship at the tax increases. One had said he would not be able to build his summer home, another that his domestic help might have to be laid off.

Recently Kerrey had spoken with the wealthiest friend he had from the state—the wealthiest friend any American had from any state— businessman Warren Buffett, who lived in Omaha. Buffett, who had accumulated personal wealth of more than $9 billion, was considered the wealthiest man in the United States and a legendary financial guru and practitioner of common sense.

The consequences of not doing anything could be serious, Buffett said. He personally might have had more spending cuts in the economic plan, but it was the right direction. He noted that it could be a costly political vote, but he still thought Kerrey should vote yes. The taxes on the wealthy were not that big a deal. Buffett believed that marginal tax-rate increases or decreases of 10 percent or so didn't affect anyone's behavior. "If anybody tells you that it's going to be a hardship for them, advise them to lower their salary to $200,000 a year and buy stocks in companies that don't issue dividends, and it'll be just fine." The bottom line of Buffett's recommendation: "Hold your nose and vote for it."

Liz Moynihan, the senator's wife, was up at the Moynihans' farm in New York State hearing reports of Kerrey's dance. She and her husband had supported and endorsed Kerrey in the early 1992 Democratic presidential primaries. They liked him, and she considered herself Kerrey's friend. She called him from their porch.

"Pat and I have talked this over. He didn't tell you what he was supposed to tell you," she said, adopting an older, maternal tone. She said she was looking out for his long-term best interest. "You can't do this to yourself. It's not a large bill," she said. "We can do more with it being passed than with it being defeated." She had been talking to Mandy Grunwald, who was also Moynihan's media adviser, and they had developed a further strategy. "You vote yes on this and you'll be liberated, and if you choose to go into permanent opposition, you can," she said. Vote no and Kerrey would ruin himself in national politics.

Some people would charge that his no vote had been motivated by spite. "They will think you did this because of New Hampshire," she said. "You don't want that argument."

Kerrey had heard some of these arguments already and they seemed to be coming out of the White House.

Liz Moynihan tried to make it clear this was not the White House, this was friendship. The interests of the party, the Senate, the country, and Kerrey himself all coincided. Her husband as the chairman of the Finance Committee would also be hurt if the plan failed. "You can't do this to Pat," she said finally.

FROM THE OTHER SIDE of the aisle, Bob Dole invited Kerrey down to the Republican cloakroom for a talk. "Vote no," Dole said. "Move to reconsider and we'll keep the reconciliation bill alive. And then we'll negotiate and try to improve it." The Senate rules allowed someone voting no to move immediately afterward to reconsider the vote. This tactic allowed the bill to be tabled but kept alive, once again open for negotiation with the White House.

Kerrey hesitated. He felt like he was in the room cutting a deal with the devil. There was an atmosphere of distrust. It wasn't just Dole alone. Kerrey didn't totally distrust the Republican leader, who seemed sincere in wanting to have a stranglehold on the Democratic president. It was the abyss between all Republicans and all Democrats. Kerrey's gut told him not to trust.

AN OUTLINE of Kerrey's spending-cut commission made its way on paper to the White House. Stephanopoulos was amazed: The totally weird side of Kerrey had been replaced by the hard-boiled negotiator. Clinton said okay to it. Gore, however, saw the plan and became upset. For five months he had been heading his own commission on "Reinventing Government," ways to streamline the federal bureaucracy and cut costs. Gore was spending half his time on it, and a Kerrey commission could kill all his efforts.

Stephanopoulos and Gore's chief of staff played with the language to shift it away from Gore's turf and onto entitlement programs. They sent it back to Mitchell for final negotiations with Kerrey. Stephanopoulos realized that the language didn't matter in the slightest. Words stopped mattering. Waiting and waiting was all they could do.

At 4 P.M., Hillary and Magaziner met with the president in the Oval

Office for two hours to get his head back into health care. Magaziner, roiling with frustration, hadn't seen Clinton since late June. The 14-hour work days had taken their toll on Magaziner, and he had acted domineering toward others in the health care task force and even angry at times. He had prepared a memo listing 18 times since February that health care had been stalled, postponed, or pushed off the agenda. The decisions had to be made quickly, and he now wanted a Camp David weekend with all the players. Hillary too was pushing hard to get decisions made quickly. But the president clearly wasn't focusing on it.

ABOUT 7 P.M. Kerrey switched: He would vote yes. Liz Moynihan and Warren Buffett had presented him with the best arguments. Practically, the plan couldn't be improved, Kerrey reasoned. What would the alternative be? Dole's? He told his staff, which had become violently opposed to the bill, of his latest decision. Almost instantly, Kerrey faced a revolt at a staff meeting. They were suddenly all against him. Kerrey went into his office and called the White House about 8:20 P.M.

Clinton was at his desk in the Oval Office. He picked up Kerrey's call, and began taking notes, biting his lower lip.

"Mr. President," Kerrey said, "I'm going to vote for it. This vote's for free."

Clinton began quietly nodding his head and finally gave a thumbs-up sign to his advisers in the room. "I appreciate it," Clinton said.

Kerrey said the decision whether to create the commission was up to the president. "If you think this is a good idea when it's all over, fine," Kerrey said. "But if you don't, there's no commitment here to do the commission."

"Thank you," Clinton said.

Kerrey then wrote out a speech in longhand. The vote was going to be very hard to explain to Nebraska. Kerrey felt no sense of elation as he went to the Senate floor. He rose and delivered an angry, personal 17-paragraph diatribe at Clinton, Congress, and himself. "My heart aches with the conclusion that I will vote yes for a bill which challenges Americans too little.

"President Clinton, if you're watching now, as I suspect you are, I tell you this: I could not and should not cast a vote that brings down your presidency." Kerrey immediately regretted saying that he could bring down the presidency. The comment was a rhetorical flourish; he didn't believe it would happen, and it was the very argument he had told Clinton he resented.

Clinton was not watching. He was tied up with phone calls to congressional leaders.

"Get back on the high road, Mr. President," Kerrey proclaimed. Taxing the wealthy was simply "political revenge," he said. "Our fiscal problems exist because of rapid, uncontrolled growth in the programs that primarily benefit the middle class." Clinton needed to return to the theme of shared sacrifice, he said, and should have said no to the deals and compromises. "I'm sympathetic, Mr. President. I know how loud our individual threats can be. But I implore you, Mr. President, say 'no' to us."

Gore, presiding in the Senate, was approached by Senator John Breaux, who had decided to support the bill in the end. "Are you going to be okay on this one?" Breaux inquired with mild sarcasm.

"I think so," Gore said. Gore approached Majority Leader Mitchell, who was on the floor, making sure everything stayed together. "I'm wavering," Gore said. Mitchell laughed. Kerrey's vote for the plan created a 50 to 50 tie. For some time, Gore had been thinking that it would be this way. He believed in what he called "the internal rationing of conscience"—that there was just enough conscience in the U.S. Senate to muster the 50 votes, but no more. Then, in his most important act as vice president to that point, Gore voted for the plan, breaking the tie.

Kerrey then went to Mitchell in private. He wanted a special session of Congress to reopen some of the matters, especially spending cuts and sacrifice. No way, Mitchell said. Kerrey demanded the commission. Howard Paster was in Mitchell's office and relayed word to Stephanopoulos in the White House.

Stephanopoulos then called Clinton, who was up in the Red Room. The president was in a good mood. He had survived, but he was mad at Kerrey's moralistic speech, which had been described to him in detail.

It was worse, Stephanopoulos said. It wasn't really a free vote. He then reported on Kerrey's last-minute insistence on the commission.

That hypocrite, that phony, Clinton said. Yet the president had to accept.

THE ROOSEVELT ROOM was filling up and soon was packed with 150 cabinet officers, White House staff, and others. Rock concert–style T-shirts, with the words "PRESIDENT CLINTON'S ECONOMIC PLAN, VICTORY AUGUST 6" emblazoned across the front, were handed out.

"Rog-er! Rog-er! Rog-er!" the chant began, summoning Altman, the leader of the War Room. The rhythmic clapping grew. Altman was pulled along, mounted a chair, and held up a T-shirt, feeling like a Wimbledon winner hoisting the victory plate. The room exploded with wild cheering. He read a David Letterman–style top-ten list: The Top Ten Reasons Why Congress Really Passed the Economic Plan. He recited them to an easy crowd: Not to offend Hillary. So congressmen won't be required to lunch with the president again. So congressmen won't have to negotiate with Bob Dole at Andrews Air Force Base. So the Clinton staff can finish high school. And the last reason—Time for summer vacation.

"Lloyd! Lloyd!" the rhythmic chant went up for Bentsen, as if for a venerated rock star in late career receiving a lifetime achievement award. The secretary of the Treasury was bubbling. "I've never seen such a great, hard-fought victory!" he said, slamming his fist in the air with pride and congratulation. It was as though all the senior-wiseman reserve drained from him in that single moment. He said he respected the work particularly of the young people. "I've seen lots of presidents and lots of victories," Bentsen said, "but this is the sweetest!"

McLarty spoke, saying that during one of the darkest moments of the battle, he had told David Dreyer, the senior communications aide, who wore the hippest modern clothes and had a small earring pierced in one ear, that he would switch neckties with him if they won. McLarty took off his conservative dark tie and Dreyer his wild brightly colored tie, and they swapped. McLarty folded his arms and brought his shoulders forward as if to conceal his new ill-matched tie.

"That's nothing," Dreyer said. "He says if we win health care, he'll wear my earring."

Sperling was summoned to speak. He said that he knew he was teased all the time about being the numbers guy, but he wanted to read some numbers anyway. He had a little sheet of paper which he held out in front of himself as he read from it nervously. Because Bill Clinton had run and was elected president, Sperling said, 5 million people who worked full time at the minimum wage would receive the earned-income-tax credit, and 10 million would receive additional benefits so that every family with a full-time working parent would be above the poverty line. Another 100,000 children would get the intensive family-preservation counseling and social services because of Clinton. Another 4.5 million children would get hunger relief through increased food stamps, 600,000 more poor women with children would get better nutrition, and 6.5 million children would be eligible for free immunization shots.

Tears came to some eyes. Altman felt a little ashamed. That was the right focus. He felt that he had been too intent on winning and had stopped thinking about the ideals. Not for the first time had he forgotten, he realized. Altman stepped forward and gave Sperling a big, emotional bear hug that was captured in a photograph.

Begala spoke next. "I want to follow up on what Gene said, and I want to make it personal. Let's all remember the faces you saw on the campaign. Those were the faces we worked for. Those faces stand for real people, and you've helped the lives of those real people. That's why we came here."

Gergen could hear the hoopla that at one point seemed to extend to the front lawn of the White House. Someone made a crack about beating the bastards, turning around the last 12 years of Reagan and Bush. It was the sort of partisan outburst that made Gergen wince. He had missed Bentsen's speech and erroneously believed that Bentsen had left, sharing Gergen's discomfort. Gergen didn't stay long, and slipped out and went home. He was one of those bastards.

CLINTON WAS BACK in Stephanopoulos's cubbyhole office. Altman gave him his T-shirt. Gore read the top-ten list to Clinton in the president's study.

The president was exhausted and drawn. He was sitting and looked as if he could not get up. It was as if his face had fallen down. His skin was dry, his eyes puffy. Little old-skin folds hung around his eyes at the bottom and the top. His eyes were small, narrow slits.

Just after 11 P.M. the president went to the North Portico at the White House. Gore, McLarty, Panetta, and Altman had followed. Bentsen had already departed. Cars could be heard in the dark, distant Washington background honking.

Clinton stepped forward and faced the cameras: "What we heard tonight at the other end of Pennsylvania Avenue was the sound of gridlock breaking. . . . After 12 long years, we can say to the American people tonight we have laid the foundation for the renewal of the American dream. . . . After a long season of denial and drift and decline, we are seizing control of our economic destiny."

The president went up to the second-floor kitchen of the residence to see Hillary.

They could begin to build people's confidence again, Clinton said. "Now," the president told his wife, "we can get on with what we really came here to do."

. . .

BY MIDNIGHT, Carville, Stephanopoulos, Greenberg, and several others were celebrating with a late-night dinner at the chic Italian restaurant Bice just off Pennsylvania Avenue, midway between the White House and the Capitol. The waiter approached them with drinks and greetings, sent over by another diner. Who? they asked. Compliments of Senator Bob Kerrey, the waiter said. It was such a strange and weird closure. They looked at each other, baffled.

Kerrey eventually drifted by; he lived on the seventh floor of the same building. He was not happy. He was tense and had one question: "Did we really do anything tonight?"

EPILOGUE

"Am I going to make it?" Clinton asked a close friend several days after the victory. The president showed no sign that he felt any sense of overwhelming accomplishment. He was worried that the plan would not work either economically or politically. "I'm exhausted now," he said. His eyes still looked like small slits, and they drifted. He fell into a chair, and it seemed he might not get up. The celebrated Clinton concentration was absent. Long gaps of ten seconds or more stalled the normal, steady flow of conversation. He just faded away in thought. The friend had never seen Clinton like this. The president seemed alone and afraid.

"The job is much tougher than I realized," Clinton said. "I did not realize the importance of communications and the overriding importance of what is on the evening television news. If I am not on, or there with a message, someone else is, with their message." Congress and the national press never gave him credit when he did something right. The atmosphere was mean and negative.

ON THE MORNING of Wednesday, August 11, Paul Begala was watching a Rose Garden ceremony that was being televised live on CNN. The president and Attorney General Janet Reno were introducing an anticrime measure. Begala noticed Senator Frank R. Lautenberg of New Jersey—one of the six Senate Democrats who had voted against Clinton's plan—among those invited. Incensed, he picked up the phone and called the White House, reaching Howard Paster. "I can't believe what you are doing!" Begala yelled.

What are you yelling about? Paster asked.

One of the turncoats is out basking in the reflected glory of Clinton and the Attorney General, Begala complained.

"No," Paster replied. That couldn't be true.

"Get out of your fucking chair," Begala said. "Get up and look out your fucking window and look what's fucking going on!"

Paster checked and came back to the phone. "It was a good idea gone awry," he attempted to explain. The White House had a standard formula for invitations, and Lautenberg had been a key supporter of the crime measure. Paster had been too busy to check.

Begala railed about incompetence. The vote list had to be on the top of Paster's desk, not in some drawer, lost to memory and history. Traitors had to be punished, supporters rewarded. The White House continued to fail at basic politics.

A MEETING WITH THE CLINTONS in the solarium that night, Wednesday, August 11, erupted into an ugly battle as factions vied for commitments from the president to devote time to health care, NAFTA, and Gore's "Revinventing Government" plan. Hillary Clinton wanted to make sure the administration didn't screw up health care reform as they had the stimulus package. The meeting lasted until midnight, and the next day Begala told the president why he was so exhausted: "The reason is we kept you up for a meeting that was embarrassing to the presidency." When Clinton asked Gergen what he thought of the meeting, Gergen replied, "I'm so depressed that I can barely speak."

Carville realized that Clinton's advisers were evenly split over what the president's next step should be. Hillary and the consultants were eager to forge ahead with health care reform. "We've been waiting patiently in line," she said at one meeting. Gergen, Bentsen, Altman, and some others whom Carville considered the Washington elite were pushing for NAFTA. Carville suggested that the administration try to cut a deal with Congress on both health care and the trade agreement. After all, Clinton was the Clinton administration almost all by himself. He could easily do two things at once. His energy was boundless; his personal efforts could carry the day.

After two years working with Clinton, Carville had concluded that the public might have its reservations about him, and they might disagree with him. But people never threw in the towel on him. They admired his goals. People knew that he worked hard and that his complicated mind was engaged. That had been the lesson of the 1992 campaign and probably would be the lesson of Clinton's presidency. But in Clintonland, as Carville came to call it, there were always surprises.

STAN GREENBERG CONTINUED to search for an analysis, or a memo, that would somehow clearly define or fix the Clinton presidency. He and the three other consultants prepared a long confidential memo, dated August 11 and entitled "The Journey," with the usual six numbered copies for Clinton, Hillary, Gore, McLarty, Gergen, and Stephanopoulos.

"One of the central problems we face is the perception that there's no coherence or principle or purpose to the president's actions," the memo stated bluntly. "People see him mired in the legislative process. They see him compromising. . . . They do not understand the journey the president is asking the country to take with him." The central lesson from the eight months was the need for some simplification. The memo proposed that "The Journey" be built on a broad theme of economic renewal for the country, with each piece of Clinton's agenda related to that overall theme.

Greenberg also presented to Clinton the latest polling and focus group research and an analysis he had done with Carville in a quarter-inch-thick report called "The Presidential Project." It stressed the notion that Congress was the new Soviet Union equivalent—and Clinton had to manage and dominate the relationship with Congress. Clinton was at first taken with the idea. But later, after dining at the White House with a group of historians who argued that the presidency was defined as much by vision as by legislation, Clinton revised his view. "Managing a relationship with Congress can't be the sum and substance of this presidency," he said afterwards. He had come to believe the presidency could be used to make dramatic moral statements.

CLINTON STILL PLUNGED into his legislative agenda, most notably on health care. In August, a thick packet of paper had landed on his desk and those of others in the White House, entitled "Presidential Level Health Care Decisions for August." Clinton had already decided that funding for reform would *not* come from any major tax hikes other than on cigarettes. The money would have to come from cuts in existing government health programs such as Medicare and Medicaid, and from reduced costs resulting from government-enforced competition.

As Clinton reviewed the numbers, he grew furious. The memo presented five scenarios for controlling costs. A table on page 5 showed that even under the most radical and aggressive scenario for government intervention, total national health care spending would still rise from the current 14 percent of the entire economy to 17 percent in the year 2000. How could he justify this to the American people? he asked. The most radical version would do no more than *slow* the rate of growth?

Also, according to the charts, total costs for 1996, his reelection year, would go up more than they would *without* reform.

Health reform could become a political loser. Clinton began to joke grimly that the savings and benefits would not be realized until, perhaps, a second Gore administration. If they couldn't save money, what's the purpose? he asked.

Clinton's key economic advisers and others also had their doubts and challenged the health care plan being devised by Hillary and Magaziner. Bentsen was disturbed that health had not been subjected to the collegial deliberative process of the economic plan, but was handled back channel with Magaziner trying to keep all the information to himself. He argued that the resulting plan was not politically attainable in Congress. Clinton could have a great victory with a smaller, less ambitious plan, and afterwards win more reforms incrementally. Altman said privately that the emerging plan was "too big, too expensive and too fast." Rubin invoked the law of unintended consequences, arguing that such rapid change for so much of the economy was impossible and that to attempt it could prompt unanticipated and harmful results. Tyson wrote memos to Hillary recommending moderation.

Gergen was mystified by the decision making. At one meeting, five possible options were to be discussed by the advisers but the more free-market options were summarily dropped. Then at the next meeting, Hillary unilaterally announced the decision for an option that called for a bigger government role than Gergen thought wise or possible. Where did this come from? he wondered.

Clinton had worked it out with Hillary and Magaziner. The president finally convened his key advisers. "We can fight like crazy about this, but when we're done and we make a decision," the president said, "we've got to pull together like we did on the economic plan. Not everybody was happy with the economic plan. Even I gave way on some things that I might have preferred differently. We have all got to go forward." Everybody nodded, and Clinton looked around the room to make sure that everybody had assented.

The centerpiece was going to be a speech to be delivered in September to a Joint Session of Congress and a national, prime-time television audience. Clinton and Hillary rejected the first draft outright, declaring that it wasn't big enough and didn't soar. "Pedestrian," Clinton said. Jeremy Rossner, the foreign policy speechwriter who had written Clinton's remarks at the recent Middle East peace signing on the White House lawn, was brought in to give the speech dramatic lift.

In the final version, Clinton compared health care reform with the latest foreign policy changes: "Miracles do happen. I mean, just a few days ago we saw a simple handshake shatter decades of deadlock in the Middle East." He also invoked the collapse of the Berlin Wall, the progress in South Africa, and the fall of the Soviet Union.

The physical setting in the House Chamber that night was ideal for Clinton. It was crowded and sweaty and had an air of importance, as if war or victory was being declared.

The TelePrompTer operators initially had the wrong speech up on the screens. Clinton's aides generally took away his eyeglasses before a major speech because they created a bulge in his pocket, so Clinton wasn't able to read his backup script. But the president knew the material and improvised until the speech was found in the computer. The mistake only seemed to add a passion and force to his delivery. Later Begala asked Clinton how it felt to be up there to give perhaps the most important speech of his life with the wrong text and poor eyesight. Clinton said, "Well, I thought, God, you're testing me. Okay."

The president received a boost in the polls afterwards. But the difference between a great speech and great legislation remained vast. Magaziner felt that by proposing a plan that was left of center, Clinton would eventually win something in the center. But Magaziner did not fully grasp that the health plan, no matter how wonderfully configured or academically sound, would get dropped into the same caldron as the economic plan. The Congress, the public, the media, and the interest groups would all have their spoons in the brew stirring at his creation.

AFTER CLINTON'S DEMOCRATS-ONLY STRATEGY on the economic plan, McLarty, Bentsen, Gergen, and others felt it was important to assemble a coalition on NAFTA that included Republicans and conservative Democrats and to continue pushing for the agreement.

Bentsen felt that the odds were that Clinton would abandon NAFTA because the labor groups in the party opposed it. In a table-pounding lead-off speech in a Cabinet Room meeting to discuss the issue, Bentsen declared that the world's perception of America hinged on going forward. Clinton's political courage was being questioned, Bentsen said, and it was absolutely imperative that he show he was a strong leader, willing to fight. The president had to demonstrate his readiness to take on an interest group in his own party. It was right, and it would give him stature. The Treasury Secretary was watching Clinton's expression, and could sense he might be gaining ground.

Secretary of State Warren Christopher next argued that Clinton's credibility was at stake. Rubin said that the business community was behind the trade agreement, and if the administration waged a full fight, so would business. Stephanopoulos took the negative side. Where were the votes? he asked. How could the administration win? If it wasn't clearly winnable, the president should not try for it but instead start developing an exit strategy, he said.

"I have to be a president beyond the borders," Clinton finally said, declaring that he would go ahead. "It is not an option to drop."

"Fine," Stephanopoulos said, holding the palms of his hands up. "As long as everyone knows what we are getting into."

Even Paster, who was worried at first, later told the president, "If you abandon NAFTA, Mr. President, there goes New Democrat."

Initially it had seemed there was no way to win on NAFTA without House Majority Leader Gephardt, who continued to oppose it. Over several weeks, McLarty had been engaged in a secret effort of phone calls and meetings to turn Gephardt around. When the Republicans who supported Clinton on NAFTA learned of McLarty's backstage efforts, they warned Paster that any compromise that could win over Gephardt would certainly cost Clinton the Republicans.

Paster finally told McLarty he felt they had enough votes for NAFTA and suggested he break off the talks with Gephardt. Stephanopoulos agreed, arguing there was no way to persuade Gephardt. McLarty continued his efforts, believing he was keeping the disagreement from getting nasty or leading to a breakdown of relations.

Paster tried to call him off again. While they had at first thought they couldn't win without Gephardt, they now believed they couldn't win with him, Paster said. Too many Republicans would jump.

"If we can just get his vote!" McLarty said.

"I'm not sure we want his vote now," Paster replied.

McLarty persisted.

"Stop this fucking thing!" Paster finally screamed.

On November 17, after a marathon of Clinton lobbying, the House approved NAFTA, 234 to 200. The winning coalition included 132 Republicans and only 102 Democrats. Several days later Paster went to tell Clinton that he was resigning from the job he had wanted his whole career. McLarty remained in the room, and Paster did not feel he could be frank with the president. The real reason he was leaving was that he no longer could work with McLarty. Paster believed that McLarty had failed to manage the White House. Its staff, the administration, the outside consultants were not coordinated. Everyone and anyone free-lanced. Paster's job of congressional liaison had been made impossible. The sole reason Paster offered publicly for his departure was that he wanted to spend more time with his family.

IN PUSHING FOR NAFTA, Gergen had taken McLarty to meet with his former boss Richard Nixon over breakfast. Nixon had argued that Clinton needed to prove he had strong beliefs, and on NAFTA it would be better to go down fighting than to compromise. "There are things worse than losing," Nixon had told the two men. Gergen later told Clinton that his determined fight on NAFTA had changed the way people viewed him. Do you really think so? Clinton asked. Gergen felt NAFTA was the turning point in Clinton's presidency: Clinton would now govern from the bipartisan center.

Immediately after the victory, Hillary convened a health care meeting in the Roosevelt Room. The subject arose of a planned show-of-affirmation meeting with the House leadership, including David Bonior, the party whip. Bonior had led the fight against NAFTA, calling it a sellout of the American worker.

"I think we ought to keep our distance from him," Gergen suggested. It was one thing to oppose NAFTA, but to lead the opposition to his own president and use the power and organization of the whip's office —the chief enforcement mechanism of party discipline—was too much.

A brief silence filled the room.

"Are you fucking crazy?" Carville piped up from the end of the table. "If David Bonior wants to come down here with his pants down, we'll kiss his ass. He's with us 95 percent of the time."

"You don't understand," Grunwald interjected. "This is the guy who will bleed for health care."

Greenberg, who was Bonior's longtime pollster, agreed. "Health care will not happen without David Bonior," he said.

"They're *exactly* right," Hillary said.

Gergen did not understand why centrist Democrats such as Boren and

McCurdy were treated like arch enemies when they opposed the president while liberals like Bonior were clasped to the administration's bosom.

Later, on his own, Clinton called Bonior. "I just want to let you know I'm thinking of you today," the president said.

Soon Gergen began referring to himself privately as "a transitional figure" whose value to Clinton was diminishing. When a published story reported that Gergen wanted to replace McLarty, Gergen went to McLarty and insisted that he never, under any circumstances, wanted to be Clinton's chief of staff.

Stephanopoulos thought that Gergen wanted to move to a foreign affairs post in the administration, noting frequent runs Gergen had made at National Security Adviser Anthony Lake. Gergen was probably responsible for a quarter of the recurring news stories about the disarray among Clinton's foreign policy team, Stephanopoulos suspected. Stephanopoulos had come to find Gergen almost intolerable. Whenever Clinton did something Republican, Gergen proclaimed that the president was standing up for principle. Whenever Clinton did something Democratic, it was caving.

Gergen felt that Clinton was an evolving figure, growing and adapting to Washington. He had not fully become the bipartisan, centrist reformer Gergen envisioned, and he frequently returned to the partisan attacks and populist themes of his campaign. More and more Hillary attacked the insurance companies and the Republicans.

Clinton's White House, Gergen felt, was surprisingly explicit in discussing matters that had been tucked away in the Republican administrations where he had worked. Clinton and his staff thought and talked a lot about the 1996 reelection effort. A campaign mentality permeated the White House, a War Room mentality. The consultants in particular needed someone and something to be against, Gergen concluded. To a certain extent, they had chosen Gergen.

ON JANUARY 21, 1994, Alan Greenspan met with Clinton and his economic advisers at the White House. "We've got a dilemma and you should understand," the Federal Reserve chairman said. The economy was growing rapidly and inflation expectations were mounting, driving up long-term rates to 6.3 percent. "We haven't made a decision, but the choices are, we sit and wait and then likely we'll have to raise short-term interest rates more. Or we could take some small increases now."

"Obviously," Clinton said, "I want to keep interest rates low, but I understand what you may have to do."

Bentsen could see that the president had said this grudgingly and was swallowing about as hard as he could. He knew Clinton recognized the importance of interest rates, economically and politically, and wanted them kept down.

Greenspan said that it was very difficult to know when to move interest rates. Much was unpredictable, and there were no formal indicators to say this was the time. "We've been flat so long," Greenspan continued, referring to the 15 months of steady 3 percent short-term rates, "we almost have to show that we can do something, that we're willing to move."

"Wait a minute!" Gore interrupted. "What about the possibility that you introduce uncertainty?" The vice president noted that, historically, a single rate increase by the Fed was followed by a series of subsequent increases that looked like a stair step on a chart. In 1988, for example, the Fed had moved the short-term rate from about 6.5 percent to nearly 10 percent in a dozen small increases. If bond traders expected a similar series of increases, Gore said, long-term rates would be driven back up. A Fed move might have the opposite effect of what Greenspan intended.

Greenspan acknowledged that was an interesting point, but said that long rates were high largely because of the inflation expectation, and that could be addressed with a move. The chairman also said that a little uncertainty in the markets would not be all bad, and if long rates went up, he did not believe they would stay up.

Afterwards the president, Gore, and Tyson said they hoped Greenspan would wait before raising short-term rates. Bentsen and Rubin thought it best for Greenspan to go ahead and do it now.

Two weeks later, the Fed raised the rate—the first increase in five years. Bentsen was almost effusive in his public comments, barely stopping short of nominating Greenspan for the Nobel Prize in Economics. The bond market was not convinced, and the long-term rates shot up. Six weeks later the Fed raised the short-term rate again. Although this time the long-term rate dropped briefly, suggesting that the Fed might have inflation under control, it soon started to rise again, climbing back up above 7 percent. The Fed raised short-term rates a third time on April 18, 1994, and the benchmark long-term rate moved to 7.4 percent —higher than at any time in Clinton's presidency.

Some in the White House found Clinton impatient and intensely inquisitive about interest rates. Bentsen realized the president was champing at the bit. Bentsen told him that it generally took about a year for interest-rate increases to have real economic bite to cool down the economy. It would be better for the Fed to move in 1994 with a cooler economy in 1995 than to wait until 1995. . . . Before Bentsen could get the words 1996 out of his mouth, the president grasped the point.

IN PREPARING the annual economic report of the president in February 1994, Laura Tyson had agreed to draft several introductory paragraphs to be included over Clinton's signature. Reflecting Clinton's views, she wrote that government should be looked at not as part of the problem but as part of the solution, as a "catalyst and promoter" of economic growth in the free market. When the draft circulated within the White House, McLarty and Gergen raised questions. Should this be said so explicitly? Would it trigger a debate about Clinton's precise economic vision? Could political opponents use it to attack Clinton as an advocate of government activism? Did it suggest that Clinton was moving off his New Democrat message?

Several discussions followed. It was finally agreed to let Clinton's economic policies speak for themselves to avoid unleashing a public debate about his overall vision. A toned-down draft was forwarded to Clinton. The president asked why it did not reflect what he wanted. Rubin, McLarty, and Gergen said it was better to do it that way, and Clinton gave his approval. Clinton told Tyson that if he had time, he was sure the vision could be put forward in acceptable language, but the deadline for the report did not permit it.

Tyson felt the economic conditions in the spring of 1994 were solid. The rapid growth of the last quarter of 1993 had been an aberration, and 1994 seemed to be settling down to a solid 3 percent. Inflation seemed under control and the only danger was an extended period of too much growth, something she did not expect.

The next year, 1995, could be weak, she thought. The deficit reduction was going to take hold even more, and it would contract the economy; and if the long-term interest rates remained high, they would also slow the economy. But more than ever she realized that the experts' knowledge of the economy was imperfect. She met at least weekly with the president, and when discussion turned to the year 1996, she realized how imperfect the tools of economic forecasting were. When it was all examined and modeled and debated, she agreed with some private economists who said the amount of projected economic growth was about the same size as the margin of error. So the projections of about 3 percent growth for 1996 meant the actual growth could turn out to be within 3 percent of that—as high as 6 percent, or as low as zero.

. . .

BoB Rubin's answer to the question of how the economy would fare in 1996 came in two parts. "The second best answer," he once told the president, "is that we've created a solid foundation with the deficit reduction and the commitment to new investments—solid growth in the range approaching 3 percent with moderate inflation.

"The first best answer: Who the hell knows?"

Rubin believed the administration had coordinated the economics and the politics pretty well. But Clinton was always calling him down with a question or a worry, one matter or another gnawing at him, causing Rubin on one occasion to declare, "He's America's first worrier."

After his successful operation of the War Room, Roger Altman became a hero to the consultants and to the Clintons and seemed a rising star in the administration, even a possibility to replace Bentsen eventually as Treasury Secretary if the elder statesman were to step down. Then, in February 1994, Altman testified before Congress about a discussion he had with White House officials that touched directly on an investigation of the Clintons' investment in an Arkansas real estate land deal called Whitewater and their relationship with an Arkansas savings and loan institution. As acting head of the Resolution Trust Corporation, the government agency assigned to clean up the S&Ls that had failed in the 1980s, Altman had met at the White House to discuss the case. He insisted he had done nothing wrong, but his testimony triggered disclosure of other White House efforts to learn about the Whitewater investigation. Soon there was a series of news stories, leaks, counterleaks, suspicions, and an expanded investigation by a special counsel. Altman's chances to succeed Bentsen appeared to sink, if not disappear. Altman publicly acknowledged that he had made a gross mistake.

Mark Gearan was spending much of his time dealing with Whitewater and other stories about Clinton's past or the statements he was alleged to have made. When a London newspaper wrote that Clinton hated British Prime Minister John Major, Clinton told Gearan, "I don't hate anyone. I forget the people I'm supposed to hate." Gearan was surprised that Clinton could maintain any composure. The White House problems, Gearan felt, were organization and discipline. The staff was too often like a soccer league of 10-year-olds. No one stuck to his part of the field during a game. The ball—any ball—would come on the field, and everyone would go chasing it down field.

GENE SPERLING HAD WORKED furiously to squeeze out more new investments for 1994. The paltry $1 billion in the initial congressional bills had been expanded to some $11 billion by taking money from other programs. For the next year's budget, money was so tight that Sperling recommended what he called a "home-run strategy" of proposing increases in only 15 top priority investments. Clinton adopted it. Much of the proposed new spending was directed at worker-retraining programs to be headed by Bob Reich. Although an investment revolution was not going to be realized in the first Clinton administration, Sperling hoped they could perhaps lay the foundation for one. "We are learning to love the half-filled cup," he said.

PANETTA REALIZED that Clinton was uncomfortable with the need to impose rigid discipline on the budget at the end of 1993. Clinton said at one meeting that they had become a government of accountants and that every issue was being decided on the numbers. The presidency was going to be reduced to being chief accountant, Clinton said.

But a month later, Panetta was fielding requests from the departments for their 1995 budgets. Secretary of State Christopher requested an additional $2 billion. "What is he doing?" Clinton asked Panetta. "There's no way we can suddenly find $2 billion out of thin air." Panetta felt that Clinton was beginning to catch on, and he was glad when the president rejected the request. When Panetta came up several billion short for the overall 1995 budget, he told the president they could claim savings on matters such as procurement reform. The claim would be a stretch, the gimmicky option, Panetta warned. Clinton declined to puff up any of the numbers, and he sat down and went through the budget carefully, ordering some real cuts.

The economic recovery and the zeal for deficit reduction led to one significant victory that remained largely unnoticed in the media. The new deficit reduction projections were beyond the deficit hawks' wildest dreams. The magic goal of cutting $140 billion from the 1997 deficit had been exceeded; projections showed a reduction of about $180 billion for that year. Clinton was on the road actually to delivering on his campaign promise to halve the deficit in four years. Few people noticed.

On February 25, 1994, Clinton invited the cabinet members to lunch at Blair House, across from the White House. After arriving late, the president slipped into a virtual monologue. Late one recent night, he said, he had been surfing through the television channels with his remote control and had hit upon a preacher speaking about values. The president said that he had been moved by the effectiveness of the preacher's deeply personal approach. He mused aloud about how he might find an equivalent appeal for presenting his program in Washington. Where were the American people in terms of basic values? Clinton asked. How might he reach into that system of beliefs?

Clinton had the distance of a professor, Panetta felt, but was seeking the intensity of a preacher. He was wondering how to mount the pulpit. At the same time, the budget director concluded that the president was trying to develop a Churchillian message to explain what the war was about. The war in Washington, Panetta knew, was waged on many fronts. It amounted to a series of daily practical choices. What weapons were going to be used? How much ammunition? Who was going to be sacrificed? The rules of political survival, the gnawing Whitewater scandal, and the stories about the Clintons' personal lives and their finances made it almost impossible to craft such a message. And Clinton, at least for the moment, seemed unable to find the high ground or establish his moral authority. For Panetta, that political reality was another stage in Clinton's slow, torturous awakening.

BEGALA CONTINUED to fight with Rubin and others over the level of populist rhetoric that should be in the president's economic messages and policies. Begala was convinced that the most popular thing Clinton had done in 1993 was to raise taxes on the rich, and the failure to exploit this had hurt the president politically. "The rich are not the heroes of our story as they were under Reagan," Begala loved to say.

Begala realized there were still management problems at the White House. In August, he had joined Clinton on a road trip to visit the flood-damaged Midwest and to meet with Pope John Paul II in Denver. While Air Force One was delayed on the runway in St. Louis, Clinton instructed Begala to go personally to the pilot and make absolutely certain they were not holding up other flights. Begala, aware that Clinton didn't want a repeat of the haircut flap from the spring, approached the pilot and requested that they call into the tower. He came back and reported to Clinton that with his own ears he had heard the tower guarantee they were delaying no one whatsoever. Clinton's eyes still showed skepticism. It wasn't that he didn't believe Begala, but perhaps somewhere in the chain of information, he seemed to be thinking, some festering problem hadn't been reported to him.

Even for the president, Begala thought, it was difficult ever to be certain. Clintonland wasn't always pretty. Begala knew that when the think-tank analysts or the professors at the Kennedy School of Government studied the history of presidential decision making, especially on the economic plan, they would probably be frightened by the chaos. Yet although it was messy, Begala felt, only one fact really mattered: Clinton had passed his economic plan.

Begala told Clinton that he should consider the narrowness of his victory on the economic plan as a badge of honor. The president had pushed the political system as far as it would go. In Washington, Begala said, gimmicks passed unanimously. The economic plan vote was close because so many powerful forces wanted it the other way and were opposed to change.

MANDY GRUNWALD, still no true believer in the bond market, nonetheless acknowledged that the lower interest rates had at least for a while helped with jobs and the economy. On health care, she felt, Clinton's decision to threaten a veto only if the final legislation did not include universal coverage had made the Clintons total pragmatists on the issue. They could now win, and she felt they were balancing their efforts in the loathsome legislative game involving all the congressional committees with regular road trips to get out the message.

Grunwald thought she was close enough to the president to identify the toughest moments of his presidency. The first was the death of his mother, Virginia Kelley, in January 1994, a loss that was still with the president months later, Grunwald was certain. Second was the death of Hillary's father. Third was the death of White House deputy counsel Vince Foster. Whatever might be said and done, even in the frightening combat of politics, Clinton knew what was lasting and what was gone forever.

IN EARLY 1994, George Mitchell surprised everyone, including the president, by announcing that he would not seek reelection. Clinton had tried to talk him out of it, since Mitchell had been such a strong ally. Mitchell insisted he just wanted a change in his life and his departure had nothing to do with Clinton.

"It was his rookie year," Mitchell said. "But I don't think that is the central factor. I think it was the significance of the tasks he undertook." Clinton could have undertaken less, at much less risk. "And it would have been politically easier and probably personally easier."

Clinton's $500 billion, five-year deficit reduction package was a huge accomplishment, Mitchell felt, more difficult than Bush's 1990 deal for the same amount. The first effort at cutting and belt-tightening and raising taxes was the easiest. The second was always much harder. The struggle grew out of the largeness of his task, not from any peculiar characteristics of the nation's capital. "The ways of Washington were the ways of Rome in the time of Julius Caesar," Mitchell said, "were the ways of Paris in the time of Napoleon or the ways of London in the time of Disraeli. There isn't much new under the sun in these things."

Asked if when the story of some of the intense struggles to get the economic plan passed were revealed, people would understand why he was quitting, Mitchell said nothing. But his face lit up, beaming for several seconds, with a large, bright smile.

AFTER THE ECONOMIC PLAN PASSED, McLarty talked to friends and colleagues about resigning or being kicked upstairs to a cabinet post. He was aware of some of the criticism of his management of the White House. "Am I the right person?" he asked several colleagues. Gergen for one counseled against leaving, and McLarty decided to say. After NAFTA passed and health care reform was introduced, the legislative accomplishments were substantial by any historic measure. He also felt that the economic plan had delivered on the basics—a better economy, increased job security, a better life or at least better opportunities for the middle class. In the end, Clinton had remained true to the spirit of his campaign. White House management also was improving, McLarty believed. Whatever the setbacks, McLarty knew something that no one could comprehend as well or fully as he. Even going back to Miss Mary's kindergarten class in Hope, Arkansas, four decades ago, he had learned a central feature of Clinton's character. It was simple, and it was what would matter in the end: Bill Clinton never gave up.

· · ·

BENTSEN HAD REPEATEDLY insisted to Clinton that it would take time for him to reap the rewards from his economic plan, for the financial markets strategy to work and interest rates to come down. But eventually the economy had turned around. By the last quarter of 1993, economic growth was soaring at 7 percent. After the passage of the economic plan, long-term interest rates fell dramatically, from about 6.5 percent to a low of 5.9 percent in October, freeing consumers and businesses to spend. Although Clinton never explicitly told Bentsen he was right, the president began citing the new economic growth numbers with great pride, and that was enough for Bentsen. When the Fed started raising rates in 1994 and the long rates jumped to 7.4 percent, consternation was apparent everywhere.

Bentsen still thought, however, that there was too much of a campaign mentality in the Clinton White House. He had seen it happen to President Jimmy Carter. The people that got a president elected were not the ones who should help him govern. He felt a president should find jobs for his valuable campaign staff elsewhere in the administration, or let them go about other business outside the White House, and bring them back only a year or so before the next campaign. Campaign people and government people were two different breeds.

The man who had worked with eight presidents and had told Dan Quayle that he was no Jack Kennedy frequently in private conversations compared Clinton with Carter. Both were highly intelligent. Clinton was even a step above Carter because he could "correlate" various ideas and issues. In many respects, Clinton was well suited to the presidency. He had a superior, inquisitive mind, especially when compared to Reagan, and was capable of genuine vision, especially when compared to Bush. But the very discord or range of opinion that Clinton craved in making his decisions often got him bogged down. Bentsen once described Clinton as the "meetingest" fellow he'd ever seen. The very fact that he wanted debate meant he could not contain his own doubt. The lapses of discipline and restraint made it hard for Clinton to act methodically, as a president must. The war for Clinton's soul, that great struggle over which ideas and approach to use to guide the nation, continued unabated. Nonetheless, Bentsen admired the president's relationship with his wife. He had never seen such a real partnership in the White House before. Hillary, however, was a lot tougher, more goal-oriented, and disciplined.

Bentsen was proud of his own work managing Treasury, bringing in experts to help reorganize the department, meticulously analyzing how he spent his own time, directing his attention to what mattered. McLarty often commented, "Why aren't we as organized as the Treasury Department?" The simple fact was that governing Arkansas was a small job. After the economic plan passed, Bentsen addressed the issue of management directly with the president. His gray hair and the quarter century he had on the president allowed him to speak frankly.

"Mr. President," Bentsen said, "you want to make every decision. You can't. You've got to delegate more." The boss needed to hear. "Mr. President, it's not the quantity of your decisions. It's the quality. I've sat beside you when somebody else is talking at one of these meetings, and I watch your eyes just fog over." Bentsen half-closed his eyes in imitation of impending sleep. "You're gone. It's because you're tired. You think you can go without sleep. You can't."

"I know you're right," Clinton replied mournfully. "I know you're right, Lloyd."

Things seemed to get better briefly. But they did not change.

THE EMPTINESS OF CONQUEST had descended on Clinton after the economic plan passed, Stephanopoulos noted. Since winning the presidency, Clinton had not taken a real vacation. He essentially had extended the campaign through the first nine months of the presidency, taking up the battle with all the urgency of FDR in the Depression or a president in war. The velocity of change in Clinton's life had been overwhelming. In the previous year, he had moved, changed jobs, worked continuously, lost his mother, shared the grief of losing Hillary's father and Vince Foster, and tried to learn to live in the fishbowl of Washington and the presidency. Not only was his present life scrutinized but everything about his past was being investigated. If Clinton were to take one of those magazine tests that measured stress, awarding so many points for various changes and traumas, he would be off the charts.

The battle to pass the economic plan had been too close, Stephanopoulos concluded. In the future, he argued, Clinton should only take on fights that he was virtually assured of winning. His own attempt to stop NAFTA, Stephanopoulos acknowledged, had been wrong. He had also made a run at Gore's "Reinventing Government" review of federal operations and spending. In the Oval Office in September, he had urged Clinton not to allow Gore to claim $108 billion in savings from his national performance review, arguing that it would unleash more deficit reduction mania. Clinton, not surprisingly, went with Gore. Clinton didn't see limits, Stephanopoulos realized.

The administration, Stephanopoulos felt, had to find a way of measuring a successful presidency. He realized it all came down to one thing:

winning reelection. Clinton had to win again in 1996. Successful presidents were reelected; failed presidents were not. Ronald Reagan, perhaps the worst modern president in Stephanopoulos's view, was widely considered successful, because, he believed, Reagan had won reelection. Yet the Clinton presidency, Stephanopoulos knew, was likely to be messy, and governing was going to be ugly. But he felt they were on the right track, and so far, Clinton had more than done his part.

ONE NIGHT IN EARLY 1994 during a discussion in the Oval Office with several aides in attendance, Clinton said that it was the ideas that had driven him. He sat forward. "I could never have survived the presidential campaign of '92—never—if it had just been a personal odyssey." Obstacles to governing abounded, he continued. "The president does not govern alone." The power of perception, he said, permeated the entire political process. "It's how other people perceive you and perceive your policies. And how they react really does matter." Clinton was asked what he thought of his role in the economy. Was he the commander in chief of the economy, as the public seemed to think?

Clinton paused some time before answering. "More like a captain of a ship," he said, grasping for the metaphor of a very old ship with oars. "That is, I can steer it, but a storm can still come up and sink it. And the people that are supposed to be rowing can refuse to row."

Clinton still had not found the theme for his presidency, a concise and compelling way to lay out "The Journey" or "The Story" as Hillary had proposed a year earlier. While drafting his State of the Union address for 1994, Clinton had told several of his aides, "I have to try to create a framework so people will understand what I'm doing." They had tried themes of economic security, or community and responsibility, but none had worked. Even after the address the White House had a group searching for a way to encapsulate his economic strategy. There were lots of topics, initiatives, directions, ideas, and words, but the description they were seeking eluded them.

As the Whitewater allegations and investigations enveloped Clinton, stories about his private life resurfaced and recirculated. "I feel like I'm in a Kafkaesque novel," he told Stephanopoulos one night. The president wavered between optimism and some level of anguish, settling on a public face of confidence. But the pain, on occasion, seeped into his public comments.

The morning of Thursday, February 3, 1994, Clinton spoke to thousands at the National Prayer Breakfast at the Washington Hilton Hotel.

His voice was weak from a cold, and he choked in a wheezing gasp a number of times. During his short remarks he paused three times, losing the natural rhythm of his speech. All elected officials, Clinton said, including himself, had abandoned certain personal characteristics—humbleness and honesty, for example. Twice, as if speaking to himself, he said it was important to learn the art and courage of self-forgiveness.

"It requires that we give our bitterness and our resentments up," he said. "We have to find the courage and the faith to forgive ourselves and to forgive our foes. . . .

"We all spend so much time obsessed with ourselves and how we stand on the totem pole and how we look in the morning paper. Five years from now it will be nothing," he said, a raspy intensity to his voice as if his conviction could will it to be so. "Five hundred years from now, the papers will be dust."

LATE IN THE WINTER OF 1994, after their first full year in the White House, Hillary Clinton felt deeply frustrated with the way she and Bill were being portrayed. She liked to think she was from what she once called "the other-shoe-will-drop school of politics." Lately, all the shoes seemed to be falling. Reading the newspapers, she tried to figure out what would stand the test of history, what was really important. She felt Bill's presidency was being trivialized. No one could ever see him or know him as well as she did. Bill was such a complex person. Nobody had described the whole man. People kept trying to chop him up into little pieces. It couldn't be done, she knew. Yes, he was an intellectual, she believed, but he was so much more complicated than that. He was also earthy, grounded, and highly personal, a temperamentally rare combination. He could quote Aeschylus and talk about the human journey one day, and the next day go bowling and slap people on the back.

Yes, Bill confused people, she thought. His style created dissonance. If people saw him being serious, they concluded that his back-slapping out in the crowds was calculated. Or if they believed he was sincere when he was hugging some old woman whose story had moved him, they didn't understand his serious purposes. She agreed with Stephanopoulos that someone would have to spend three months straight with Bill to see each piece and get it right. It had been a long time since the country had a president with these dimensions. Nearly all the great presidents had been complex human beings, misunderstood in their own times.

After her own speeches and public appearances, she was the first to call the White House. "What do the wires say?" she asked, insisting on precise details.

When the going was particularly harsh, however, Hillary just stopped reading the newspapers. As the one who managed the family finances, she came under intense scrutiny and criticism in Whitewater. She tried at times to see the lighter side, joking that she was living in a bunker. She was going through what she called one of her "not-reading phases" in March 1994 because of what she called "this little Whitewater thing." Most distressing was that she and Bill were being charged with being greedy, of having used his office as governor and her law practice to wheel and deal in a real estate venture to get rich. But they lost money. Yes, they would prove it. The disclosure that she had made nearly $100,000 trading in the highly speculative commodity futures market in the late 1970s also upset her.

Part of what she and Bill were up against, she theorized, was that people were still trying to absorb the 1980s. The public, Congress, and journalists worked on timelines, she had concluded. All had been surprised and caught short by the Savings and Loan scandal of that earlier decade. She and Bill were being hammered on Whitewater because the public, Congress, and media all had failed to pay attention to the S&L crisis early on. Now it seemed everyone was obsessed with it. It was a kind of payback time. The president was trying to turn around the greed of the 1980s, change the values, move the country into a new era, still unknown and still not fully defined.

In a larger sense—and maybe this was what it all meant—she and Bill were transitional figures. She was a transitional First Lady, taking on a new, bolder role as woman, mother, and policy maker. Bill was a transitional president for a new generation. They were paying the price of being transitional figures. She tried to convince herself that she didn't resent that, and that she understood that was what happened when you were on a historical cusp. But it made their jobs so much harder. It was almost as if they didn't yet have the language to communicate effectively with people. Everyone was playing catch-up.

She felt that people had voted for change, but in a nebulous way. They didn't know exactly what change meant. They could not agree on an agenda. Although Bill was trying to begin to present pieces of what change meant, she felt, the story was so big that people could only grasp small pieces. It all became tied up with the unfinished business of the past. As people worked through the political, cultural, and social changes, they were bound to have their resentments. The more personal they made those resentments, the better they felt. Of course, others missed the entirety of Clinton, of his presidency, of his journey, and of the times they lived in. Nobody else understood. Nobody else really knew. She knew.

To those who thought there was too much of a campaign mentality in the White House, she said, "I think you have to run a campaign for policy just like you do for elections." She, Bill, and the staff couldn't go off on a hilltop by themselves, come down with answers, and expect them to be accepted. They had to sell the public and Congress. As she spoke and answered questions around the country, she found that some confused her vigorous advocacy on behalf of certain points of view, especially on health care, with inflexibility, or, of all things, idealism.

This was politics. Bill and she felt that the barrage of attacks—both on their policies and on them personally—were politically motivated. Too much of the media had become tools of the political opposition. On her good days she tried not to take it personally. "It's not personal," she said at one point, as if trying to convince herself. *"I mean it really isn't."* On her bad days, there was no other way to take it, as she crossed the pain threshold.

She connected the current troubles to a call that she remembered Bill telling her about in the summer of 1991, just as he was deciding to run for president. She recalled that he reported a direct threat from someone in the Bush White House, warning that if he ran, the Republicans would go after him. "We will do everything we can to destroy you personally," she recalled that the Bush White House man had said. It was the same organized opposition, she felt, that had attacked him during the campaign and was now trying to tear down his presidency. Others from the campaign and the White House, however, remembered the call very differently—as neither stark nor threatening. The story had grown much better in the telling and in her memory. One campaign veteran thought it might be apocryphal or the message something between a political chat and a threat. She was not viewing things with her usual cold and clear eye. She was talking, at times, as if they were being persecuted.

She told herself that the avalanche descending upon them could not be motivated simply by a fear of Bill personally. No, these people were afraid of his *ideas,* she concluded. He was trying to overturn their philosophy and all their work. The vehemence of the attacks reinforced her belief that Bill and she were on the right track, fighting vast and entrenched interests. She even tried at times to see the intensity of the working-over they were getting as a great compliment.

They had done much since the day in August 1991 when she awoke with the realization that he would run and win. In the spring of 1994, they were out publicly talking up the successes—the economic plan, trade agreements, other legislation, and health care, which was still to come. In private they talked about the pressures and attacks. So on one hand it was better than ever; on the other, worse than ever.

"We're going to keep on going," he said to her one day. "They're never going to stop us."

ACKNOWLEDGMENTS

Simon & Schuster and *The Washington Post* once again supported me with patience and trust. Richard E. Snyder, the chairman of Paramount Publishing, is the tough boss and devoted friend every author seeks. At the *Post*, Leonard Downie, Jr., the executive editor, and Robert G. Kaiser, the managing editor, allowed me once again to plunge into an examination of the decision making behind the daily news. No two editors in American journalism care more about the profession and the quest for the fullest, fairest presentation of events. I owe special thanks to Kaiser, one of the best editing hands in the business, for reading an early draft of the manuscript and providing excellent guidance and advice.

Steve Luxenberg, the assistant managing editor for projects at the *Post*, also helped me focus the project and better understand my own information. I have been a beneficiary of his calm and probing intellect a thousand times. Lucy Shackelford, the master researcher at the *Post*, is thanked for many large and small assists. Joe Elbert and his great photo staff at the *Post* provided the pictures; Jennifer Belton, head of news research, Margot Williams, and their staff, which keeps the best library and photo library around, provided constant assistance. Olwen Price was of invaluable help.

Virtually all the information in this book comes from my own reporting. David Greenberg, my assistant, and I consulted and read hundreds of newspaper and magazine articles. *The Washington Post,* the

Wall Street Journal, The New York Times, The Los Angeles Times, and other daily newspapers cover economic policy making and the White House with exceptional skill. Special thanks to *Post* colleague David Maraniss, who understands Clinton better than any other writer. Much gratitude to other reporters at the *Post,* including Ann Devroy, Ruth Marcus, Dan Balz, John M. Berry, Al Kamen. Thanks and respect to David Ignatius and his talented staff of financial reporters. *Newsweek, U.S. News & World Report,* and *Time* magazine also provided much information and background; the weekly magazines do some of the most comprehensive reporting on the White House and economics. *Mad as Hell: Revolt at the Ballot Box, 1992* by Jack W. Germond and Jules Witcover was the campaign book we relied on. It is impossible to write about politics without using the great bible, *Almanac of American Politics 1994,* by Michael Barone and Grant Ujifusa.

Simon & Schuster went all-out to expedite publication of this book. I want to thank Carolyn K. Reidy, Michael Jacobs, Victoria Meyer, Eric Steel, Frank Metz, Eve Metz, Marcia Peterson, Lydia Buechler, Jackie Seow, and Sarah Baker. David Greenberg and I want to thank Ann Adelman for her careful and perceptive copyediting.

Alice Mayhew, my book editor and friend for two decades and seven books, threw herself into the task with the determination and zeal of ten. She is truly the great iron editor. A lover of knowledge, politics, and life, Alice bears down on chapters, paragraphs, sentences, words—and ideas—with both her towering intellect and a mighty pen.

Robert B. Barnett once again was counselor, agent, and lawyer. Ed Williams would even be prouder. It seems there is now little political business in Washington that Bob is not party to. Because he has worked with President Clinton, he did not read the manuscript until it was completed.

Hundreds of people served as sources for this book, ranking high and low and in between. I thank every one of them. Those closest to the center will, I hope, recognize the care that I've tried to bring to the task. It is not the way any of them singly would have written it.

Tali, the best daughter, is off to college this year, and her thoughts will be welcomed on any future project. She will be missed and always welcome home. Rosa Criollo again cared for all of us so well at Q Street.

Elsa Walsh, my wife and best friend, tolerates my work habits and much else in me. She provided the most useful read of the manuscript, and a regular dialogue on the book's progress. One of our pals recently pronounced at dinner that I am "a hard case." True words. Elsa has grace and selfless love. She is the best and easiest case.

INDEX